MW00675111

Coursebook

to accompany

13TH EDITION

ECONOMICS

PRIVATE AND PUBLIC CHOICE

prepared by

Russell S. Sobel

JAMES D. GWARTNEY
Florida State University

RICHARD L. STROUP
Montana State University

RUSSELL S. SOBEL
West Virginia University

DAVID A. MACPHERSON
Trinity University, San Antonio TX

SOUTH-WESTERN
CENGAGE Learning·

Australia • Brazil • Japan • Korea • Mexico • Singapore • Spain • United Kingdom • United States

SOUTH-WESTERN
CENGAGE Learning

Coursebook to accompany
Economics: A Private and Public Choice, 13 edition

James D. Gwartney, Richard L. Stroup, Russell S. Sobel, David A. Macpherson

Prepared by Russell S. Sobel

Vice President of Editorial, Business: Jack W. Calhoun

Publisher: Joe Sabatino

Sr. Acquisitions Editor: Steve Scoble

Sr. Developmental Editor: Susan Smart

Sr. Marketing Manager: John Carey

Marketing Communications Manager: Sarah Greber

Associate Content Project Manager: Jana Lewis

Media Editor: Deepak Kumar

Sr. Manufacturing Buyer: Sandee Milewski

Production Service: OffCenter Concept House

Sr. Art Director: Michelle Kunkler

Photography Manager: Deanna Ettinger

Text Permissions Manager: Mardell Glisnki-Schultz

Internal Designer: OffCenter Concept House

Cover Designer: c miller design

Cover Image: © Reza Estakhrian/Getty Images, Inc.

© 2011, 2008 South-Western, Cengage Learning

ALL RIGHTS RESERVED. No part of this work covered by the copyright hereon may be reproduced or used in any form or by any means—graphic, electronic, or mechanical, including photocopying, recording, taping, Web distribution, information storage and retrieval systems, or in any other manner—except as may be permitted by the license terms herein.

For product information and technology assistance, contact us at **Cengage Learning Customer & Sales Support, 1-800-354-9706**

For permission to use material from this text or product, submit all requests online at
www.cengage.com/permissions
Further permissions questions can be emailed to
permissionrequest@cengage.com

ISBN-13: 978-0-538-45226-7
ISBN-10: 0-538-45226-9

South-Western Cengage Learning
5191 Natorp Boulevard
Mason, OH 45040
USA

Cengage Learning products are represented in Canada by Nelson Education, Ltd.

For your course and learning solutions, visit www.cengage.com
Purchase any of our products at your local college store or at our
preferred online store **www.ichapters.com**

Printed in Canada
1 2 3 4 5 6 7 13 12 11 10

Preface

We are often asked why we call this book a *Coursebook* rather than a "study guide." We use this title because we feel the *Coursebook* goes well beyond the typical study guide in at least three ways:

1. *Critical Analysis.* We stress questions that require students to develop and use the economic way of thinking to come up with the answers, rather than having students passively choose between a group of prepared alternatives.

2. *Readings.* We include short, interesting readings by a broad spectrum of economists to provide a real-world context for applying the economic way of thinking to important issues.

3. *Explained Answers.* Except for the open-ended discussion questions, we include explanations of why a particular answer is correct and the alternatives incorrect.

In writing this *Coursebook,* we have attempted to strike a balance between economic reasoning and mechanics. Often a supplementary workbook is little more than a set of mechanical exercises. Such exercises lack substance and meaning for the student who has not yet acquired a firm foundation in the economic way of thinking. Our teaching experience has shown that stressing real-world situations, presenting actual data, providing selected short readings, and explaining why particular answers are correct—as we have done in the *Coursebook*—illuminate the power, and utility, of economic reasoning.

The *Coursebook* has been structured to maximize the student's comprehension of the concepts presented in each chapter of *Economics: Private and Public Choice,* Thirteenth Edition. The first section of each chapter is composed of approximately fifteen true/false questions. Although this section has a realistic flavor, mechanics primarily are emphasized. When possible, students are tested on their ability to reject common economic fallacies or "Myths of Economics," as they are often referred to in the text. The second section of problems and projects generally contains about five problems that emphasize both mechanics and economic reasoning. The problems and projects are specifically designed to foster the economic way of thinking by guiding students through a series of smaller, logical steps when approaching each larger economic problem. The third section contains approximately twenty-five multiple-choice questions of the type familiar to most students. We have tried to maximize the usefulness of these questions in preparing students for tests by making these questions similar in wording, context, and logic to the ones available to instructors in the test bank that accompanies the book. They represent a fair mix of questions designed to test mechanics and economic thinking. Finally, each chapter contains approximately five discussion questions that are intended to provoke further speculation on economic issues.

The *Coursebook* also serves as a reader, presenting a "Perspectives in Economics" section in about half of the chapters. These articles are readable and engaging, will reinforce the classroom presentation of economic lessons, and will expand on important concepts discussed in the text. Following each selection are questions asking the student to evaluate the position of the author. Is the reasoning sound? Is it opinionated? Does empirical evidence support the author's contention? This feature of the *Coursebook* again highlights the usefulness of economics in our everyday lives.

Answers to virtually every question are provided in the "Answer Key" at the back of the *Coursebook*. The answers are followed by an explanation of why that particular answer is correct. Students who take the time to master these questions—and who understand the rationale behind each answer—should do very well in introductory economics classes.

We would like to express our appreciation to Joab N. Corey, Kerry A. King, Keri M. Cowan, A. H. Studenmund, and Mary Hirschfeld for their contributions to this and previous editions of the *Coursebook*; Sheryl Nelson of OffCenter Concept House for her help in production and composition; Susanna Smart and Jana Lewis of Cengage; and especially Terri and Reagan Sobel for their patience, support, and understanding.

Russell S. Sobel
James D. Gwartney
Richard L. Stroup
David A. Macpherson

Contents

Making the Grade in Economics

Here are some hints that will help you to greatly improve your grade in economics.

Do your coursebook for each chapter. Students who use the coursebook generally average exam grades at least one letter grade higher than those who do not use it. The coursebook questions will likely be very similar to what will be on your exams. If you have trouble with the wording, or don't understand why the right answers are indeed right, get help. Have a friend, your instructor, or a tutor help you with the specific questions.

Learning this "economic way of thinking" is more important than being able to memorize definitions. However, being familiar with the key terms and the jargon of economics will help. These terms, with their definitions, can be found in the margins of your textbook.

When grading your answers, ask yourself, "Did I miss several questions all regarding the same idea?" The quickest way to fail an exam is to miss a key concept that accounts for several exam questions. The coursebook should enable you to find these problem spots before your exam, so you can correct them. Get additional help on these problem spots.

Use the coursebook to improve the effectiveness of your study time. Suppose you get all the questions on opportunity cost correct, while you miss several questions on scarcity. Additional study time should focus on learning what you missed, not on restudying what you know. The coursebook can help you figure out which is which.

Do not focus too much on the specific example. Economics is a set of ideas that can, and should, be applied consistently. The law of demand (from Chapter 3) states that as the price of a good rises, consumers will buy less of it. So what will happen if the price of funerals in your town rises, will the quantity of funerals purchased rise, fall or stay the same? Students often deduce that death is unavoidable, so the quantity of funerals purchased will stay the same. WRONG! The world is full of substitutes: You can be buried in another town, or you could be cremated and have your ashes thrown over the ocean.

Because the specific example generally doesn't matter, a few key words generally determine the answer. Above, the key idea being tested is "a higher price causes . . ." find these key words in each question and ask what idea from the chapter is being tested. It isn't knowledge of the funeral home industry! That wasn't in the chapter.

Finally, remember what you already know from the real world. You have lived your entire life in an economy, and economic theory is meant to explain and give insights into the real world. Most students would know before ever taking economics that monopolies charge higher prices or that recessions are characterized by higher unemployment rates. Always double check the answer you get by applying economic theory against what you already know. Generally go with your first instinct on a question; students often read too much into questions when they overanalyze them.

The Economic Approach

CHAPTER 1

TRUE OR FALSE

T F

☐ ☐ 1. According to the economic guidepost that incentives matter, if there is an increase in the benefit derived from an activity, individuals will be more likely to choose that activity.

☐ ☐ 2. The opportunity cost of attending an economics class is the money spent on transportation (gasoline, parking, etc.) plus the cost of the books for the class.

☐ ☐ 3. Resources are inputs used to produce goods and services. They include human resources (such as labor), physical resources (such as capital), and natural resources (such as land).

☐ ☐ 4. The value of a good is objective; it is the same to everyone.

☐ ☐ 5. Economic activity often has secondary effects that are not initially observable.

☐ ☐ 6. Because public education is freely provided to students, it is by definition not a scarce good.

☐ ☐ 7. One's time is scarce and thus must be rationed among alternative activities.

☐ ☐ 8. If you like pizza and steak equally well, economizing behavior suggests you will purchase whichever is more expensive.

☐ ☐ 9. A good is scarce if human desire for it exceeds the amount freely available from nature.

☐ ☐ 10. In economics, the term *ceteris paribus* means that everything is changing.

T F

☐ ☐ 11. The following is a positive economic statement: "An increase in the minimum wage will increase unemployment among unskilled workers."

☐ ☐ 12. The following is a positive economic statement: "The government should increase its funding of welfare programs to help the poor."

☐ ☐ 13. The following is an example of marginal thinking: "I was going to buy a taco and a drink, but the value meal with two tacos and a drink costs only $.30 more and has one additional taco."

☐ ☐ 14. Whenever two events frequently happen together, this necessarily implies that one causes the other.

☐ ☐ 15. Economics assumes people will generally make decisions with limited information because information is costly to obtain.

PROBLEMS AND PROJECTS

1. The text lists eight guideposts to the economic way of thinking. They are summarized below.

Guidepost 1: The use of scarce resources is costly; decision makers must make trade-offs. ("There is no such thing as a free lunch.")

Guidepost 2: Individuals choose purposefully; they try to get the most from their limited resources.

Guidepost 3: Incentives matter—choice is influenced in a predictable way by changes in incentives.

Guidepost 4: Individuals make decisions at the margin.

Guidepost 5: Although information can help us make better choices, its acquisition is costly.

Guidepost 6: Beware of the secondary effects—economic actions often generate indirect as well as direct effects.

Guidepost 7: The value of a good or service is subjective.

Guidepost 8: The test of a theory is its ability to predict.

Read each of the statements below and indicate in the blank space to the left of the statement the number of the guidepost that best accounts for the statement.

___ a. The luxury tax placed on expensive boats in 1990 was meant to increase the tax burden on the rich, but it ended up hurting many blue-collar manufacturing workers in the boat industry as they lost their jobs when boat sales fell substantially.

___ b. I will usually not stop to pick up a penny laying on the ground but will stop to pick up a dollar bill.

___ c. Although I would really like to buy that $100 name-brand shirt, I will instead buy a less expensive, $30 shirt and save the $70 for something else.

___ d. The Food and Drug Administration should stop requiring all new drugs for AIDS to be exhaustively tested for safety and effectiveness before approving their use. People who might have benefited from the drug are dying during the years required for the approval process.

___ e. I hate tomatoes, but my wife loves them. On the other hand, I love onions, and my wife hates them. When we go out to eat and order a salad, I give her my tomatoes and she gives me her onions.

___ f. Bill Gates spends hours each week caring for and growing grapes to make his own wine. That sure is some expensive wine!

___ g. Long ago people used to believe the earth was the center of the solar system, with the sun and the other planets orbiting around the earth. The sun-centered solar system was originally considered a radical theory that finally gained acceptance because it better predicted the positions of the planets observed in the night sky.

___ h. I love the beach, but because it is a six-hour drive, I don't go very often. However, each year when I visit my grandmother, I drive to the beach because she lives only one hour away from it.

2. Each of the following statements ignores or violates one of the eight guideposts to economic thinking (listed above in question 1). In each case, identify the guidepost and explain how it has been violated.

___ a. Before voting in an election, each voter should learn everything possible about the issues and candidates involved.

___ b. Reducing the prices of necessities would clearly benefit the poor. Therefore, it would help the poor if the government passed a law requiring landlords to reduce by half the rental rates for any tenant who makes less than $10,000 per year.

___ c. Full scholarships make education free.

___ d. Because I get the same satisfaction from reading a book, seeing a movie, or hearing a concert, there should be no reason for me to prefer one choice over the other.

___ e. Because criminals are irrational, increasing the punishment associated with a crime will not affect the amount of the crime committed.

___ f. Joe declares, "I'm not going to class today; I'd rather go to the beach." Sam responds, "But Joe, you are forgetting to consider the money you've already paid for tuition and books for the class."

___ g. I'm trying to find a ticket for Saturday's sold-out game, but everyone I call wants at least $75 for their ticket. Don't these people understand that their tickets are only worth the $15 price they originally paid for them?

___ h. Economics tries to explain the lower birth rate among educated women as being due to them having a higher opportunity cost of having children. This cannot be true because the decision to have a baby has nothing to do with economics.

3. The text discusses four common pitfalls to avoid in the economic way of thinking.
   (1) Violation of the *ceteris paribus* condition can lead one to draw the wrong conclusion.
   (2) Good intentions do not guarantee desirable outcomes.
   (3) Association is not causation.
   (4) The fallacy of composition: What's true for one might not be true for all.

Indicate which pitfall applies to each of the following statements. Briefly explain each case.

___ a. Because everyone buys a lottery ticket in hopes of winning a prize, the perfect lottery would pay back $1 to each player, making everyone a winner, instead of giving the money as only one big prize.

___ b. The price of typewriters has fallen over the last 10 years, but less typewriters are sold today than 10 years ago. This rejects the economic theory that people buy more as the price falls.

___ c. In the past, students who earn A's in my class tend to be the ones who come up after class and ask questions. Perhaps I should require everyone to come up and ask questions to improve student grades.

___ d. Senator Mackenzie cares about eliminating poverty. Therefore, his proposal to increase the minimum wage will definitely help the poor.

4. [Note to students: The following problem relates to the addendum at the end of Chapter 1 on understanding graphs.] Exhibit 1 shows data on the relationship between gas consumption of a new Chevrolet and the number of miles traveled.

   a. Graph the relationship between miles traveled and gas consumption in the space provided. Measure miles traveled on the horizontal axis (x axis) and gasoline consumption on the vertical axis (y axis). Label the graph clearly.

   b. Is there a direct or inverse (that is, positive or negative) relationship between gasoline consumption and distance traveled?

   c. What is the slope of the line? How is it related to the miles per gallon obtained in the Chevrolet (that is, how many miles can be traveled on a gallon of gas)?

EXHIBIT 1

Total Distance Traveled (miles)	Amount of Gasoline Consumed (gallons)
0	0
75	5
150	10
225	15
300	20
375	25
450	30

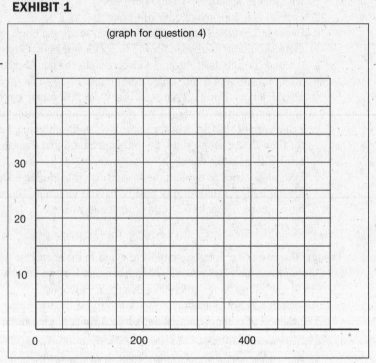

(graph for question 4)

5. [Note to students: The following problem relates to the addendum at the end of Chapter 1 on understanding graphs.] Exhibit 2 shows how the quantity of melons purchased by consumers depends on the price of melons and on average consumer income.

   a. In the space provided, graph the relationship between price and quantity purchased if income is $10,000. Label this curve D_1.

   b. Are price and quantity purchased directly or inversely related to those with average incomes of $10,000 per year?

   c. Graph the relationship between price and quantity purchased if income is $15,000. Label this curve D_2.

   d. If price is fixed at 4 cents per pound, and consumer income rises from $10,000 to $15,000 per year, how much will quantity purchased change?

   e. For a person with an income of $15,000 per year, if the price rises from 4 cents to 5 cents per pound, how much will quantity purchased change?

EXHIBIT 2

Quantity Purchased (thousands of tons per year)

Price (cents per pound)	For average income of	
	$10,000/year	$15,000/year
1	900	1,100
2	800	1,000
3	700	900
4	600	800
5	500	700
6	400	600

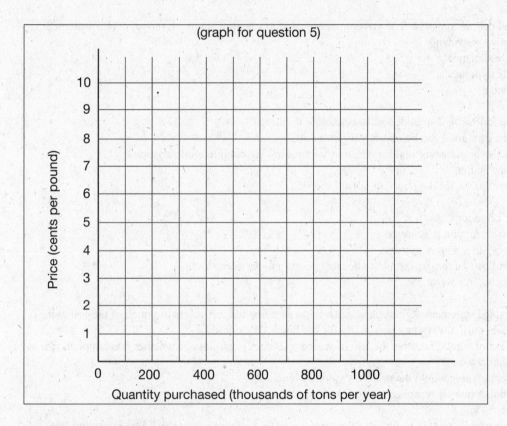

(graph for question 5)

MULTIPLE CHOICE

1. Which of the following is true?
    a. Scarcity and poverty are basically the same thing.
    b. Poverty implies that some basic level of need has not been attained.
    c. Scarcity is the result of prices being set too high.
    d. All of the above are true.

2. Economics is the study of how
    a. individuals make choices because of scarcity.
    b. to succeed in business.
    c. to make money in the stock market.
    d. the morals and values of people are formed.

3. When an economist states a good is scarce, she means that
    a. production cannot expand the availability of the good.
    b. it is rare.
    c. desire for the good exceeds the amount that is freely available from nature.
    d. people would want to purchase more of the good at any price.

4. When economists say an individual displays economizing behavior, they simply mean that the individual is
    a. making a lot of money.
    b. purchasing only those products that are cheap and of low quality.
    c. learning how to run a business more effectively.
    d. making choices to gain the maximum benefit at the least possible cost.

5. "The national debt is too large. The government must stop spending so much money." This statement is
    a. a normative statement.
    b. a positive statement.
    c. a testable hypothesis.
    d. both b and c.

6. Which of the following is a guidepost to economic thinking?
    a. The value of a good can be objectively measured.
    b. Individuals should never make a decision without having complete information.
    c. Incentives matter.
    d. Goods are scarce for the poor but not for the rich.

7. Competitive behavior
    a. occurs as a reaction to scarcity.
    b. occurs only in a market system.
    c. occurs only when the government allocates goods and services.
    d. always generates waste.

8. In economics, the statement, "There is no such thing as a free lunch," refers to which of the following?
    a. Individuals must always pay personally for the lunch they consume.
    b. Production of a good requires the use of scarce resources regardless of whether it is supplied free to the consumers.
    c. Restaurant owners would never give away free lunches.
    d. All good theories are testable.

9. "If income were redistributed in favor of the poor, we would eliminate scarcity." The preceding statement is
    a. essentially correct.
    b. incorrect because scarcity has already been eliminated among the poor in wealthy countries such as the United States.
    c. incorrect; it fails to recognize that poverty will be present as long as resources are scarce.
    d. incorrect; it confuses the elimination of poverty with the elimination of the constraint imposed by scarcity.

10. Which of the following is not scarce?
    a. an individual's time
    b. air
    c. pencils
    d. automobiles

11. People make decisions at the margin. Thus, when deciding whether to purchase a second car, they would compare
    a. the total benefits expected from two cars with the costs of the two cars.
    b. the additional benefits expected from a second car with the total cost of the two cars.
    c. the dollar cost of the two cars with the potential income that the two cars will generate.
    d. the additional benefits of the second car with the additional costs of the second car.

12. The basic difference between macroeconomics and microeconomics is that
    a. macroeconomics looks at how people make choices, and microeconomics looks at why they make those choices.
    b. macroeconomics is concerned with economic policy, and microeconomics is concerned with economic theory.
    c. macroeconomics focuses on the aggregate economy, and microeconomics focuses on small components of that economy.
    d. macroeconomics is associated with the fallacy of composition, and microeconomics has little to do with the fallacy of composition.

13. The highest valued alternative that must be given up in order to choose an action is called its
    a. opportunity cost.
    b. utility.
    c. scarcity.
    d. *ceteris paribus.*

14. Which of the following actions is consistent with the basic economic postulate (the guidepost) that incentives matter?
    a. Consumers buy fewer potatoes when the price of potatoes increases.
    b. A politician votes against a pay raise for himself because most of his constituents are strongly opposed to it and would vote against him in the next election.
    c. Farmers produce less corn because corn prices have declined.
    d. All of the above.

15. If Susan bought nine gallons of gasoline at $1.50 per gallon, the car wash cost $1, but if she bought 10 gallons of gasoline, the car wash was free. Given that Susan is going to get the car wash, the marginal cost of the tenth gallon of gasoline is
    a. zero.
    b. $.50.
    c. $1.00.
    d. $1.50.

16. Positive economics differs from normative economics in that
    a. positive economics deals with how people react to changes in benefits, and normative economics deals with how people react to changes in costs.
    b. positive economic statements are testable, and normative statements are not.
    c. positive economic statements tell us what we should be doing, and normative economics tells us what we should have done.
    d. positive economic statements focus on the application of the theory, and normative economic statements are theoretical.

17. Which of the following represents a normative statement?
    a. Incentives matter.
    b. The temperature in this room is 120 degrees.
    c. It is too hot in this room.
    d. People will buy less butter at $1.50 per pound than they will at $1.00 per pound.

18. The economic way of thinking stresses that
    a. changes in personal costs and benefits will exert a predictable influence on the choices of human decision makers.
    b. only direct monetary costs matter in making decisions.
    c. if a good is provided free to an individual, its production will not consume valuable scarce resources.
    d. secondary effects are not important to consider when making decisions.

19. Which of the following is a positive economic statement?
    a. The federal minimum wage should be raised to $6.50 per hour.
    b. The United States spends too much on national defense.
    c. Higher rates of investment lead to higher rates of economic growth.
    d. Economics is more interesting to study than history.

20. When economists use the term *ceteris paribus,* they indicate
    a. the causal relationship between two economic variables cannot be determined.
    b. the analysis is true for the individual but not for the economy as a whole.
    c. all other factors are assumed to be constant.
    d. their conclusions are based on normative economics rather than positive economic analysis.

21. In economics, the benefit (or satisfaction) that an individual gets from an activity is called
    a. scarcity.
    b. utility.
    c. opportunity cost.
    d. *ceteris paribus.*

DISCUSSION QUESTIONS

1. When a good is scarce, there is not enough of it freely available from nature to satisfy human desires for the good. Thus, some means of rationing the limited quantity among those who desire it is necessary. A market system allows prices to perform this rationing function. Prices simply rise until the number of people willing to buy is equal to the quantity available. Can you think of other rationing systems other than price? Contrast the secondary effects of the alternative rationing systems with price rationing.

2. List three things that are not scarce. List three things that are commonplace but still scarce. How did you decide whether an item was scarce or not?

3. "Economics is of limited relevance. Most people will not be directly involved in management or the production of material goods. They will not put much money in the stock market. Understanding the economic approach will be of limited value to the typical student." Do you agree or disagree with this view? Be honest. Explain your reasoning.

4. "The minimum wage makes it more expensive for businesses to hire unskilled labor. As a result of the higher cost, businesses will hire fewer unskilled workers. Because unskilled workers find it harder to get jobs under a minimum wage, we should eliminate the minimum wage." Indicate the positive and normative aspects of these three statements.

5. "Under our plan, health care in the United States will now be free. No citizen will be denied medical care because of an inability to pay. The program will be funded by increasing the employer's tax on the wages of his employees."
    a. Will health care really become free to society? If so, why? If not, who do you think will end up paying for it?
    b. Will the total amount of health care consumption rise or fall? Do you consider this change in health care consumption desirable or not? Explain.

PERSPECTIVES IN ECONOMICS

Economics in One Lesson

by Henry Hazlitt

[Reprinted with permission from Henry Hazlitt, *Economics in One Lesson*, (New York: Crown, 1979) pp. 15–17 (abridged).]

Economics is haunted by more fallacies than any other study. This is no accident. The inherent difficulties of the subject would be great enough in any case, but they are multiplied a thousandfold by a factor that is insignificant in, say, physics, mathematics or medicine—the special pleading of selfish interests. While every group has certain economic interests identical with those of all groups, every group has also interests antagonistic to those of all other groups. While certain public policies would in the long run benefit everybody, other policies would benefit one group only at the expense of all other groups. The group that would benefit by such policies, having such a direct interest in them, will argue for them plausibly and persistently. It will hire the best buyable minds to devote their whole time to presenting its case. And it will finally either convince the general public that its case is sound, or so befuddle it that clear thinking on the subject becomes next to impossible.

In addition to these endless pleadings of self-interest, there is a second main factor that spawns new economic fallacies every day. This is the persistent tendency to see only the immediate effects of a given policy, or its effects only on a special group, and to neglect to inquire what the long-run effects of that policy will be not only on that special group but on all groups. It is the fallacy of overlooking secondary consequences.

In this lies the whole difference between good economics and bad. The bad economist sees only what immediately strikes the eye; the good economist also looks beyond. The bad economist sees only the direct consequences of a proposed course; the good economist looks also at the longer and indirect consequences. The bad economist sees only what the effect of a given policy has been or will be on one particular group; the good economist inquires also what the effect of the policy will be on all groups.

From this aspect, therefore, the whole of economics can be reduced to a single lesson, and that lesson can be reduced to a single sentence. The art of economics consists in looking not merely at the immediate but at the longer effects of any act or policy; it consists in tracing the consequences of that policy not merely for one group but for all groups.

DISCUSSION

1. Rephrase Hazlitt's lesson in your own words. Is it really possible to reduce the whole of economics to one sentence?

2. Which "Guideposts to Economic Thinking" corresponds to Hazlitt's lesson? Explain your choice(s).

3. Can you think of applications of Hazlitt's lesson in your own life? What are they?

Some Tools of the Economist

CHAPTER 2

TRUE OR FALSE

T F

☐ ☐ 1. The opportunity cost of washing your car is the discomfort and drudgery associated with the task.

☐ ☐ 2. Time is a component of opportunity cost.

☐ ☐ 3. For most students, the largest component of the cost of college is the opportunity cost of forgone earnings.

☐ ☐ 4. In each trade there is a winner and a loser; trade cannot make both parties better off.

☐ ☐ 5. The law of comparative advantage helps explain why fathers often have their 12-year-old sons mow the lawn even though the fathers could do it in less time.

☐ ☐ 6. Private property rights give owners a strong incentive to disregard the wishes of others when using or employing their property.

☐ ☐ 7. Property that is privately owned tends to be much better cared for and better conserved for the future than property that is not privately owned.

☐ ☐ 8. Middlemen add to the buyer's cost without producing anything of value.

☐ ☐ 9. A country gains by importing products that are relatively expensive for them to produce, while exporting products that are relatively inexpensive for them to produce.

☐ ☐ 10. The principle of comparative advantage causes both individuals and nations to specialize in the production of those things for which they are the lowest opportunity cost producer.

T F

☐ ☐ 11. All economies must make decisions about what to produce, how to produce it, and to whom to distribute the goods produced.

☐ ☐ 12. Capitalism is the use of the political process and government planning to allocate goods and resources.

☐ ☐ 13. If an economy is operating efficiently, to produce more of one good it must produce less of another.

☐ ☐ 14. An increase in technology shifts the production possibilities curve inward.

☐ ☐ 15. Creative destruction refers to the ongoing process of entrepreneurial discovery and innovation in which new products and methods of production are continuously replacing old ones.

PROBLEMS AND PROJECTS

1. Susan is a 30-year-old, high-school graduate currently earning $20,000 at her job. She rents an apartment and pays for all of her own expenses (food, rent, transportation to and from work, etc.). She is considering quitting her job and enrolling in the local university to earn a college degree. The brochure for the local university gives the following table of the average cost of attending the university.

    Using the economic tools of opportunity cost and the marginal way of thinking that you have learned in Chapters 1 and 2, evaluate Susan's cost of going to college relative to the table.

EXHIBIT 1

	Per Year	Total for 4 Years
Tuition and fees	$2,191	$8,764
Books and supplies	$552	$2,208
Room and board	$4,434	$17,736
Transportation	$557	$2,228
Total	$7,734	$30,936

a. What important component of her cost of going to college is omitted from the table? (Hint: Think of opportunity cost.)

b. Are transportation and room and board (housing and food) really costs of going to college? Are they relevant costs in making her decision? (Hint: Use the marginal way of thinking.)

c. Adjust the table according to your answers to a and b. What is her relevant 1-year and 4-year costs of going to college?

d. What percent of this total cost is due to her forgone earnings?

e. Because a person's earnings usually increase with age, can you think of a reason why people generally chose to go to college when they are younger instead of waiting?

2. The text lists the following four important factors and incentives created by private property rights.

   (1) Private owners can gain by employing their resources in ways that are beneficial to others, and they bear the opportunity cost of ignoring the wishes of others.
   (2) Private owners have a strong incentive to care for and properly manage what they own.
   (3) Private owners have an incentive to conserve for the future—particularly if the property is expected to increase in value.
   (4) Private owners have an incentive to lower the chance their property will cause damage to the property of others.

   Now read each of the statements below and indicate in the blank space to the left of the statement the number of the above feature or incentive of private property rights that best accounts for the statement.
   ___ a. Before selling their home, most people fix it up and do needed repairs.
   ___ b. You cause an automobile accident and must pay to repair the damage to the other automobile.
   ___ c. When sharing an apartment with others, the common areas such as the living room and kitchen are usually not kept as clean as each person keeps their own room.
   ___ d. John and Mary love to eat popcorn and watch movies on their DVD player. However, they note that when they put the popcorn in one big bowl it gets eaten more quickly than if it is divided and each gets their own bowl of popcorn.
   ___ e. Cows, pigs, and chicken are slaughtered in massive quantities each year for human benefit. Whales and African elephants are also killed for human benefit, but at much lower rates. However, whales and elephants are facing extinction while cows, pigs, and chicken are everywhere.
   ___ f. People generally take better care of housing that they own than housing that they rent.
   ___ g. Sam uses spray paint to paint his car pink and purple and puts bumper stickers all over the outside of the car. When he goes to sell it, he has trouble finding a buyer and ends up getting a much lower price than the average used value for his make and model car.

3. Bob needs to go from Atlanta to Miami. A bus ticket costs $200, and the bus takes 56 hours, while an airplane ticket costs $450 and takes 6 hours.
   a. What is the marginal cost of taking the plane? That is, how much more additional money does the plane ticket cost over the bus?
   b. What is the marginal benefit of taking the plane? That is, how many hours does he save over taking the bus?
   c. For 50 hours of Bob's time to be worth $250, how much must he value his time?
   d. If Bob's value of his time is $8 per hour, should he fly or take the bus?

EXHIBIT 2

Sam's Weekly Production Possibilities		Larry's Weekly Production Possibilities	
Tables	Chairs	Tables	Chairs
5	0	4	0
4	2	3	1
3	4	2	2
2	6	1	3
1	8	0	4
0	10		

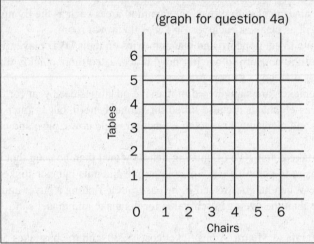

(graph for question 4a)

4. Sam and Larry operate a furniture shop. They specialize in the production of tables and chairs. The data representing their respective production possibilities schedules are presented in Exhibit 2.
   a. Plot the data given in the exhibit for Larry in the graph to graphically show his production possibilities curve.
   b. If Larry produces no tables and instead devotes all of his time to producing chairs, how many chairs can he produce? If Larry produces one table, how many chairs can he produce with his remaining time? How many chairs did Larry have to give up to produce this one table?
   c. If Sam produces no tables and instead devotes all of his time to producing chairs, how many chairs can he produce? If Sam produces one table, how many chairs can he produce with his remaining time? How many chairs did Sam have to give up to produce this one table?
   d. Who gives up the fewest chairs to produce one table (that is, who has the comparative advantage in producing tables, or equivalently, who is the lowest opportunity cost producer of tables)?
   e. Using the same process as above in parts b through d, can you find both Larry's and Sam's opportunity cost of producing one chair? Who has the comparative advantage in producing chairs?
   f. Sam currently produces 2 tables and 6 chairs, and Larry produces 1 table and 3 chairs. Total production is 3 tables and 9 chairs. Using your answers to parts d and e, allow Larry and Sam to specialize in the area of their comparative advantage and see how much they can produce in total if they specialize. Is it more or less total output than now?

EXHIBIT 3

	Hours of Work Required per Ton of	
	Coffee	Tobacco
United States	15	45
Brazil	25	50

5. The following questions relate to the data given in Exhibit 3 on the hours of work required to produce tons of coffee and tobacco in the United States and Brazil.
   a. If it takes the United States 15 hours to produce a ton of coffee and 45 hours to produce a ton of tobacco, how many tons of coffee must the United States give up to produce one ton of tobacco? (Hint: How many tons of coffee could be produced in the same 45 hours?)
   b. How many tons of coffee must Brazil give up to produce one ton of tobacco?
   c. Which country has the lowest opportunity cost (in terms of forgone coffee) of producing tobacco?
   d. Which country has the lowest opportunity cost (in terms of forgone tobacco) of producing coffee?
   e. What implications does this have for trade between the United States and Brazil?

6. Exhibit 4 shows the production possibilities curve for growing wheat and corn.

EXHIBIT 4

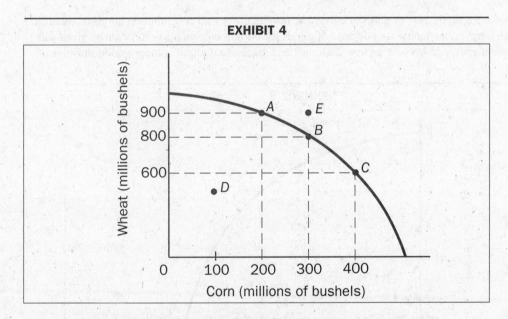

   a. Are resources efficiently employed at point A? At point B? At point D?
   b. At point A, how much wheat is being produced? How much corn?
   c. To increase corn production from A to B, how much wheat must be sacrificed? What is the opportunity cost of one bushel of corn when production moves from point A to B?
   d. Can the country produce 900 million bushels of wheat and 300 million bushels of corn (the output shown at point E)?

7. The division of labor enhances the value that citizens contribute to an economy. Each of the five statements below is a potential answer to a question about the division of labor; read them before going on.

   (1) According to the laws of physics, matter is neither created nor destroyed, it is only rearranged. Manufacturing reshapes matter; distribution relocates it. Both activities, done wisely, rearrange matter in a way that increases its value.
   (2) Deciding which activities to undertake and how to undertake them are risky and costly decisions.
   (3) "You measure the worth of a ballplayer by how many fannies he puts in the seats." (George Steinbrenner, baseball team owner).
   (4) For jobs that are not inherently pleasant, groups of workers left on their own may not accomplish much.
   (5) Lots of activities generate value without being exchanged in the marketplace.

   Now read each of the questions below and indicate in the blank space to the left of the question the number of the statement above that best answers the question.
   ___ a. How can a baseball player ever be worth over $6 million a year?
   ___ b. Why not buy direct more often and cut out the wasteful middleman?
   ___ c. Why do so many house spouses just "sit at home" instead of going out and getting a "real" job?
   ___ d. Why don't we encourage more labor-managed firms so we can eliminate unproductive jobs like shift leaders and supervisors?
   ___ e. Why does the compensation of presidents and owners of corporations often rise and fall with the profitability of their firms instead of being fixed like most salaries?

8. Exhibit 5 contains a production possibility curve, but instead of for two consumption goods as usual, it is specified in terms of a country's production of goods for current consumption (*C*) such as pizza and beer, and investment (*I*) goods such as new buildings and machines. Output is measured in millions of units.

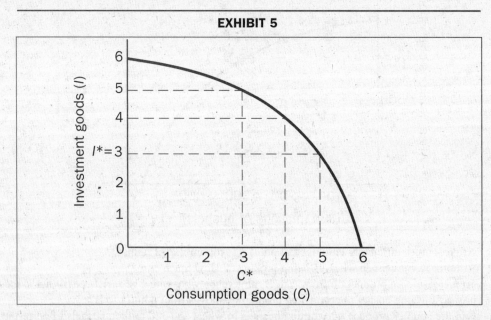

EXHIBIT 5

$C^* = 3$ indicates the minimum level of the consumption good *C* that must be produced in order to avoid starving its citizens.

$I^* = 3$ indicates the amount of the investment good *I* necessary to replace capital equipment and resources that wear out each year. If investment falls short of I^*, the economy's production possibilities curve will shrink from its present position. If investment exceeds I^*, the economy's production possibilities curve will expand.

   a. What will be the consumption/investment good production point(s) if the country wants to (1) grow as rapidly as possible without starving its citizens or (2) enjoy as much consumption as possible without reducing its future production capabilities?

b.   Circle the portion of the production possibilities curve that corresponds to all points that have both more *I* than is needed for replacement and more *C* than is required to avoid starvation.

MULTIPLE CHOICE

1. The opportunity cost to the United States of placing a man on the moon was
   a.   the loss of government revenues that were allocated to the mission.
   b.   the cost of all production involved in the space program.
   c.   the loss of utility from the highest valued bundle of products that had to be forgone because of the moon mission.
   d.   less than zero, because the long-run benefit of the project will be greater than the cost.

2. When Benjamin Franklin wrote, "Remember that time is money!" he understood
   a.   the incentives created by property rights.
   b.   the law of comparative advantage.
   c.   the concept of opportunity cost.
   d.   that watches cost money.

3. An airline ticket from Seattle to Miami costs $525. A bus ticket is $325. Traveling by plane will take 5 hours, compared with 25 hours by bus. Thus, the plane costs $200 more but saves 20 hours of time. (Hint: Note how we are "thinking at the margin" here by looking at the changes.) Other things constant, an individual will gain by choosing air travel if, and only if, each hour of her time is valued at more than
   a. $10 per hour.
   b. $13 per hour.
   c. $20 per hour.
   d. $105 per hour.

4. Which of the following best describes the implications of the law of comparative advantage? If each person sells goods for which he or she has the greatest comparative advantage in production and buys those for which his or her comparative advantage is least, the
   a.   total output available to each person can be expanded by specialization and exchange.
   b.   total output will fall.
   c.   buyers of goods will gain at the expense of sellers.
   d.   sellers of goods will gain at the expense of buyers.

5. Keri decided to sleep in today rather than attend her 9 A.M. economics class. According to economic analysis, her choice was
   a.   irrational, because economic analysis suggests you should always attend classes that you have already paid for.
   b.   irrational, because oversleeping is not in Keri's self-interest.
   c.   rational if Keri has not missed any other classes.
   d.   rational if Keri values sleep more highly than the benefit she expects to receive from attending the class.

6. Which of the following is not one of the basic economic questions that all economies must answer?
   a.   What will be produced?
   b.   To whom will the goods produced be allocated?
   c.   How will goods be produced?
   d.   Which government agency will set the prices of the goods produced?

7. The owners of private property will
    a. use their property for selfish ends, taking no account of the impact their behavior has on others.
    b. use their property in ways that others value because the market will generally reward them with profits (or a higher selling price) if they do so.
    c. find very little incentive to take care of the property or conserve it for the future.
    d. lose profits when they take the wishes of others into consideration.

8. Ken values his boat at $5,000, and Monica values it at $8,000. If Monica buys it from Ken for $7,000, which of the following is true?
    a. Ken gains $2,000 of value, and Monica gains $1,000 of value.
    b. Ken gains $7,000 of value, and Monica loses $7,000 of value.
    c. Ken gains $7,000 of value, and Monica gains $3,000 of value.
    d. Ken and Monica both gain $7,000 of value.

9. When collective decision making (the political process) is used to resolve economic questions regarding the allocation of resources,
    a. decentralized decision making is present.
    b. central planning and political bargaining will replace market forces.
    c. individual preferences are of no importance.
    d. economic equality will result.

10. The law of comparative advantage suggests that
    a. individuals, states, and nations can all benefit if they trade with others.
    b. free trade among nations is harmful to an economy.
    c. each economy should strive to be self-sufficient.
    d. each country should attempt to produce roughly equal amounts of all goods.

11. When resources are being used wastefully or inefficiently, the
    a. production possibilities curve shifts inward.
    b. production possibilities curve shifts outward.
    c. economy is operating at a point inside its production possibilities constraint.
    d. economy is operating at a point outside its production possibilities constraint.

12. Which of the following is a transaction cost?
    a. price of a ticket to a concert
    b. price of food eaten before a concert
    c. time spent standing in line to buy the concert ticket
    d. price of a T-shirt at the concert

13. Middlemen, such as grocers, stockbrokers, and realtors,
    a. specialize in reducing transactions costs.
    b. provide nothing of value to either the buyer or the seller.
    c. have no effect on economic output in society.
    d. do not exist in capitalist economies.

14. Private property rights exist when property rights are
    a. exclusively controlled by the owner or owners.
    b. transferable to others.
    c. protected by legal enforcement.
    d. all of the above.

15. When an economy is operating efficiently, the production of more of one good will result in the production of less of some other good because
    a. consumers do not want more of both goods.
    b. resources are limited (scarce) and efficiency implies that all are already in use.
    c. the production possibilities curve shifts inward as more of one good is produced.
    d. technological improvement can only improve the production of a single good.

16. Which of the following would allow the production possibilities curve for an economy to shift outward?
    a. a better social organization of economic activity, such as conversion from socialism to capitalism
    b. an increase in the labor force or resource base
    c. more investment leading to better technology and more innovation
    d. all of the above

17. "If I didn't have a date tonight, I would save $10 and spend the evening playing tennis." The opportunity cost of the date is
    a. the other things that could be purchased with the $10.
    b. the other things that could be purchased with the $10 plus the forgone value of a night of tennis.
    c. dependent upon how pleasant a time one has on the date.
    d. the forgone value of a night of tennis.

EXHIBIT 6

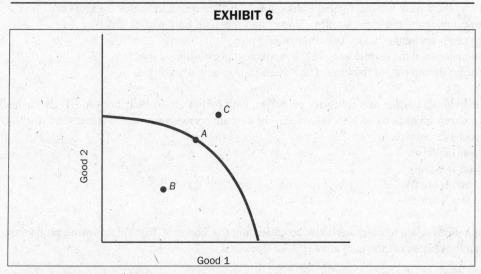

18. Use Exhibit 6 to answer the following question: In the above figure showing the production possibilities curve,
    a. A is efficient.
    b. B is inefficient.
    c. C is unattainable.
    d. all of the above are true.

19. Dr. Jones, a dentist, is choosing between driving and flying from Pittsburgh to New York City. If Jones drove, she would have to close her office four hours earlier than if she flew by airplane. Her expected income (after taxes) from her practice is $50 per hour. Assuming all other factors are equal, if Jones was a rational decision maker, she would drive if the price differential (air cost minus driving) was greater than
    a. $50.
    b. $100.
    c. $150.
    d. $200.

20. According to the law of comparative advantage,
    a. each producer should strive toward self-sufficiency in order to maximize the total production of the economy.
    b. each product should be produced by the lowest opportunity cost producer in order to maximize output.
    c. one should never compare one's abilities with those of another.
    d. each product should be produced by the individual who can produce more of that product than any other individual.

21. "The economic wealth of this country was built primarily by some individuals profiting from a transaction, whereas others were harmed by that transaction." This statement indicates the speaker
    a. fails to comprehend the idea that all voluntary trades benefit both parties involved.
    b. fails to comprehend the fallacy of composition.
    c. fails to understand the significance of the production possibilities curve.
    d. uses the economic way of thinking. The statement is essentially correct.

22. (I) When individuals engage in a voluntary exchange, both parties are made better off. (II) By channeling goods and resources to those who value them most, trade creates value and increases the wealth created by a society's resources.
    a. I is true; II is false.
    b. I is false; II is true.
    c. Both I and II are true.
    d. Both I and II are false.

The next two questions relate to the material in the addendum to Chapter 2. Use the following production possibilities data for Lebos and Slavia to answer these questions.

LEBOS		SLAVIA	
FOOD	CLOTHING	FOOD	CLOTHING
0	8	0	8
2	6	1	6
4	4	2	4
6	2	3	2
8	0	4	0

23. Which of the following is correct?
    a. In Lebos, the opportunity cost of producing one unit of food is equal to one unit of clothing.
    b. In Slavia, the opportunity cost of producing one unit of food is equal to two units of clothing.
    c. The opportunity cost of producing food in Lebos is less than the opportunity cost of producing food in Slavia.
    d. All of the above are correct.

24. Which of the following is correct?
    a. Lebos has the comparative advantage in both goods.
    b. Slavia has the comparative advantage in food.
    c. Lebos has the comparative advantage in food.
    d. Lebos has the comparative advantage in clothing.

25. The process by which new products and methods of production are continuously replacing old ones is known as:
    a. opportunity cost.
    b. the production possibilities frontier.
    c. creative destruction.
    d. the fallacy of composition.

DISCUSSION QUESTIONS

1. As an individual, you will ultimately take part in determining how your economy answers its three basic economic decisions: What will help you choose what you should produce, how you should produce it, and for whom you should produce it? Are these answers at all interrelated?

2. Consider the cost of this economics course to you.
    a. About how much money did you spend on tuition and books for this course? When did you incur these costs?
    b. What is the cost of actually attending the class once you've paid your tuition and purchased your books?
    c. Use your answer to part b to comment on the following quote: "I could earn $15 if I worked during today's economics class, but tuition averages out to $20 per lecture, so I can't afford to go. If only I went to a university where tuition is lower, I could skip class and earn the money." Do you agree or disagree? Explain your answer.

3. Explain why it is often efficient for faculty members with training in computer programming to hire student programmers to do their computer work.

4. Consider the following quote by a medical doctor who knows something about economics: "It doesn't make sense for me to care for my own lawn when my opportunity cost is $80 per hour."
    a. Do you agree with the doctor's view? Explain.
    b. Would you be surprised to find this doctor's lawn exquisitely maintained? Explain.

5. When the Khmer Rouge came to power in Cambodia in 1975, they sought to eliminate the evils of money. One part of their strategy was to eliminate those jobs that dealt primarily in money rather than the production of goods and services. In other words, they got rid of the "middlemen." What would happen to an economy that had no middlemen? What would happen to the standard of living of the average consumer? Explain.

Unfair Competition with the Sun

by Frederic Bastiat

[From Frederic Bastiat, "Petition of the Manufacturers of Candles, Wax-Lights, Lamps, Candlesticks, Street Lamps, Snuffers, Extinguishers, and of the Producers of Oil, Tallow, Resin, Alcohol, and Generally, of Everything Connected with Lighting." To messieurs the members of the Chamber of Deputies.]

Gentlemen,—You are on the right road. You reject abstract theories, and have little consideration for cheapness and plenty. Your chief care is the interest of the producer. You desire to protect him from foreign competition, and reserve the national market for national industry.

We are suffering from the intolerable competition of a foreign rival, placed, it would seem, in a condition so far superior to ours for the production of light that he absolutely inundates our national market with it at a price fabulously reduced. The moment he shows himself our trade leaves us—all consumers apply to him; and a branch of native industry, having countless ramifications, is all at once rendered completely stagnant. This rival, who is no other than the sun, wages war to the knife against us, and we suspect that he has been raised up by perfidious Albion (a good policy as times go); inasmuch as he displays towards that haughty island a circumspection with which he dispenses in our case.

What we pray for is, that it may please you to pass a law ordering the shutting up of all windows, skylights, dormer windows, outside and inside shutters, curtains, blinds, bull's-eyes, in a word, of all openings, holes, chinks, clefts, and fissures, by or through which the light of the sun has been in use to enter houses, to the prejudice of the meritorious manufactures with which we flatter ourselves we have accommodated our country—a country, which, in gratitude, ought not abandon us now to a strife so unequal.

We trust, Gentlemen, that you will not regard this our request as a satire, or refuse it without at least previously hearing the reasons which we have to urge in its support.

And, first, if you shut up as much as possible all access to natural light, and create a demand for artificial light, which of our French manufacturers will not be encouraged by it?

We foresee your objections, Gentlemen, but we know that you can oppose to us none but such as you have picked up from the effete works of the partisans of Free Trade. We defy you to utter a single word against us which will not instantly rebound against yourselves and your entire policy.

You will tell us that, if we gain by the protection which we seek, the country will lose by it, because the consumer must bear the loss.

We answer:

You have ceased to have any right to invoke the interest of the consumer for, whenever his interest is found opposed to that of the producer, you sacrifice the latter. You have done so for the purpose of encouraging workers and those who seek employment. For the same reason you should do so again.

You have yourselves obviated this objection. When you are told that the consumer is interested in the free importation of iron, coal, corn, textile fabrics—yes, you reply, but the producer is interested in their exclusion. Well, be it so; if consumers are interested in the free admission of natural light, the producers of artificial light are equally interested in its prohibition.

If you urge that the light of the sun is a gratuitous gift of nature, and that to reject such gifts is to reject wealth itself under pretense of encouraging the means of acquiring it, we would caution you against giving a death-blow to your own policy. Remember that hitherto you have always repelled foreign products, because they approximate more nearly than home products to the character of gratuitous gifts.

Nature and human labour cooperate in various proportions (depending on countries and climates) in the production of commodities. The part which nature executes is very gratuitous; it is the part executed by human labour which constitutes value, and is paid for.

If a Lisbon orange sells for half the price of a Paris orange, it is because natural, and consequently gratuitous, heat does for the one what artificial, and therefore expensive, heat must do for the other.

When an orange comes to us from Portugal we may conclude that it is furnished in part gratuitously, in part for an onerous consideration; in other words, it comes to us at half-price as compared with those of Paris.

Now, it is precisely the gratuitous half (pardon the word) which we contend should be excluded. You say, How can national labour sustain competition with foreign labour, when the former has all the work to do, and the latter only does one-half, the sun supplying the remainder. But if this half, being gratuitous, determines you to exclude competition, how should the whole, being gratuitous, induce you to admit competition? If you were consistent, you would, while excluding as hurtful to native industry what is half gratuitous, exclude a fortiori and with double zeal, that which is altogether gratuitous.

One more, when products such as coal, iron, corn, or textile fabrics are sent us from abroad, and we can acquire them with less labour than if we made them ourselves, the difference is a free gift conferred upon us. The gift is more or less considerable in proportion as the difference is more or less great. It amounts to a quarter, a half, or three-quarters of the value of the product, when the foreigner only asks us for three-fourths, a half or a quarter of the price we should otherwise pay. It is as perfect and complete as it can be, when the donor (like the sun is furnishing us with light), asks us for nothing. The question, and we ask it formally, is this: Do you desire for our country the benefit of gratuitous consumption, or the pretended advantages of onerous production?

Make your choice, but be logical; for as long as you exclude as you do, coal, iron, corn, foreign fabrics, in proportion as their price approximates to zero what inconsistency it would be to admit the light of the sun, the price of which is already at zero during the entire day!

DISCUSSION

1. What does the Bastiat reading have to do with this chapter? [Hint: The text states that the law of comparative advantage applies to nations as well as to individuals.] Does comparative advantage mean that all trade is good? Explain your answer.

2. Do you think that individuals or industries ever need protection from competition? If so, how would we decide whether an industry (like the lighting industry or the automobile industry) deserves to be protected from competition?

3. What economic arguments can be made against the proposal?

Supply, Demand, and the Market Process

CHAPTER 3

TRUE OR FALSE

T F

☐ ☐ 1. Consumers will purchase fewer tacos at higher prices than at lower prices if other factors remain the same.

☐ ☐ 2. If the price of bananas increased, the demand for substitutes such as oranges and apples would increase.

☐ ☐ 3. The law of supply reflects the willingness of producers to expand output in response to an increase in the price of a product.

☐ ☐ 4. When consumer purchases of a good are highly responsive to a change in the price of a good, the demand for that good is said to be relatively inelastic.

☐ ☐ 5. An increase in demand for coffee would cause its price to rise and producers to expand output.

☐ ☐ 6. A reduction in the supply of beef would cause the price of beef to fall.

☐ ☐ 7. Hamburgers and hot dogs would be considered substitutes, while peanut butter and jelly would be considered complements.

☐ ☐ 8. If Terri would be willing to pay up to $50 for a pair of jeans and finds them for $30, her purchase would give her $20 in consumer surplus.

☐ ☐ 9. If an increase in the price of pizza resulted in fewer pizzas being sold, this would be considered a reduction in quantity demanded, not a reduction in demand.

☐ ☐ 10. Three factors that will each cause the supply curve for Napa county wine to shift to the left include a drought in Napa county, higher wages for Napa county grape pickers, and lower prices for Napa county wine.

T   F

☐   ☐   11.   If an increase in the cost of lumber resulted in fewer new homes being produced, this would be considered a reduction in quantity supplied, not a reduction in supply.

☐   ☐   12.   An increase in the price of lumber used in the construction industry would cause housing prices to rise and the demand for housing to decline.

☐   ☐   13.   An increase in consumer income would cause the demand for new cars to increase.

☐   ☐   14.   Government regulation is the only way to coordinate economic activity in complex societies like the United States with millions of individuals buying and selling goods and services.

PROBLEMS AND PROJECTS

EXHIBIT 1

Price (1)	Initial Quantity Demanded (2)	Quantity Supplied (3)	New Quantity Demanded (4)
$ 6	60	20	80
9	50	30	70
12	40	40	60
15	30	50	50
18	20	60	40

1.   Exhibit 1 presents hypothetical supply and demand schedules for shoes in a local market area.

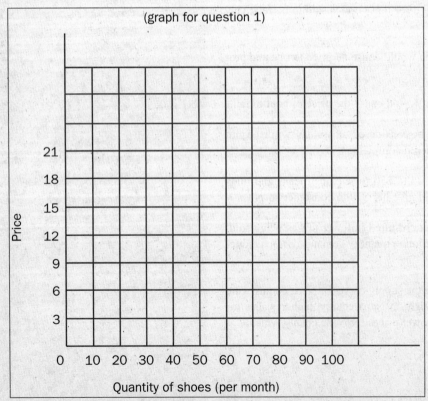

(graph for question 1)

Price

21
18
15
12
9
6
3

0   10   20   30   40   50   60   70   80   90   100

Quantity of shoes (per month)

a.   Graph the initial demand curve (column 2) on the chart to the left.
b.   Graph the initial supply curve (column 3) on the chart to the left.
c.   What is the initial equilibrium price?
d.   The region experiences a boom and consumer income increases, causing an increase in demand. The new demand schedule is indicated in column 4. Graph the new demand curve in the chart.
e.   What is the new equilibrium price?
f.   What has happened on the demand side of the market? Is it a change in demand or a change in quantity demanded?
g.   What has happened on the supply side of the market? Is it a change in supply or a change in quantity supplied?

EXHIBIT 2

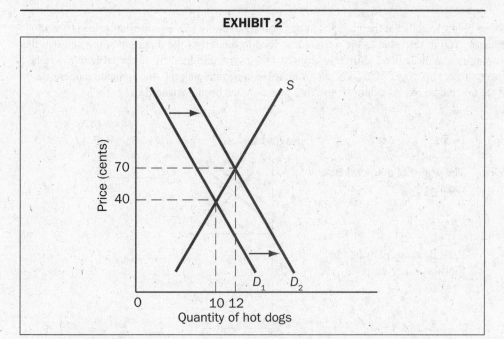

2. As indicated by Exhibit 2, the initial demand for hot dogs is D_1. The supply is S.
    a. What is the initial equilibrium price? quantity sold?
    b. Hamburgers are a substitute for hot dogs. Higher hamburger prices cause the demand for hot dogs to increase to D_2. What is the new equilibrium price? quantity sold?
    c. Suppose instead of hamburger prices rising, hot dog bun prices have fallen. Would the impact of the lower hot dog bun prices on the market for hot dogs be the same?

3. The pricing system sends out signals that influence the decisions of producers and consumers. Understanding the secondary effects of a change in market conditions is essential if one is to understand how a market system works. Suppose that the price of gasoline rose sharply. What do you think would happen to
    a. the demand for smaller, more fuel efficient cars relative to large cars?
    b. the demand for other leisure goods (such as home swimming pools), relative to cross-country driving vacations?
    c. employment in the tourism industry? (hint: higher gas prices increase the cost of traveling)
    d. the prices of consumer goods that require transportation?
    e. the demand for alternative energy sources (such as solar power) and the incentive to produce them?
    f. the incentive to find and develop new oil reserves to produce gasoline?
    g. the price of electricity, firewood, and other substitute fuels?

4. Use the diagrams below to indicate the changes in demand (D), supply (S), equilibrium price (P), and equilibrium quantity (Q) in response to the events described to the left of the diagrams. First show in the diagrams how supply and/or demand shift in response to the event, and then fill in the table to the right of the diagrams using a plus sign (+) to indicate an increase, a negative sign (−) to indicate a decrease, and 0 to indicate no change. As an example, the first question has been answered.

	Market	Event	Diagrams	D	S	P	Q
a.	Automobiles	The wages of autoworkers increase.		0	−	+	−
b.	Oranges	Frost destroys half the Florida orange crop.		—	—	—	—
c.	Butter	There is a decrease in the price of margarine (a substitute for butter).		—	—	—	—
d.	Lumber	Lower interest rates cause a housing construction boom.		—	—	—	—
e.	Wine	A technological advance lowers the cost of growing grapes.		—	—	—	—

5. Exhibit 3 illustrates two different demand curves with different slopes, D_1 and D_2.
    a. If the price rises from $5 to $15, by how much will consumer purchases fall if the demand curve is given by D_1?
    b. If the price rises from $5 to $15, by how much will consumer purchases fall if the demand curve is instead given by D_2?
    c. Which of the demand curves represents consumers being more responsive in their purchases to a change in the price of the good?
    d. Which of the demand curves would be considered relatively elastic? Which would be considered relatively inelastic?

EXHIBIT 3

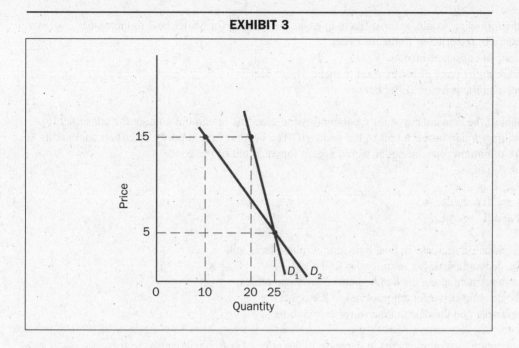

MULTIPLE CHOICE

1. If the price of tickets to the World Series were set below the equilibrium price,
   a. the quantity demanded would be smaller than the quantity supplied.
   b. the demand for World Series tickets would be highly responsive to the price.
   c. there would be no transactions between buyers and sellers of the tickets.
   d. the number of persons seeking to obtain tickets to World Series games would be greater than the number of tickets available.

2. Which of the following would cause the price of automobiles to rise?
   a. a decrease in the wages of autoworkers
   b. a reduction in the price of bus travel
   c. an increase in the price of gasoline
   d. an increase in consumer income

3. Which of the following would be the best example of consumer surplus?
   a. Jane pays $30 a month for phone service even though it is worth $70 to her.
   b. Sam refuses to pay $10 for a haircut because it is only worth $8 to him.
   c. Fred buys a car for $4,000, the maximum amount that he would be willing to pay for it.
   d. When Sue purchases a candy bar for $.50, she uses a $20 bill to pay for it.

4. If cigars and cigarettes are substitute goods, an increase in the price of cigars would result in
   a. an increase in the demand for cigarettes.
   b. a decrease in the price of cigarettes.
   c. a decrease in the demand for cigarettes.
   d. a decrease in the demand for cigars.

5. Which of the following would most likely cause the current demand for DVD players to fall?
   a. an increase in consumer income
   b. an increase in the price of DVD players
   c. an increase in the price of Blu-ray players, a substitute good
   d. the expectation that the price of DVD players will decrease sharply during the next six months

6. Which of the following would be most likely to cause the demand for Miller beer to increase?
    a. an increase in the price of Budweiser beer
    b. a decrease in consumer income
    c. a decrease in the price of barley used to make Miller beer
    d. a decrease in the price of Miller beer

7. (I) The height of the demand curve for a commodity indicates the maximum amount the consumer would be willing to pay for each unit of the good. (II) The height of the supply curve for a commodity indicates the minimum price the seller would accept for each unit of the good.
    a. I is true; II is false.
    b. I is false; II is true.
    c. Both I and II are false.
    d. Both I and II are true.

8. All things constant, a decrease in bus, train, and airplane fares will
    a. shift the demand curve for automobiles to the left.
    b. cause a movement along the demand curve for automobiles.
    c. shift the demand curve for automobiles to the right.
    d. have no impact on the demand curve for automobiles.

9. If coffee and cream are complements, a decrease in the price of coffee will cause
    a. the demand for cream to decrease.
    b. the demand for cream to increase.
    c. the demand for coffee to increase.
    d. no change in the demand for cream; only quantity demanded would be affected.

10. If the market price is above the equilibrium price, there will be a tendency for price to decrease, causing
    a. the quantity demanded to decrease and the quantity supplied to increase until they are equal.
    b. the quantity demanded to increase and the quantity supplied to decrease until they are equal.
    c. both quantity demanded and quantity supplied to decrease until they are equal.
    d. both quantity demanded and quantity supplied to increase until they are equal.

11. According to the law of supply, as the price of a good decreases
    a. buyers will buy more of the good.
    b. sellers will produce more of the good.
    c. buyers will buy less of the good.
    d. sellers will produce less of the good.

12. John advertises his used car for $3,000 in the newspaper. He would be willing to sell his used car for as low as $2,000. He is offered $2,600 for it from a buyer and accepts it. In this trade, John receives
    a. producer surplus of $3,000.
    b. producer surplus of $2,600.
    c. producer surplus of $600.
    d. consumer surplus of $400.

13. Economic efficiency requires that
    a. individuals take all actions within their power.
    b. only long-lasting, high-quality products be produced.
    c. income be distributed equally among individuals.
    d. all economic activity generating more benefits than costs to individuals in the economy be undertaken.

14. If the demand for beer increased, what would be the effect on the equilibrium price and quantity of beer?
    a. price increases, quantity decreases
    b. price decreases, quantity decreases
    c. price increases, quantity increases
    d. price decreases, quantity increases

EXHIBIT 4

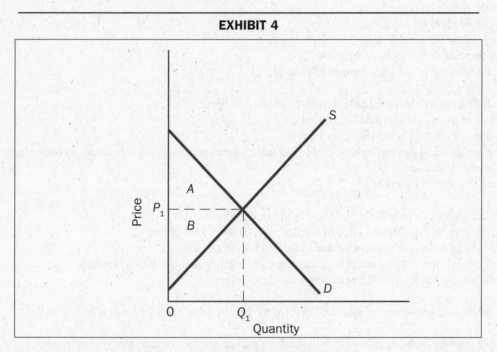

15. In Exhibit 4, there are two triangular areas indicated by the letters A and B. Which of the following is true?
    a. A represents consumer surplus; B represents producer surplus.
    b. A represents producer surplus; B represents consumer surplus.
    c. Both areas A and B represent consumer surplus.
    d. Both areas A and B represent producer surplus.

16. "Falling consumer income from the recent recession has hurt automakers in more ways than one. Not only have sales of new cars fallen, but car prices have fallen as well. As a result, the major automakers have announced cutbacks in production and layoffs of workers." Which of the following places these statements in the proper economic terminology within the context of the supply and demand model? [Note: It may help to graph this first.]
    a. a decrease in demand and a decrease in supply
    b. a decrease in demand and a decrease in quantity supplied
    c. a decrease in quantity demanded and a decrease in quantity supplied
    d. a decrease in quantity demanded and a decrease in supply

17. "If gasoline were taxed, the price of gasoline would rise. Consequently, the demand for gasoline would fall, causing the price to fall to the original level." This statement is
    a. essentially correct.
    b. incorrect—after the demand falls, the price would fall but to some level higher than the original level.
    c. incorrect—demand and quantity demanded are confused. The price increase would reduce quantity demanded, not demand.
    d. incorrect—after the demand falls, the price would fall but to some level lower than the original level.

18. Over the past 20 years both the quantity of health care provided and health care prices have been rising rapidly. Economic theory would suggest that the observed data could best be explained as
    a. an increase in supply, while demand remained relatively constant.
    b. a decrease in both supply and demand.
    c. an increase in demand, while supply remained relatively constant.
    d. a sharp increase in both supply and demand.

19. A decrease in the supply of a good will
    a. decrease the demand for the good.
    b. cause the price of the good to fall.
    c. lead to an increase in the price of the good.
    d. increase the quantity of the good bought and sold.

20. Which of the following would most likely decrease the price of beef?
    a. lower prices of grains used to produce cattle feed
    b. higher prices for chicken, a substitute for beef
    c. a cow disease that destroys millions of cattle (and makes their meat unfit for consumption) before they are ready for market
    d. an increase in consumer income

21. A decrease in the price of flour will shift the supply curve for donuts
    a. leftward, causing the equilibrium price to increase and quantity to decrease.
    b. leftward, causing the equilibrium price and quantity to decrease.
    c. rightward, causing the equilibrium price to decrease and equilibrium quantity to increase.
    d. rightward, causing the equilibrium price and quantity to increase.

22. When Adam Smith said economic activity was directed by an "invisible hand," he was referring to the fact that
    a. competitive markets motivate altruistic individuals to pursue productive activities that only serve their private interests.
    b. when economic activity is directed by competitive markets, the actions of self-interested individuals will generally serve the public interest.
    c. invisible forces will lead to economic chaos unless wise central planning directs economic activity.
    d. scarcity is largely the result of invisible forces that would be eliminated if individuals were free to pursue their own self-interests.

23. A hurricane damaged much of the housing in Miami. Shortly thereafter, the price of plywood rose significantly. The events suggest that
    a. a decrease in the supply of plywood caused the price of plywood to rise.
    b. an increase in the supply of plywood caused the price of plywood to rise.
    c. a decrease in the demand for plywood caused the price of plywood to rise.
    d. an increase in the demand for plywood caused the price of plywood to rise.

24. If the demand for a good increases, which of the following will generally occur in a market setting?
    a. The price of the good will decrease.
    b. The supply of the good will increase.
    c. The quantity supplied will increase.
    d. Producer profits will fall.

25. A freeze in Florida devastates the orange crop at the same time a new study is released showing the health benefits of vitamin C (leading consumers to want to buy more orange juice). How will the equilibrium price and quantity of orange juice change in response to the combination of these two events?
    a. Equilibrium quantity will decrease, equilibrium price will increase.
    b. Equilibrium price will decrease, the effect on quantity is ambiguous.
    c. Equilibrium price will increase, the effect on quantity is ambiguous.
    d. Equilibrium quantity will increase, the effect on price is ambiguous.

DISCUSSION QUESTIONS

1. In an effort to increase the number of students going to college, the federal government is considering legislation that would give a large tax credit to low-income families with college tuition payments. What impact would the legislation have on the
   a. number of students attempting to enroll in college?
   b. price of tuition for other students?
   c. salaries earned by college graduates?
   d. wage rates in low-skilled occupations that only require a high school degree?
   e. salaries earned by college professors?

2. Consider the following statement: "Campus parking permits and meters are inefficient and unfair. Campus parking should be free, with parking spaces allocated on a first-come, first-served basis."
   a. Is "free" parking that requires time to hunt for a space (or requires students to get into school earlier) really free?
   b. Is "free" parking more efficient than permit or meter parking? In other words, is rationing the spaces by price more or less efficient than rationing them by the cost of student time?
   c. With "free" parking, who, if anyone, gains? Who loses?
   d. Would you favor "free" parking on your campus? Why or why not?

3. Explain what is wrong with the following reasoning: "When meat prices rise due to a decrease in the supply of meat, the demand for meat decreases, so meat prices end up falling."
   a. Suppose a price is temporarily above its equilibrium level. How do you think producers figure out the price is in fact "too high"? Explain how a lower price causes both production and consumption adjustments to help correct the situation.
   b. Suppose a price is temporarily below its equilibrium level. How do you think producers figure out the price is in fact "too low"? Explain how a higher price causes both production and consumption adjustments to help correct the situation.

4. People often use the term "demand" when they actually mean "quantity demanded"; the same is true of "supply" and "quantity supplied."
   a. What causes a change in quantity demanded but not a change in demand?
   b. With market-determined prices, can the following statement be true? "The demand for oil is expected to exceed supply by 2050."
   c. How can you rephrase the statement of part b so that it makes economic sense?

5. Define both consumer and producer surplus, and give an example of each. Define economic efficiency, and show graphically how it relates to the consumer and producer surplus areas within a supply and demand graph.

6. There are some occasions when shortages or surpluses appear. For example, there is routinely a shortage of tickets to "hot" concerts or sporting events—people who want the tickets at the listed price are unable to get them. Can you think of any other situations you have seen where the market had either a shortage or a surplus (in other words, out of equilibrium)? Was the situation temporary? What caused the problem? Was the price set too high or too low?

7. During the recent financial crisis, the federal government provided significant bailouts to many struggling companies including banks and automobile companies. How would the normal profit and loss system of the market have worked in these cases had the government not provided these taxpayer subsidies? Do you think that the government's interference with the profit and loss system will have significant unintended consequences?

PERSPECTIVES IN ECONOMICS

The Use of Knowledge in Society

by Friedrich A. Hayek

[Abridged from "The Use of Knowledge in Society," *American Economic Review,* volume 35, number 4, September 1945, pp. 519–530. Reprinted with permission.]

What is the problem we wish to solve when we try to construct a rational economic order?

On certain familiar assumptions the answer is simple enough. If we possess all the relevant information, if we can start out from a given system of preferences and if we command complete knowledge of available means, the problem which remains is purely one of logic.

This, however, is emphatically not the economic problem which society faces. The reason for this is that the "data" from which the economic calculus starts are never for the whole society "given" to a single mind which could work out the implications, and can never be so given.

The peculiar character of the problem of a rational economic order is determined precisely by the fact that the knowledge of the circumstances of which we must make use never exists in concentrated or integrated form, but solely as the dispersed bits of incomplete and frequently contradictory knowledge which all the separate individuals possess. The economic problem of society is thus not merely a problem of how to allocate "given" resources—if "given" is taken to mean given to a single mind which deliberately solves the problem set by these "data." It is rather a problem of how to secure the best use of resources known to any of the members of society, for ends whose relative importance only these individuals know. Or, to put it briefly, it is a problem of the utilization of knowledge not given to anyone in its totality.

If we can agree that the economic problem of society is mainly one of rapid adaptation to changes in the particular circumstances of time and place, it would seem to follow that the ultimate decisions must be left to the people who are familiar with these circumstances, who know directly of the relevant changes and of the resources immediately available to meet them. We cannot expect that this problem will be solved by first communicating all this knowledge to a central board which, after integrating all knowledge, issues its orders. We must solve it by some form of decentralization. But this answers only part of our problem. We need decentralization because only thus can we ensure that the knowledge of the particular circumstances of time and place will be promptly used. But the "man on the spot" cannot decide solely on the basis of his limited but intimate knowledge of the facts of his immediate surroundings. There still remains the problem of communicating to him such further information as he needs to fit his decisions into the whole pattern of changes of the larger economic system.

There is hardly anything that happens anywhere in the world that might not have an effect on the decision he ought to make. Be he need not know of these events as such, not of all their effects. It does not matter for him why at the particular moment more screws of one size than of another are wanted, why paper bags are more readily available than canvas bags, or why skilled labor, or particular machine tools, have for the moment become more difficult to acquire. All that is significant for him is how much more or less difficult to procure they have become compared with other things with which he is also concerned, or how much more or less urgently wanted are the alternative things he produces or uses. It is always a question of the relative importance of the particular things with which he is concerned, and the causes which alter their relative importance are of no interest to him beyond the effect on those concrete things of his own environment.

Fundamentally, in a system where the knowledge of the relevant facts is dispersed among many people, prices can act to coordinate the separate actions of different people in the same way as subjective values help the individual to coordinate the parts of his plan. It is worth contemplating for a moment a very simple and commonplace instance of the action of the price system to see what precisely it accomplishes. Assume that somewhere in the world a new opportunity for the use of some raw material, say tin, has arisen, or that one of the sources of supply of tin has been eliminated. It does not matter for our purpose—and it is very significant that it does not matter—which of these two causes has made tin more scarce. All that the users of tin need to know is that some of the tin they used to consume is now more profitably employed elsewhere, and that in consequence they must economize tin. There is no need for the great majority of them even to know where the more urgent need has arisen, or in favor of what other needs they ought to husband the supply. If only some of them know directly of the new demand, and switch resources over to it, and if the people who are aware of the new gap thus created in turn fill it from still other sources, the effect will rapidly spread throughout the whole economic system and influence not only all the uses of tin, but also those of its substitutes and the substitutes of these substitutes, the supply of all the things made of tin, and their substitutes, and so on; and all this without the great majority of those instrumental in bringing about these substitutions knowing anything at all about the original cause of these changes. The whole acts as one market, not because any of its members survey the whole field, but because their limited individual fields of vision sufficiently overlap so that through many intermediaries the relevant information is communicated to all.

We must look at the price system as such a mechanism for communicating information if we want to understand its real function. The most significant fact about this system is the economy of knowledge with which it operates, or how little the individual participants need to know in order to be able to take the right action. In abbreviated form, by a kind of symbol, only the most essential information is passed on, and passed on only to those concerned. It is more than a metaphor to describe the price system as a kind of machinery for registering change, or a system of telecommunications which enables individual producers to watch merely the movement of a few pointers, as an engineer might watch the hands of a few dials, in order to adjust their activities to changes of which they may never know more than is reflected in the price movement.

Of course, these adjustments are probably never "perfect" in the sense in which the economist conceives of them in his equilibrium analysis. But I fear that our theoretical habits of approaching the problem with the assumption of more or less perfect knowledge on the part of almost everyone has made us somewhat blind to the true function of the price mechanism and led us to apply rather misleading standards in judging its efficiency. The marvel is that in a case like that of a scarcity of one raw material, without an order being issued, without more than perhaps a handful of people knowing the cause, tens of thousands of people whose identity could not be ascertained by months of investigation, are made to use the material or its products more sparingly; i.e., they move in the right direction. This is enough of a marvel even if, in a constantly changing world, not all will hit it off so perfectly that their profit rates will always be maintained at the same constant or "normal" level.

I have deliberately used the word "marvel" to shock the reader out of the complacency with which we often take the working of this mechanism for granted. I am convinced that if it were the result of deliberate human design, and if the people guided by the price changes understood that their decisions have significance far beyond their immediate aim, this mechanism would have been acclaimed as one of the greatest triumphs of the human mind. Its misfortune is the double one that it is not the product of human design and that the people guided by it usually do not know why they are made to do what they do. But those who clamor for "conscious direction"—and who cannot believe that anything which has evolved without design (and even without our understanding it) should solve problems which we should not be able to solve consciously—should remember this: The problem is precisely how to extend the span of our utilization of resources beyond the span of the control of any one mind; and, therefore, how to dispense with the need of conscious control and how to provide inducements which will make the individuals do the desirable things without anyone having to tell them what to do.

The price system is just one of those formations which man has learned to use (though he is still very far from having learned to make the best use of it) after he had stumbled upon it without understanding it. Through it not only a division of labor but also a coordinated utilization of resources based on an equally divided knowledge has become possible. The people who like to deride any suggestion that this may be so usually distort the argument by insinuating that it asserts that by some miracle just that sort of system has spontaneously grown up which is best suited to modern civilization. It is the other way round: man has been able to develop that division of labor on which our civilization is based because he happened to stumble upon a method which made it possible. Had he not done so he might still have developed some other, altogether different, type of civilization, something like the "state" of the termite ants, or some other altogether unimaginable type. All that we can say is that nobody has yet succeeded in designing an alternative system in which certain features of the existing one can be preserved which are dear even to those who most violently assail it—such as particularly the extent to which the individual can choose his pursuits and consequently freely use his own knowledge and skill.

DISCUSSION

1. What does the Hayek reading have to do with this chapter? How does it relate to Adam Smith's invisible hand principle?

2. Are prices an effective mechanism to communicate information? Do they save people time in having to acquire information about events to adjust their behavior?

3. Do the signals sent by price changes cause people to adjust their behavior in ways that are consistent with what is best for society in the face of the new events?

Supply and Demand: Applications and Extensions

TRUE OR FALSE

T F

1. Wage rates and interest rates are both market prices determined by the relative supply and demand in those markets.

2. If the demand for housing increased, the demand for resources used to produce housing (such as lumber) would fall.

3. The benefits of a $20 government textbook subsidy program to students will be the same regardless if the subsidy is directly paid to students or if it is paid to bookstores.

4. Black markets operate outside the legal system and thus suffer from a higher incidence of defective products and use of violence.

5. If a landlord is faced with a government-imposed price ceiling set below the equilibrium level, a common response would be to improve the quality of housing in order to attract new tenants.

6. Because the demand for tobacco is relatively inelastic, a subsidy to tobacco farmers will provide little benefit to tobacco consumers.

7. If the government imposed a price ceiling of $1 on compact discs, there would be a surplus of compact discs.

8. Shortages arise when prices are legally set above the equilibrium level.

9. The minimum wage increases unemployment among unskilled workers.

T F

☐ ☐ 10. As illegal drug markets illustrate, the lack of contract and private property right enforcement causes harmful secondary effects that keep these black markets from operating as smoothly as legal markets.

☐ ☐ 11. The individuals on whom a tax is imposed are always the ones who end up bearing the burden of the tax.

☐ ☐ 12. The actual burden of a tax does not depend on the original legal (or statutory) assignment of the tax, but it does depend upon the elasticities of demand and supply.

☐ ☐ 13. Because taxes reduce the number of mutually beneficial trades in a market, they create an excess burden (or deadweight loss) in addition to the direct revenue burden of the tax.

☐ ☐ 14. A proportional tax is one in which everyone pays the same dollar amount of taxes regardless of income.

☐ ☐ 15. When marginal tax rates are very high, the Laffer curve suggests that lowering tax rates will result in an *increase* in tax revenue.

PROBLEMS AND PROJECTS

1. Exhibit 1 shows the job market for accountants. Using Exhibit 1(i), show how an increase in the number of students majoring in accounting would affect the wage rate and employment of accountants. Using Exhibit 1(ii), show how a tax reform that vastly increased the simplicity of the tax code would affect the wage rate and employment of accountants.

EXHIBIT 1

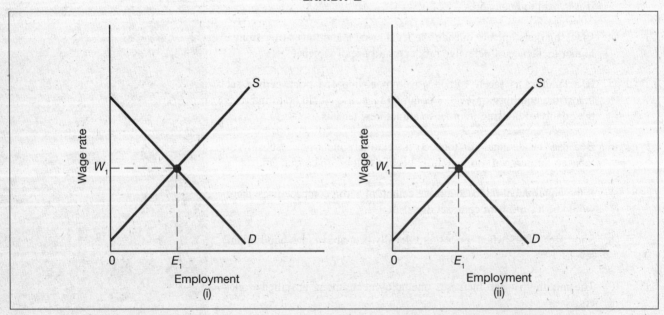

EXHIBIT 2

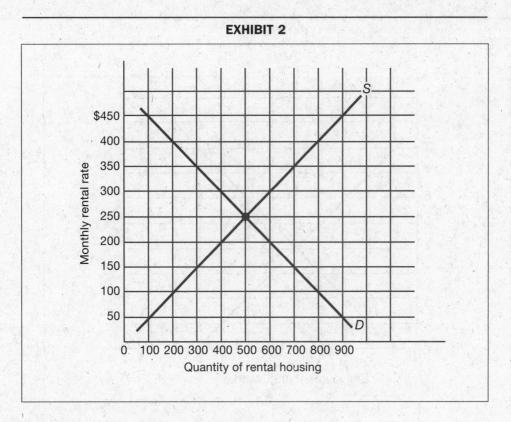

2. Exhibit 2 shows the market for rental housing in a college town.
   a. Indicate in the diagram the equilibrium price and quantity for rental housing.
   b. If a law is passed setting a maximum monthly rental rate at $100, what would happen to the quantity of rental housing supplied? the quantity demanded? Is there a surplus or a shortage?
   c. What would you expect to happen to the rate of new rental housing construction in the future?
   d. What would you expect to happen to the quality of rental housing in the area?
   e. With so many renters hunting after only a very limited number of apartments, what criterion do you think landlords will use to ration the apartments now that they are forbidden by law from rationing them by price?

EXHIBIT 3

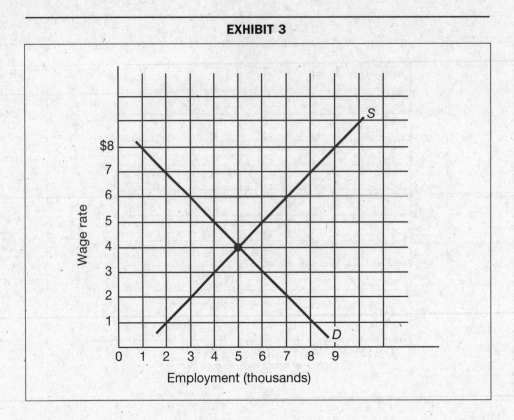

3. Exhibit 3 shows the market for unskilled labor.
    a. Indicate in the diagram the equilibrium wage and level of employment for unskilled labor.
    b. Suppose a minimum wage of $6 per hour is enacted for unskilled labor. What would happen to the number of workers searching for jobs in this market (that is, the quantity of labor supplied)? What would happen to the number of job openings available at this higher wage rate (that is, the quantity of labor demanded)?
    c. Does the imposition of the minimum wage create a shortage or a surplus of labor?
    d. Are the workers who are able to retain their jobs at this higher wage better off or worse off?
    e. Are the workers who are now no longer able to find jobs at this higher wage better off or worse off?

4. Exhibit 4 shows how a $1 per beer tax, statutorily imposed on beer sellers, affects the market for beer. Use Exhibit 4 to answer the following questions.
    a. What was the original price of beer prior to the imposition of the tax?
    b. What is the new price that a consumer must pay for a beer after the imposition of the tax on sellers? How much has the price to consumers risen?
    c. After selling a beer at the new market price, the seller must send the government $1 in tax for the beer. What is the new net (after-tax) price the seller receives from selling a beer? How much has the price a seller receives fallen?
    d. Who has borne the larger share of the actual burden of the tax, beer buyers or sellers?
    e. How much revenue has the government raised from this tax? Shade in the area that represents tax revenue in the exhibit.
    f. How much has this tax reduced beer consumption? Shade in the area in Exhibit 4 representing the losses to buyers and sellers from the reductions in these trades (that is, the area representing the deadweight loss of the tax).
    g. Show in Exhibit 4 how the market would have appeared had an equal tax have been imposed on buyers instead of sellers (so that there would be a tax amount added on your purchase, just as is

EXHIBIT 4

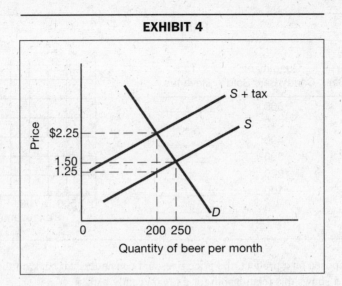

the regular consumer sales tax). What would have been the new market price of beer? How much would sellers have received per beer sold? How much would consumers pay for a beer considering both the price of a beer and the additional $1 tax?

h. How would the actual burden of the tax differed had the tax been imposed on buyers rather than sellers?

5. Reagan currently makes $50,000 in taxable income and pays $10,000 in taxes on her income. Her boss offers her a promotion that would double her taxable income to $100,000 per year.
   a. What is Reagan's current average tax rate on her income?
   b. Suppose that at her new level of income ($100,000) she will owe $15,000 in taxes. What will be her new average tax rate? What is the marginal tax rate on this additional income? What percent of her additional income does she get to keep in the form of additional take-home pay? Is this tax code regressive, proportional, or progressive?
   c. Explain how in part b (above) the tax is regressive even though she is now paying more taxes than before ($15,000 in taxes as opposed to her old taxes of $10,000).
   d. Instead, now suppose that at her new level of income ($100,000) she will owe $20,000 in taxes. What will be her new average tax rate? What is the marginal tax rate on this additional income? What percent of her additional income does she get to keep in the form of additional take-home pay? Is this tax code regressive, proportional, or progressive?
   e. Instead, now suppose that at her new level of income ($100,000) she will owe $35,000 in taxes. What will be her new average tax rate? What is the marginal tax rate on this additional income? What percent of her additional income does she get to keep in the form of additional take-home pay? Is this tax code regressive, proportional, or progressive?
   f. Instead, now suppose that at her new level of income ($100,000) she will owe $60,000 in taxes. What will be her new average tax rate? What is the marginal tax rate on this additional income? What percent of her additional income does she get to keep in the form of additional take-home pay? Is this tax code regressive, proportional, or progressive? Under this final case, would you suggest she take the promotion if it required additional responsibilities and longer work hours?

EXHIBIT 5

Tax per Candy Bar	Quantity of Candy Bars Sold	Tax Revenue
$0	600	$_____
1	500	_____
2	400	_____
3	300	_____
4	200	_____
5	100	_____
6	0	_____

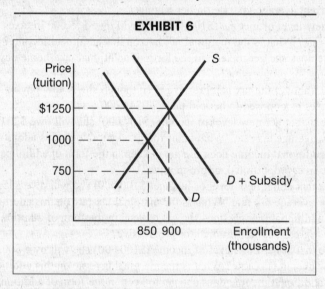

6. When a tax is imposed on a product, the price rises and consumers cut back on their purchases of the product. Exhibit 5 shows this relationship for a tax on candy bars.
   a. For each tax rate, calculate the total tax revenue raised by the tax and put your numbers in the spaces provided in the Exhibit 5.
   b. Now, using your answers from part a, plot the relationship between the tax rate and tax revenue in the space provided. Connect the data points with a curved line; this is the Laffer curve for the candy bar tax.
   c. If the government's objective was to maximize the revenue from this tax, what tax rate should be chosen?
   d. If the current tax rate on candy bars was $5, what would you suggest the government do if it wanted to increase its revenue, lower or raise the candy bar tax?

EXHIBIT 6

7. Exhibit 6 shows the impact of a $500 tuition subsidy for college students on college tuition and enrollment. Answer the following questions regarding the impact of the subsidy.
   a. In this program, is the subsidy paid directly to the student or to the college they attend? (Hint: You can tell by which curve is shifted.)
   b. What is the amount of the subsidy?
   c. How much was the average tuition before the subsidy program was enacted? How does the tuition price charged by colleges change in response to the subsidy program?
   d. How does the subsidy program affect the cost of attending college, taking into account the subsidy?
   e. If only some subset of students was eligible for the subsidy (low-income students, for example), how would other students who don't qualify for the program be affected?

MULTIPLE CHOICE

1. An increase in the demand for a product will cause output to
   a. increase and both the demand for and prices of the resources used to produce the product to increase.
   b. increase and both the demand for and prices of the resources used to produce the product to decrease.
   c. decrease; the demand for the resources used to produce the product will remain constant.
   d. decrease; the price of resources used to produce the product will decrease.

2. Which of the following is a true statement regarding the economic impact of a subsidy?
   a. The distribution of the benefits from a subsidy will depend on whether the subsidy is legally granted to the buyer or seller.
   b. When demand is relatively inelastic, the benefits of a subsidy will mainly accrue to sellers.
   c. When supply is relatively elastic, the benefits of a subsidy will mainly accrue to buyers.
   d. When demand is relatively elastic, the benefits of a subsidy will mainly accrue to buyers.

3. The average tax rate (ATR) is defined as
   a. taxable income divided by tax liability.
   b. change in tax liability divided by change in taxable income.
   c. tax liability divided by taxable income.
   d. change in taxable income divided by change in tax liability.

4. During the imposition of price controls in the 1970s, long gasoline lines were common. In the absence of price controls, markets would have eliminated such excess demand by
   a. allowing the price to rise, so gas was rationed to those willing to pay the most for it.
   b. increasing the gap between supply and demand.
   c. allowing price to decline, so the poor could afford to buy more gas.
   d. mandating a 50-mile-per-hour speed limit to reduce consumption.

5. If an increase in the government-imposed minimum wage pushes the price (wage) of unskilled labor above market equilibrium, which of the following will most likely occur in the unskilled labor market?
   a. an increase in demand for unskilled labor
   b. a decrease in the supply of unskilled labor
   c. a shortage of unskilled labor
   d. a surplus of unskilled labor

6. With a price ceiling above the equilibrium price,
   a. quantity demanded would exceed quantity supplied.
   b. quantity supplied would exceed quantity demanded.
   c. the market would be in equilibrium.
   d. the equilibrium price would be expected to fall over time.

7. Rent controls generally fix the price of rental housing below market equilibrium. Economic analysis suggests these controls
   a. are effective in helping the poor find housing.
   b. improve the quality of housing available to consumers.
   c. create a surplus of rental housing.
   d. reduce the future supply of rental housing.

8. Because illegal drug markets operate outside the legal system,
   a. the quality of these drugs has increased.
   b. the sellers of illegal drugs earn less money.
   c. there is less violence in these markets than if they were legal.
   d. none of the above.

9. Currently, federal and state gasoline taxes (imposed statutorily on the sellers of gasoline) amount to about $.45 per gallon. Suppose the current price of gasoline is $1.20 per gallon, and that if the tax was not in place, the price would be only $.80.
    a. The full incidence of the tax is falling on consumers.
    b. The full incidence of the tax is falling on suppliers.
    c. A $.05 burden is being borne by sellers and $.40 by consumers.
    d. A $.05 burden is being borne by consumers and $.40 by sellers.

10. The deadweight loss resulting from levying a tax on an economic activity is
    a. the tax revenue directed to the government as the result of the tax.
    b. the loss of potential gains from trade from activities forgone because of the tax.
    c. the increase in the price of an activity as the result of the tax levied on it.
    d. the marginal benefits derived from the expansion in government activities made possible by the increase in tax revenues.

11. Suppose there is an increase in the excise tax imposed on cigarettes, a good for which the demand is relatively inelastic. The short-run burden of the tax increase will be borne primarily by
    a. consumers, because the increase in market price will be large relative to the increase in the excise tax.
    b. firms, because the increase in market price will be large relative to the increase in the excise tax.
    c. consumers, because the increase in market price will be small relative to the increase in the excise tax.
    d. firms, because the increase in market price will be small relative to the increase in the excise tax.

12. An income tax is regressive if
    a. the tax liability of high-income recipients exceeds the tax liability of those with low incomes.
    b. the tax liability of high-income recipients is less than the tax liability of those with low incomes.
    c. high-income recipients pay a higher percentage of their incomes in taxes than those with low incomes.
    d. high-income recipients pay a lower percentage of their incomes in taxes than those whose incomes are low.

13. Use the table below to choose the correct answer.

INCOME	TAX LIABILITY
$10,000	$1,000
20,000	2,000
30,000	3,000
40,000	4,000

For the income range illustrated, the tax shown here is
    a. regressive.
    b. proportional.
    c. progressive.
    d. progressive up to $30,000 but regressive beyond that.

14. In the mid-1940s, the marginal income tax rate in the top income tax bracket was 94 percent. In the 1960s, the top rate was lowered to 70 percent, and in the 1980s, the top rate was again lowered to 28 percent. The data show that as a result of these tax rate reductions, tax revenue (particularly from the rich) increased. This is consistent with the idea illustrated with the
    a. Laffer curve.
    b. production possibilities curve.
    c. supply of loanable funds curve.
    d. demand for unskilled labor curve.

15. The Laffer curve illustrates the principle that
    a. when tax rates are quite high, reducing tax rates will increase tax revenue.
    b. when tax rates are quite low, reducing tax rates will increase tax revenue.
    c. when tax rates are quite high, reducing tax rates will decrease tax revenue.
    d. increasing tax rates always increases tax revenue.

16. If Joan pays $5,000 in taxes when she earns $20,000 and must pay $12,000 in taxes when she earns $30,000, she faces a marginal tax rate in this income range of
    a. 25 percent.
    b. 30 percent.
    c. 40 percent.
    d. 70 percent.

17. A legal minimum wage is an example of
    a. the invisible hand principle.
    b. a price floor.
    c. a price ceiling.
    d. a fringe benefit.

18. Both price floors and price ceilings, when effective, lead to
    a. shortages.
    b. surpluses.
    c. an increase in the quantity traded.
    d. a reduction in the quantity traded.

19. If there was an increase in the excise tax on beer, what would be the effect on the equilibrium price and quantity of beer?
    a. price increases, quantity decreases
    b. price decreases, quantity decreases
    c. price increases, quantity increases
    d. price decreases, quantity increases

20. The more elastic the supply of a product, the more likely it is that the burden of a tax will
    a. fall on sellers.
    b. fall on buyers.
    c. fall equally on both buyers and sellers.
    d. be borne by the public sector, and not by market participants.

DISCUSSION QUESTIONS

1. Many uninformed people believe that the reductions in the income tax rates during the 1980s were the cause of the large budget deficits during that period. However, data show that the effect of the tax rate reductions was to increase tax revenue, not lower it.
    a. Use the Laffer curve to illustrate how a reduction in tax rates can increase tax revenue.
    b. Explain in words how it is possible to obtain more revenue when tax rates are lowered. (Hint: What must happen to the tax base?)
    c. Had the tax rate reductions not have been enacted, would the budget problems have been worse or better?

2. Evaluate the following statements. "Currently there are 100,000 six-packs of soda sold per year in our state. We are going to impose a $10 tax on each six-pack and require that the seller of the soda pays the tax. In this way we will raise $1,000,000 for the state budget, and none of the burden will be borne by our state consumers."
    a. Will the tax raise $1,000,000 in revenue? Explain.
    b. How much revenue would you expect the state to get from this tax?
    c. Is it true that consumers will bear none of the burden of this tax because it is legally imposed on the sellers? Show this using a graph.

3. Consider the health care industry. We could allow the market to allocate health care through the price mechanism (rationing by price), or we could have the government set the price of health care at a low level so that it would be "affordable" for all citizens. Assume that when the government sets a low price for health care, health care services are allocated on a first-come, first-served basis (rationing by waiting).
    a. What type of waste occurs with rationing by waiting?
    b. Suppose there is a surge in demand for health care services. Which rationing system provides health care providers with better information and incentives? Explain.
    c. Health care involves a variety of services including preventive care (checkups and diagnostic procedures), treatment of illness and injuries, expensive and/or experimental procedures to care for the critically ill and injured, and plastic surgery or other elective procedures. What mix of these services would you expect to see in a system rationed by price? What mix of health care services would you expect to see in a system rationed by waiting? (Hint: Who would get more health care in a system rationed by price? by waiting?)
    d. What other rationing schemes are possible? What effects would they have on the efficiency of health care delivery? What effects would they have on the mix of health care services provided?
    e. Why should health care be rationed at all? Why not provide unlimited health care to everyone?

4. In an effort to control rising prices during the 1970s, many governments adopted price controls, fixing prices (and wages) for extended periods of time and thereby caused shortages of some goods and surpluses of others. Respond to the following statement: "Shortages are a disadvantage of price controls, but surpluses are an offsetting advantage."

5. Market prices coordinate economic activity by providing the proper incentives and bringing into harmony the desires of buyers and sellers. Explain how market prices coordinate the following:
    a. the markets for labor in terms of job seekers and employment offerings.
    b. the desires of the buyers and sellers of a product of your choosing.

PERSPECTIVES IN ECONOMICS

The Drug Problem

by Randall G. Holcombe

[Abridged from "The Drug Problem," Chapter 10 in Randall G. Holcombe, *Public Policy and the Quality of Life*. (Westport, CT: Greenwood Press, 1995). Reprinted with permission.]

The public policy response to the drug problem has been to make recreational drug use illegal and then to enforce drug laws by arresting both users and sellers, even going overseas to nations supplying the underground drug markets to try to stop the supply at the source. The war on drugs is now decades old, and there is no evidence that the war is being won, or can be won.

As the very limited success of the war on drugs shows, drug use will continue to be extensive although drugs are illegal. Along with the law enforcement campaign against underground drug markets has come a public relations campaign to dissuade people from drug use. The public relations campaign appears more successful than the law enforcement campaign, and public relations campaigns can help to curtail the use of both illegal drugs and legal drugs such as alcohol and tobacco. This shows that there are alternative strategies to legal prohibition for those who want to use the government to reduce drug use. The costs of continuing to make recreational drug use illegal are many. The war on drugs is taking its toll on the individual rights our Constitution was designed to protect. Many of the negative consequences if illegal drug use stem from the fact that illegal drugs are illegal rather than that they are drugs. Because of the history of the legal prohibition on recreational drug use, it is reasonable to consider alternatives to help solve many of the problems that are a part of the drug problem.

The creation of illegal markets for recreational drugs has the obvious effect of making prices higher than they would be with legal markets. Higher prices contribute to property crime because high prices can push users into criminal activity to finance their drug purchases. The news often portrays drug users as criminals who steal to support their habit but rarely shows stories of alcoholics who steal to support their addictions. One reason is that alcohol prices are not forced upward artificially by legal prohibition.

Before considering some of the pros and cons of legalization, consider the question of whether it would ever be possible to win the war on drugs. One of the problems often cited in fighting the war on drugs is that users tend to be relatively insensitive to the price of drugs. If drugs become more costly, users will engage in various types of theft to acquire them. In the terminology of economists, the demand for recreational drugs is relatively inelastic, so that even a relatively large increase in the price will result in only a small decrease in the quantity of drugs demanded by users.

If users in the recreational drug market do not want to alter their consumption habits very much in response to price changes, consider the results of winning some battles in the war on drugs. Surely, sellers in the black market for drugs will charge whatever the market will bear, and if government efforts succeed in removing a small percentage of the supply of drugs from the market, competition among buyers for drugs will push prices up by a greater percentage than the decline in quantity, with the result that the drug market will take in more total money by selling fewer drugs.

Trade in illegal markets creates huge profits that entice people into the market. Legalization would take the glamour out of drug dealing, it would eliminate the problems produced by the profitability of dealing, and it would be more likely to keep children out of the drug market.

Another disadvantage to users of trading in illegal markets is that there is no legal protection for the transaction. This means, at a minimum, that there is no recourse in case of a faulty product but also means that a buyer risks being the victim of other crimes in an attempt to purchase drugs. Users might be reluctant to tell the police that they were robbed by someone from whom they were trying to buy drugs.

One major disadvantage to drug users of trading in illegal markets is that their activities make them criminals. There are several negative side effects. First, there is a stigma attached to drug use simply because it is illegal. One need only remember the 1980s to recall that Judge Douglas Ginsberg's nomination to the Supreme Court was torpedoed because he had used marijuana. There was no evidence that it had affected his legal activities or his judgment in any other way. Simply the stigma attached to marijuana use was enough to keep him off the Supreme Court. If, instead, he had admitted to trying bourbon there would have been no issue raised.

This stigma will also make users more reluctant to seek treatment. People must admit not only that they cannot seem to get off drugs but also that they have been violating the law. Legalization would make it easier for people to seek treatment for drug problems if they desired it.

Another negative aspect of the profits generated by drug prohibition is they create an opportunity for corrupting law enforcement officers. Law enforcement is not a notably high-paid profession, and drug profits can be spent to pay law enforcement officers for protection or to look the other way while drug dealers transact their business.

Corruption of law enforcement officers is most serious with victimless crimes, such as drug sales, prostitution, gambling, and the like. Crimes with victims, like assault and burglary, have individuals who want to cooperate with law enforcement officers and who have an incentive to monitor the law enforcement system to see that justice is done. With victimless crimes nobody directly involved in the activity wants law enforcement. If an individual who commits an assault is able to buy his way out of an arrest, the assault victim will want to call that corruption to the attention of someone higher up in the political chain of command. The potential problems would be severe enough that there would be a high likelihood that the corrupt law enforcement officer would not benefit from the corrupt activity. With victimless crimes, nobody directly involved in the crime has an incentive to complain about corrupt activity. Therefore, corruption is more likely.

Corruption may not be the major problem related to the legal enforcement of drug crimes. Incentives in the legal system may lead law enforcement officers to pursue drug crimes at the expense of other types of crime, with the result that other crimes increase. The most obvious incentive is that often property confiscated by law enforcement officers through drug arrests remains with the law enforcement agency. Law enforcement officers will have more incentive to pursue these types of crimes if the budgets of their agencies can be directly enhanced as a result.

The incentives are structured so law enforcement officers can benefit from putting more law enforcement effort into drug crimes and less effort into property crimes. As a result of reduced effort fighting property crimes, robbery and burglary will become less risky, and crime rates in those areas will increase.

Dealing in illegal drugs is a very profitable business for the dealers, but it is a business that has no access to legal protection. Whereas the legal system is, for the most part, designed to protect property and to defend the rights of individuals to engage in voluntary exchange and retain ownership over what they receive through market transactions, in the drug market, the legal system is worse than neutral toward protecting participants. Rather than just not offering those transactions any protection, the legal system actively seeks to confiscate any money and goods exchanged in the market. Because the government's legal system is openly hostile to drug markets those who participate in those markets must take steps to actively protect themselves.

Non-users suffer considerably because drugs are bought and sold on black markets, which offers no legal protection to those who deal in them. There is big money to be made dealing in drugs, and, without legal protection, those dealing in the markets must find ways to protect themselves. This is what leads to the gang warfare, the drive-by shootings, and the unsafe neighborhoods filled with criminal activity.

The consequences of the illegal profits in drug markets are overwhelmingly negative. The location of drug markets tends to be in poorer neighborhoods and in inner cities. The resulting crime harms those who do not participate in the markets but have a limited ability to move from the area. However, in poor neighborhoods, there is also the negative side effect of the incentives established by drug markets. In areas where unemployment may be high and employed people work for relatively low wages, much more money can be made by dealing in drugs than working in legal markets. The people with the new cars and the people with the gold chains will likely be those involved in the drug market. This entices others to enter the market and makes those who deal in drugs neighborhood role models. Why work for low wages, if one can find a job at all, when by working for dug dealers one can make more money?

If recreational drugs were legal, there would be no high profits to lure individuals into the market. There would still be drug users, to be sure, but those individuals would tend to be the losers—the equivalent of the skid row alcoholic—rather than the people to envy. Without the illegal profits, those involved in drugs would no longer look like role models to individuals in drug-infested neighborhoods. This is one

argument for legalization. If all drugs were legalized, the drug culture would not look nearly as attractive because it would be stripped of its excess profits caused by government efforts to reduce supply.

If drugs were legalized, their quality would be controlled better because they would be sold in commercial markets. Firms would have an incentive to develop reputations for quality, and drugs would be packaged in standardized doses, which would reduce the incidence of accidental overdoses. Because drugs would be sold under brand names, sellers would have an incentive to distinguish their products and to be concerned about the health of their customers.

If drugs were legalized, there would not be the same incentives to produce drugs in concentrated doses. Transportation is more costly for illegal drugs because they must be concealed from law enforcement officers. Drugs that can contain more doses in a given volume will be more valuable, and one of the motivations of designer drugs is to allow easier transportation through more concentrated doses. Using alcohol as an example, high-proof liquor was more often produced than beer with low alcohol content during prohibition. Legalization would result in drugs that are not as strong.

If drugs were legalized, there would be an incentive for research and development in the recreational drug industry to produce designer drugs that cause better feelings but with fewer harmful side effects. The designer drug industry today shows the possibilities for research and development in recreational drugs, but, as just noted, the incentives today are to produce more concentrated drugs rather than less harmful drugs. This push toward less harmful designer drugs would be amplified if drug manufacturers were allowed to advertise their products.

Finally, if drugs were legalized, manufacturers would have an incentive to innovate because they could take advantage of patent protection and other legal protections that would go to producers in any legal industry. As it is, the incentives do not exist because drugs are illegal.

Legalization would bring the same benefits to users and non-users. Violence and unpredictable behavior from drug use should be reduced because of better information about drugs, quality control, increased variety, and the tendency for drugs to be packaged in less potent forms. Accidental deaths should fall, which would reduce costs to those with drug users in the family. Thus, the effects of drug use should be less burdensome to non-users if drugs were legalized.

Earlier, it was argued that the demand for recreational drugs is relatively inelastic meaning that a reduction in the price would not cause large increases in consumption. This suggests that legalization would have relatively little effect on drug use taking only the money price into account. For some people, however, the violation of drug laws might appear as a powerful and prohibitive deterrent because legalization would entice people who never had a desire to do so to try recreational drugs.

An important argument in favor of legalization, regardless of how many new users would be created, is that in a free society people should have the right to behave as they choose as long as their behavior does not harm others. People engage in many activities that are hazardous to their health, but society does not ban skydiving or motorcycle riding. One of the casualties of the war on drugs has been individual rights.

This discussion of drug policy considers a controversial issue but one that is worthwhile considering within the context of an examination of public policy and the quality of life. For one thing, a general framework should be able to deal with controversial issues, but a larger reason is that the issue of drug policy directly confronts the issue of the degree to which individual freedom contributes to the quality of life. Freedom is important enough to the quality of life to want to defend it as a goal of its own, but the protection of individual freedoms also indirectly enhances the quality of life. Freedom allows people to pursue their own interests as they understand them, and it allows them to profit from activities that benefit others. The protection of individual rights is necessary for a market system to operate, and the market system has proven itself to be an indispensable component in enhancing the welfare of a nation's citizens.

DISCUSSION

1. Using a demand and supply diagram, show how drug enforcement policies aimed at reducing the supply of drugs affect the price of drugs and the quantity traded. How do the effects on price and quantity compare with policies aimed at reducing demand (such as education and "Just say no" campaigns)?

2. Do you think the demand for illegal drugs is fairly inelastic? What does this imply about the ability to reduce consumption by supply-side policies that increase the price of drugs?

3. Police departments have a fixed amount of resources that must be allocated across different crimes and laws that must be enforced. Use a production possibilities curve to show how increased enforcement of drug laws reduces the enforcement of other laws. What effect does this have on the amount of these other crimes committed?

4. If drugs were made legal, what do you think would happen to the following?
    a.   the quantity of drugs consumed
    b.   the profits of drug sellers
    c.   the amount of gang violence
    d.   the presence of street corner drug dealers (Hint: Could they compete with Wal-Mart?)
    e.   the quality of drugs in terms of side effects and tainted products
    f.   the number of users willing to admit their problem and get help

5. During prohibition in the 1920s, alcohol was made illegal. As a result, gangsters controlled the alcohol trade, the murder rate rose substantially, high-potency moonshine was created, and deaths from tainted alcohol rose. Compare and contrast each of these with (1) the current market and usage of alcohol now that it is legal again (are these problems gone or at least reduced?), and (2) with the current market and usage of illegal drugs.

Difficult Cases for the Market and the Role of Government

TRUE OR FALSE

T F

☐ ☐ 1. The total social cost of an action includes the costs to the voluntary participants and any costs imposed on third parties.

☐ ☐ 2. When production of a good results in externalities that impose a cost on others, the output level of the good often exceeds the socially ideal amount.

☐ ☐ 3. It is often difficult to exclude nonpaying customers from receiving the benefits of a public good.

☐ ☐ 4. Anything provided by the government (the public sector) is called a public good.

☐ ☐ 5. When an activity generates external costs, government intervention in the form of establishing private property rights or imposing a tax that would reduce the level of the activity could improve economic efficiency.

☐ ☐ 6. National defense is an example of a public good.

☐ ☐ 7. Poor information on the part of buyers is very seldom a factor in real-world markets.

☐ ☐ 8. Spillover, or third-party effects, are the same thing as externalities.

☐ ☐ 9. Getting accurate information is often difficult for consumers, but sellers offering good products have an incentive to provide this information to consumers.

☐ ☐ 10. *Consumer Reports* is an example of a government solution to the problems for the market created by information costs.

T F

☐ ☐ 11. Externalities are the result of poorly defined or poorly enforced private property rights.

☐ ☐ 12. Externalities can be either negative (costs) or positive (benefits).

☐ ☐ 13. The free-rider problem occurs when it is easy to exclude nonpaying customers.

☐ ☐ 14. A productive government uses price controls, tariffs, and quotas to increase the intensity of competition in the market for goods and services.

☐ ☐ 15. When the production of a good or service generates external benefits, market forces may supply an amount smaller than would be consistent with economic efficiency.

☐ ☐ 16. Economics highlights the fact that there is an optimal amount of any activity to undertake. It is possible to both do too little or too much of a worthwhile activity.

PROBLEMS AND PROJECTS

1. Public goods are goods that are both (1) nonrival in consumption (or "joint in consumption") and (2) nonexcludable. For each of the goods listed below, indicate whether it meets each of these criterion with a "yes" or a "no" in the space provided. In the final column, indicate whether the good is a public good or a private good based upon your answers.

Good	Nonrival in Consumption	Nonexcludable	Public Good or Private Good
a. National defense	_____	_____	_____
b. An indoor rock concert	_____	_____	_____
c. Mail & package delivery	_____	_____	_____
d. A cup of coffee	_____	_____	_____
e. A radio broadcast	_____	_____	_____
f. A movie at a theatre	_____	_____	_____
g. A taco	_____	_____	_____
h. A toll road	_____	_____	_____

2. Exhibit 1 shows the supply and demand schedules for pulp paper in Academia, a hypothetical country.
    a. Diagram the supply and demand curves and show the equilibrium price and quantity for pulp paper in Academia.
    b. Suppose the production of pulp paper results in external pollution costs of $20 per ton produced. In your diagram, show a supply curve that includes these external costs. What are the socially ideal (efficient) price and quantity for pulp paper? Show these in your diagram.
    c. Explain in your own words why the private market equilibrium you found in part a is inefficient.
    d. Suppose the government levies a tax of $20 per ton on producers of pulp paper. How will this affect the market? How will the outcome compare with efficiency?

EXHIBIT 1

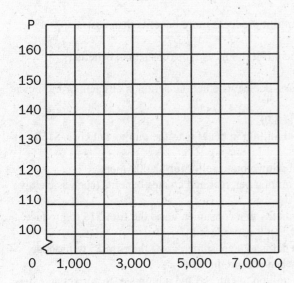

PRICE (PER TON)	QUANTITY (TON/YEAR)	
	DEMANDED	SUPPLIED
$150	1,000	7,000
140	2,000	6,000
130	3,000	5,000
120	4,000	4,000
110	5,000	3,000
100	6,000	2,000

3. Exhibit 2 depicts the market for baseball teams, with the total number of teams on the horizontal axis and the price of each team (in millions of dollars) on the vertical axis.
   a. Diagram the supply and demand curves and determine the values of the free market equilibrium price and quantity.
   b. Some have argued that a baseball team generates external benefits for a city by increasing the city's morale and pride and by bringing in extra tourist revenue. Suppose the value of these external benefits turns out to be $24 million per team. Use your diagram from part a to depict these externalities. What is the efficient total number of baseball teams?
   c. What type of policy could a city government use to attract a baseball team?
   d. Suppose there really are no external benefits associated with baseball teams but that city governments subsidize them anyway. Will the resulting outcome be consistent with economic efficiency? Explain.

EXHIBIT 2

PRICE (MILLIONS)	QUANTITY DEMANDED	QUANTITY SUPPLIED
$68	17	35
62	20	32
56	23	29
50	26	26
44	29	23
38	32	20
32	35	17

4. The book presents the following two conditions as necessary for economic efficiency:

    Rule 1: Undertaking an economic action is efficient if it produces more benefits than costs.

    Rule 2: Undertaking an economic action is inefficient if it produces more costs than benefits.

    Using these criterion, for each of the following cases, decide whether the action is efficient or inefficient and which rule applies.
    a. Buying a pair of jeans for $25 that you value at $30
    b. Building a new public park that generates $100 million in benefits to the public, but costs $150 million in tax revenue to build
    c. Making a $1,500 repair to your home that will allow you to sell it for $2,000 more
    d. Operating a recycling program that costs $50 million per year and creates benefits (such as energy savings) of $20 million per year
    e. The production of a good that yields $20 in benefits to a consumer, costs the firm $15 to produce, and generates $10 in external pollution costs when it is produced
    f. The production of a good that yields $20 in benefits to a consumer, costs the firm $5 to produce, and generates $10 in external pollution costs when it is produced
    g. Imposing a tax that costs the government $10 million to enforce and administer to correct an externality that was generating $5 million in external costs
    h. Purchasing an issue of *Consumer Reports* magazine for $3 that contains a review of writing pens to help you decide whether to purchase a Bic pen or a Papermate pen, both of which cost 50 cents
    i. Purchasing an issue of *Consumer Reports* magazine for $3 that contains a review of new automobiles to help you decide whether to purchase a Ford Explorer or a Jeep Cherokee

MULTIPLE CHOICE

1. Which one of the following would *reduce* the efficiency of the market process?
    a. promoting competitive markets
    b. protecting persons from fraud and theft
    c. providing a stable monetary environment
    d. protecting consumers by imposing legally mandated price ceilings

2. It is difficult for the market process to provide public goods because
    a. private firms generally cannot undertake large-scale projects.
    b. it will be difficult to get potential consumers to pay for such goods because there is not a direct link between payment for and receipt of the good.
    c. consumers do not really want public goods, even though such goods are best for them.
    d. individuals are generally made worse off by the production of public goods.

3. Which of the following are ways in which the private market provides consumers with valuable information to help them make better decisions?
    a. brand names
    b. franchising
    c. private sector certification firms and consumer report magazines
    d. all of the above

4. Which of the following are the four major factors that may undermine the ability of the invisible hand to produce market efficiency?
    a. externalities, private goods, poorly informed buyers or sellers, lack of competition
    b. public goods, externalities, lack of competition, poorly informed buyers or sellers
    c. competition, poorly informed buyers or sellers, externalities, public goods
    d. public goods, lack of competition, well-informed buyers and sellers, externalities

5. Which of the following activities is least likely to give rise to external costs or benefits?
    a. spraying to control mosquitos in your backyard
    b. driving one's car during rush hour
    c. inoculating your children during a flu epidemic
    d. buying a hamburger and eating it for lunch

6. Driving your automobile in Los Angeles during the rush hour causes externalities because
    a. it adds congestion and pollution from auto exhaust, reducing the welfare of others.
    b. gasoline is scarce and you must pay for it.
    c. gasoline is a public good.
    d. your actions will benefit others even though you will be unable to charge them for the service.

7. Criteria of ideal economic efficiency requires that (I) all actions generating more social benefit than cost be undertaken and (II) no actions generating more social cost than social benefit be undertaken.
    a. Both I and II are true.
    b. Both I and II are false.
    c. I is true; II is false.
    d. II is true; I is false.

8. Which of the following "goods" is the best example of a pure public good?
    a. highways
    b. national defense
    c. mail delivery
    d. welfare programs

9. In the absence of government intervention, goods with external costs tend to be
    a. overproduced.
    b. underproduced.
    c. efficiently produced.
    d. offset by goods generating external benefits.

10. The absence of well-defined and enforceable private property rights often
    a. causes people to work together for the common good.
    b. improves society because it avoids the selfish actions of private property owners.
    c. causes difficulties for society due to externalities.
    d. brings about efficiency by providing incentives to conserve resources.

11. The major distinction between private and public goods is that
    a. private goods are goods produced by private firms whereas public goods are goods produced by government—the public sector.
    b. unlike private goods, public goods are nonexcludable—it is difficult or impossible to prevent non-paying customers from receiving the good.
    c. unlike private goods, public goods are nonrival in consumption—the consumption of a unit by one person does not detract from the amount available to others.
    d. both b and c are correct.

12. New products provide a classic case of the consumer information problem. However, in some cases consumers partially solve the problem by trusting the "brand name" of the producer of the new product. Because firms spend millions of dollars advertising and maintaining their brand names, the likelihood of a "brand name" firm intentionally selling a dangerous or shoddy new product is
    a. high because big firms are always after a quick dollar.
    b. high because their brand name is a communal property right.
    c. low because big firms do not make mistakes.
    d. low because the firm with a brand name has a lot to lose if word spreads about bad consumer experiences.

13. A public good is defined as a good with which of the following characteristics?
    a. non-rivalry, rivalry
    b. excludability, rivalry
    c. non-rivalry, non-excludability
    d. rivalry, non-excludability

14. Which of the following correctly describes an *external benefit* resulting from an individual's purchase of a winter flu shot?
    a. The flu shot is cheaper than the cost of treatment when you get the flu.
    b. The income of doctors increases when you get the flu shot.
    c. The flu shot reduces the likelihood of others catching the flu.
    d. The flu shot reduces the likelihood you will miss work as the result of sickness; therefore, you will earn more income.

15. Which of the following would be a protective function of government?
    a. providing national defense
    b. welfare programs and income redistribution
    c. mail delivery
    d. all of the above

16. Consider two goods—one that generates external benefits and another that generates external costs. A competitive market economy would tend to produce too
    a. much of both goods.
    b. little of both goods.
    c. much of the good that generates external benefits and too little of the good that generates external cost.
    d. little of the good that generates external benefits and too much of the good that generates the external cost.

17. Externalities are due to which of the following?
    a. poorly defined or enforced private property rights
    b. individuals not caring sufficiently about the welfare of others
    c. the choice of a capitalist, rather than socialist, economy
    d. poor information on the part of buyers and sellers

18. The problem created when it is difficult to exclude nonpaying customers is called the
    a. consumption-payment link problem.
    b. free-rider problem.
    c. public sector dilemma.
    d. asymmetric information problem.

19. General agreement exists that the legitimate economic functions of government include
    a.   protection against invasions from a foreign power.
    b.   provision of goods that cannot easily be provided through markets.
    c.   the maintenance of a framework of rules within which people can interact peacefully with one another.
    d.   all of the above.

DISCUSSION QUESTIONS

1. Provide a specific example for each of the reasons why unregulated markets might fail to be efficient. For each case explain how government intervention might promote efficiency.

2. List as many goods as you can think of that have substantial public good characteristics that are provided by the private sector. Try weather forecasts and radio broadcasts for starters. Pick two of these goods and answer the following questions: How does the market cope with the public goods aspect of the good? Does the market produce enough of the good? Would government provision of the good be more efficient?

3. For decades, smokers were free to smoke almost everywhere—at work, at parties, on airplanes, and in restaurants. Today, smokers face increasing restrictions about where they can smoke. Some of these restrictions are the result of government policy, but many have arisen without legislation and are simply imposed by private companies (such as airlines, restaurants, and private employers). The latter set of restrictions represent a nongovernmental solution to the externalities created by smokers. Can you think of other activities that generate negative externalities that are regulated in a similar manner?

4. Your decision about which college to attend is an example of a nonrepeat, major purchase about which few individuals have full information. Do you feel like you made a good choice? Is there any way for you to know that you made the best choice? What sources did you use to obtain information about the various colleges and universities? How many of these sources were provided by the market? by the government? Does poor information pose a problem for the market for higher education?

5. In general, it has been argued that private sector markets will allocate too few resources to public goods like national defense. Do you think the public sector allocates too few, too many, or just the right amount of resources to such goods? What is your evidence? How should you go about determining the socially optimal amount of public goods to produce? Does government intervention necessarily imply that the good will be produced efficiently?

6. Consider each of the following quotes:

    "Following the example set by the ending of Prohibition, we should legalize marijuana, cocaine, and certain other drugs we have failed to control. Excise taxes and punishments could hold drug use to tolerable levels and discourage their use prior to engaging in activities that might harm others." (Gary Becker, economist)

    "Drug use is out of control in our society. Making it legal would only reinforce the erroneous perception that drugs such as marijuana and cocaine can be used without consequences." (Lee I. Dogoloff, Executive Director, American Council for Drug Education)

Assume you are the vice president of the United States and have to cast a vote to break a tie in the Senate on the issue of legalization of marijuana and cocaine. In a single paragraph, state your decision, and carefully and clearly support your position. Be sure to address both points of view expressed above.

7.   "If it's worth doing, it's worth doing it to the best of your ability." Discuss, from an economic point of view, the validity of this statement. Use a graph to illustrate your answer.

The Economics of Collective Decision Making

TRUE OR FALSE

T F

☐ ☐ 1. Well-organized special interest groups may be able to use the political process for their own gain even though the action is inefficient and results in a net social loss.

☐ ☐ 2. The shortsightedness effect implies that a policy providing immediate, readily identified benefits at the expense of costs in the future that are difficult to identify tends to be very attractive to a legislator seeking reelection.

☐ ☐ 3. Logrolling and pork-barrel legislation are rules designed to prevent individual legislators from getting special interest policies for their districts passed.

☐ ☐ 4. Rent seeking is when an individual spends time and money in an effort to influence government policy in their favor.

☐ ☐ 5. When an individual votes, they will attempt to gain all available information about the candidate and the issues involved.

☐ ☐ 6. The efficiency of the political process would be enhanced if the costs of government action (taxes) were more closely linked to the benefits people receive from government action.

☐ ☐ 7. Government failure strengthens the case for use of the market system.

☐ ☐ 8. An individual voter has a strong economic incentive to fight special interest legislation with his or her own time and money because such legislation is costly to all members of society.

☐ ☐ 9. The majority of government income transfer programs are directed toward the poor.

T   F

☐   ☐   10. The assumption that politicians behave in a self-interested fashion is premised largely on the fact that politicians who fail to do so will often also fail to be reelected.

☐   ☐   11. A voter usually must choose among candidates whose positions represent complex bundles of goods, services, and costs to the voter.

☐   ☐   12. When voters pay in proportion to benefits received, all voters gain from productive (i.e., efficient) government action.

☐   ☐   13. The exchange between politicians of political support for issues (vote trading) is called pork-barrel legislation.

☐   ☐   14. Even if a policy is inefficient, government is likely to enact it if the benefits are concentrated in a small interest group and if the costs are widespread.

☐   ☐   15. Even if a policy is efficient, government is *not* likely to enact it if the costs are concentrated in a small interest group and if the benefits are widespread.

☐   ☐   16. The market and public sector are similar in that individuals must pay exactly for the benefits they receive.

☐   ☐   17. Scarcity is not present in the public sector because the government pays for all goods and services it provides free to citizens.

☐   ☐   18. The direction of budgeted funds to specific programs, projects, and locations is referred to as earmarking.

PROBLEMS AND PROJECTS

1. Exhibit 1 presents data on the benefits received by three voters for two different proposals up for vote, A and B. Also shown in the table are two possible tax-sharing arrangements for each project. The equal tax is if they split the total cost of the project equally, whereas the benefit tax is the case where each person pays the same percent of the total tax bill as the percent of the benefits they receive from the project.

   a. Proposal A creates a total benefit of $200, and the total cost of the project (as shown by the total tax needed) is $150. Is project A efficient? Is project B efficient?

EXHIBIT 1

	PROPOSAL A			PROPOSAL B		
VOTER	BENEFIT	EQUAL TAX	BENEFIT TAX	BENEFIT	EQUAL TAX	BENEFIT TAX
Adam	$140	$50	$105	$5	$40	$6
Bob	40	50	30	50	40	60
Cathy	20	50	15	45	40	54
Totals	$200	$150	$150	$100	$120	$120

b. Suppose only the equal tax plans are considered and majority rule is used to make the decisions. Would proposal A pass (win majority approval) under the equal tax-sharing arrangement? Would proposal B pass under the equal tax-sharing arrangement?

c. Are the outcomes in part b consistent with the criterion of efficiency in part a?

d. Under the benefit tax shown, each taxpayer is assessed the same proportion of the total tax as the proportion of the benefits they receive from the project. For example, Bob receives one-half the benefits from project B ($50 of $100), so is charged one-half the total tax ($60 of $120). Under the benefits tax plan, would proposal A pass? Would proposal B pass under the benefits tax?

e. Are the outcomes in part d consistent with the criterion of efficiency in part a? If you want government to pass only efficient projects, would it be better to use equal taxes or taxes in proportion to benefits received?

2. Exhibit 2 shows the net benefits (benefits minus tax cost) from three different government projects for three districts.

EXHIBIT 2

	NET BENEFITS (+) OR COSTS (−) TO DISTRICT		
REPRESENTATIVE OF DISTRICT	NEW ROAD IN DISTRICT A	NEW PARK IN DISTRICT B	NEW DAM IN DISTRICT C
A	$+10	$−5	$−2
B	−6	+9	−2
C	−6	−5	+13
Totals	−2	−1	+9

a. By looking at the Totals row at the bottom of the table, which of these projects are efficient? Which are inefficient?

b. If each project was put up for vote individually (by majority rule), which would pass? Which would fail?

c. Suppose you were the representative of district A and wanted to get your new road passed. You only need one more vote for a majority. Would both you and the representative of district B be willing to "trade" votes to get your projects passed? That is, would you be willing to vote for B's park if he voted for your road? Would he agree to the trade as well?

d. Now consider a "pork-barrel" bill that contained all three projects. How would each representative vote on the total bill containing all three projects?

3. Consider the supply and demand for public sector action, and decide whether each of the following illustrates

(1) rent-seeking behavior by private parties,

(2) vote-seeking behavior by elected officials, or

(3) the rational ignorance effect.

____ a. Members of Congress rejected bills that would have restricted the lobbying activities of political action coalitions (PACs).

____ b. Election results are often distorted by poorly informed voters and low voter turnouts.

____ c. Liquor wholesalers in most states have lobbied for state laws that compel retailers to buy their liquor supplies only from the nearest available wholesaler instead of shopping around.

____ d. Many voters support import tariffs and quotas on foreign goods even though such protectionism costs consumers billions of dollars.

____ e. A steel company sends a $50 million campaign contribution to a legislator in a year in which a bill is being debated that would affect the steel industry.

4. Exhibit 3 shows the classification of government actions into four types depending upon how concentrated or widespread the benefits and costs of the action are.

EXHIBIT 3

		Distribution of benefits	
		Widespread	Concentrated
Distribution of costs	Widespread	Type 1	Type 2
	Concentrated	Type 4	Type 3

---

a. For which types of action is government likely to work the best (that is most consistent) with economic efficiency?

b. For which type of action is government likely to have a bias toward adopting the actions even if they are inefficient?

c. For which type of action is government likely to have a bias against adopting the actions even if they are efficient?

Classify each of the following as type 1, 2, 3, or 4 according to the Exhibit 3.

d. A $1 tax on every citizen to provide large subsidies to tobacco farmers

e. A 10 percent tax on the profits of major gasoline retailers (BP, Shell, Exxon, etc.) to finance government-funded research on solar energy

f. An increase in the income tax to finance an increase in national defense spending

g. A $5 increase in student tuition to finance increases in professor salaries

h. A law allowing consumers to buy prescription drugs on the advice of their pharmacist without a visit to a medical doctor (who are strongly represented by the American Medical Association)

i. A 1 percent increase in Social Security taxes on current workers to finance large benefit increases for those currently receiving Social Security payments

j. Reductions in subsidies to sugar farmers to finance the increases in Social Security benefits

MULTIPLE CHOICE

The following quotation relates to questions 1 and 2.

> "The ideal policy, from the viewpoint of the state, is one with identifiable beneficiaries, each of whom is helped appreciably, at the cost of many unidentifiable persons, none of whom is hurt very much."
> (George Stigler, *A Dialogue on the Proper Economic Role of the State*)

1. This statement is probably
   a. incorrect because voters are well informed on a wide range of political issues.
   b. incorrect because the political process dilutes the influence of special interest groups, because like other citizens, their members have only one vote.
   c. correct because the well-informed voter will favor policies that cater to the views of small groups of people.
   d. correct because voters who have a strong personal interest in an issue will tend to support candidates who cater to their views, whereas most other voters ignore the issue.

2. Which of the following groups does the above quotation suggest would have the most influence on public sector action?
   a. taxpayers
   b. nonunion workers
   c. special interest groups
   d. consumers

3. Economists use the term *shortsightedness* effect to describe which one of the following phenomena?
   a. Politicians tend to support actions that have immediate and easily recognized current benefits.
   b. Individuals are apt to spend their income on goods that bring immediate personal benefits.
   c. Voters elect politicians on the basis of campaign promises, regardless of what they may do once they are in office.
   d. Politicians support the programs of special interest groups in order to get elected; however, special interest support may be detrimental later, costing politicians popularity after the programs are implemented.

4. Economic theory leads us to expect that the typical voter will be uninformed on many issues because
   a. most issues are so complex that voters will be unable to understand them.
   b. even though information is free, most voters do not care.
   c. information is costly, and the individual voter casting a well-informed vote can expect negligible personal benefit.
   d. citizen apathy about political matters is inevitable, except when decisions are made by referendum.

5. Public choice theory suggests that politicians will be most likely to favor redistribution of income from
   a. the rich to the poor.
   b. disorganized individuals to well-organized special interest groups.
   c. middle-income taxpayers to both the rich and the poor.
   d. well-organized business and labor groups to consumers.

6. Giving local governments more power is less dangerous than giving the same power to the national government because
   a. local governments generally have more strict constitutional rules they must operate under.
   b. it is easier to vote in local elections than national elections.
   c. only national-level governments are allowed to use coercive force.
   d. higher exit options exist at the local level—it is easier for people to move away from a bad local government.

7. Assume that you are a member of the U.S. House of Representatives from your home state and district. Which of the following best explains why you have a strong incentive to get the federal government to finance pork-barrel projects in your district?
    a. Most of the benefits of pork-barrel projects within your district will accrue to your constituents, whereas most of the costs will be imposed on voters from other districts.
    b. Most of the costs of pork-barrel projects within your district will be imposed on your constituents, whereas most of the benefits will accrue to voters from other districts.
    c. Pork producers are a powerful political lobby that will influence the actions of legislators in all districts.
    d. This is a trick question; in a representative democracy, there is little incentive for legislators to support pork-barrel projects.

8. The theory of public choice
    a. analyzes the likelihood that various public sector alternatives will be instituted.
    b. assumes that economic incentives influence the choices of voters.
    c. applies the tools of economics to the collective decision-making process.
    d. is all of the above.

9. When analyzing public sector decision making, economic theory assumes that voters, politicians, and government officials will
    a. respond to changes in personal benefits and costs when making public sector choices.
    b. pursue the public interest even when it conflicts with their private interests.
    c. pursue primarily public interests because competition is less intense in the public sector.
    d. do none of the above.

10. Public choice theory indicates that competitive forces between candidates in elections provide a politician with a strong incentive to offer voters a bundle of political goods that she believes
    a. is best for the economic and political situations the country faces.
    b. will most likely clear the legislative process.
    c. will increase the welfare of society.
    d. will increase her chances of winning elections.

11. When voters pay in proportion to the benefits received from an economic action of the government, if the government activity is productive,
    a. all voters will gain.
    b. only a smaller proportion of voters will gain.
    c. less than a simple majority of voters will gain.
    d. approximately 50 percent of the voters will gain.

12. In which case is the political process most likely to result in the acceptance of productive programs and rejection of unproductive political activities?
    a. when the benefits are highly concentrated and costs widespread among voters
    b. when the costs are highly concentrated and the benefits widespread among voters
    c. when both the benefits and costs are widespread among voters
    d. when the benefits accrue primarily in the future, whereas the costs are more visible during the current period

13. When is representative democracy most likely to lead to the adoption of an inefficient government program?
    a. when the program provides substantial benefits to a small proportion of voters and the costs are widespread among voters
    b. when both the benefits and costs of the program are widespread among voters
    c. when the program is financed by a user charge
    d. when a close relationship exists between the personal benefits received from the program and the tax cost imposed on each voter

14. Legislators often gain by bundling a number of projects benefiting local districts at the expense of general taxpayers. Such legislation is called
    a.   market failure legislation.
    b.   the rational ignorance effect.
    c.   public goods legislation.
    d.   pork-barrel legislation.

15. Which of the following refers to when legislators trade votes on legislation?
    a.   logrolling
    b.   the special interest effect
    c.   rational ignorance
    d.   the shortsightedness effect

16. Which of the following is a predictable side effect of increased government activity (e.g., taxes and subsidies) designed to redistribute income among citizens?
    a.   improvement in the operational efficiency of government agencies
    b.   budget surpluses
    c.   reduction in the poverty rate
    d.   an increase in rent-seeking activity

17. Legislation that offers immediate and easily recognized benefits, at the expense of uncertain costs that are in the distant future (such as financing by government debt), is often enacted even when economic inefficiency results. This can be expected because of
    a.   a lack of incentive for operational efficiency in the public sector.
    b.   market failure.
    c.   the special-interest effect.
    d.   the shortsightedness effect.

18. Public choice analysis indicates that
    a.   because government action provides public goods, it always increases the wealth of the citizenry.
    b.   unconstrained democratic governments often enact special-interest programs that waste resources and impair the standard of living.
    c.   constitutional rules limiting public-sector activity generally lower the economic efficiency of the overall economy.
    d.   Politicians and voters are better able to judge the public interest than their own private interest.

19. Which of the following is true about the market and public sectors?
    a.   Competitive behavior is present in both sectors.
    b.   The public sector utilizes the price mechanism more than the private sector.
    c.   In both sectors, individuals always pay for the goods and services they consume.
    d.   There is more free choice for individual consumers in the public sector than in the private sector.

20. Despite many differences, the market and public sectors are *similar* in which one of the following respects?
    a.   In both sectors, income (or power) is distributed on the basis of the same criterion.
    b.   Consumers in the market sector and voters in the public sector are equally well informed.
    c.   Voluntary exchange, rather than compulsion, is characteristic of both sectors.
    d.   It will be costly to use scarce goods, whether through the private or the public sector.

21. Which of the following is legally permitted to use coercive force to modify the actions of adults against their will?
    a.   banks
    b.   corporations
    c.   governments
    d.   all of the above

22. Senator Spendall is able to use his position on an important committee to set aside government funding specifically for a new bridge in his hometown. This is an example of
    a. earmarking.
    b. logrolling.
    c. pork-barrel legislation.
    d. the invisible hand principle.

DISCUSSION QUESTIONS

1. Do you find the public choice theory of political behavior convincing? What do you see as its strengths? its weaknesses? Do you think most politicians are motivated by personal self-interest? Cite evidence in support of your answer.

2. Why are well-organized special interest groups likely to be politically powerful? Why will vote-seeking politicians have an incentive to cater to their views?

3. "Government bureaucrats are only as important as the size of their departments, so they will always spend their entire budget allocation to avoid having their budgets cut in the next year."
    a. Do you agree with this quote? Why or why not?
    b. If bureaucrats act this way, what are the implications for the efficiency of government-run bureaus? Will they minimize their costs?

4. What are the major factors that contribute to market failure? What are the major factors that contribute to government failure? Which type of failure do you think is more common? more costly?

5. In recent years there has been a widespread discontent with the large size of income transfer programs in the United States. Welfare programs for the poor are subject to much heated criticism, whereas other transfer programs, like farm subsidies, are less often and less heatedly criticized. At the same time, large transfer programs like Social Security and Medicare are labeled as politically "untouchable." What explains why there is a greater clamor to cut welfare programs rather than farm subsidy programs? To what extent can public choice theory explain the difference? In an era when many are calling for substantial reductions in income transfer programs, why is it considered politically impossible to cut Social Security or Medicare?

Taking the Nation's Economic Pulse

TRUE OR FALSE

T F

☐ ☐ 1. Gross domestic product (GDP) is a measure of the market value of all final goods and services that were produced domestically during a year.

☐ ☐ 2. The consumer price index (CPI) and the GDP deflator are price indexes used to convert nominal values to real values when attempting to correct data for the effects of inflation.

☐ ☐ 3. If you paid $800 for a used motorcycle last year, the sale contributed $800 toward last year's GDP.

☐ ☐ 4. One way to raise GDP would be for everyone to give up their leisure time and spend more time working.

☐ ☐ 5. Gross investment measures all expenditures on investment, whereas net investment subtracts depreciation to arrive at only expenditures on new investment. Thus, net investment excludes expenditures for replacement of worn-out capital equipment.

☐ ☐ 6. When Social Security payments are given to retired persons, this transfer payment is added to GDP.

☐ ☐ 7. If domestic citizens live and work in foreign countries, their income is counted as part of GDP.

☐ ☐ 8. If Joe buys 100 shares of stock at $5 each, GDP rises by $500.

☐ ☐ 9. Increases in real output give rise to increases in real income and thus increase a nation's standard of living.

T   F

☐   ☐   10.   If one wanted to measure the change in the annual output of goods and services between 1995 and 2000, nominal GDP would be a more reliable indicator than real GDP.

☐   ☐   11.   During a period of rising prices (inflation), the increase in nominal GDP will be larger than the increase in real GDP.

☐   ☐   12.   If a person gets a 2 percent raise in their nominal salary in a year in which consumer prices rise by 5 percent, their real income (or real purchasing power) falls by 3 percent.

PROBLEMS AND PROJECTS

1.   Exhibit 1 presents economic data for the United States (in billions of dollars) for 2008.
   a.   Calculate GDP using the expenditure approach by adding up the data in the left set of columns.
   b.   Calculate GDP using the resource cost-income approach by adding up the data in the right set of columns.
   c.   Explain why the same result for GDP can be obtained by either adding up spending in the economy or by adding up income in the economy.
   d.   Gross investment includes all investment expenditures. However, these expenditures can be divided into (1) expenditures to replace current capital equipment that has worn out and (2) net investment expenditures on new additions to capital equipment. Find net investment expenditures by subtracting depreciation from gross private investment.
   e.   In Exhibit 1, net exports are negative. Explain why this is negative.
   f.   Economists use several other measures of economic activity that you can derive from the data:
   (1) gross national product, equal to gross domestic product minus the net income of foreigners.
   (2) net national product, equal to gross national product minus depreciation.
   (3) national income, equal to net national product minus indirect business taxes.

EXHIBIT 1

EXPENDITURE APPROACH		RESOURCE COST-INCOME APPROACH	
Personal consumption expenditures	$10,058	Employee compensation	$8,055
		Proprietors' income	1,072
Gross private investment	1,994	Rents	64
Government consumption and gross investment	2,882	Corporate profit	1,477
		Interest income	683
Net exports	–669	Indirect business taxes	1,080
		Depreciation	1,967
		Net income of foreigners	–133

EXHIBIT 2

PERSON	YEAR	HOURLY WAGE (NOMINAL)	CONSUMER PRICE INDEX (CPI)	REAL HOURLY WAGE (IN BASE YEAR DOLLARS)
Bob's grandfather	1961	$0.75	29.9	_____
Bob's father	1981	3.00	90.9	_____
Bob	2001	6.50	177.1	_____

2. Exhibit 2 shows the hourly wage earned by Bob when he was 20 years old in 2001 and his father and grandfather when they were the same age. The consumer price index (CPI) for each year is also given.
   a. Convert all of the wages shown to their real value in the base year of the CPI (the year when the price index was equal to 100, which is now defined as an average of 1982 through 1984). Place your answers in the spaces provided in Exhibit 2.
   b. Who had the highest real wage? Who was able to buy the most goods and services with the money they earned from an hour's work?
   c. Now, consider the grandfather who made $0.75 per hour in 1961. Using the CPI for 1961 and the CPI for 2001, figure out the grandfather's real salary in 2001 dollars. Note that this shows how much a person would need to earn in 2001 to have an identical real salary to a person earning $0.75 in 1961.

3. Exhibit 3 shows actual data for the U.S. economy between 1990 and 1993.
   a. Fill in the missing information in the left half of Exhibit 3 regarding the values of nominal GDP, the GDP deflator, and real GDP.
   b. Fill in the missing information in the right half of Exhibit 3 regarding the percentage changes in these variables. (Hint: Recall the percent change formula is [(new value – old value) ÷ old value].)
   c. Given that the percentage change in the GDP deflator is the inflation rate for that year, what can you say about inflation during this period? Did it rise or fall?
   d. Explain why the percentage growth in real GDP was smaller than the percentage change in nominal GDP for these years.
   e. Interpreting your results for the percentage changes in real GDP, what can you say about the state of the economy during 1991? during 1992?

EXHIBIT 3

	NOMINAL GDP (BILLIONS)	GDP DEFLATOR (1996 = 100)	REAL GDP (BILLIONS OF 1996 DOLLARS)	PERCENTAGE CHANGE FROM PREVIOUS YEAR		
				NOMINAL GDP	GDP DEFLATOR	REAL GDP
1990	$5,803	86.5	$6,709	5.7%	3.8%	1.8%
1991	_____	89.7	6,673	3.2	3.7	_____
1992	6,319	_____	6,883	_____	2.3	3.1
1993	6,642	94.0	_____	5.1	_____	2.7

4. In the blank preceding each event described below, indicate whether the event would increase (+) or cause no change (0) in measured GDP for the United States.

     ___ a. Mary cleans her house.

     ___ b. Mary hires someone to clean her house.

     ___ c. Jim sells cocaine on the black market and earns $30,000 per year.

     ___ d. Rachel buys $5,000 worth of IBM stock from Steve.

     ___ e. A burglar steals your stereo.

     ___ f. You buy a new stereo to replace the one that was stolen.

     ___ g. You purchase a German clock by mail order from a German company.

     ___ h. Instead of paying for your dinner at a local restaurant, you wash dishes for them in exchange for your meal.

     ___ i. Gary receives a $1,000 social security check from the government.

     ___ j. The federal government buys a new stealth bomber for $2 billion.

     ___ k. You lose $500 playing blackjack in your dorm.

     ___ l. You wreck your car and pay $5,000 to have it repaired.

     ___ m. You buy an antique desk from a friend for $300.

     ___ n. You buy some flour to make a loaf of bread.

     ___ o. IBM purchases some new equipment for $10 million.

     ___ p. You pay your landlord $300 for this month's rent.

     ___ q. A hurricane destroys a family's home, and they pay $100,000 to rebuild it.

MULTIPLE CHOICE

1. Real GDP refers to nominal GDP
    a. minus gifts to other countries.
    b. minus total unemployment compensation.
    c. adjusted for price changes.
    d. adjusted for unemployment changes.

2. Assume that between 1995 and 2000 nominal GDP increased from $1,000 to $2,500, and the index of prices increased from 100 to 200. Which of the following expresses GDP for 2000 in terms of 1995 prices?
    a. $1,000
    b. $1,250
    c. $2,500
    d. $5,000

3. Which of the following transactions would be counted toward this year's GDP?
    a. General Motors purchases 10,000,000 tires from Firestone.
    b. A 300-year-old painting is sold for $12 million.
    c. A street gang earns $2 million from selling illegal drugs.
    d. Your real estate agent earns $5,000 commission when you sell your 100-year-old house for $100,000.

4. The consumer price index (CPI) and the GDP deflator are designed to measure the degree to which
    a. there have been changes in the proportions of national income generated by (and thus earned by) the rich relative to the poor.
    b. the cost of purchasing a bundle of goods has changed over time.
    c. consumption patterns have changed with time.
    d. consumer prices have risen over and above increases in worker wages.

5. If you wanted to take 2000 nominal GDP and convert it to 1995 prices, you would take 2000 nominal GDP and
   a. multiply it by (GDP deflator$_{1995}$ ÷ GDP deflator$_{2000}$).
   b. multiply it by (GDP deflator$_{2000}$ ÷ GDP deflator$_{1995}$).
   c. divide it by GDP deflator$_{2000}$.
   d. divide it by (GDP deflator$_{2000}$ + GDP deflator$_{1995}$).

6. Which of the following would *not* be counted as part of this year's GDP?
   a. the increase in the value of an antique automobile that was restored this year
   b. the value of a new automobile at its sale price
   c. the value of a used car at its sale price
   d. a family's replacement of a worn-out washing machine with a new one

7. Jim, a U.S. citizen, gets a summer job working in Germany. His summer earnings
   a. would count as part of U.S. GDP and German GNP.
   b. would count as part of U.S. GNP and German GDP.
   c. would count as part of U.S. GDP but would have no effect on Germany's GNP or GDP.
   d. would be double-counted, raising both U.S. GDP and German GDP.

Use the following information to answer questions 8 and 9.

Personal consumption expenditures	$900
Personal taxes	180
Government consumption and gross investment	300
Interest income	60
Exports	40
Imports	75
Depreciation	60
Gross investment	200

8. What is this country's net exports?
   a. 35
   b. −35
   c. 115
   d. −115

9. What is this country's gross domestic product?
   a. 1,225
   b. 1,305
   c. 1,365
   d. 1,440

10. Which of the following is *not* a problem or shortcoming of GDP?
    a. Goods produced in one period that are sold in the following period fail to get counted in any period.
    b. It tends to understate the growth of economic welfare because it does not fully and accurately account for improvements in the quality of products.
    c. GDP is not an accurate measure of welfare because it makes no adjustment for harmful side effects (such as pollution) or destructive acts of nature.
    d. GDP understates output because it fails to include nonmarket production such as that which takes place in the household or in illegal markets.

11. If you were required to write a paper for your history class (or a report for your job) in which you were using dollar valued data across different years, you would
    a. use a price index to remove the effects of inflation to have reliable data measuring changes in the real value of things.
    b. never attempt to correct for inflation because inflation is a key indicator of economic activity.
    c. tell your teacher or boss that you never learned how to correct data for inflation.
    d. assume that prices did not change during the period you are studying.

12. Suppose that nominal GDP increased by 3 percent, but the real GDP increased by only 1 percent during that same period. Which of the following best explains the phenomenon?
    a. Prices increased by approximately 1 percent.
    b. Prices increased by approximately 2 percent.
    c. Prices increased by approximately 3 percent.
    d. Prices increased by approximately 4 percent.

13. If tax rates were raised substantially, we would expect which of the following scenarios to result?
    a. Measured GDP would fall relative to the actual amount of true economic activity.
    b. Measured GDP would come closer to reflecting the actual amount of true economic activity.
    c. GDP would increase by the amount of the new tax revenue because of the higher level of government spending it allows.
    d. Personal consumption expenditures would rise, while government spending would fall.

14. Which of the following would increase U.S. GDP?
    a. The city government of New York buys file cabinets directly from a Mexican company.
    b. A Mexican citizen buys stock in a U.S. company.
    c. A Japanese automobile company produces cars within the U.S.
    d. A U.S. automobile company produces cars in a foreign country.

15. You buy one hundred shares of IBM stock at $100 per share and pay $250 commission. How much will this transaction add to GDP?
    a. zero
    b. $250
    c. $10,000
    d. $10,250

16. If a used-car dealer purchases a used car for $1,000, restores it, and resells it for $1,500, the dealer contributes
    a. value added equal to $500, but nothing is added to GDP.
    b. value added equal to $500, and consequently $500 is added to GDP.
    c. nothing to production because only existing goods are involved.
    d. value added equal to $1,500, but only $500 is added to GDP.

17. Gross domestic product is the sum of
    a. the purchase price of all goods and services exchanged during the period.
    b. the purchase price of all final goods and services produced domestically during the period.
    c. the purchase price of all goods and services produced during the period minus depreciation of productive assets during the period.
    d. the purchase price of all final goods and services produced by a country's citizens during the period.

18. If the base year for the GDP deflator is 1996, the value of the GDP deflator for 1996
    a. is 10.
    b. is 100.
    c. is 150.
    d. cannot be determined from the data given.

19. If the base year for the GDP deflator is 2000 and the value of the GDP deflator in 2003 was 107, this indicates that the general level of prices
    a. declined between 2000 and 2003.
    b. was approximately 7 percent lower in 2003 than in 2000.
    c. was approximately 7 percent higher in 2003 than in 2000.
    d. was approximately 107 percent higher in 2003 than in 2000.

20. Your grandfather tells you he earned $0.65 per hour at his job when he was a boy in 1929. Given that the CPI was 17.1 in 1929 and 215.3 in 2008, how much would you have had to make in 2008 to have the same real hourly wage as your grandfather?
    a. $0.65
    b. $3.80
    c. $8.18
    d. $11.12

21. Assume that between 2000 and 2010 the money GDP of an economy increased from $3 trillion to $8 trillion and that the appropriate index of prices increased from 100 to 200. Which of the following expresses GDP for 2000 in terms of 2010 prices?
    a. $1 trillion
    b. $3 trillion
    c. $4 trillion
    d. $6 trillion

22. Suppose that Mike earned $15,000 in 2008 and $15,600 in 2009. If the consumer price index was 100 in 2008 and 103 in 2009, by approximately what percent did Mike's *real* salary increase?
    a. 1 percent
    b. 3 percent
    c. 4 percent
    d. 5 percent

23. In a country where many families make their own clothes, GDP will be understated because the clothes making represents
    a. economic bads.
    b. leisure.
    c. the underground economy.
    d. nonmarket production.

24. The *primary* value of GDP lies in its ability to
    a. reflect the welfare of a society relative to a previous period.
    b. compare the quality of a nation's products between two periods widely separated in time.
    c. indicate short-term changes in the output rate of a nation.
    d. indicate how much leisure time the people of a nation have.

25. If the Consumer Price Index in 2008 was 150 and the CPI in 2009 was 165, the rate of inflation between 2008 and 2009 would be:
    a. 9.09 percent.
    b. 10 percent.
    c. 15 percent.
    d. 110 percent.

DISCUSSION QUESTIONS

1. What is the difference between the income approach to calculating GDP and the expenditure approach? Why do both methods yield the same answer?

2. Would you expect real GDP to grow faster or slower over time than nominal GDP? Why? Which do you think better measures changes in the level of economic activity? Why?

3. What are some of the deficiencies of GDP as a measure of aggregate output? Consider the following statement: "In terms of measuring *changes* in the level of economic activity, these deficiencies are not important as long as the present method of measuring GDP is applied consistently over time."
    a. Is this statement correct if the structure of our economic activity (the way we operate and the types of things we produce) is fairly stable over time? Why or why not?
    b. Two major changes in recent years include sizeable increases in (1) efforts to control pollution and (2) the proportion of households with two working parents who pay for services such as child care, housecleaning, and gardening. Is the above quotation correct under these circumstances? Why or why not?

4. Suppose that a farmer grows $0.30 worth of wheat and sells it to a miller who makes it into flour. The miller then sells it for $0.50 to a baker who makes bread with it and sells the bread to a customer for $0.75. How much GDP results from this chain of events? If intermediate transactions were counted at their market sales prices, how much GDP would be reported? What is wrong with counting the intermediate transactions?

5. Until recently, Gross National Product was the most frequently cited measure of the aggregate output of an economy. What is the main difference between GDP and GNP? Do you agree with the choice to switch (that is, do you think GDP is the preferred measure)? Why or why not?

6. Think of three events that would raise GDP but that would make people in the economy worse off. Given that increases in GDP do not always reflect an improvement in living standards, why does anyone care about GDP? What is GDP really designed to measure, welfare or production?

PERSPECTIVES IN ECONOMICS

GDP: Pluses and Minuses

Morgan Guaranty Trust Company

[From Morgan Guaranty Survey, June, 1970, pp. 9–13. Reprinted with permission of the Morgan Guaranty Trust Company.]

The gross domestic product in recent years has basked in the warm glow of nearly universal praise. Economists, quite naturally, have been freest with the encomiums. Where else but the GDP could they get in one tidy number a measure of the growth in the mammoth U.S. economy? Businessmen, though not entirely persuaded of the value of statistics, especially esoteric statistics, nevertheless have been known to quote the GDP—possibly because of its powers to impress audiences with the speaker's grasp of the "big picture." Politicians, too, have been extravagant in their admiration of GDP, most especially when it was rising at a brisk pace. Even the ubiquitous cocktail party has paid homage to the GDP as assorted junior executives, research assistants, housewives, and dancing instructors have pronounced on the latest GDP numbers with a solemn and knowing air.

Now all that seems to be changing. GDP increasingly is coming under attack. Dr. Arthur F. Burns, Chairman of the Federal Reserve Board, told Congress recently: "The gross domestic product—which has been deceiving us all along—is a good deal lower than we think it is." Richard A. Falk, a professor of international law at Princeton, told a Congressional committee not long ago: "If the U.S. were to double its GDP, I would think it would be a much less livable society than it is today." And Representative Henry S. Reuss of Wisconsin warned earlier this year that "as our GDP grows, national pollution also grows every year."

Such comments suggest a need to take a new hard look at GDP, at what it is and—equally significant—what it is not.

Amoral GDP. At the outset, it is important to realize that GDP is an estimate of the market value of goods and services produced. The unit of account is always dollars. What is equally important to remember is the GDP measures only those goods and services which are exchanged for money in the market place. In other words, what people, or business, or government are willing to pay for gets into the national income and product accounts. Few distinctions are made among the types of expenditures. Thus, the dollars spent in dedicated pursuit of a cancer cure carry the same weight in the GDP as the wages of lackadaisical ecdysiast. Official compilers of the GDP routinely calculate money spent for medical care, new homes, whiskey, tobacco, and plastic objects d'art. To those who object on aesthetic or even moral grounds, the standard reply is that GDP measures what people actually buy, not what they ought to buy. The latter is thought by economists to be more the province of a higher occupational order, such as saints. It should be noted, however, that the accounting rules are not entirely indifferent to moral considerations. Hence, GDP does not include

economic activity from illegal operations—such as a bookie parlor, an illicit still, or a doxy's den.

Janus-Faced GDP. Thus it is clear that estimating the value of the nation's total spending depends on application of some fairly rigid—some would say arbitrary—rules of inclusion and exclusion. Economic scholars over the years have discussed ways to improve the GDP. Their suggestions can be conveniently split into two groups, the "pluses" and the "minuses." The former school argues that more items should be added to the accounts when striking a total. This school thinks that the GDP, by excluding nonpaid items such as work done by housewives, significantly understates the nation's output. Those in the "minuses" group, while not necessarily unreceptive to the other group's proposals, nevertheless see a different set of deficiencies. They charge that GDP is overstating national income and progress because it does not, for example, take account of the deterioration of the environment.

At present, the "minuses" school seems to be dominating the headlines. Dr. Burns, for example, while strongly backing maximum production, is suggesting that the nation develop and stress a more meaningful net domestic product, or NDP. This is GDP *after* deducting the value of capital goods used up in the production process. Such depreciation or capital consumption currently is running about $80 billion a year. From this NDP (published quarterly along with GDP data), Dr. Burns would additionally deduct some unspecified amount that would represent depreciation in the environment.

To illustrate the point, assume that a manufacturer flushes waste products into a river. If $1,000 were spent to remove the sludge from the waterway, such spending would increase GDP by a like amount. If no effort is made to deal with the pollution, there is no effect on GDP. Economists argue that this is improper since, in fact, the situation is analogous to the depreciation of capital assets. In the waterway case, however, the fixed asset is the environment and its depreciation is called pollution. What is wrong with present accounting procedures, according to these analyses, is that pollution has not been removed from GDP in the calculations of NDP.

Admittedly, adjusting GDP accounting rules to embrace allowances for social values presents some abstruse conceptual problems. Until fairly recently, such social costs were not overwhelmingly important. The elements of the environment were so vast that they appeared to be inexhaustible. Air, for example, was considered to be a "free good." Although air is necessary to life, it was so abundantly available that no one could sell it at a positive price. As a consequence, the destruction of the usefulness of such a prevalent commodity imposed no costs on society.

Now, of course, things are different. There is much concern about the air these days as more and more people in urban areas have come to realize that they cannot breathe deeply without some risk to lung tissue. Air no longer is "free": There is some "cost" to the user.

But how much do you deduct from GDP for dirty air? Or for streams that no longer support fish or waterfowl? Or for a scenic view bulldozed out of existence? For such as these (the list could easily be expanded), any reasonable person would agree that some deduction should be made. But how much? Calculated in what way?

Goodies and Baddies. The only practical method so far discovered is to follow the simple test of marketability—can it be sold for a price? Presumably, if people want breathable air, drinkable water, and the noise levels of a sternly supervised library, then they will spend the money needed to pay for it all. Such spending is included in the GDP. But the offsetting "depreciation" that makes these expenditures necessary is not now deducted from GDP in arriving at NDP. This is not to say, of course, that the market value approach to calculating environmental depreciation would be easy to apply or entirely satisfactory. But inspired intellectual effort surely could produce a method to account for what one observer has called "man-made-bads" to offset the "man-made-goods" that go into the GDP.

It is undoubtedly true, as Dr. Burns states, that a GDP which does not take account of environmental pollution overstates growth and progress of the nation. The affluent society, measured by an expanding GDP, is not so affluent as the official numbers indicate.

Or is it? There are, after all, a number of sizable "pluses" not in the GDP which could be added. If this were done, the "minus" of environmental pollution might very well be more than offset.

The single largest item not counted in GDP is the value of work done in the home by housewives. However, much of this may appear as an antifeminist manifestation, suitable for protestations by women's liberation groups, the plain fact is that placing a value on home tending presents some very tricky problems in estimation. Besides, unpaid productive work done by husbands in the home, too, does not get into the GDP. An example of such work would be the turning of a basement into a finished playroom. Only the purchased material would swell GDP; the husband's work would add nothing to GDP even though his house would increase in value as a consequence of the added playroom. However, if the housewife or husband hired someone to clean the house or finish off the basement, such spending would find its way into GDP.

Other examples of "pluses" that are left out: no allowance is made in GDP for volunteer work, and it is only the out-of-pocket cost, rather than the time spent or the wisdom acquired, that measures the contribution of education. Similarly, no estimates are made of the "income" received by people from services in the public sector—such as use of a park, highway, or library. People receive benefits from such facilities year after year, and yet GDP records only the initial cost when the facility is built and its subsequent maintenance. Here again there are immense problems of estimation. Not all people have access to public facilities, the quality of which, in any case, varies widely all across the nation.

Finally, GDP treats the value of spending on consumer durable goods in different ways depending on their ownership. For instance, money spent by an auto rental agency for its fleet of automobiles is included in the GDP. So is money spent by people and businesses to rent the autos year after year. On the other hand, money spent by an individual purchasing a car for himself gets into the GDP only once—as a personal consumption expenditure at the time of purchase, even though the buyer will get a stream of services, no different from those he would get from a rental auto, for several years. In other words, the "service income" to the owner of any consumer durable good—auto, refrigerator, washing machine, TV—is left out of GDP.

An exception is made in the case of an owner-occupied house. Since the rent on rented dwellings goes into GDP, the comparable service enjoyed by homeowners from their own dwellings is also included so that the total is not subject to variation resulting merely from changes in the proportion of home ownership. Homeowners simply are regarded as landlords who rent to themselves at going local rates. If all consumer durable goods were to be treated the same way as housing, the result, of course, would be a larger GDP.

Policies that would produce no growth in GDP undoubtedly would hold down pollution. But "costs" to society would be heavy. For one thing, antipollution efforts themselves cost money. Only increased production can provide the resources to tackle pollution—and to reduce poverty, keep up the nation's defenses, meet housing needs, and a thousand other things. Suggestions that consumption of goods be restricted to lessen pollution have a surface kind of logic. But, in practice, what goods would be restricted? From the hands of what groups of people? Would this require the setting up of a new agency: The Department of Consumer Privation? The nation's poor do not have the feeling that they are consuming to an excessive degree. Nor do the millions in the middle class who, after paying taxes and making the mortgage payment, are barely able to keep their heads above water. They would find little comfort if the quagmire that engulfed them when GDP stopped growing were a little purer.

Those who are asking whether the nation can survive with pollution are asking the wrong question. It is unfortunate but true that the nation cannot survive without pollution. The answer is not to jettison growth and push for an anemic GDP, but rather to channel economic growth in new directions. More resources and more talent can be applied to reducing pollution to tolerable levels. In the case of automobiles, for example, increased inputs of capital and labor to produce autos that do not emit noxious fumes would be more sensible than closing down assembly lines to produce fewer automobiles. In short, there need not be a basic contradiction between growth and a livable environment. It is not necessary or even possible to choose one and abandon the other.

DISCUSSION

1. What does the author mean when he says that "air no longer is 'free': There is some 'cost' to the user"?

2. The author appears to belittle the concern of many economists that omitting the value of work done in the home causes a sexist bias in GDP calculations. With whom do you agree? Why?

3. Which group do you agree with considering the improvement of GDP, the "pluses" or "minuses"?

4. Which concerns about GDP revolve around its ability to accurately measure current production versus around its ability to measure economic well-being? Is there a difference? Is there value in having a separate measure of both, or can one measure perform both functions?

Economic Fluctuations, Unemployment, and Inflation

TRUE OR FALSE

T F

1. The term business cycle refers to the fluctuations in economic output known as expansion, boom, contraction, and recession.

2. Inflation decreases the purchasing power of the dollar.

3. During a recession, both frictional and structural unemployment will be zero.

4. If the actual current rate of unemployment is equal to the natural rate of unemployment, actual employment will be equal to the full-employment level and actual GDP will be equal to potential GDP.

5. A nonworking student or a retired person is not counted as unemployed in the official figures.

6. If a country has a population of 100 of which 75 are employed, the unemployment rate must be 25 percent.

7. Potential GDP is the level of output associated with the full employment of resources.

8. When the economy is in a recession, unemployment will be higher than the natural rate and actual GDP will be below potential GDP.

9. Inflation can be harmful to an economy when it lowers the willingness of individuals to enter into long-term contracts and requires individuals to devote resources toward protecting themselves against the effects of the inflation.

10. The natural rate of unemployment is composed of frictional unemployment and cyclical unemployment, but structural unemployment is excluded.

T F

☐ ☐ 11. Inflation is a sustained increase in the general level of prices in an economy.

☐ ☐ 12. If the price index rose from 120 to 132, the inflation rate would be 12 percent.

☐ ☐ 13. Through time, inflation hurts the average worker because it raises the prices of consumer goods without increasing their income.

☐ ☐ 14. The labor force is equal to the number employed plus the number unemployed.

☐ ☐ 15. The GDP of an economy can never exceed the potential GDP level.

PROBLEMS AND PROJECTS

1. Classify the following workers as either F, frictionally unemployed; S, structurally unemployed; C, cyclically unemployed; or O, out of the labor force.
    ___ a. A worker moves to a new town and has spent two weeks searching for a new job.
    ___ b. Environmental regulations have resulted in a coal miner losing his job. He has not been able to find a job that he can perform with his current skills.
    ___ c. A mother is reentering the labor force after having a baby but has not yet found work.
    ___ d. An auto worker is laid off because of a sharp decline in GDP during the last six months.
    ___ e. A 40-year-old man quits his current job to return to college and get his degree. He does not currently hold a job.
    ___ f. An airline pilot is laid off after an economic slowdown caused by a sharp reduction in the demand for air transportation.
    ___ g. After unsuccessfully searching for a job for eight weeks, a woman decides to stop looking for work.
    ___ h. A person retires after working for his employer for 20 years.

EXHIBIT 1

Country	Population	Employed	Unemployed	Labor Force	Unemployment Rate	Labor Force Participation Rate	Employment to Population Ratio
Abos	200	100	50	___	___	___	___
Bela	100	76	4	___	___	___	___
Copa	100	54	6	___	___	___	___

2. Exhibit 1 presents data on the population, employment, and unemployment in three hypothetical countries.
    a. Using the data supplied, calculate and fill in the labor forces of the countries.
    b. Using your results, find the unemployment rates for the countries.
    c. Based upon the unemployment rates, which country has the best performing economy and which has the worst?
    d. Now find the labor force participation rates for the countries.
    e. Calculate the employment to population ratios for each country.
    f. Explain why these "employment rates" from part e are not simply 100 percent minus the unemployment rates.

3. For each of the situations listed, look at the data given and classify the economy as either R, in a recession; F, at full employment; or B, in an economic boom.

___ a. An economy with a natural rate of unemployment of 5 percent currently has an actual unemployment rate of 7 percent.

___ b. An economy with a full employment (or potential) level of GDP equal to $5 billion has an actual GDP of $4 billion.

___ c. An economy with a natural rate of unemployment of 5 percent currently has an actual unemployment rate of 5 percent.

___ d. An economy with a potential GDP of $2 billion has an actual GDP of $3 billion.

MULTIPLE CHOICE

1. Frictional unemployment results from
   a. not enough jobs in the economy.
   b. not enough employers.
   c. not enough employees.
   d. scarce information about job opportunities and the time it takes to acquire that information.

2. The definition of the unemployment rate is
   a. the number of persons in the country who are not employed.
   b. the number of persons in the civilian labor force who are not employed.
   c. the percentage of persons in the country who are not employed.
   d. the percentage of persons in the civilian labor force who are not employed.

3. Inflation is best described as
   a. high prices.
   b. a sustained increase in the general level of prices as indicated by a price index.
   c. an increase in the purchasing power of money.
   d. an increase in the price of a particular good or service that is necessary for all consumers.

4. The natural rate of unemployment equals
   a. the sum of frictional and structural unemployment.
   b. frictional unemployment.
   c. full employment minus all those unemployed.
   d. the sum of frictional and cyclical unemployment.

5. The labor force participation rate is
   a. the number of persons employed divided by the number of persons unemployed.
   b. the number of persons 16 years of age and older who are either employed or actively seeking work divided by the total noninstitutional population 16 years of age and older.
   c. the number of persons employed divided by the number of persons 16 years of age and older.
   d. the number of persons who are actively seeking work divided by the number of persons who are employed.

6. Structural unemployment means that
   a. employment in the construction industry is insufficient.
   b. there are simply not enough jobs to go around.
   c. worker qualifications do not match available jobs.
   d. jobs are plentiful, but workers are scarce.

7. Actual GDP
   a.   is greater than potential GDP during recessions.
   b.   is less than potential GDP during recessions.
   c.   and potential GDP have identical meanings.
   d.   is equal to potential GDP during economic booms.

8. During periods of high and variable inflation, which of the following is unlikely to occur?
   a.   Resources will be diverted from economically productive activities toward activities designed to protect individuals from inflation.
   b.   Individuals will find it difficult to know whether a price change is due to the general inflation or due to shifts in supply or demand in a given market.
   c.   Individuals will want to make long-term contracts in order to enjoy the benefits of higher prices.
   d.   Some resources will be wasted as suppliers have to reprint menus and price catalogues to reflect the new, higher prices.

9. In a properly operating, dynamic economy,
   a.   the unemployment rate should remain near zero.
   b.   we would expect to have some unemployment due to normal structural and frictional factors.
   c.   the rate of unemployment will be very high during economic booms.
   d.   the employment/population ratio should average 100 percent.

10. The period of declining growth in real GDP between the peak of the business cycle and the trough is called the
    a.   contractionary phase.
    b.   boom.
    c.   expansionary phase.
    d.   lost phase.

11. Which of the following will most likely occur during the expansionary phase of a business cycle?
    a.   Real GDP rises and unemployment falls.
    b.   Real GDP declines and inflation rises.
    c.   Interest rates rise and the number of business failures rise.
    d.   Inflation rises and employment falls.

12. In the early 1990s, the U.S. government substantially reduced defense expenditures. The resulting unemployment of defense-related workers, who possessed skills no longer needed by the economy, is an example of
    a.   cyclical unemployment.
    b.   frictional unemployment.
    c.   seasonal unemployment.
    d.   structural unemployment.

13. Which of the following would be officially classified as unemployed?
    a.   a school administrator who has been working as a substitute teacher one day per week while looking for a full-time job in administration
    b.   a mathematician who returned to graduate school after failing to find a job the last four months
    c.   a 60-year-old former steel worker who would like to work but has given up actively seeking employment
    d.   None of the above would be officially classified as unemployed.

Use the following data to answer the next four questions.

Population	200 million
Number employed	120 million
Number unemployed	30 million

14. What is the labor force of the economy?
    a. 30 million
    b. 120 million
    c. 150 million
    d. 200 million

15. What is the unemployment rate of the economy?
    a. 15 percent
    b. 20 percent
    c. 60 percent
    d. 75 percent

16. What is the labor force participation rate of the economy?
    a. 25 percent
    b. 60 percent
    c. 75 percent
    d. 80 percent

17. What is the employment/population ratio of the economy?
    a. 25 percent
    b. 60 percent
    c. 75 percent
    d. 80 percent

18. (I) Changes in the age composition of the labor force will affect the natural rate of unemployment (for example, an increase in the relative number of youthful workers). (II) Institutional changes such as an increase in the minimum wage may increase cyclical unemployment but will not affect the natural rate of unemployment.
    a. Both I and II are true.
    b. I is true; II is false.
    c. I is false; II is true.
    d. Both I and II are false.

19. Which of the following is true?
    a. During a boom, the natural rate of unemployment falls below the actual rate of unemployment.
    b. During a boom, the output of the economy will exceed its long-run potential output.
    c. During a boom, there will be widespread unemployment.
    d. During a boom, the actual rate of unemployment will exceed the natural rate of unemployment.

20. The natural rate of unemployment
    a. is fixed; it cannot be changed with public policy.
    b. fluctuates substantially over the business cycle.
    c. is associated with the economy's maximum sustainable output rate.
    d. declines when youthful workers (under age 25) become a larger proportion of the labor force.

DISCUSSION QUESTIONS

1. a. What is inflation? How is it measured? What would a negative inflation rate mean?
    b. Could you predict what would happen to the price of swimsuits and the price of coats during a hot, dry summer, all else equal? How would these changes affect the overall inflation rate? Explain both answers.

2. List the major factors that determine the natural rate of unemployment. Based on those factors, do you expect the natural rate of unemployment to rise or fall over the next decades?

3. If you were to ask most people what the optimal rate of unemployment was, they would be likely to respond "Zero, of course!" Do you agree? What drawbacks might zero unemployment have for workers? For firms? For the economy as a whole?

4. In 1998, the U.S. unemployment rate was 4.5 percent. Was the economy in a recession or boom? Explain your reasoning.

5. When Ronald Reagan took office, the nation's unemployment rate was 7.4 percent. When it reached 9.8 percent two years later, Reagan joked that he would take responsibility for the 2.4 percent increase in the unemployment rate during his term if the Democrats would accept blame for the other 7.4 percent. Should Reagan's joke be taken literally? Explain.

6. Respond to each of the following statements:
    a. "We could eliminate the economic cost of recessions by setting up unemployment compensation so that all unemployed workers receive the same income that they earn when working."
    b. "We could eliminate the economic cost of inflation by indexing all payments, such as wages, interest, retirement benefits, and taxes."

PERSPECTIVES IN ECONOMICS

The Efficiency Costs of Inflation: Myth and Reality

by Alan S. Blinder

[Reprinted with permission from Alan S. Blinder, *Soft Hearts: Tough Minded Economics for a Just Society* (Reading, MA: Addison-Wesley, 1987), pp. 45–51 (abridged).]

It is pretty clear that inflation is unloved. The question is why. More precisely, is the popular aversion to inflation based on fact and logic or on illusion and prejudice? After all, public opinion also lines up solidly behind the existence of flying saucers, angels, and extrasensory perception.

Economists, naturally, have been thinking about, studying, and trying to measure the social costs of inflation for decades. A central conclusion of the research is that the costs of inflation depend very much on whether it proceeds at a steady, predictable rate or is volatile and takes people by surprise.

Unexpected changes in inflation are widely decried because they capriciously create and destroy large chunks of wealth. When borrowers pay back loans in cheaper dollars then they borrowed, they reap a bonanza at the expense of lenders. During hyperinflation, the wealth redistributions from inflation swamp all other sources of wealth creating. The profit to be made by designing and marketing useful products becomes trivial next to the rewards for clever cash management. Accordingly, entrepreneurial talent is channeled into outsmarting inflation rather than outsmarting the competition. When that happens, the invisible hand is amputated.

Similar things happen in the more moderate inflations we are used to in the United States, though on a muted scale. Americans who provided for their retirement by purchasing long-term bonds in the 1950s and 1960s saw the purchasing power of their savings decimated by the unexpectedly high inflation in the 1970s. In stark contrast, Americans who acquired fixed-interest mortgages at 3 percent and 4 percent interest rates in the 1950s and 1960s discovered to their delight that inflation reduced their mortgage payments to insignificance.

Winners and losers arise whenever there are large swings in the inflation rate. And the resulting redistributions of wealth are rank violations of the principle of (horizontal) equity. Because they are the product of neither the smooth functioning of an efficient market economy nor deliberate government interventions to assist the poor, the arbitrary redistributions caused by unanticipated changes in inflation deserve their bad reputation.

One example is especially important. When people are uncertain about the future course of inflation, long-term contracts calling for payment in dollars become hard to write and even harder to live by. Again, the case of hyperinflation makes the point graphically: When contracts lasting more than a few days become infeasible because no one can predict what money will buy, the economy is in deep trouble. But even modest inflation creates substantial uncertainties and engenders insecurity. In terms of today's money, the repayment of principal on a $1 million five-year corporate bond will be worth $1 million if inflation is zero, $822,000 if inflation averages 4 percent a year over the five years, and $681,000 if inflation averages 8 percent. If no one knows what the average inflation rate will be, both the corporation and prospective bond buyers are taking a big gamble by entering into such a contract.

Rather than bear such risks, nervous investors may deem it wiser to put their money into something tangible—like real estate, precious metals, rare coins, or expensive works of art. Such investments, of course contribute nothing to productivity and economic growth. And so, it is argued, fears of inflation undermine the mainspring of economic prosperity. This charge, if true, would constitute a genuine and serious cost of inflation. But is it? On close examination, the argument founders on the same fallacy I mentioned earlier: failure to remember that every transaction has both a buyer and a seller.

Suppose I purchase a $25,000 painting rather than invest $25,000 in the bond market. The seller of the painting gets $25,000 in cash. What will he do with it? Surely he will not stuff it in his mattress. More likely, he will invest it in the bond market, or in the stock market, or deposit it in the bank. At that point, the funds are back in the financial system—where they can be channeled into productive investments. But what if the seller of the painting invests his money in, say, old coins? Then it may be the coin seller who puts the funds back into circulation. Eventually, however, someone must do so, for the supply of collectibles is fixed and every transaction has both a buyer and a seller. Society as a whole cannot buy more collectibles. Thus, though I may put my savings to an unproductive use, someone else will bail society out.

Nonetheless, the risks of inflation do pose a critical question: How much should society pay to avoid assuming such risks? People spend considerable sums on life insurance, fire insurance, and health insurance. Therefore, it is perhaps believable that the body politic knowingly and willingly pays the large premiums it does to insure itself against the risks of inflation. Millions of Americans, however, eagerly wager small sums in lotteries, at racetracks, and in casinos—suggesting a certain fondness for taking a chance. So, while the costs that stem from an uncertain future price level are genuine and potentially large, they are hard to translate into dollars and cents and may not amount to much.

More important, we could easily eliminate this risk if we really wanted to. All we need do is write long-term contracts with escalator clauses, as some businesses already do. In these so-called indexed contracts, the amount of money that will change hands in the future is not fixed in dollars, but is tied to the behavior of some price index, such as the Consumer Price Index.

The number of dollar bills that will change hands is not known in advance, but the purchasing power of those dollars is.

This simple device would eliminate the risks that stem from an unpredictable future price level. Yet businesses and individuals acting in their own self-interest rarely choose to do so. The apparent reluctance to write indexed contracts suggest that people are willing to pay only small premiums to insure themselves against long-term inflation risks. Yet society pays huge premiums for anti-inflation insurance when it keeps millions of people unemployed. Something seems amiss here.

There is one further cost that a believer in the principle of efficiency should be aware of. In a market economy, the relative prices of different commodities guide the allocation of resources. If a severe frost reduces the Brazilian coffee crop, the price of coffee will rise relative to, say, the price of tea. Consumers pursuing their own best interests will buy less coffee and more tea. Similarly, more resources will be thrown into coffee production and less into tea. All this activity is as it should be, because nature has made coffee scarcer.

But variable and uncertain inflation makes relative prices hard to monitor because the dollar ceases to serve as a reliable measuring rod. A consumer goes to the store and finds that coffee costs 10 percent more than it did last week. Does that mean coffee has become 10 percent more expensive relative to tea? Or does it just mean that inflation has raised all prices by 10 percent? More information is needed to make an intelligent decision.

As with other costs of inflation, this cost can be colossal in a hyperinflation. If the price level rises 40 percent a week on average, but rises 70 percent in some weeks and 10 percent in others, the fact that coffee prices rise 10 percent in a week tells consumers little about the price of coffee relative to other commodities. But what is a mountain in a hyperinflation is only a molehill in a single-digit inflation. If the typical weekly price increase is only one-tenth of 1 percent (which is roughly what a 5 percent annual inflation rate means), then a 10 percent increase in the price of coffee strongly suggests that coffee has become 9.9 percent more expensive relative to most other goods. Dollar prices are almost as useful to shoppers under low inflation as under zero inflation.

Can that be all there is to the costs of inflation? The inefficiencies caused by hyperinflation are, of course, monumental, but the costs of moderate inflation that I have just enumerated seem meager at best.

I am forced to conclude that inflation's most devout enemies exhibit verbal hysteria. Inflation does indeed bring losses of efficiency. It also makes people feel unsure and unhappy. We would no doubt be better off without it. But, on close examination, the costs that attend the low and moderate inflation rates experienced in the United States and in other industrial countries appear to be quite modest—more like a bad cold than a cancer on society. And the myth that the inflationary demon, unless exorcised, will inevitably grow is exactly that—a myth. There is neither theoretical nor statistical support for the popular notion that inflation has a built-in tendency to accelerate.

As rational individuals, we do not volunteer for a lobotomy to cure a head cold. Yet, as a collectivity, we routinely prescribe the economic equivalent of lobotomy (high unemployment) as a cure for the inflationary cold. Why?

DISCUSSION

1. Blinder's main conclusion is that inflation is less harmful to the economy than most people think it is. Do you agree? Which of his arguments are convincing? With which do you disagree? Explain.

2. Economists generally agree that inflation has higher costs if it is variable (and cannot be predicted accurately) than if it is steady. If you knew exactly what next year's inflation rate was going to be, how could you protect yourself?

3. If Blinder is right, what implications do his conclusions have for the proper objective of government policy?

An Introduction to Basic Macroeconomic Markets

TRUE OR FALSE

T F

☐ ☐ 1. The vertical LRAS curve indicates that by increasing the price level in the economy, technology will be improved so real output will increase as well.

☐ ☐ 2. When the economy is in long-run equilibrium, actual output will equal potential GDP.

☐ ☐ 3. A trade deficit is when a country's exports of goods and services are greater than its imports.

☐ ☐ 4. If interest rates rise, bond prices will increase.

☐ ☐ 5. Saving is disposable income that is not spent on consumption.

☐ ☐ 6. The aggregate demand curve shows the inverse relationship between the demand for goods and services and the money (or nominal) interest rate.

☐ ☐ 7. The real interest rate equals the money (or nominal) interest rate plus an inflationary premium.

☐ ☐ 8. When U.S. citizens make investments in foreign countries, this would be considered an "outflow of capital" from the United States.

☐ ☐ 9. One reason the aggregate demand curve slopes downward is the increase in real wealth that comes about when aggregate prices fall while the money supply remains constant.

☐ ☐ 10. When the U.S. dollar appreciates, it is less expensive for foreigners to buy U.S. goods and services.

T F

☐ ☐ 11. In the loanable funds market, the true "price" paid by borrowers (demanders) and earned by lenders (suppliers) of money is the real interest rate.

☐ ☐ 12. When the foreign exchange market and loanable funds market are in equilibrium, injections will equal leakages in the circular flow of income.

☐ ☐ 13. The key markets in the circular flow of income are the goods and services market, the resource market, the loanable funds market, and the foreign exchange market.

☐ ☐ 14. The money available in an economy for investment loans comes from household savings.

☐ ☐ 15. The aggregate demand curve slopes downward for the same reason that all other demand curves slope downward.

☐ ☐ 16. A sudden increase in the willingness of individuals to save would cause the market interest rate to rise.

☐ ☐ 17. If the current exchange rate is one dollar equals three Mexican pesos, the cost of purchasing a 60 peso product in dollars is $20.

☐ ☐ 18. An increase in foreign demand for products made in the United States would cause the dollar to appreciate.

PROBLEMS AND PROJECTS

1. Consider the data in Exhibit 1.
    a. For each of these three years, draw an aggregate demand/aggregate supply diagram in which you show a short-run aggregate supply curve, a long-run aggregate supply curve, and an aggregate

EXHIBIT 1

YEAR	ACTUAL GDP (BILLIONS OF 2000 DOLLARS)	POTENTIAL GDP (BILLIONS OF 2000 DOLLARS)	PRICE LEVEL (GDP DEFLATOR)	UNEMPLOYMENT RATE (PERCENT)
1997	8,736	8,736	95	4.9
2000	9,952	9,590	100	4.0
2008	$11,801	$12,041	122	7.2

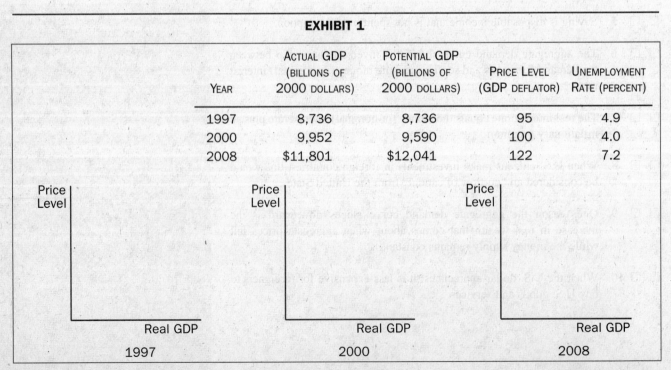

Price Level   Price Level   Price Level

                Real GDP   Real GDP   Real GDP

        1997   2000   2008

demand curve. Label the appropriate values for total output and the price level. (Hint: Remember that actual output occurs at the intersection between AD and SRAS.)

b.   Based upon this data, what is the economy's natural rate of unemployment?

c.   In which of these cases is the unemployment rate greater than the natural rate of unemployment? In which cases does actual output fall below potential GDP? Are they the same? In what part of the business cycle would you consider the economy?

d.   In which of these cases is the unemployment rate less than the natural rate of unemployment? In which cases does actual output exceed potential GDP? Are they the same? In what part of the business cycle would you consider the economy?

e.   In which of these cases is the unemployment rate equal to the natural rate of unemployment? In which cases does actual output equal potential GDP? Are they the same? In what part of the business cycle would you consider the economy?

2.   Consider the information in Exhibit 2.

a.   Fill in the blanks by calculating the real interest rate for each of the years listed. Was the real interest rate constant, rising, or falling between 2001 and 2004? Was the real interest rate constant, rising, or falling between 1998 and 2001? (Hint: The prime interest rate is a well-publicized rate that banks charge some of their better customers and is a good measure of the money rate of interest. Also, because we do not know what rates of inflation were expected, assume that the actual inflation rates are good guesses for the inflationary premiums in those years.)

EXHIBIT 2

	1979	1982	2001	2004
Prime interest rate	12.7%	14.9%	6.9%	4.3%
Inflation rate	11.3%	6.1%	2.8%	2.7%
Real interest rate	___	___	___	___

b.   Assuming all else constant, what effect would the change in real interest rate between 1979 and 1982 have had on the willingness of consumers and businesses to borrow money? Between 2001 and 2004?

3.   Exhibit 3 contains hypothetical information about the AD and SRAS curves giving the appropriate values for real GDP (in billions of dollars) at different price levels (P).

a.   Plot the data in an AD-AS diagram in the space provided. What is the current equilibrium level of real GDP? What is the price level?

b.   Suppose the level of full-employment real GDP is $330 billion. Add a LRAS curve to your diagram.

c.   Is this economy currently experiencing full employment, a recession, or a boom? Explain briefly.

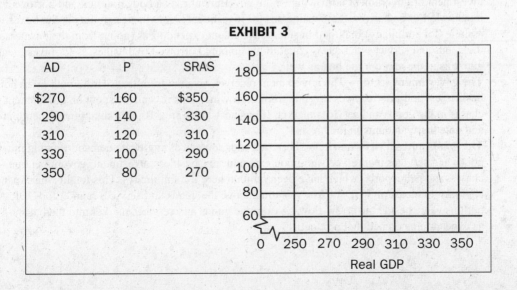

EXHIBIT 3

AD	P	SRAS
$270	160	$350
290	140	330
310	120	310
330	100	290
350	80	270

4. Understanding the difference between real and nominal (or "money") interest rates is important but can sometimes be confusing. The easiest way to understand the difference is to consider loaning your friend $100 because he is having a party tonight and wants to buy ten large pizzas that cost $10 each. He will repay you in one year. The nominal (or money) interest rate is the percent difference in the dollar amount of money he repays you relative to what you loaned him. The real interest rate is the percent difference between the quantity of pizza that can be purchased now (at today's prices) with the money you loan him relative to the quantity of pizza that you will be able to buy when the money is repaid (at future prices). Use this analogy to answer the following questions.

    a. You tell your friend he can borrow the $100 today if he gives you back $100 one year from now. What money (or nominal) interest rate are you charging him?

    b. If inflation causes the price of a large pizza to increase from $10 to $20 by the time he repays you, how many pizzas will you be able to buy with the $100 when it is repaid? Is the real interest rate positive, negative, or zero?

    c. Suppose that instead of specifying the loan in dollars, you specify it in pizza. You will lend him enough for ten pizzas today if he returns enough money to buy ten pizzas next year. What real interest rate are you charging him? If the price of pizzas rises to $20, how much will he owe you?

    d. Suppose that both you and your friend expect the price of pizzas to double from $10 to $20 between now and next year. You both agree to a written contract in which you loan him $100 today if he repays you $200 next year. If inflation turns out to be higher than you both expected, and the price of pizza rises to $25, are you (the lender) better or worse off when he repays you with $200? Is your friend (the borrower) better or worse off? What has changed relative to what you expected, the real or nominal interest rate, or both?

    e. If both you and your friend had known in advance that the inflation rate would be higher (as in part d) and that pizza prices would rise to $25, how might the contract you agreed to in part d have changed? Would the real or nominal interest rate, or both, have been different?

5. Exhibit 4 shows a simplified version of the circular flow diagram with the international sector omitted. Beside each arrow is a box with a letter corresponding to the question letter relating to that box. A few boxes are already done as examples. Follow the questions below to fill in the remaining boxes. (Hint: For every market or sector, the total of all the arrows coming in must equal the total of all flowing out.)

    a. **The household sector**—At the lower right, national income is earned by households supplying their resources in the resource market (wage income from supplying labor, for example). Part of this income is taken by the government in taxes and the remaining disposable income must be either spent on consumption or saved. Of the $100 of income earned by households, $10 is paid out in taxes to the government and $70 is spent on consumption. How much is household saving? Note this amount in the box for net saving.

    b. **The loanable funds market**—Household net saving is available to the economy for either business investment or government borrowing. If the government runs a budget deficit and borrows $5, how much is left to be borrowed by businesses for investment? Note these amounts in the boxes. Also, assume (for simplicity) that total business investment expenditures (going from the businesses into the goods and services market) is equal to the amount borrowed by businesses for investment and note this in the appropriate box as well.

    c. **The government sector**—The government receives revenue from taxes (from both households and businesses) and also receives revenue from borrowing. This revenue is spent on government purchases in the goods and services market. If business taxes are $10, find total government purchases and note these amounts in the boxes.

    d. **The goods and services market**—There are four sources of aggregate demand flowing into the goods and services market: consumption expenditures, business investment, government purchases, and net exports (which have been omitted here for simplicity). This total is the expenditure approach to measuring GDP. Write this total above the goods and services market for GDP. Also, put this value beside the arrow flowing from the goods and services market into the business sector as expenditures on national product.

e. **The business sector**—Businesses receive revenue from the expenditures on goods and services (top left arrow). They also have money flowing in from the loanable funds market that they have borrowed for investment. The money flowing out is in the form of taxes to the government, money spent on investment goods in the goods and services market, and resource payments to factors of production (workers, etc.). Find the remaining total resource payments flowing from businesses into the resource market.

f. **The resource market**—This is where we started by assuming that households received $100 of national income from supplying their resources. Does your total from part e above going into the resource market match the outflow that we began with? Given your answers above, what do you think is the primary determinant of household income?

EXHIBIT 4

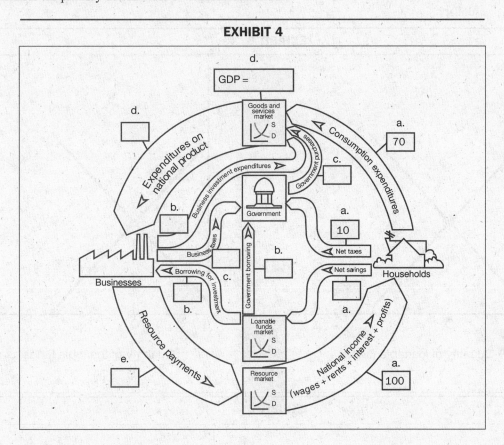

6. Using your knowledge from working problem 5, answer the following questions. You might need to refer back to Exhibit 4 to answer these.

a. In a later chapter, we will discuss several theories about how government borrowing affects the economy. Returning to the diagram, suppose government borrowing increases from $5 to $10. What must change to bring the loanable funds market back into equality so that the money coming in equals the money flowing out?

b. If households decide to spend more of their income on consumption, and save less, what will happen to the level of investment in the economy (assume government borrowing does not change)? Because economic growth requires investment, what does this tell you about the relationship between economic growth and household savings? If you were a politician in favor of increasing economic growth what would you propose?

7.   a. Exhibit 5 shows the market for loanable funds. Using Exhibit 5(i), show how a decrease in the num-
         ber of persons seeking new automobile loans would affect the interest rate and quantity of loans.
         Using Exhibit 5(ii), show how an increase in the desire of households to save their income would
         affect the interest rate and quantity of loans.
     b. Exhibit 6 shows the foreign exchange market for the Mexican peso. Using Exhibit 6(i), show how
         an increase in the desire of Americans to go on vacation to Mexico would affect the value of the
         peso and the quantity exchanged. In Exhibit 6(i), has the peso appreciated or depreciated relative
         to the U.S. dollar? Using Exhibit 6(ii), show how an increase in the desire of Mexicans to purchase
         foreign-made goods (for instance, U.S. automobiles) would affect the value of the peso and the
         quantity exchanged. In Exhibit 6(ii), has the peso appreciated or depreciated relative to the U.S.
         dollar?

EXHIBIT 5

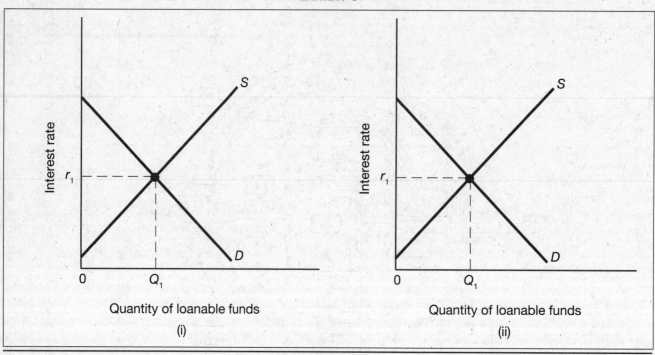

EXHIBIT 6

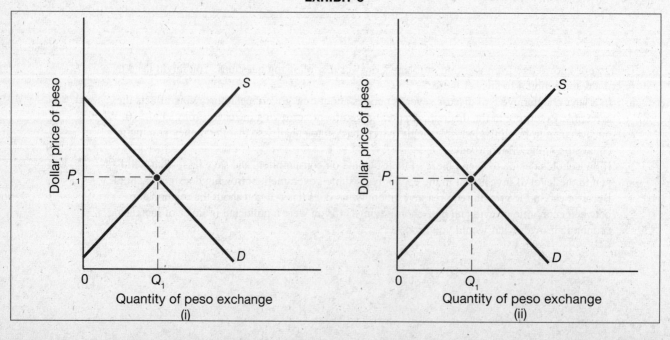

MULTIPLE CHOICE

1. Within the aggregate demand/aggregate supply framework, the quantity on the horizontal axis in the aggregate goods and services market represents the
    a. total amount of government spending.
    b. total real output (real GDP) of the economy.
    c. total unemployment of the economy.
    d. price level of the economy.

2. In the loanable funds market, the true burden of borrowers and the true yield to lenders is the
    a. real (inflation adjusted) interest rate.
    b. nominal (money) interest rate.
    c. inflation rate.
    d. inflation premium rate (in money terms).

3. When AD is equal to SRAS at an output level equal to the LRAS curve,
    a. we are at long-run macroeconomic equilibrium.
    b. we are at the natural rate of unemployment.
    c. both a and b are true.
    d. neither a nor b is true.

4. Your grandmother gives you a $100 savings bond that will mature in fifteen years. The bank tells you that they will buy it from you today at a price of $24. If interest rates rise in the near future, the value of your bond
    a. will fall and it will be worth less than $24.
    b. will rise and it will be worth more than $24.
    c. will remain unchanged at $24.
    d. This is a trick question; the value of a $100 bond is always $100.

5. If the expected rate of inflation is zero, the
    a. real interest rate must also equal zero.
    b. money (nominal) interest rate must also equal zero.
    c. real interest rate must equal the money interest rate.
    d. economy is likely to experience high inflation in the near future.

6. Which of the following is the primary factor that coordinates the actions of borrowers and lenders in the loanable funds market?
    a. inflation rate
    b. unemployment rate
    c. the government
    d. interest rate

7. Which of the following statements about the circular flow diagram is not correct?
    a. Households receive income from the resource market; they save some of it and spend the rest of it on domestic or foreign goods and services.
    b. The loanable funds market takes net household savings and channels it in part to the government and in part to businesses for investment.
    c. Expenditures on GDP are equal to consumption plus government purchases plus investment plus net exports (exports minus imports).
    d. The net inflow of capital from foreign economies must always be positive and equal to the amount of business investment.

8. The circular flow of income is coordinated by the
   a. goods and services market, resources market, foreign exchange market, and loanable funds market.
   b. consumption market, investment market, stock market, and government market.
   c. government market, household goods market, bond market, and business market.
   d. financial market, corporate market, stock market, and loanable funds market.

9. As prices rise, a fixed money supply will be able to buy fewer goods and services. This effect is due to a(n)
   a. reduction in the interest rate.
   b. increase in aggregate demand.
   c. decline in the purchasing power of money.
   d. increase in income.

10. The aggregate demand curve slopes downward to the right because
    a. as prices decrease, the real value of the fixed quantity of money increases and thereby stimulates consumer spending.
    b. a lower price level reduces the price of domestic goods relative to foreign goods, increasing net exports (the international substitution effect).
    c. a lower price level reduces the demand for money and lowers the real interest rate, stimulating consumption and investment spending (the interest rate effect).
    d. all of the above are correct.

11. Which of the following is true regarding an unanticipated increase in inflation?
    a. Both borrowers and lenders will be better off.
    b. Both borrowers and lenders will be worse off.
    c. Borrowers will be better off and lenders will be worse off.
    d. Borrowers will be worse off and lenders will be better off.

12. Suppose people anticipate that inflation will be 4 percent during the next several years. If the real rate of interest is 5 percent, the money rate of interest must be
    a. 1 percent.
    b. 4 percent.
    c. 5 percent.
    d. 9 percent.

13. Suppose you are earning 5 percent nominal interest on your savings account. If the rate of inflation is 3 percent, the real rate of interest you are earning is
    a. 2 percent.
    b. 3 percent.
    c. 5 percent.
    d. 8 percent.

14. In 1999, the nominal interest rate on a 30-year bond was around 5.85 percent. Assuming that investors have set these contracts expecting a real interest rate of 3 percent, what is the average rate of inflation that investors in the market are expecting over the next thirty years?
    a. 2.85 percent
    b. 3 percent
    c. 5.85 percent
    d. 8.85 percent

15. Which of the following situations would you prefer if you planned to borrow money?
    a. The nominal interest rate is 5 percent, and future prices are expected to be stable.
    b. The nominal interest rate is 9 percent, and expected inflation is 7 percent.
    c. The nominal interest rate is 4 percent, and expected inflation is 1 percent.
    d. The nominal interest rate is 25 percent, and expected inflation is 22 percent.

16. If the dollar price of the English pound goes from $1.50 to $2.00, the dollar has
    a. appreciated, and the English will find U.S. goods cheaper.
    b. appreciated, and the English will find U.S. goods more expensive.
    c. depreciated, and the English will find U.S. goods cheaper.
    d. depreciated, and the English will find U.S. goods more expensive.

17. A depreciation of a nation's currency would cause
    a. the nation's imports to increase and exports to decline.
    b. the nation's exports to increase and imports to decline.
    c. both imports and exports to decline.
    d. both imports and exports to rise.

18. If the value of a nation's imports exceeds exports, the nation has a
    a. government budget deficit.
    b. trade surplus.
    c. trade deficit.
    d. negative net capital flow.

19. The long-run aggregate supply curve is vertical, reflecting the fact that
    a. changes in price have no effect on output in the long run. In the long run, the price of goods and the price of resources move together and firms have no incentive to change their output.
    b. fluctuations in inflation cannot be anticipated in the long run, so future prices have no effect on output.
    c. changes in price affect output a lot in the long run because in the long run firms can adjust factory sizes to meet changing demand conditions.
    d. changes in price have a large effect on output because they lead to highly variable interest rates, and business is hard to conduct under those circumstances.

20. Which of the following accurately indicates the relationship between the short-run and long-run aggregate supply curves?
    a. In the short run, aggregate supply is sloped upward to the right, and in the long run, it is vertical.
    b. In the short run, aggregate supply is vertical, and in the long run, it is sloped upward to the right.
    c. In the short run, aggregate supply is downward sloping, but in the long run, it is sloped upward to the right.
    d. In the short run, aggregate supply is sloped upward to the right, but in the long run, it is downward sloping.

21. If the current price level in the goods and services market is higher than what was expected, output will be
    a. at the economy's long-run capacity.
    b. below the economy's long-run capacity.
    c. above the economy's long-run capacity.
    d. equal to the expected rate of inflation minus net exports.

22. (I) If long-run equilibrium is present in the goods and services market, the current price level will equal the price level buyers and sellers anticipated.
    (II) When an economy is in long-run equilibrium, the actual rate of unemployment will equal the natural rate of unemployment.
    a. Both I and II are true.
    b. Both I and II are false.
    c. I is true; II is false.
    d. I is false; II is true.

23. A trade surplus is when
    a. imports are greater than exports of goods and services.
    b. exports are greater than imports of goods and services.
    c. imports are equal to exports of goods and services.
    d. there is a positive net inflow of foreign capital.

24. (I) Fiscal policy involves altering government tax and spending policies.
    (II) Monetary policy encompasses those actions that alter the money supply.
    a. Both I and II are true.
    b. Both I and II are false.
    c. I is true; II is false.
    d. I is false; II is true.

25. Suppose business decision makers become more optimistic about future economic conditions and desire additional funds to expand their plant capacity. What is the likely effect on the loanable funds market?
    a. The demand for loanable funds will rise and the interest rate will rise.
    b. The demand for loanable funds will fall and the interest rate will fall.
    c. The supply for loanable funds will rise and the interest rate will fall.
    d. The supply for loanable funds will fall and the interest rate will rise.

DISCUSSION QUESTIONS

1. Respond to the following statement: "It is impossible to produce more than what economists refer to as 'potential GDP.'" Use the aggregate supply/aggregate demand diagram to depict a situation where the economy is producing past potential GDP. How is it possible for the economy to produce at that point?

2. "The burden of inflation falls heavily on savers and creditors, for example, upon wealthy bondholders." (Campbell McConnell, *Economics,* 6th ed. [New York: McGraw-Hill, 1975], p. 380.) Under what circumstances is this statement likely to be correct? incorrect?

3. Consider the natural rate of unemployment.
    a. What do economists mean by the natural rate of unemployment? Do you really believe there is such a thing as a natural rate of unemployment? Explain your answer.
    b. What reasons can you think of to explain why the natural rate of unemployment seems to have been higher in the United States than in Japan for most of the years since World War II?
    c. What ways can you think of to lower the natural rate of unemployment in the United States?
    d. If the natural rate of unemployment in the United States did fall, what would happen to the long-run aggregate supply curve?

4. Different loans have different interest rates. What are some of the types of interest rates that you know of? In considering how interest rates rise and fall, is it a major flaw in our model of the loanable funds market to consider just one interest rate for the economy?

5. In order to calculate the real rate of interest, we must somehow come up with an inflationary premium that is based on our expectation of inflation in the future. Do you have such an expectation? Do your friends? Would an inflation rate of 20 percent surprise you? If so, does that imply that you do or do not have some sort of expectation about future rates of inflation?

6. Market prices coordinate economic activity by providing the proper incentives and bringing into harmony the desires of buyers and sellers. Explain how market prices coordinate the following:
    a. the actions of those wanting to save with those wanting to borrow.
    b. the relationship between a country's imports and exports.
    c. the markets for labor in terms of job seekers and employment offerings.

Dynamic Change, Economic Fluctuations, and the AD-AS Model

CHAPTER 10

TRUE OR FALSE

T F

☐ ☐ 1. An anticipated change differs from an unanticipated change in that an anticipated change is foreseen by decision makers.

☐ ☐ 2. A decrease in real wealth, such as might be caused by a stock market crash, would decrease short-run aggregate supply.

☐ ☐ 3. A reduction in the real rate of interest would increase aggregate demand because it would increase business investment and consumer (consumption) spending.

☐ ☐ 4. Any factor, such as a technological advance, that shifts the long-run aggregate supply curve also similarly shifts the short-run aggregate supply curve.

☐ ☐ 5. Aggregate demand would fall if either the expected rate of inflation fell, foreign incomes fell, or the exchange rate value of the dollar fell (the dollar depreciated).

☐ ☐ 6. An unanticipated reduction in aggregate demand would cause the price level to fall and real output (real GDP) to fall as well.

☐ ☐ 7. An increase in resource prices (such as the price of oil) would cause a decrease in the long-run aggregate supply curve.

☐ ☐ 8. Adverse supply shocks that decrease short-run aggregate supply include major earthquakes, wars, and other natural disasters.

☐ ☐ 9. An unanticipated increase in short-run aggregate supply would cause the price level to fall and real output (real GDP) to fall as well.

T   F

☐ ☐ 10. During a recession, wages, resource prices, and the real interest rate will fall, helping to bring the economy back out of the recession.

☐ ☐ 11. When the economy is in a short-run equilibrium above the full employment level (an economic boom), rising resource prices will help the economy to "self-correct," redirecting it back to full employment at a higher price level.

☐ ☐ 12. Economic booms are sustainable in the long run because changes in aggregate demand are caused by changes in permanent income.

☐ ☐ 13. All economists agree that the self-correcting mechanism works very rapidly.

☐ ☐ 14. Once decision makers anticipate a given rate of inflation and build it into long-term contracts, an actual rate of inflation that is less than expected is essentially the equivalent of a reduction in the price level when price stability (zero inflation) is anticipated.

PROBLEMS AND PROJECTS

1. Use the aggregate demand/aggregate supply diagrams below to illustrate the changes in aggregate demand (AD), short-run aggregate supply (SRAS), long-run aggregate supply (LRAS), the price level (P), and real gross domestic product (RGDP) in response to the events described to the left of the diagrams. First show in the diagrams how AD, SRAS, and/or LRAS shift and then fill in the table to the right of the diagrams using + to indicate an increase (a shift to the right), – to indicate a decrease (a shift to the left), and 0 to indicate no change. (Hint: Only focus on the new short-run equilibrium and do not worry about any future long-run changes.)

EVENTS	DIAGRAMS	AD	SRAS	LRAS	P	RGDP

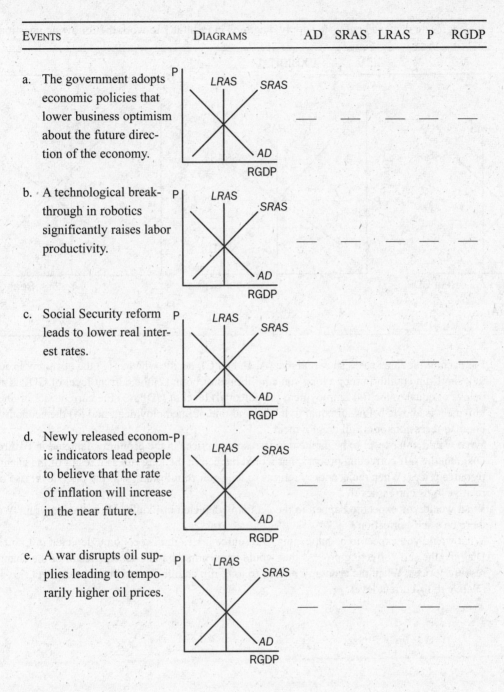

a. The government adopts economic policies that lower business optimism about the future direction of the economy.

    — — — — —

b. A technological breakthrough in robotics significantly raises labor productivity.

    — — — — —

c. Social Security reform leads to lower real interest rates.

    — — — — —

d. Newly released economic indicators lead people to believe that the rate of inflation will increase in the near future.

    — — — — —

e. A war disrupts oil supplies leading to temporarily higher oil prices.

    — — — — —

2.   Use the aggregate demand/aggregate supply diagrams in Exhibit 1 to work the following questions.

EXHIBIT 1

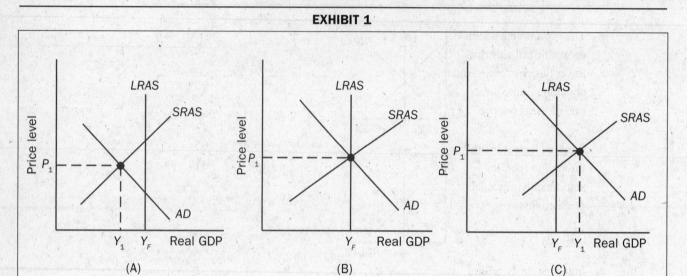

(A)   (B)   (C)

a.   For each of the three cases shown above (A, B, and C), decide whether (1) the economy is currently in a short-run equilibrium or a long-run equilibrium or both; (2) the current level of GDP is above, below, or equal to the full-employment (or potential) level of GDP; (3) the current rate of unemployment is above, below, or equal to the natural rate of unemployment; and (4) the economy is in a boom, a recession, or at full employment.

b.   What would you expect to be happening to resource prices in the economy depicted in Exhibit 1A? Diagram the self-correcting process that would happen in the long run as a result of the changing resource prices. When the economy returns to long-run equilibrium, will the price level rise or fall relative to its current level?

c.   What would you expect to happen to the economy depicted in Exhibit 1B in the long run? Would there be a self-correction?

d.   What would you expect to be happening to resource prices in the economy depicted in Exhibit 1C? Diagram the self-correcting process that would happen in the long run as a result of the changing resource prices. When the economy returns to long-run equilibrium, will the price level rise or fall relative to its current level?

3. Using an AD/AS model, decide what happens to the price level, the output level, and unemployment in each of the following cases. Assume that the economy is initially in long-run equilibrium and the events initially catch people by surprise (the changes are unanticipated). Use + to indicate an increase, – to indicate a decrease, and 0 to indicate no change.

Event	Price Level	Output (Real GDP)	Unemployment Rate
a. Interest rates fall.	_____	_____	_____
b. The stock market crashes.	_____	_____	_____
c. The dollar depreciates.	_____	_____	_____
d. Severe flooding in agricultural areas.	_____	_____	_____
e. World oil prices fall (oil is a resource).	_____	_____	_____
f. A major technological advance occurs.	_____	_____	_____
g. The expected rate of inflation rises. (Hint: This shifts both AD and SRAS.)	_____	_____	_____
h. Consumers and businesses become pessimistic about the future direction of the economy.	_____	_____	_____
i. Foreign economies fall into recession.	_____	_____	_____

4. Use the diagrams in Exhibit 2 to label each of the statements below as (T) true or (F) false.

EXHIBIT 2

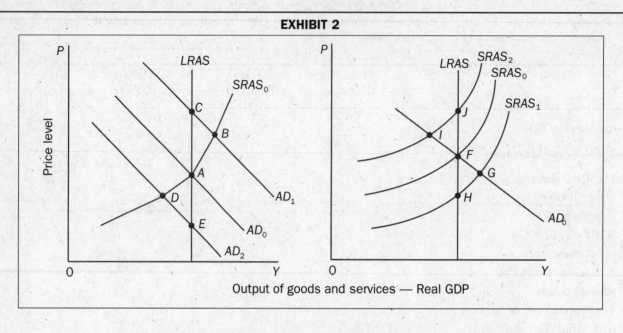

Output of goods and services — Real GDP

___ a. B and G represent economic booms, while D and I represent recessions.
___ b. A and F are points of long-run equilibrium.
___ c. Beginning from A, a decline in the real interest rate would move the economy toward D.
___ d. Beginning from F, an increase in resource prices would move the economy toward I.
___ e. At B, there will be a tendency for resource prices to fall, moving the economy toward C.
___ f. At I, there will be a tendency for resource prices to fall, moving the economy toward J.
___ g. Beginning from A, if foreign economies (with whom this economy trades) went into recessions, the economy would move toward D.
___ h. If a stock market crash moved the economy from A to D, the self-correcting mechanism of resource prices would tend to move the economy toward E in the long run.
___ i. If the world price of oil rose, moving the economy from F to I, the self-correcting mechanism of resource prices would tend to move the economy toward J in the long run.
___ j. A movement from F to G represents a decrease in short-run aggregate supply.
___ k. A movement from B to A represents a decrease in short-run aggregate supply.
___ l. If the economy was currently in a recession at D, a decrease in real interest rates could move the economy out of the recession and toward A.

MULTIPLE CHOICE

1. Which of the following will reduce aggregate demand?
    a. an increase in real wealth
    b. lower real incomes in foreign economies with whom an economy trades
    c. increased consumer and business optimism about the future
    d. an increase in the expected rate of inflation

2. An increase in the long-run aggregate supply curve shifts
   a. both LRAS and AD to the right.
   b. both LRAS and SRAS to the right.
   c. both LRAS and AD to the left.
   d. only LRAS to the right.

3. During recessions, interest rates tend to fall because
   a. consumers attempt to borrow money to make up for their falling income.
   b. business borrowing for investment purposes tends to fall during recessions.
   c. lower real resource prices create profit opportunities for banks.
   d. recessions shift the economy's long-run aggregate supply curve to the left.

4. In the short run, equilibrium output in the goods and services market may be either above or below the full-employment level, but in the long run, it
   a. must be less than full-employment output.
   b. must be greater than full-employment output.
   c. must be equal to full-employment output.
   d. depends on aggregate demand, not just long-run aggregate supply.

5. Which of the following is most likely to result from an unanticipated increase in short-run aggregate supply due to favorable weather conditions in agricultural areas?
   a. an increase in the inflation rate
   b. an increase in the unemployment rate
   c. a decrease in the price level
   d. a decrease in the natural rate of unemployment

6. Which of the following is most likely to accompany an unanticipated reduction in aggregate demand?
   a. an increase in the price level
   b. a decrease in unemployment
   c. an increase in real GDP
   d. an increase in the unemployment rate

7. Which of the following is most likely to accompany an unanticipated increase in short-run aggregate supply?
   a. an increase in real GDP
   b. a decrease in real GDP
   c. an increase in the price level
   d. an increase in the unemployment rate

8. In the aggregate demand/aggregate supply model, an economy operating below its long-run potential capacity will experience
   a. falling real wages and resource prices that will increase SRAS, moving the economy back toward full employment.
   b. rising interest rates that will increase SRAS, moving the economy back toward full employment.
   c. inflation that will stimulate additional spending and thereby restore full employment.
   d. a prolonged economic depression unless consumer optimism is increased.

For questions 9 through 12, assume that the economy is in
long-run equilibrium in the aggregate demand/aggregate
supply model and that some sort of event takes place. In
each case, mark the most likely impact of the event on
the aggregate demand/aggregate supply diagram given in
Exhibit 3.

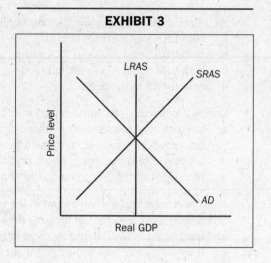

EXHIBIT 3

9. Good weather allows agricultural output to double.
   a. The aggregate demand curve would shift to the
      right.
   b. The aggregate demand curve would shift to the left.
   c. The short-run aggregate supply curve would shift to
      the right.
   d. The short-run aggregate supply curve would shift to
      the left.

10. There is an increase in the expected rate of inflation.
    a. The aggregate demand curve would shift to the right.
    b. The short-run aggregate supply curve would shift to the left.
    c. The price level would rise and real GDP would remain the same.
    d. All of the above are correct.

11. Consumers and businesses all suddenly decide that the future looks much better than it previously had.
    a. The aggregate demand curve would shift to the right.
    b. The aggregate demand curve would shift to the left.
    c. The short-run aggregate supply curve would shift to the right.
    d. The short-run aggregate supply curve would shift to the left.

12. A major technological advance occurs.
    a. The aggregate demand curve would shift to the right.
    b. The aggregate demand curve would shift to the left.
    c. Both the short-run and the long-run aggregate supply curves would shift to the right.
    d. Both the short-run and the long-run aggregate supply curves would shift to the left.

13. Which of the following would not cause a shift in the short-run aggregate supply curve?
    a. a major technological advance
    b. a decrease in the real interest rate
    c. a decrease in the expected rate of inflation
    d. an increase in resource prices

14. If an economy is in equilibrium at a given price level and a given output level, the aggregate demand/
    aggregate supply (AD/AS) model indicates that an unanticipated decrease in aggregate demand will cause
    a. real output to decline.
    b. the price level to fall.
    c. unemployment to increase.
    d. all of the above.

15. Which of the following is most likely to accompany a fully anticipated reduction in short-run aggregate
    supply?
    a. an increase in the price level
    b. a decrease in the price level
    c. a decrease in real GDP
    d. both a and c

16. During the 1990s, a financial crisis spread throughout Asia causing those economies to drop into recessions. Other things constant, how would such a decrease in the income of foreign trading partners have influenced the price level and output of the United States?
    a. Both real output and the price level would have fallen.
    b. Both real output and the price level would have risen.
    c. Real output would have fallen, and the price level would have risen.
    d. Real output would have risen, and the price level would have fallen.

17. Which of the following will most likely occur in the United States as the result of an unexpected rapid growth in real income in Japan and Europe?
    a. a short-run increase in U.S. employment and output
    b. a short-run decrease in U.S. employment and output
    c. a short-run decline in prices in the United States
    d. a reduction in the natural rate of unemployment in the United States

18. If there is an unanticipated increase in aggregate demand, which of the following is most likely to occur?
    a. an increase in the price level (inflation)
    b. an increase in the rate of unemployment
    c. a reduction in the growth rate of real GDP
    d. a decrease in LRAS to restore full-employment

19. Which of the following will most likely increase the economy's long-run aggregate supply?
    a. advances in technology
    b. unfavorable weather conditions in agricultural areas
    c. an increase in the expected inflation rate
    d. a low rate of investment

20. If improvements in education and training programs increased the productivity of persons in the labor force,
    a. aggregate demand would decrease.
    b. short-run aggregate supply would increase, but long-run aggregate supply would not change.
    c. long-run aggregate supply would increase, but short-run aggregate supply would not change.
    d. Both short-run and long-run aggregate supply would increase.

21. If an economy was initially in long-run equilibrium, an unanticipated increase in aggregate demand will tend to cause
    a. an increase in unemployment.
    b. a decrease in the price of resources.
    c. a reduction in real output that will spiral downward into a prolonged recession.
    d. a temporarily high level of output and employment that cannot be maintained.

22. When an economy is in a recession,
    a. strong demand for investment funds will push interest rates upward.
    b. strong demand for resources will push the prices of resources upward.
    c. weak demand for investment funds will cause the real interest rate to decline.
    d. the unemployment rate will be less than its natural rate.

23. Which of the following statements is most consistent with the view that the economy has a self-corrective mechanism?
    a. When the economy is in a recession, it will remain there until the government steps in to bring the economy out of the recession.
    b. When the economy is in a recession, falling resource prices and declining interest rates will direct the economy back to full employment.
    c. During economic booms, interest rates will fall, causing the economy to fall into a recession.
    d. In a market economy, resource prices, such as wages, can only increase; they can never decrease.

24. Which of the following factors contributed to the 2008 economic recession in the United States?
    a. Housing wealth fell causing consumers to become more pessimistic about the economy.
    b. The stock market plummeted causing the real wealth of Americans to decrease.
    c. As the recession spread to other countries, falling incomes abroad depressed aggregate demand in the United States even more.
    d. All of the above were contributing factors.

DISCUSSION QUESTIONS

1. Recent improvements in the quality of South Korean goods have made Americans more willing to "buy Korean."
    a. Use an AD/AS diagram to show the impact of this development on the U.S. economy.
    b. What happens to the price level as the economy moves to its short-run equilibrium and then corrects to its new long-run equilibrium? What happens to inflation?
    c. Can one-time shocks such as this cause persistent inflation? Why or why not?

2. The topic of tax rate changes will not be dealt with specifically until the following chapters, but you will not be surprised to hear that taxes have a profound effect on the economy. Could you analyze the impact of an income tax reduction on the economy with the AD/AS diagram? How?

3. Explain the self-correcting mechanisms present in a market economy. Specifically state how these work to bring an economy out of a recession. Do all economists agree on the speed with which the self-correcting mechanisms work? What implications does this debate have for government policy?

4. The economy is highly complex, and each of the main aggregate markets (the goods and services market, the resources market, and the loanable funds market) affect each other. Keeping that in mind, what should happen to real interest rates during a recession? Does it matter what caused the recession? Does it matter whether the drop in income was expected or unexpected? whether the drop in income is expected to be temporary or permanent? What should happen to money interest rates? Will they always move with real interest rates? Why or why not?

5. Shifts in aggregate demand and short-run aggregate supply are usually given more attention than shifts in long-run aggregate supply. Do you think this emphasis is appropriate? Which is really more important to an economy? If you had a choice between a policy that would increase aggregate demand, one that would increase short-run aggregate supply, or one that would increase long-run aggregate supply, which one would you choose?

6. How would each of the following influence the equilibrium level of output and employment? Explain your answer.
    a. an increase in planned saving
    b. the expectation of a recession in the near future
    c. the expectation of accelerating inflation during the next twelve months
    d. an increase in government spending
    e. a decline in the income tax

Fiscal Policy: The Keynesian View and Historical Perspective

CHAPTER 11

TRUE OR FALSE

T F

☐ ☐ 1. Fiscal policy is the use of government tax and expenditure policy to influence the economy.

☐ ☐ 2. A change in fiscal policy usually changes the full-employment level of output, allowing for a permanently higher level of real output.

☐ ☐ 3. Keynesians believe that wages and prices are inflexible—especially in the downward direction.

☐ ☐ 4. If government borrowing pushes up interest rates, private borrowing for consumption and investment will increase, further expanding the economy.

☐ ☐ 5. Automatic stabilizers are programs that tend to automatically carry out countercyclical fiscal policy—promoting a budget deficit during a recession and a budget surplus during a boom—without the need for discretionary government action.

☐ ☐ 6. A budget surplus means that tax revenues exceed government expenditures.

☐ ☐ 7. Fiscal policy is not subject to timing problems—it has an immediate effect on the economy.

☐ ☐ 8. Running a budget surplus would be considered restrictive fiscal policy, whereas a budget deficit is expansionary fiscal policy.

☐ ☐ 9. Modern theories suggest that fiscal policy is much more effective for stabilizing the economy than early Keynesian theories suggested.

☐ ☐ 10. Keynes believed that full employment would be automatically achieved because of flexible wages and prices.

☐ ☐ 11. In a simple Keynesian model, the expenditure multiplier equals one divided by one minus the marginal propensity to consume.

T   F

☐   ☐   12.   Keynes believed that changes in output, rather than in prices, direct the economy to equilibrium.

☐   ☐   13.   The marginal propensity to consume (MPC) is defined as the total amount of consumption in the economy divided by the change in disposable income.

☐   ☐   14.   An increase in disposable income, other things being equal, will cause consumption to increase.

☐   ☐   15.   According to Keynes, the main determinant of current consumption is current disposable income.

☐   ☐   16.   The Keynesian model shows a positive relationship between income and net exports.

☐   ☐   17.   Because disposable income can only be consumed or saved, the knowledge of an economy's aggregate consumption function will permit one to calculate the economy's aggregate saving function with respect to disposable income.

☐   ☐   18.   In the Keynesian model, output would rise if planned aggregate expenditures were above output. In that situation, firms would find their inventories falling unexpectedly, and they would raise output in response.

PROBLEMS AND PROJECTS

1.   Refer to Exhibit 1 to answer the following questions.
   a.   Is the economy depicted (at point A) in a recession, a boom, or at full employment?
   b.   If no government action was taken, at which point would the economy return to long-run equilibrium with the self-correcting mechanism (changing resource prices affecting SRAS)? Show the curve shifting and note the new equilibrium point in the figure.
   c.   What would a Keynesian suggest be done to government taxes or spending to help the economy out of the recession? Would this be consistent with running a budget deficit, budget surplus, or balanced budget?
   d.   If the policies in part c were adopted, under the Keynesian view, at what point would the economy return to long-run equilibrium? Show the curve shifting and note the new equilibrium point in the figure.
   e.   How do your answers to parts b and d differ? That is, what is different when fiscal policy is used to restore full employment relative to when the economy restores full employment through a self-correction?

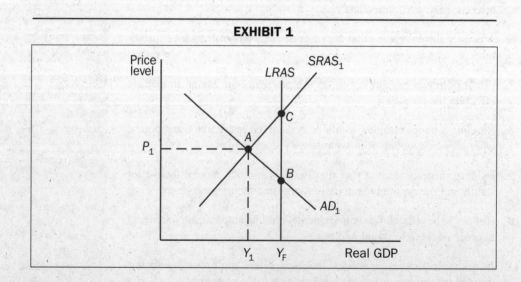

EXHIBIT 1

2. Use the diagram given in Exhibit 2 to answer the following questions.
    a. Is the economy depicted (at point A) in a recession, a boom, or at full employment?
    b. According to the Keynesian view, what should be done with government taxes and/or spending to restore full employment? Is this consistent with running a budget deficit, a budget surplus, or a balanced budget?
    c. Suppose these policies are enacted, but during the time it takes for the impact of these policies to be felt, the economy has already self-corrected. First, show in the diagram where the economy would be if the self-correcting mechanism worked, then shift aggregate demand consistent with the impact of the policies enacted.
    d. What has been the effect of this policy? If these timing problems happen frequently, does it suggest that fiscal policy works to stabilize or destabilize the economy?

EXHIBIT 2

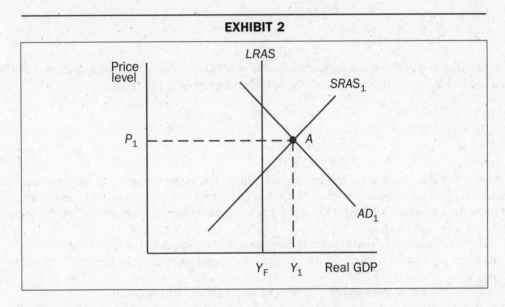

3. Calculate the marginal propensity to consume for the following situations:
    a. Consumption increases by $2,000 when disposable income increases by $3,000.
    b. Consumption increases from $6,000 to $7,000 when disposable income increases from $8,000 to $9,500.
    c. Disposable income increases from $9,000 to $10,000, but consumption remains the same.
    d. Disposable income increases by $4,000 causing savings to increase by $1,000. (Hint: Disposable income must be either spent or saved.)

4. Calculate the expenditure multiplier for all four cases in question 3 above.

MULTIPLE CHOICE

1. The expenditure multiplier is used to calculate the change in
    a. spending caused by a change in income.
    b. equilibrium income resulting from a change in interest rates.
    c. equilibrium income resulting from an independent change in spending.
    d. investment caused by a change in consumption.

2. Which of the following is a major insight of the Keynesian model?
   a. Changes in output, as well as changes in prices, play a role in the macroeconomic adjustment process, particularly in the long run.
   b. A general overproduction of goods relative to total demand is impossible because production creates its own demand.
   c. The responsiveness of aggregate demand to changes in supply will be directly related to the availability of unemployed resources.
   d. Fluctuations in aggregate demand are an important potential source of business instability.

3. If the MPC is 3/4, the simple expenditure multiplier is
   a. 4.00.
   b. 1.33.
   c. 1.75.
   d. 0.75.

4. If consumption equals 800 when disposable income is 1,000, and then consumption increases to 1,000 when disposable income increases to 1,300, the marginal propensity to consume is
   a. 8/10.
   b. 10/13.
   c. 2/3.
   d. 3/4.

5. "If there is unemployment, the average wage rate will decline as the unemployed workers choose lower wages rather than going without a job. The demand curve for labor slopes downward and to the right so that more workers would be hired at the lower wage rate, restoring full employment." According to the Keynesian view, this quote is
   a. incorrect because widespread unemployment would cause wages to rise, not decline.
   b. incorrect because the demand for labor, other things constant, will not be negatively related to wages.
   c. incorrect because wages and prices tend to be highly inflexible downward.
   d. essentially correct.

The following information is relevant to the next two questions:

Assume IBM decides, despite an ongoing recession, to build a new branch for computer analysis in Bozeman, Montana. The plant expects to spend $12 million to hire the necessary employees, all of whom move in from out of state to take the jobs.

6. If the marginal propensity to consume of the newly employed workers was 3/4, what would be the total change in income that would result from the operation of the plant for one year?
   a. $12 million
   b. $48 million
   c. $9 million
   d. $27 million

7. If Bozeman citizens decided to spend more than 3/4 of the additional income,
   a. the MPC would decrease.
   b. the expenditure multiplier would decrease.
   c. the expansion in income would be larger.
   d. aggregate expenditures would decline.

8. If the federal government runs a budget deficit in order to finance an increase in spending, where do the funds to finance the spending come from?
    a. increased personal income taxes
    b. additional money printed by the Federal Reserve
    c. additional bonds issued by the U.S. Treasury
    d. the financial assets of the members of Congress who are legally responsible for the deficit

9. When the federal government is running a budget surplus,
    a. government revenues exceed government expenditures.
    b. government expenditures exceed government revenues.
    c. the economy must be in a recession.
    d. additional government borrowing will decrease the size of the national debt.

10. If a fiscal policy change is going to exert a stabilizing impact on the economy, it must
    a. be expansionary.
    b. be restrictive.
    c. be timed correctly.
    d. keep the federal budget in balance.

11. Automatic stabilizers are government programs that tend to
    a. reduce the ups and downs in aggregate demand without legislative action.
    b. bring expenditures and revenues automatically into balance without legislative action.
    c. signal Congress that legislative changes are needed.
    d. increase tax collections automatically during a recession.

12. When the economy enters a recession, automatic stabilizers create
    a. higher taxes.
    b. more discretionary spending.
    c. larger budget deficits.
    d. larger budget surpluses.

13. In the Keynesian model, the primary determinant of consumer spending is
    a. the interest rate.
    b. disposable income.
    c. expectations of inflation.
    d. the stage of the business cycle.

14. Which of the following is most likely to lead to an increase in current consumption?
    a. an increase in personal income tax rates
    b. an increase in one's expected future income
    c. a decrease in one's marginal propensity to consume
    d. an increase in the interest rate

15. If the economy is operating at a point where the aggregate expenditure line lies below the 45-degree line (AE = GDP),
    a. total spending is more than total output.
    b. unwanted business inventories will increase.
    c. businesses will reduce their future production.
    d. both b and c are correct.

16. Keynesian analysis suggests that if planned spending (aggregate demand) were $700 billion but GDP was $800 billion,
    a. businesses would accumulate inventories, and output would fall.
    b. output would rise, incomes would rise, and tax revenues would automatically increase.
    c. production would be stimulated, and output would increase, unless the full-capacity output was less than $950 billion.
    d. the Federal Reserve would eventually lower interest rates.

17. In the Keynesian aggregate expenditure model, the equilibrium level of income is achieved when
    a. the employment rate equals approximately 96 percent.
    b. actual saving equals actual investment.
    c. planned aggregate expenditures exceed actual output.
    d. actual output equals planned aggregate expenditures.

18. Keynesian countercyclical budget policy suggests that
    a. a budget deficit is needed if the economy is operating at less than full employment.
    b. a budget deficit should be planned during an inflationary boom.
    c. the budget must be balanced if the national debt is growing more rapidly than the economy.
    d. the budget should always be in balance

19. According to Keynesian theory, which of the following would most likely stimulate an expansion in real output if the economy were in a recession?
    a. an increase in tax rates
    b. a balanced budget
    c. a budget deficit
    d. a budget surplus

20. The Keynesian macroeconomic model was highly popular for several decades following World War II because it provided an explanation for
    a. the strong economic recovery following the end of the war.
    b. the high inflation rates of the 1950s.
    c. the prolonged unemployment of the 1930s.
    d. the high rate of investment during the Great Depression.

21. John Maynard Keynes and his followers argued that the Great Depression was primarily the result of
    a. excessive government spending.
    b. large budget deficits.
    c. the perverse monetary policies of the Fed.
    d. insufficient aggregate spending on goods and services.

22. If output is less than full employment in the Keynesian model, what is needed to restore full employment?
    a. an increase in the price level
    b. an increase in aggregate demand
    c. a reduction in government expenditures
    d. an increase in aggregate supply

23. According to the Keynesian view, if policy makers thought the economy was about to fall into a recession, which of the following would be most appropriate?
    a. a reduction in government expenditures
    b. an increase in government expenditures or reduction in taxes, financed by borrowing
    c. a balanced federal budget
    d. an increase in taxes

24. In the Keynesian model, equilibrium occurs when
    a. the real and nominal interest rates are equal.
    b. total spending is equal to current output.
    c. the general price level is constant.
    d. the money supply is growing at a constant rate.

DISCUSSION QUESTIONS

1. "A reduction in tax rates will lead to a decline in tax revenues and an increase in the size of the budget deficit. The deficit spending will be inflationary. Thus, there is little reason to believe that a tax cut will be able to alter the real output rate of an economy." Evaluate each of these three sentences.

2. A leading politician once said, "The government budget should always be balanced, so a tax cut does not make sense without a cut in spending." Would you favor a balanced budget amendment? Why or why not?

3. What do you find most convincing about the economic theory of John Maynard Keynes? least convincing? On the whole, do you think the influence of Keynes has been good or bad?

4. What are the reasons that wages might be inflexible downward? Do you think that such inflexibility is an empirically important feature of our economy? What sort of empirical evidence could you look for in order to answer this question?

Fiscal Policy, Incentives, and Secondary Effects

TRUE OR FALSE

T F

☐ ☐ 1. The crowding-out effect refers to the hypothesis that high marginal tax rates crowd personal consumption out of the marketplace and therefore reduce the effectiveness of fiscal policy.

☐ ☐ 2. According to the new classical view, fiscal policy is generally impotent—it has little or no effect on the economy or aggregate demand.

☐ ☐ 3. Despite the very different fiscal policies followed, the economic records of both the expansions of the 1990s and 2000s and the recessions of 1990–1991 and 2001 suggest that fiscal policy has not had much of an influence on the U.S. economy in recent decades.

☐ ☐ 4. The supply-side view is that higher marginal tax rates tend to decrease work effort reducing aggregate supply.

☐ ☐ 5. Ricardian equivalence (the new classical view) holds that an increase in government spending financed by borrowing (debt) has an identical effect on the economy as if the spending were financed by an increase in current taxes instead.

☐ ☐ 6. Keynesians and non-Keynesians are in agreement that proper timing of discretionary fiscal policy is easy to achieve, but rather unimportant.

☐ ☐ 7. Keynesians and non-Keynesians now agree that automatic stabilizers reduce fluctuations in aggregate demand and help direct the economy toward full employment.

☐ ☐ 8. Over the years, Keynesians and non-Keynesians have come to agree that fiscal policy is much more potent than the early Keynesian view implied.

☐ ☐ 9. Many non-Keynsians believe that increased government spending will be less likely to bring the economy out of a recession because it will be motivated by political considerations rather than by profits and losses.

☐ ☐ 10. The increase in government debt caused by expansionary policy in times of a severe recession will lead to higher future interest payments and tax rates, which are beneficial for long-term growth.

☐ ☐ 11. A tax cut is likely to be more effective at pulling an economy out of a recession than an increase in government spending because a reduction in tax rates will increase the incentive to earn, invest, produce, and employ others.

☐ ☐ 12. The paradox of thrift states that an increase in savings and reduction in consumption may reduce the overall demand for goods and services, causing businesses to reduce output and layoff workers, which could lead to less total savings.

PROBLEMS AND PROJECTS

1. Label each of the following statements as most likely to be made by a Keynesian (K), a believer in the crowding-out view (CO), a new classical economist (NC), or supply-sider (SS).
   ___ a. "Expansions in government spending financed by borrowing (debt) are a highly effective way to increase aggregate demand in the economy."
   ___ b. "Large budget deficits cause high real interest rates that reduce private spending and investment."
   ___ c. "There is no link between budget deficits and interest rates; higher deficits are simply matched by higher savings."
   ___ d. "The expansionary effect of increased government spending will be completely offset by reductions in private consumption; thus, fiscal policy has no effect on aggregate demand."
   ___ e. "The expansionary effect of increased government spending financed with debt will be at least partially offset by the negative effects of higher interest rates caused by government borrowing."
   ___ f. "Lower marginal tax rates stimulate people to work, save, and invest, resulting in more output and a larger tax base."
   ___ g. "The primary use of fiscal policy should not be to counter short-run business cycle fluctuations but rather to promote long-run growth in the economy."
   ___ h. "Whenever the economy is in a recession, expansionary fiscal policy should be employed to restore full employment."

2. Decide whether an increase in government spending financed by a budget deficit (borrowing) would increase (+), decrease (−), or have no effect (0) on each of the following economic variables under the view given in the question.
   ___ a. the real interest rate under the crowding-out view
   ___ b. the real interest rate under the new classical view
   ___ c. private borrowing for investment under the crowding-out view
   ___ d. personal saving under the new classical view
   ___ e. foreign capital investment in the United States under the crowding-out view
   ___ f. U.S. net exports under the crowding-out view
   ___ g. aggregate demand under the Keynesian view
   ___ h. aggregate demand under the crowding-out view
   ___ i. aggregate demand under the new classical view

MULTIPLE CHOICE

1. Expansionary fiscal policy financed by government borrowing can lead to
    a.   higher interest rates and lower private investment under the crowding-out view.
    b.   an increase in aggregate demand under the Keynesian view.
    c.   no change in aggregate demand under the new classical view.
    d.   all of the above.

2. The crowding-out effect implies that budget deficits will
    a.   increase real interest rates and lower the future stock of private capital.
    b.   decrease real interest rates and increase the future stock of private capital.
    c.   increase the productivity of workers in the future.
    d.   lead to higher levels of income for workers in the future.

3. The crowding-out effect suggests that
    a.   expansionary fiscal policy causes inflation.
    b.   high marginal tax rates crowd out tax deductions.
    c.   the demand stimulus effects of a budget deficit will be weak because the borrowing to finance the deficit will lead to higher interest rates.
    d.   a budget surplus will cause the economy to slip into a major recession.

4. The new classical model implies that the effect of government increasing expenditures by debt financing
    a.   has the same effect as if it was financed by raising current taxes.
    b.   is highly expansionary on aggregate demand and the economy.
    c.   will result in higher real interest rates.
    d.   will result in lower personal savings.

5. The new classical model implies that a shift to a more expansionary fiscal policy will
    a.   stimulate aggregate demand and employment.
    b.   retard aggregate demand and employment.
    c.   increase the real rate of interest.
    d.   exert little or no impact on the real interest rate, aggregate demand, and employment.

6. According to the new classical view, a $20 billion increase in government expenditures financed by a budget deficit will
    a.   stimulate output by $20 billion.
    b.   stimulate output more than $20 billion.
    c.   stimulate output but by less than $20 billion.
    d.   leave output unchanged.

7. Other things constant, an increase in marginal tax rates will
    a.   decrease the supply of labor and reduce its productive efficiency.
    b.   decrease the supply of capital and decrease its productive efficiency.
    c.   encourage individuals to buy goods that are tax deductible instead of those that are more desired but nondeductible.
    d.   do all of the above.

8. Which of the following statements is true?
    a.   The empirical evidence indicates that countries with higher marginal tax rates have higher economic growth rates.
    b.   Unlike other policies, supply-side tax cuts have their full impact on an economy instantaneously.
    c.   The supply-side effects of changes in marginal tax rates take place over lengthy time periods.
    d.   In the 1960s and 1980s, when the marginal tax rates were reduced, the share of income taxes paid by high-income taxpayers fell.

9. The modern consensus view of fiscal policy stresses
    a. that the federal government should always balance its budget.
    b. that offsetting factors make fiscal policy much less potent than the Keynesian view suggested.
    c. that proper timing of fiscal policy is very difficult to achieve, rendering fiscal policy less useful as a stabilization tool.
    d. that both b and c are true.

10. Which of the following is the best explanation of how expansionary fiscal policy can crowd out net exports?
    a. Expansionary fiscal policy leads to high budget deficits. Foreigners become concerned about the stability of the United States and stop buying American goods as a result.
    b. When the government spends more, some of its spending is on foreign goods. As imports rise, net exports fall.
    c. The higher interest rates associated with expansionary fiscal policy attract foreign investors. To buy U.S. financial assets, foreigners bid up the real exchange rate, which in turn causes net exports to fall.
    d. The cut in taxes associated with expansionary fiscal policy stimulates aggregate supply. As aggregate supply rises, consumers have a greater incentive to purchase domestic goods, causing imports to fall and net exports to drop.

11. Which of the following groups would be least likely to support a balanced budget amendment to the U.S. Constitution?
    a. Keynesians
    b. new classicals
    c. supply-siders
    d. believers in the crowding-out view

12. "Expansionary fiscal policy will tend to substantially increase current real output." Which of the following models would tend to support such a statement?
    a. the Keynesian model and the new classical model, but not the crowding-out model
    b. the Keynesian model and the crowding-out model, but not the new classical model
    c. the Keynesian model, but not the crowding-out and new classical models
    d. all three models

13. According to the Keynesian view, expansionary fiscal policy will have its greatest impact
    a. when planned aggregate expenditures equal total output.
    b. during a strong economic expansion.
    c. when widespread unemployment is present.
    d. during a period of severe inflation.

14. Keynesian critics would argue that expansion in government debt during a recession would lead to
    a. consumer optimism and a substantial increase in private consumption and investment.
    b. higher future interest payments and tax rates.
    c. lower future interest payments and tax rates.
    d. a strong recovery and substantial future economic growth.

15. Why might increases in government spending be ineffective during a recession?
    a. The level of aggregate demand will not affect output and employment during a recession.
    b. Increases in government spending cannot stimulate aggregate demand.
    c. According to the Keynesian view, fiscal policy will be largely ineffective during a recession.
    d. Recessions often reflect a coordination problem related to the composition of aggregate demand, not just its level.

16. Which of the following is a potential drawback of an expansion of government spending projects during a recession?
    a. Spending projects are easily reversed once the economy has recovered.
    b. Government spending projects are not included in the calculation of GDP.
    c. Those benefiting from spending projects will lobby for a continuation of these projects long after the economy has recovered.
    d. Government spending projects will not encourage rent-seeking activity.

17. According to the paradox of thrift, if many families decided to save an additional $200 a month, this would lead to
    a. an increase in both saving and output.
    b. an increase in loanable funds and a reduction in interest rates, leading to an expansion in investment.
    c. a reduction in total output with little or no increase in total saving.
    d. an increase in total saving and no change in total output.

18. How will a high level of saving impact long-run economic growth?
    a. Saving will drive interest rates higher, and thereby increase the returns to investment and stimulate growth.
    b. Saving provides the source of investment capital that allows businesses to expand production and the economy to grow.
    c. Saving will reduce consumption, and thereby retard economic growth.
    d. Saving will reduce the funds available for investment and thereby retard entrepreneurship and economic growth.

19. A person's marginal tax rate determines the percentage of
    a. taxes that are allocated to the repayment of government debt.
    b. additional earnings that the individual is permitted to keep.
    c. the individual's total income that must be paid in taxes.
    d. additional taxable income allocated to saving rather than investment.

20. Other things constant, a reduction in marginal tax rates will tend to increase aggregate supply because the lower taxes will increase
    a. disposable income, which will induce an increase in consumption and aggregate supply.
    b. business optimism, which will increase both investment and aggregate supply.
    c. savings, which will lead to lower interest rates, an increase in consumption, and an increase in aggregate supply.
    d. the attractiveness of productive activity relative to leisure and tax avoidance.

21. Increases in government expenditures and large budget deficits are projected for 2010–2019. The crowding-out and new classical views indicate this fiscal policy will lead to
    a. lower interest rates and tax rates that will enhance economic growth.
    b. higher interest rates and tax rates that will slow economic growth.
    c. increases in aggregate demand that will lead to strong economic growth.
    d. high rates of future inflation.

DISCUSSION QUESTIONS

1. Explain the New Classical position on the effect of tax cuts in your own words. What are the main criticisms of the New Classical position? Think of some empirical work that you could do that would help you decide whether to accept or reject the New Classical position. Some economists in this debate have done research on the extent to which people leave bequests to their children and their reasons for leaving these bequests. How could such research have any bearing on the debate on the New Classical position?

2. The large reductions in marginal tax rates enacted during the Reagan administration were followed by a long boom. How would a Keynesian explain this result? a supply-sider? Use the AS/AD diagram to illustrate their explanations. Is there any way we could tell whose explanation is correct?

3. "Government spending financed by budget deficits pushes up real interest rates. The higher real interest rates cause private borrowing for consumption and investment to fall. In addition, the inflow of foreign capital will cause an appreciation of the U.S. dollar, reducing net exports. Thus, in the aggregate demand equation $(AD = C + I + G + NX)$, whenever G is increased the other three variables fall." Evaluate and discuss each of these sentences using diagrams where possible to explain your answer. What views are consistent with this statement, and which are not?

4. As the economy plunged into the recent recession, the Bush administration responded with a huge increase in federal spending (financed through deficits), including a $168 billion stimulus package and another $700 billion to bailout troubled financial institutions. When Obama took over in 2009, he added another stimulus package of $787 billion. What might a Keynesian say about the correctness of this course of action? How about a non-Keynesian?

Money and the Banking System

CHAPTER 13

TRUE OR FALSE

T F

☐ ☐ 1. M1 is the broadest definition of the money supply because it includes all currency and checkable deposits.

☐ ☐ 2. Liquidity refers to how easily an asset can be converted into purchasing power, thus money is the most liquid of all assets.

☐ ☐ 3. Money serves three basic functions: It is a medium of exchange, a store of value, and a unit of account.

☐ ☐ 4. Fiat money is money that is backed by gold or some other valuable commodity.

☐ ☐ 5. All money that is deposited in a bank must be kept by the bank in its vault in case the customer wants to withdraw the money.

☐ ☐ 6. If the reserve requirement was 5 percent, and you deposited $100 in your bank account, the bank would have to keep $95 in required reserves.

☐ ☐ 7. A reserve requirement of 25 percent implies a potential deposit expansion multiplier of 4.

☐ ☐ 8. If the reserve requirement was 25 percent, and the Federal Reserve System (Fed) wanted to expand the money supply by $800 using open market operations, it would buy $200 worth of bonds.

☐ ☐ 9. Because money is defined in specific units ($5 and $20 bills for example), the value of money never changes.

☐ ☐ 10. The purchasing power of money falls when the price level rises.

☐ ☐ 11. Raising the reserve requirement is one way in which the Fed can reduce the money supply.

T   F

☐ ☐ 12. If the Federal Reserve extended fewer loans to banks, it would increase bank reserves, encourage banks to make more loans, and consequently, increase the money supply.

☐ ☐ 13. When the Fed sells bonds on the open market, it results in an increase in the money supply.

☐ ☐ 14. When the U.S. Treasury issues and sells new bonds to the general public, it results in a decrease in the money supply.

PROBLEMS AND PROJECTS

1. For each of the following, write M1 to indicate that the item is included in the M1 money supply and M2 to indicate that it is included only when the definition is expanded to M2. Write neither to indicate that the item is not a part of either the M1 or M2 money supply.
    _____ a.   a $100 bill
    _____ b.   a $10,000 six-month certificate of deposit with your bank
    _____ c.   a $10,000 retirement account invested in stocks
    _____ d.   a $50 traveler's check
    _____ e.   a $5,000 credit line on an American Express credit card
    _____ f.   a quarter
    _____ g.   a $1 off coupon clipped from the Sunday newspaper
    _____ h.   a $100 balance in a noninterest-earning checking account
    _____ i.   a $200 balance in an interest-earning savings account
    _____ j.   a $10,000 U.S. Treasury bill

2. Suppose the Fed wished to increase the money supply by $50 billion to head off a coming recession. Also assume that the reserve requirement is 20 percent and banks hold no excess reserves.
    a.   What is the deposit expansion multiplier?
    b.   If the Fed wanted to use open market operations, should it buy or sell bonds?
    c.   How many dollars' worth of bonds should it buy or sell?
    d.   Rework parts a, b, and c using a value for the reserve requirement of 10 percent. Does the multiplier rise or fall? To accomplish the same increase, will the Fed now have to buy/sell more or less bonds?

3. For each of the following, indicate whether the result will create an increase (+), decrease (–), or have no change (0) in the money supply and the national debt.

	MONEY SUPPLY	NATIONAL DEBT
a. The Fed sells $100 million of government securities (bonds) to the general public.	_____	_____
b. Government spending exceeds tax revenue, so the U.S. Treasury responds by issuing $100 million of new bonds and sells them to the general public.	_____	_____
c. Government spending exceeds tax revenue, so the U.S. Treasury responds by issuing $100 million of new bonds and sells them to the Fed.	_____	_____
d. Jim sells his five-year $100 U.S. savings bond to his friend Sarah for $80.	_____	_____
e. Worried about terrorist attacks, bank customers withdraw their money from their accounts and store the cash in their houses.	_____	_____
f. The Fed buys $20 million of government securities from the general public.	_____	_____
g. The federal government runs a $100 billion surplus and uses the money to pay off the national debt by buying (retiring) bonds.	_____	_____

4. Assume the required reserve ratio for the U.S. banking system is 20 percent and that banks keep no excess reserves. Suppose the Fed buys a $10,000 U.S. government security from the public.
    a. Will the action by the Fed increase or decrease the money supply?
    b. Complete the following table to track the change in the money supply resulting from the Fed's action through the first four rounds of the multiplier process. (Hint: Find the totals using the multiplier, not by adding up the numbers.)

	BANK (DEMAND) DEPOSITS	REQUIRED RESERVES	EXCESS RESERVES (NEW LOANS)
Round 1	_____	_____	_____
Round 2	_____	_____	_____
Round 3	_____	_____	_____
Round 4	_____	_____	_____
Remaining rounds	. . .	. . .	. . .
Total	_____	_____	_____

MULTIPLE CHOICE

1. If the Fed used "open market operations" to decrease the money supply, it
   a. increased the federal funds rate.
   b. issued more federal government debt.
   c. sold U.S. government securities (bonds) to the general public.
   d. increased the required reserve ratio.

2. Suppose the Fed buys $10 million of U.S. securities from the public. Assume a reserve requirement of 5 percent and that all banks hold no excess reserves. The total impact of this action on the money supply will be
   a. an increase of $200 million.
   b. a decrease of $200 million.
   c. a decrease of $10 million.
   d. an increase of $10 million.

3. In the United States, the control of the money supply is the responsibility of the
   a. Federal Reserve System (the Fed).
   b. the president.
   c. the U.S. Treasury.
   d. the U.S. Congress.

4. Measuring the money supply has become more difficult in recent years due to
   a. the reduced use of pennies in transactions.
   b. the U.S. Congress continuing the process of decreasing the independence of the Fed.
   c. the volume of transactions conducted with credit cards has escalated.
   d. debit cards and electronic money coming into widespread use.

5. Suppose a bank receives a new deposit of $500. The bank extends a new loan of $400 because it is required to hold the other $100 on reserve. What is the legal required reserve ratio?
   a. 10 percent
   b. 15 percent
   c. 20 percent
   d. 25 percent

6. Fiat money is defined as
   a. the money of U.S. citizens deposited at banks and other financial institutions outside the United States.
   b. money spent on Italian sports cars.
   c. money that has little intrinsic value; it is neither backed by nor convertible to a commodity of value.
   d. vault cash plus deposits at the Fed.

7. The most frequently used tool of the Fed to control the money supply in recent years has been
   a. changes in the premiums charged for FDIC deposit insurance.
   b. open market operations.
   c. changes in the discount rate.
   d. changes in reserve requirements.

8. The federal funds rate is the interest rate
   a. banks pay when they borrow money from each other.
   b. the federal government pays on the national debt.
   c. the Fed charges banks when banks need to borrow from the Fed.
   d. the federal government charges foreign banks.

9. The three basic functions of money are
    a. fiat, *seigniorage*, and debt.
    b. a medium of exchange, a store of value, and a unit of account.
    c. a standard of pay, a coincidence of wants, and a measure of the value of time.
    d. demand deposits, other checkable deposits, and time deposits.

10. If the Federal Reserve wanted to expand the supply of money to head off a recession, it could
    a. decrease the reserve requirements.
    b. lower taxes.
    c. sell U.S. securities in the open market.
    d. increase the discount rate.

11. The larger the reserve requirement, the
    a. larger the potential deposit multiplier.
    b. smaller the potential deposit multiplier.
    c. more profitable the banks will be.
    d. larger the proportion of an additional deposit that is available to the bank for the extension of additional loans.

12. The total expansion in the money supply can be less than is predicted by the deposit expansion multiplier if
    a. banks choose to hold some excess reserves rather than lending all excess reserves.
    b. some individuals prefer to hold cash instead of depositing their money in banks.
    c. instead of a monopoly banking system, there are many banks.
    d. both a and b are correct.

13. When economists say that money serves as a unit of account, they mean that money
    a. allows people to avoid barter (trading goods for other goods) by using money.
    b. is always issued in fixed denominations (for example $1, $5, $10, $20 bills).
    c. allows people to value all goods and services in terms of one commodity (money), rather than in terms of several commodities.
    d. makes it easier for people to maintain value across time by letting them save it in the form of money, rather than in the form of physical goods that might depreciate over time.

14. The value (purchasing power) of each unit of money
    a. does not depend on the amount of money in circulation.
    b. tends to increase as the money supply expands.
    c. increases as prices rise.
    d. is inversely related to prices (in other words, money's value falls as prices rise and vice versa).

15. Which of the following is not a component of the M1 money supply?
    a. demand deposits
    b. large-denomination (more than $100) bills
    c. interest-earning checking deposits
    d. outstanding balances on credit cards

16. Which of the following compose the M2 money supply?
    a. currency only
    b. currency, demand deposits, other checkable deposits, and traveler's checks
    c. M1 plus large denomination time deposits
    d. M1 plus savings deposits, small-denomination time deposits, and money market mutual funds (retail)

17. The difference between the total reserves that a bank holds and the amount that is required by law are called
    a. excess reserves.
    b. nonborrowed reserves.
    c. borrowed reserves.
    d. actual reserves.

18. A reserve requirement of 20 percent implies a potential money deposit multiplier of
    a. 1.
    b. 5.
    c. 20.
    d. 80.

19. Suppose the Fed sells $100 million of U.S. government securities (bonds) to the public. How will this affect the money supply and the national debt?
    a. The money supply will increase; the national debt will decrease.
    b. The money supply will decrease; the national debt will increase.
    c. The money supply will increase; the national debt will be unaffected.
    d. The money supply will decrease; the national debt will be unaffected.

20. Suppose the U.S. Treasury issues and sells $100 million of U.S. government securities (bonds) to the public. How will this affect the money supply and the national debt?
    a. The money supply will increase; the national debt will decrease.
    b. The money supply will decrease; the national debt will increase.
    c. The money supply will be unaffected; the national debt will increase.
    d. The money supply will be unaffected; the national debt will decrease.

21. Which of the following is not part of the M1 money supply?
    a. paper bills (currency)
    b. travelers' checks
    c. savings deposits
    d. coins

22. As the Fed increased its asset holdings and the volume of loans to financial institutions during the latter half of 2008, the result was
    a. a vast increase in the monetary base and in the excess reserves of the commercial banking system.
    b. a substantial increase in short-term interest rates.
    c. a sharp decrease in the monetary base, as well as a depletion of the excess reserves of the commercial banking system.
    d. an increase in the volume of loans extended by commercial banks and a sharp increase in the inflation rate.

23. Which of the following correctly indicates how the Fed could use the interest rate it pays commercial banks on their excess reserves to influence the money supply?
    a. If the Fed wanted to increase the money supply, it could increase the interest rate it pays banks on their excess reserves.
    b. When the Fed reduces the interest rate paid on excess reserves, it increases the incentive of commercial banks to hold excess reserves.
    c. If the Fed wanted to decrease the money supply, it could increase the interest rate paid on excess reserves.
    d. When the Fed increases the interest rate it pays on excess reserves, this encourages banks to extend more loans and thereby increase the money supply.

24. Rather than using the purchase and sale of only government bonds in the conduct of open market operations, in 2008 the Fed also began buying and selling
    a. stock options so it would be able to gain from the expected rebound in the stock market.
    b. real estate in the Washington D.C. area.
    c. corporate bonds, commercial paper, and mortgage-backed securities from commercial banks and other financial institutions.
    d. future contracts for goods like grains, metals, and crude oil, which could be expected to increase in price substantially if the inflation rate rose rapidly in the future.

DISCUSSION QUESTIONS

1. Would you be better off if the amount of
   a. food and clothing you have suddenly doubles?
   b. food and clothing everyone has suddenly doubles?
   c. money you have suddenly doubles?
   d. money everyone has suddenly doubles?
   Explain the difference in your answers to parts b and d.

2. "Because our currency can no longer be exchanged for gold, it is only a matter of time until people realize that a dollar bill is worthless. Exchanging pieces of paper that are not backed by valuable minerals cannot go on forever." Do you agree or disagree? Explain.

3. Consider the following paradoxes:
   a. Paradox 1: When the Treasury sells government securities to the public, the money supply does not change, but when the Fed sells government securities to the public, the money supply falls.
   b. Paradox 2: When the Treasury buys government securities from the public, the national debt falls, but when the Fed buys government securities from the public, the national debt does not change.
   Because both the Federal Reserve Board and the Treasury Department are part of the government, how can you explain these paradoxes?

4. Consider the following questions about fractional reserve banking.
   a. Why do banks need to hold only a fraction of the demand deposits of their customers on reserve?
   b. If the Fed stopped setting required reserve ratios, would bank reserves drop to zero? Why or why not?
   c. Why don't banks keep all of their customer deposits on reserve?
   d. If fractional reserve banking were outlawed and banks had to keep all customer deposits on reserve, would depositors pay more or less for the banking services they receive? Explain.

5. How free do you think the Federal Reserve is from political pressure? What are the advantages of having an independent central bank? What are the disadvantages? Why do countries with less independent central banks tend to have more inflation? Why would government officials "want" more inflation than the authorities of the central bank "want"?

6. So far we have presented two "multipliers," the deposit expansion multiplier in this chapter and the expenditure multiplier in Chapter 10. What is the difference between the two? Explain.

PERSPECTIVES IN ECONOMICS

How the Federal Reserve Decides How Much Money to Put into the Economy

by Edwin L. Dale Jr., Special to *The New York Times*
[From *The New York Times,* May 6, 1976. Copyright © by
The New York Times Co. Reprinted by permission.]

WASHINGTON, May 4—Only one thing is entirely agreed, accepted and understood about the somewhat mysterious and often controversial subject of the Government's monetary policy, which is conducted by the semi-independent Federal Reserve Board.

This is that the Fed, as it is commonly known, can create money out of thin air by writing a check on itself without any deposits to back that check. It can do so in unlimited amounts. And only it can do so—the Treasury cannot.

Yesterday, Arthur F. Burns, chairman of the Federal Reserve Board, disclosed to Congress the Fed's intentions and targets for the creation of money in the year ahead. But he gave his targets in the form of range, not a precise number, and he is the first to admit that he and his colleagues are not at all certain what exactly is the "right" amount of money to create for the good of the nation's economy.

The Government's "printing press" is literally in the Bureau of Engraving and Printing, which turns out currency notes in amounts that depend on the public's demand for them. But the true printing press is a little known man named Alan R. Holmes who sits in an office every day, under instructions and guidelines, from a powerful body of the Federal Reserve known as the Open Market Committee, on how much money to create.

Orders Securities. Mr. Holmes creates money by placing an order in the money market for Treasury bills or other Government securities. He pays for them by writing a check on the Federal Reserve Bank of New York. If the order is for $100 million, an additional $100 million in cash suddenly flows into the economy, possessed originally by the people who sold the Government securities to the Fed.

Mr. Holmes can "extinguish" money, too. If he places a sell order in the market, the Fed sells securities to a money market dealer or bank and gets a check in payment. The amount of money in that check essentially vanishes. The buyer of the securities from the Fed has less cash, but the Fed, in effect, tears up the check.

How much money Mr. Holmes creates makes a good deal of difference to the performance of the economy—the rate of inflation, the expansion of production and jobs, interest rates and indeed general well-being—because the amount of money affects how rapidly the wheels of the economy turn.

But what Mr. Holmes does is cause of controversy because the creation of additional money is also linked by economists to inflation. Friedrich Hayek, the Pulitzer Prize-winning Austrian economist, asserts unequivocally that "inflation is an all monetary phenomenon." Mr. Hayek has innumerable followers. While other economists think his view is a little oversimplified, nearly all of them agree that "money matters."

What is more, the check that Mr. Holmes writes is only the beginning of the process of creating money. That initial $100 million starts a process by which the nation's money supply—currency plus deposits in banks—will grow not by $100 million but by some multiple of that amount.

It is at this point that things begin to get a little more complicated. In brief, the "multiplier" effect arises from the way the nation's—any advanced nation's—banking system works. It is called a "fractional reserve" system and it works this way:

Suppose that Salomon Brothers receives Mr. Holmes's check on the Federal Reserve Bank of New York and deposits it in Citibank, where deposits are now higher than $100 million.

Under the Fed's "reserve requirement" regulations, which are crucial to the multiplier process, Citibank must deposit about $15 million of this in its "reserve" account at the Fed. But then it can, and does, lend the remaining $85 million to, say, the United States Steel Corporation, which needs money to pay wages while it waits for its inventories of steel to be bought.

U.S. Steel gets the money from Citibank and deposits it at the Pittsburgh National Bank, and the multiplying process goes on. Pittsburgh National puts about $13 million in its reserve account at the Fed and uses the remaining $72 million to buy notes of the city of Boston, which deposits this income in the First National Bank of Boston.

At this point Mr. Holmes's original $100 million has already become $257 million, as follows:

- Salomon Brothers has $100 million more cash (but correspondingly less in Treasury bills).
- U.S. Steel has $85 million more cash (but a debt to Citibank).
- Boston has $72 million more cash (but a debt to Pittsburgh National).

The process continues until, with a 15 percent reserve requirement, Mr. Holmes's original check for $100 million eventually adds more than $600 million to the total of bank deposits in the nation, the nation's money supply. And that money, obviously, can be and is spent. Sometimes more spending is desirable to bring forth production and add to jobs, but by no means always.

The more money there is in circulation, the easier it is for sellers to raise prices, whether to cover higher wages and other costs or to increase profits, because customers around the nation have more to spend. When prices go up all over, this is inflation. But it is impossible to know precisely just how much money is enough or how much is too much at any given time. But there is obviously a point of "too much," as all of history teaches.

For policy makers, there are the two following questions:

- What targets for Mr. Holmes should the Open Market Committee, which consists of seven members of the Federal Reserve Board and the presidents of five of the twelve regional Federal Reserve banks, establish? The relationship of the money supply to the economy at large, including inflation, is by no means clear, even to the experts.

- Because Mr. Holmes's buying and selling affects short-term interest rates as well as the money supply, which should he concentrate on?

At the bottom, the nation's central bank is controversial, and frequently unpopular, because it is a "naysayer." Whenever inflation rears its head, the job of the Fed is to slow the creation of money and, for a while at least, that often means higher interest rates and sometimes a cutback in production and a loss of jobs.

Switching of Funds. The right policy will always be a matter of judgement. But at the moment the problem of setting the target for Mr. Holmes is complicated by what Mr. Burns calls the "new financial technology," such as those little electronic "tellers" that many banks now make available to their depositors. Among other services, they permit immediate switching of funds from savings to checking accounts by the push of a button and even payment of some bills, such as utilities bills, directly out of savings.

The "money supply" as long defined means currency plus checking accounts (known in the jargon as M1). There were fairly well-established relationships between the growth of M1 and the overall courage of the economy, including the rate of inflation, but now that people, and business, too, have learned to use savings accounts as almost the equivalent of checking accounts, those relationships have gone awry.

"Our equations are all fouled up," a high Federal Reserve official concedes.

The report of the Open Market Committee on its meeting of last January disclosed that the panel, puzzled by a slow growth in money but a rapid growth in the economy, threw up its hands and simply gave Mr. Holmes an unusually wide "target range" for money growth in the period immediately ahead. This meant that he was not to take any special action to create or extinguish money as long as M1 growth stayed within a very wide band.

The Fed also keeps track of and sets targets for M2, which includes savings accounts. But Mr. Holmes cannot tell when he writes one of his checks how much of the ultimate deposits will be in checking or savings accounts. Thus his art will always be imprecise and his results subject to criticism. At present, the Fed does not know whether M1 or M2 is the more important measure, though in the end it controls the growth of both.

The interest rate problem is a different one.

When Mr. Holmes intervenes in the market to buy or sell Government securities, he not only changes the amount of money in the economy but, unavoidably, also affects what are called "money market interest rates"—the rates on very short-term instruments such as Treasury bills.

Rate on Bank Loans. The impact of his intervention decisions shows up first in the most sensitive and closely watched of all rates, called the "Federal funds" rate, which is the interest rate charged on loans from one bank to another. In daily operations some banks wind up short of their required reserve deposits with the Federal Reserve and some have an excess, and this gives rise to overnight loans from one bank to another.

Eventually, a rising prime rate brings along with it higher interest rates to ordinary consumers and other borrowers.

Sometimes, as occurred last week, Mr. Holmes is instructed to intervene in such a way as to "nudge up" the Federal funds rate himself, as a signal that the Federal Reserve feels the money supply is growing too rapidly. In either case, whether he "lets" the rate go up or pushes it up himself, the result is higher interest rates. And these days that often means a quick drop in the stock market, as happened in the last few days.

Every time Mr. Holmes writes a check, he adds to bank reserves and makes the Federal funds interest rates "easier" —that is, lower or less likely to rise.

DISCUSSION

1. Explain how the Federal Reserve System is actually creating money when Alan Holmes places an order in the money market for Treasury bills or other government securities. How will this money supply change affect employment and output?

2. The article refers to "the multiplier." Is this the deposit expansion multiplier that we talked about in this chapter or the multiplier we covered in Chapter 10?

3. Who actually decides to expand the money supply—the Treasury, Alan Holmes, the Open Market Committee, or the Board of Governors of the Federal Reserve Board?

Modern Macroeconomics and Monetary Policy

CHAPTER 14

TRUE OR FALSE

T F

☐ ☐ 1. The money (nominal) interest rate is the opportunity cost of holding money balances.

☐ ☐ 2. If the demand for money does not shift, an increase in the money supply would lower the interest rate in the short run.

☐ ☐ 3. If other factors remain unchanged, lower real interest rates make more investment projects worthwhile.

☐ ☐ 4. In the long run, a higher rate of growth in the money supply will generally cause a higher rate of inflation and an increase in money (nominal) interest rates.

☐ ☐ 5. Based on the equation of exchange ($MV = PY$), the quantity theory of money states that an increase in the money supply (M) will cause a proportional increase in output, or real GDP(Y).

☐ ☐ 6. The supply curve of money is vertical because the quantity of money supplied is strongly influenced by changes in the interest rate.

☐ ☐ 7. According to the Taylor rule, the lower the inflation rate and the smaller the current level of output is relative to the potential level of output, the more restrictive the monetary policy needed for the achievement of full employment with price stability.

☐ ☐ 8. Monetarists believe that instability in the supply of money is the major cause of fluctuations in real GDP.

☐ ☐ 9. Because the Federal Reserve can make decisions much more quickly than can Congress, monetary policy, unlike fiscal policy, is not subject to timing problems.

T F

☐ ☐ 10. If the velocity of money is constant and an economy's real output tends to grow at 3 percent, a stable 5 percent growth rate for the money supply would be consistent with an inflation rate of 8 percent.

☐ ☐ 11. If the Fed expands the supply of money by buying bonds, this action would be considered restrictive monetary policy.

☐ ☐ 12. If an expansion in the money supply is fully anticipated, it will cause an increase in the price level (inflation) but no change in real GDP even in the short run.

☐ ☐ 13. Unanticipated changes in the money supply can affect real output in the short run, but in the long run, the effect is the same as if the policy had been anticipated.

☐ ☐ 14. Expansionary monetary policy helped fuel the credit expansion and run up in housing prices, which set up the economy for the financial crisis of 2008.

PROBLEMS AND PROJECTS

1. The equation of exchange ($MV = PY$) is a useful formula for understanding the relationships between the money supply (M), the velocity of money (V), the price level (P), and real GDP(Y). In addition, because $P \times Y$ is equal to nominal GDP, the formula can be written as $MV = GDP$, where GDP is nominal GDP. Further, sometimes we use the "growth rate version" of this equation, which is $\%\Delta M + \%\Delta V = \%\Delta P + \%\Delta Y$, where %Δ stands for "percent change." This final version relates the growth rate of the money supply ($\%\Delta M$) to the growth rate of velocity ($\%\Delta V$), the inflation rate ($\%\Delta P$), and the growth rate of real output ($\%\Delta Y$). To summarize, we have three versions of this equation:

(I) $MV = PY$
(II) $MV = GDP$
(III) $\%\Delta M + \%\Delta V = \%\Delta P + \%\Delta Y$

Answer each of the following questions, and indicate which version of the equation you used.
a. In 2000, nominal GDP in the United States was $9,963 billion and the M2 money supply was $4,945 billion. What was the velocity of the M2 money supply in 2000?
b. If the money supply is 600, velocity is 5, and the price index is 100, what is real GDP?
c. If the velocity of money remains constant (so, $\%\Delta V = 0$), real output grows at 3 percent, and the money supply grows at 7 percent, what is the inflation rate?
d. If the velocity of money remains constant, real output grows at 3 percent, and the money supply grows at 1 percent, what is the inflation rate?
e. If the velocity of money remains constant and real output grows at 3 percent, what rate of growth in the money supply would be consistent with a policy of zero inflation?
f. Suppose currently, the money supply is 20, the velocity of money is 4, the price level is 8, and real GDP is 10. If the Fed doubles the money supply and both velocity and real output remain unchanged, what will be the new price level?
g. Suppose the money supply is 100, the velocity of money is 3, the price level is 5, and real GDP is 60. An unanticipated increase in the money supply to 200 increases real GDP to 100 in the short run, but then real GDP returns to 60 in the long run. Assuming the velocity of money remains constant, what will happen to prices in the short run? in the long run?

2. Exhibit 2 below illustrates the macroeconomy initially in equilibrium at the real GDP level of Y_1, price level of P_1, and nominal and real interest rates of i_1 and r_1, respectively.
    a. Suppose the Fed conducts an open market sale of bonds. Show the short-run impact of this sale in the money balances and loanable funds markets. Briefly explain the changes you make in the diagrams. Assume the policy is unanticipated.
    b. Now show the short-run impact of these changes on real GDP and the price level in the AD/AS model at the far right. Again, explain briefly the changes you make in the diagram.

EXHIBIT 2

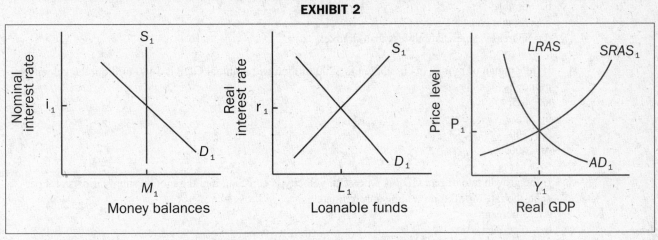

3. Exhibit 3 illustrates the macroeconomy in equilibrium initially at real GDP level Y_f (the full-employment level) and price level P_1. Suppose the Fed increases the money supply.
    a. If the policy is unanticipated, and the increase in the money supply raises aggregate demand in the second period to AD_2, what will be the short-run impact on real GDP and the price level? Explain briefly.
    b. Will the change in real GDP you described in part a be sustainable in the long run? Explain, modifying the diagram as necessary to reflect the long-run impact of this policy.

EXHIBIT 3

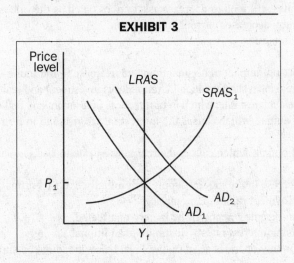

MULTIPLE CHOICE

1. A decrease in the nominal (or money) interest rate would
    a. encourage people to hold smaller money balances.
    b. encourage people to hold larger money balances.
    c. force the Fed to increase the money supply.
    d. cause the real interest rate to rise.

2. According to monetarists, which of the following would most likely eliminate inflation?
   a. a steady increase in federal expenditures at an annual rate of approximately 3 percent
   b. indexing of wages, taxes, and pensions to the rate of inflation
   c. a steady expansion in the money supply at a rate no greater than the long-run growth of real output
   d. a steady 3 percent increase in the size of the budget deficit

3. Given the strict quantity theory of money, if the quantity of money doubled, prices would
   a. fall by half.
   b. double.
   c. remain constant.
   d. increase somewhat but less than double.

4. If the amount of money in circulation is $200 million and nominal GDP is $400 million, the velocity of money is
   a. 0.5.
   b. 2.
   c. 200.
   d. 400.

5. If the growth rate of real GDP is 3 percent, velocity is constant, and the money supply grows at 9 percent, the rate of inflation will be approximately
   a. 3 percent.
   b. 6 percent.
   c. 9 percent.
   d. 12 percent.

6. When the Fed unexpectedly increases the money supply, it will cause an increase in aggregate demand because
   a. real interest rates will fall, stimulating business investment and consumer purchases.
   b. the dollar will appreciate on the foreign exchange market, leading to a decrease in net exports.
   c. lower interest rates will tend to decrease asset prices (such as the prices of homes), which decreases wealth and thereby decreases current consumption.
   d. all of the above are true.

7. The most likely short-run impact of an unanticipated decrease in the money supply is a(n)
   a. decrease in the real interest rate, which in turn reduces investment and real GDP.
   b. increase in the real interest rate, which in turn reduces investment and real GDP.
   c. increase in real output, which causes the interest rate to rise and in turn reduces investment and real GDP.
   d. decrease in real output, which causes the real interest rate to rise.

8. An unanticipated increase in the money supply will initially exert its primary impact on
   a. output and employment rather than on prices.
   b. prices; output and employment will be largely unaffected.
   c. interest rates; rising interest rates will stimulate additional saving.
   d. prices if the economy operates at an output level below its long-run supply constraint.

9. Which of the following is true?
   a. An unanticipated shift to a more expansionary monetary policy will temporarily stimulate output and employment.
   b. Persistent growth of the money supply at a rapid rate will cause inflation.
   c. Both a and b are true.
   d. None of the above are true.

10. In the short run, an unanticipated increase in the money supply will
    a. increase interest rates and shift the aggregate demand curve to the left.
    b. increase interest rates and shift the aggregate demand curve to the right.
    c. lower interest rates and shift the aggregate demand curve to the left.
    d. lower interest rates and shift the aggregate demand curve to the right.

11. Suppose the economy is experiencing full employment. An unanticipated increase in the money supply
    will
    a. raise real GDP and the price level in the short run, but in the long run will cause no change in real
        GDP and only a higher price level.
    b. lower real GDP and the price level in the short run, but in the long run will cause no change in real
        GDP and only a lower price level.
    c. cause no change in real GDP in either the short run or long run but will increase the price level.
    d. cause the price level to rise in the short run but will increase real GDP in the long run.

12. In the equation of exchange, V stands for
    a. velocity, or the annual rate at which money changes hands in the purchase of final products.
    b. the investment component of aggregate demand.
    c. the amount of money in circulation.
    d. a constant equal to 3.1416, discovered by classical economists.

13. The demand curve for money
    a. would shift if the interest rate changed.
    b. shifts with an increase in the reserve requirement.
    c. shows the relationship between the quantity of money demanded and the interest rate.
    d. is a relationship between the quantity of investment demanded and the interest rate.

14. Classical economists, who adhered to the quantity theory of money, believed that an increase in the
    money supply would cause
    a. a proportional change in velocity.
    b. a proportional change in real GDP.
    c. a proportional change in prices.
    d. no effect on velocity, prices, or real GDP.

15. When the Fed unexpectedly increases the money supply,
    a. real interest rates will rise, and the foreign exchange value of the dollar will appreciate.
    b. real interest rates will rise, and the foreign exchange value of the dollar will depreciate.
    c. real interest rates will fall, and the foreign exchange value of the dollar will appreciate.
    d. real interest rates will fall, and the foreign exchange value of the dollar will depreciate.

16. The Taylor rule was designed to provide a measure of
    a. the real interest rate.
    b. the consistency of monetary policy with price stability and full employment.
    c. the inflation rate that will minimize the rate of unemployment.
    d. the growth rate of excess reserves available to commercial banks.

17. If the actual federal funds rate is 1 percent when the target rate called for by the Taylor rule is 5 percent,
    this indicates that
    a. monetary policy is overly expansionary, and a shift toward a more restrictive policy would be
        appropriate.
    b. monetary policy is too restrictive, and a shift to a more expansionary policy would be appropriate.
    c. monetary policy is unable to influence interest rates.
    d. current monetary policy is on target, and no policy shift is needed.

18. Which of the following contributed to the dramatic rise in housing prices between 2002 and mid-year 2006?
    a.   the low interest rate policy of the Federal Reserve
    b.   the Fed's restrictive monetary policy, which led to high interest rates
    c.   the tightening of loan standards by commercial lenders
    d.   the substantial excess reserves of commercial banks

19. During the nine months following July 2008, the Fed doubled the monetary base and generated huge excess reserves within the commercial banking system. This policy increases the danger of
    a.   a contraction in the money supply that will increase the length and severity of the recession.
    b.   rapid future growth of the money supply and inflation.
    c.   higher future interest rates, which will increase the length and severity of the recession.
    d.   a credit contraction because banks are unable to extend future loans.

20. Which of the following will make it difficult for the Fed to institute shifts in monetary policy in a manner that will promote economic stability?
    a.   the inability of the Fed to alter the money supply
    b.   the long and variable time lags between shifts in monetary policy and its impact on output and employment
    c.   a velocity rate of money that is relatively constant
    d.   the inability of the Fed to shift monetary policy without the approval of Congress

21. Which of the following interest rates will be most affected by a shift to a more restrictive monetary policy?
    a.   rate on a 30-year home mortgage
    b.   rate on a 20-year Treasury bond
    c.   rate on a 10-year bank loan
    d.   rate on a three-month certificate of deposit

DISCUSSION QUESTIONS

1.   In the previous chapter, we discussed the emergence of two new forms of money: debit cards and electronic money. How might these new forms of money affect the demand for money? How might they affect velocity? As these new money forms emerge, what impact might they have on the effectiveness of monetary policy?

2.   Susan, who always likes to be prepared for the unexpected, keeps $200 in cash in a drawer at her house in case of emergency. If the money, or nominal, interest rate is 10 percent, how much does it cost Susan to hold this money balance each year? How much would it cost her if the interest rate was 50 percent? Do you think she would be likely to hold a smaller money balance if the interest rate was that much higher?

3.   Government regulations and two huge government sponsored mortgage lenders, Fannie Mae and Freddie Mac, made credit for housing finance both abundantly available and easily accessible between the years 2002 and 2006. Starting in 2007, the housing market experienced a bust that helped lead to the financial crisis of 2008. How does this relate to what you learned about the short-run and long-run effects of expansionary monetary policy?

4.   The monetarists believe that changes in the money supply can, and do, have large effects on real GDP. However, they also are very "nonactivist" in believing that the Fed should not actively try to direct the economy with monetary policy. Explain the reasoning behind this apparent contradiction. Be sure to address the problem of proper timing in your answer.

5.   An expansion in the money supply eventually results in an increase in aggregate demand. Discuss the possible means by which the increase in the money supply is transmitted to the economy in this manner.

Stabilization Policy, Output, and Employment

CHAPTER 15

TRUE OR FALSE

T   F

☐ ☐ 1. At least three kinds of lags seriously complicate the timing of discretionary policy; these lags are the recognition lag, the administrative lag, and the impact lag.

☐ ☐ 2. A major difference between activists and nonactivists is that activists believe policy makers can use monetary and fiscal policy in response to changing economic conditions in a manner that will promote economic stability.

☐ ☐ 3. Nonactivists believe that the use of discretionary fiscal and monetary policy in response to changing economic conditions is likely to do more harm than good.

☐ ☐ 4. As it was originally developed by economist A.W. Phillips, the Phillips curve analysis indicates that higher inflation causes the rate of unemployment to rise.

☐ ☐ 5. The high accuracy of complex economic forecasting models allows us to predict every recession and expansion of the economy in advance.

☐ ☐ 6. The administrative lag for fiscal policy is much longer than for monetary policy.

☐ ☐ 7. The index of leading indicators is the single most widely used forecasting tool for the economy.

☐ ☐ 8. Whereas the public tends to credit (as well as blame) the president for the state of the economy, economists would be more likely to credit (or blame) the Fed.

☐ ☐ 9. According to the modern Phillips curve analysis, unemployment will fall below the natural rate when inflation is less than expected (overestimated).

T   F

☐   ☐   10.   Under adaptive expectations, a shift to more expansionary policy will cause output to rise in the short run but not in the long run.

☐   ☐   11.   Under rational expectations, a shift to more expansionary policy will likely cause little or no change in output, even in the short run, as decision makers quickly adjust to the new policy.

☐   ☐   12.   The adaptive- and rational-expectations theories differ in two major respects: (1) how quickly people adjust to a change and (2) the likelihood of systematic forecasting errors.

☐   ☐   13.   People with rational expectations base their expectations on more information than do people with adaptive expectations.

☐   ☐   14.   People with adaptive expectations base their expectations for the future on whatever has happened in the recent past.

☐   ☐   15.   According to the modern Phillips curve analysis, when inflation is greater than anticipated, unemployment falls below the natural rate.

☐   ☐   16.   When people overestimate inflation, it means that actual inflation is higher than what was expected.

☐   ☐   17.   Expansionary policies will generally lead to inflation without permanently reducing unemployment below the natural rate.

PROBLEMS AND PROJECTS

1.   Tammy is a great believer in adaptive expectations. Last year, when the inflation rate was 10 percent, she bought a new car with a loan that carried a nominal interest rate of 13 percent. Unfortunately, at least for her, this year's inflation rate is only 4 percent. For Tammy, calculate the following. (Hint: Remember the real interest rate is the nominal interest rate minus the inflation rate.)
     a.   the rate of inflation she expected
     b.   the real interest rate she expected to pay
     c.   the real interest rate she actually paid this year
     d.   Has the fall in the inflation rate made her happy or unhappy (at least with respect to the interest rate she is paying on her car)?

2.   Using Exhibit 1, indicate the appropriate equilibrium for each of the following situations. Throughout the question, assume that the self-correcting mechanism operates through changes in resource prices (shifts in the short-run aggregate supply curve) only.
     a.   If the economy is in recession at point A, the economy, if left to itself, would eventually adjust to a long-run equilibrium at which point?
     b.   If the economy is in recession at point A, what policy recommendations might an activist make?
     c.   If the policy recommendations of the activist in part b are adopted quickly and impact the economy long before the self-correcting mechanism starts working, where would the economy end up? (Hint: Assume people have adaptive expectations, so the policy is unanticipated.)
     d.   If the policy recommendations of the activist in part b are adopted but do not impact the economy until after the self-correcting mechanism has taken place, where would the economy end up?

EXHIBIT 1

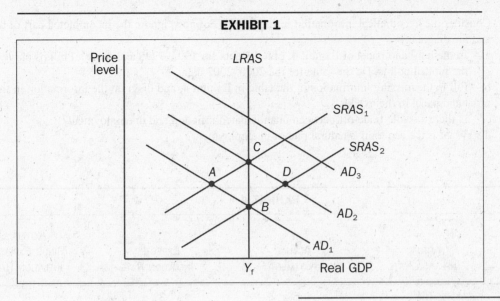

3. Assume the economy depicted in Exhibit 2 is in equilibrium at point A (AD_1 and $SRAS_1$).
   a. Would an expansionary monetary policy designed to increase aggregate demand from AD_1 to AD_2 and move the economy to point B be effective in the long run?
   b. Is there any way the economy could be moved to point B on a sustainable basis? (Hint: Think about ways of shifting *LRAS*.)

4. The economy depicted in Exhibit 3 is originally in equilibrium at point A (AD_1 and $SRAS_1$), and expansionary monetary and fiscal policies are conducted that increases aggregate demand from AD_1 to AD_2. For this question, assume no lags in policy (the effects are immediate).
   a. Where would the economy move in the short run if people form their expectations adaptively?
   b. Where would the economy move in the long run if people form their expectations adaptively?
   c. Where would the economy move in the short run if people form their expectations rationally and had correctly anticipated the policy?
   d. Where would the economy move in the long run if people form their expectations rationally and had correctly anticipated the policy?
   e. In light of your answers, assess the following statement: "In the long run, the effects of the policy are the same regardless of how expectations are formed or whether the policy is anticipated or unanticipated. There is only a difference in the short-run effects."

EXHIBIT 2

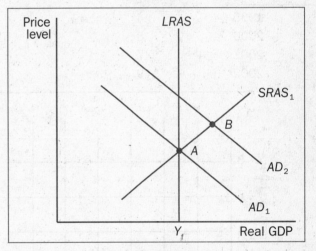

EXHIBIT 3

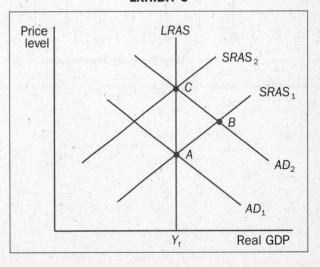

5. Consider the hypothetical information in Exhibit 4. (For now, ignore the incompleted part of the table and the diagram.)

  a. In the left-hand panel of Exhibit 4, plot the data for 1993–1995 and draw a Phillips curve through the plotted points. Do the same for the 2000–2002 data.

  b. Fill in the missing information in the table in Exhibit 4, and diagram the information in the right-hand panel in the exhibit.

  c. Is there a stable trade-off between unanticipated inflation and unemployment?

  d. What is the economy's natural rate of unemployment?

EXHIBIT 4

YEAR	ACTUAL INFLATION RATE	ACTUAL UNEMPLOYMENT RATE	EXPECTED INFLATION RATE	ACTUAL MINUS EXPECTED INFLATION RATE
1993	3%	5%	3%	_____ %
1994	2	8	3	_____
1995	4	4	2	_____
2000	8	5	8	_____
2001	7	8	8	_____
2002	9	4	7	_____

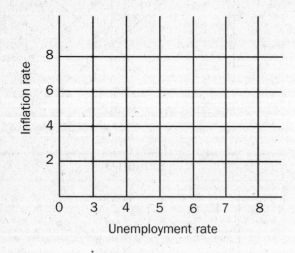

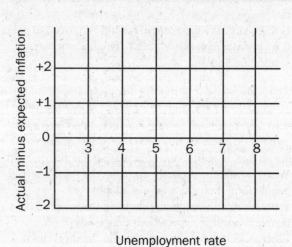

MULTIPLE CHOICE

1. The index of leading indicators is
    a. an alphabetical listing of all the most popular indicators in the economy for a given month.
    b. a composite index of indicators that provides information on the future direction of the economy.
    c. an alphabetical listing of the most important indicators of the current economic well-being of the U.S. economy.
    d. a composite index of the most important indicators of the current economic well-being of the U.S. economy.

2. The Phillips curve depicts the relationship between
    a. the federal debt and unemployment.
    b. wage rates and aggregate demand.
    c. the equilibrium level of income and the employment rate.
    d. inflation and unemployment.

3. During the 1960s, most economists believed macropolicy
    a. that caused inflation would permanently reduce unemployment.
    b. that caused inflation would permanently increase unemployment.
    c. could not be utilized to reduce unemployment.
    d. did not affect inflation.

4. The modern view of the Phillips curve indicates that expansionary macroeconomic policy
    a. will reduce the unemployment rate if policy makers are willing to accept the required rate of inflation.
    b. will reduce the unemployment rate only when people underestimate the inflationary effects of the expansionary policy.
    c. will reduce the unemployment rate only when people overestimate the inflationary effects of the expansionary policy.
    d. will reduce the unemployment rate if people accurately anticipate the inflationary effects of the expansionary policy.

5. The interval between the recognition of a need for a policy change and when the policy change is instituted is called the
    a. recognition lag.
    b. impact lag.
    c. policy lag.
    d. administrative lag.

6. Which of the following is true?
    a. When the inflation rate is steady—when it is neither rising nor falling—the actual rate of unemployment will equal the economy's natural rate of unemployment.
    b. When the inflation rate is higher than was anticipated, unemployment will exceed the natural rate.
    c. Demand stimulus policies will lead to inflation without permanently reducing the unemployment rate.
    d. Both a and c are true; b is false.

7. Use the table below to choose the correct answer.

TIME PERIOD	ACTUAL INFLATION
1	4%
2	4%
3	6%
4	8%

According to the adaptive expectations hypothesis, at the beginning of period 3, decision makers would expect inflation during period 3 to be
a. 4 percent.
b. 5 percent.
c. 6 percent.
d. 8 percent.

8. The theory according to which individuals weigh all available evidence when they formulate their expectations about economic events (including information concerning the probable effects of current and future economic policy) is called
a. the adaptive expectations hypothesis.
b. the permanent income theory.
c. the rational expectations hypothesis.
d. Laffer curve analysis.

9. The rational expectations hypothesis implies that discretionary macropolicy may be
a. relatively ineffective, even in the short run.
b. relatively effective in the short run but ineffective in the long run.
c. effective both in the short run and long run.
d. effective in the long run because decision makers will continually make systematic, predictable errors.

10. Under *adaptive* expectations, which of the following will likely be an initial effect of an unanticipated shift to a more restrictive macroeconomic policy?
a. a short-run decrease in output and a long-run decrease in inflation
b. no change in output even in the short run, only a permanent decrease in inflation
c. a short-run decrease in inflation and a long-run decrease in output
d. lower inflation and lower output in the long run

11. Under *rational* expectations, which of the following will likely be an initial effect of an unanticipated shift to a more restrictive macroeconomic policy?
a. a short-run decrease in output and a long-run decrease in inflation
b. no change in output even in the short run, only a permanent decrease in inflation
c. a short-run decrease in inflation and a long-run decrease in output
d. lower inflation and lower output in the long run

12. When persons overestimate inflation (when actual inflation is lower than was expected), actual unemployment will
a. exceed the natural rate of unemployment.
b. equal the natural rate of unemployment.
c. fall below the natural rate of unemployment.
d. decrease if the government is running a budget deficit and increase if a budget surplus is present.

Use the Modern Expectational Phillips curve diagram in Exhibit 5 to answer the next two questions.

EXHIBIT 5

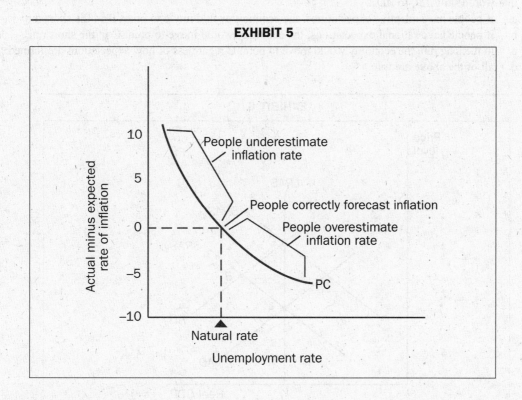

13. According to the modern expectational Phillips curve, unemployment will temporarily be above the natural rate of unemployment when
    a. any inflation is present.
    b. people expected inflation to be higher than what actually occurred.
    c. people expected inflation to be lower than what actually occurred.
    d. people correctly anticipated the inflation rate.

14. According to the modern expectational Phillips curve, actual unemployment will generally fall below the natural rate of unemployment if
    a. inflation falls to zero.
    b. inflation exceeds what was anticipated by decision makers.
    c. inflation is less than anticipated by decision makers.
    d. people fully anticipate the inflationary side effects of expansionary macroeconomic policies.

15. According to the adaptive expectations hypothesis,
    a. people will adapt to whatever income they are earning.
    b. the more people save, the less total savings will be available to the economy.
    c. the anticipated rate of inflation is based on the actual rates of inflation experienced during the recent past.
    d. the expected rate of inflation is adapted to macropolicy changes.

16. An individual who had rational expectations would be most likely to
    a. ignore information about all current policies of both the government and the Fed.
    b. always disagree with the expectations of someone who believed in adaptive expectations.
    c. use all pertinent information when formulating views about the future.
    d. never anticipate stable prices because monetary authorities continually expand the supply of money rapidly.

17. If the economy were currently operating at point A in Exhibit 6 and expansionary policy were enacted that would shift AD_1 to AD_2,
    a. if people have adaptive expectations, the economy would move to point B in the short run.
    b. if people have rational expectations, the economy would move to point C in the short run.
    c. in the long run, the economy would move to point C regardless of how expectations are formed.
    d. all of the above are true.

EXHIBIT 6

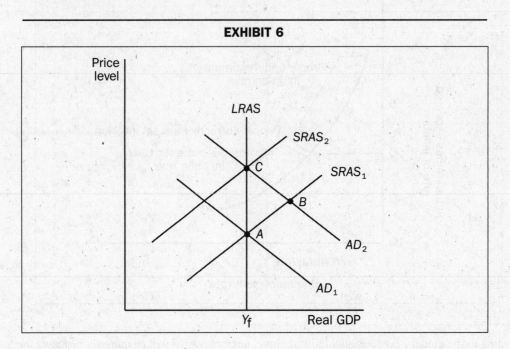

18. When there is an abrupt reduction in the rate of inflation,
    a. the actual rate of unemployment will tend to fall below the natural rate.
    b. the actual rate of unemployment will tend to rise above the natural rate.
    c. the actual and natural rate of unemployment will generally be equal.
    d. the natural rate of unemployment will tend to rise.

19. The index of leading indicators has
    a. turned down prior to six of the eight recessions since 1959.
    b. turned up prior to each of the periods of inflation since 1959.
    c. turned down prior to each of the eight recessions since 1959, but it has also falsely forecasted several others.
    d. turned down only eight times since 1959, and each downturn has been followed by a recession.

20. Which combination of signals is indicative that Fed policy is restrictive and that a shift to a more expansionary policy is in order?
    a. Commodity prices are falling, and the dollar is appreciating.
    b. The unemployment rate is low, and the inflation rate is high.
    c. Commodity prices are rising, and the dollar is depreciating.
    d. The index of leading indicators is rising, and the unemployment rate is low.

21. Most economists agree that
    a. fiscal policy is a more effective stabilization tool than monetary policy.
    b. price stability is the proper goal of monetary policy.
    c. monetary policy should focus on reducing unemployment, while fiscal policy should focus on the control of inflation.
    d. discretionary macro-policy can easily be instituted in a manner that will promote economic stability.

22. Between 1983 and 2007, the U.S. economy was in recession
    a. approximately 33 percent of the time.
    b. approximately 20 percent of the time.
    c. 17 months.
    d. This is a trick question; there was no recession during this period.

23. Stop-go policy that shifts between expansionary monetary policy and restrictive monetary policy will most likely
    a. promote economic stability and attract investment.
    b. lead to price stability because the restrictive policies will offset the effects of expansionary policies.
    c. create an environment of uncertainty, which will result in economic instability.
    d. help promote economic stability because changes in monetary policy will quickly exert a predictable impact on the economy.

DISCUSSION QUESTIONS

1. A few years ago, MIT economist Robert Solow gave a public lecture titled, "What Do Economists Know, If Anything?" Following the lecture, a member of the audience asked Professor Solow, "I'm a meteorologist and what I want to know is, how come you guys get paid more than I do?"
    a. Is economic forecasting useful? Why or why not?
    b. If there were no administrative and impact lags, would forecasting be more or less useful? Explain.
    c. Is it realistic to expect to *ever* be able to forecast unexpected events? If so, how? If not, how, if at all, can forecasting still be useful?
    d. If we made more use of centralized planning instead of markets, would forecasting be easier or harder? more or less useful?

2. It appears that persons marketing economic forecasts have sometimes oversold the ability of economists in this area. Why do you think that competition between forecasters hasn't driven bad forecasters out of the business?

3. There is a distinct psychological side to the argument between activism and nonactivism. In particular, which side seems to be almost "fatalistic" in its acceptance of the economic future? Which side wants to intervene and "do something," even if that something can potentially make things worse? Do you think it possible that some economists choose sides on this issue because of their personalities rather than on the basis of economic theory?

4. Suppose you were president of the United States and were faced with the activist/nonactivist debate. How would you go about making up your mind? Would the lack of a clear unified message from the economics profession make you more or less likely to make decisions based on political rather than economic grounds? Does this seem to be happening in the real world?

5. What are some of the methods currently used to shorten the various time lags of macroeconomic policy making? What other methods can you think of that might help? What are the odds that your ideas would be passed by Congress or approved by the federal bureaucrats?

6. Answer the following question both from the perspective of an activist and from the perspective of a non-activist: "Is economic instability the result of the natural tendencies of a market economy or the errors of policy makers?"

7. Prior to the experience of the 1970s, most economists and policy makers believed that a lower rate of unemployment could be attained if we were willing to live with a higher rate of inflation.
    a. Discuss this trade-off within the context of the original Phillips curve.
    b. How did the experience of the 1970s change this view?
    c. What does modern economic analysis suggest about this relationship? Be sure to address the role of expectations in your answer.

8. For each of the following, (1) discuss how the unemployment rate will change, particularly with respect to the natural rate; (2) show using a Phillips curve diagram; and (3) discuss whether the outcome is sustainable in the long run.
    a. Inflation is lower than was expected.
    b. Inflation is higher than was expected.
    c. Inflation is equal to what was expected.

CURRENT DEBATES IN ECONOMICS

Should We Use Activist Macropolicy?

Yes, We Should Use Activist Macropolicy: Activist Government: Key to Growth

by Walter H. Heller
[Reprinted from *Challenge*, March/April 1986. Copyright © 1986. Reprinted with permission of M. E. Sharpe, Inc., Armonk, New York 10504. Abridged.]

In a period when government activism, especially in economic affairs, is under attack—indeed, when President Reagan, charming, disarming, and sometimes alarming, tells the country that the government's impact on the economy is somewhere between baneful and baleful and that the greatest contribution he can make is to get government's clammy hands out of our pockets and government monkeys off our backs—against that background, the Joint Economic Committee's 40th anniversary is an especially appropriate time to take stock of the role government has played and should play in the economy.

Down Memory Lane . . . The early postwar years were really vintage years in our fiscal policy annals. We ran appropriate surpluses (that alone shows I'm dealing in ancient history) in 1947 and 1948. Then, in mid-1950, the Joint Economic Committee, in one of its finest hours, recognized the inflationary potential of the Korean War and led the charge to reverse gears, i.e., to take a tax cut that was halfway through the congressional mill and help convert it to a tax increase. As has been true so often, it was providing the intellectual leadership in Congress on economic policy. . . .

But the 1953–1960 period, with three recessions in seven years, was hardly activist policy at its best, especially during the 1950–1960 period of overly tight fiscal-monetary policy.

The Good Times. Then came the Golden Sixties, truly watershed years with a revitalizing of the Employment Act of 1946. President Kennedy asked us to return to the letter and spirit of that Act. He ended equivocation about the intent of the Act by translating its rather mushy mandate into a concrete call for meeting the goals of full employment, price stability, faster growth, and external balance—all within the constraints of preserving economic freedom and choice and promoting greater equality of opportunity. He went on to foster a rather weak-kneed antirecession program in 1961 and a powerful growth-promoting tax-cut program in 1962–1964. In that process, I counted six firsts for presidential economics:

- He was the first president to commit himself to numerical targets for full employment, namely 4 percent unemployment, and growth, namely 4.5 percent per year.

- He was the first to adopt an incomes policy in the form of wage-price guideposts developed by his Council of Economic Advisers. The guideposts, flanked by sensible supply-side tax measures to stimulate business investment, by training and retraining programs, and the like, helped maintain a remarkable record of price stability 1961–1965, namely, only 1.2 inflation per year.

- He was the first president to shift economic policy focus from moderating the swings of the business cycle to achieving the rising full-employment potential of the economy.

- In that process, he moved from the goal of a balanced budget over the business cycle to a balanced budget at full employment.

- He was the first president to say, as he did in January 1963, that budget deficits could be a positive force to help move a slack or recession-ridden economy toward full employment.

- As a capstone, he was the first president to say that a tax cut was needed, not to cope with recession (there was none), but to make full use of the economy's full-employment potential. . . .

Those were the halcyon days of economic policy. Aided and abetted by the Fed, the 1964 tax cut worked like a charm. In mid-1965, just before the July escalation in Vietnam, we saw the happy combination of an inflation rate of only 1.5 percent; unemployment coming down steadily, to 4.4 percent; defense expenditures continuing their four-year decline from 9 percent of GNP in 1960 to 7 percent of GNP in 1965; and the cash budget running $3 billion in the black.

The Downturn Begins. Then came the dark years of Vietnam, in economics as well as foreign policy. Unlike 1950–1951, we did not reverse gears in spite of the timely warnings of the Joint Economic Committee and of most of the economists, both inside and outside the government, who were advising President Johnson. . . . He did not propose a tax increase until early 1967, and no tax action was completed until 1968, long after the inflation horse was out of the barn. . . .

As I put it in testimony before the JEC in July 1970, "There are no magic formulas, no pat solutions, no easy ways to reconcile full employment and price stability. No modern, free economy has yet found the combination of policies that can deliver sustained high employment and high growth side by side with sustained price stability." That was all well and good, as far as it went, but in light of the experience of the 1970s, it did not go nearly far enough.

The policy travails of the seventies are too well known to require lengthy review:

- First, there was the Nixon fiasco of freezes and phases serving as a facade for pumping up the economy with tax cuts, spending increases, and a rapid run-up in the money supply, with surefire consequences of an over-heated economy.

- Superimposed on that were the supply shocks in 1973–1974—oil prices quadrupling, food prices jumping 40 percent in two years, other world raw-material prices doubling in about the same time—that served to consolidate stagflation.

The shocks, of course, were not just to the price level, but the economics profession, led by Keynesians. We learned the sad lesson that as to wages and prices, what goes up, propelled by overstimulative monetary-fiscal policy and a series of external shocks, does not necessarily come down when the fiscal-monetary stimulus and supply shocks subside. We have since learned a lot about sticky wages and prices that stay in high orbit even without visible means of fiscal-monetary support. At least they stayed there until we administered a dose of sadomasochism, better known as the double-dip recession of the eighties, the deepest since the Great Depression.

One should not recite the economic sins of the seventies without acknowledging one bright fiscal episode, namely, the tax rebate and tax cut enacted in the second quarter of 1975. Granted, it was a bit late to blunt the recession, but it provided a welcome boost to an economy that had fallen into what, until topped by the recession of the early eighties, was the deepest postwar recession. The 1975 tax cut was a winner in both size and timing.

As one surveys the whole postwar period, activist economics and New Deal intrusions into the marketplace can surely take credit not only for building in strong defenses against depression but also for 25 years (1948–1973) of high-octane operation of the economy and sharply reduced instability. Within the framework, one can criticize antirecession fiscal policy as often too little and too late, monetary policy as sometimes too easy and other times overstaying tightness. The far-too-late and considerably-too-little tax increase to finance the war in Vietnam, coupled with excessive monetary ease in 1967–1968, has to go down in the annals as one of the flat failures of postwar fiscal-monetary policy. And the stagflation experience of the 1970s still hangs like a pall over expansionary policy today.

Still, it is worth reminding ourselves that even in the face of high performance of the economy, inflation in the 1949–1972 rose above 6 percent only once (during the Korean War), and averaged only 2.3 percent. If inflation was the price of activism in public economics, it was a long time in coming.

No, We Should Not Use Activist Macropolicy Economic Policy: The Old Tools Won't Work

by Marc Levinson
[Reprinted with permission from *Business Monthly,* January 1987. Copyright © 1987 by Goldhirsch Group, Inc. Abridged.]

Since the advent of the New Deal more than half a century ago, the federal government has actively helped shape the course of the economy. Its ability, at least in the short run, to pump up the economy in hard times and slow it down when inflation began to boil up has been unquestioned. As recently as 1981, when a sharp cutback in money supply growth pushed the country into recession, or 1983, when the stimulative effects of a tax cut brought the economy back to health, the old elixirs worked as they had in the past.

But in 1986, things were different. Heady growth in the money supply, repeated cuts in the Federal Reserve Board's discount rate and record federal budget deficits all failed to juice the lackluster economy. The old linkages between the government's actions and the economy's responses have changed in ways economists do not fully understand. As a result, the government's economic tools have been partially blunted. Contends Lawrence Chimerine, chairman of Chase Econometrics, "The ability of policy changes to improve the economy is much smaller than ever."

The reason: the growing internationalization of the U.S. economy. Flexible exchange rates and the resulting mushrooming of international capital markets have made traditional economic policies act in unexpected ways. "No one has a reliable theory of exchange rates," says Paul Krugman, a professor of international economics at the Massachusetts Institute of Technology. "That makes it very difficult to be sure of the effects of macroeconomic policy."

These international connections make it increasingly difficult to aim economic weapons at purely domestic targets. Even thinking of "domestic" in terms of economic problems is misleading. "The problem is global overcapacity and global underconsumption," contends Steve Quick, an economist with the Joint Economic Committee of Congress. "But we have no tools. We have no global fiscal policy. We have no global monetary policy." Adds Harold Rose, chief economist of Britain's Barclays Bank: "It's very hard to see how we can get out of these problems by macroeconomic policy alone."

Certainly, the assumption that the government can "fine tune" the economy has been in disrepute since the early 1970s, when policy makers were helpless as they faced high unemployment and high inflation at the same time. But faith in the government's ability to deal with one of these problems at a time has remained strong. Now, however, the government's very ability to achieve some domestic goals—3 percent growth in output, 4 percent unemployment—appears increasingly limited. The jury is still out on whether these limitations are a temporary phenomenon or a permanent fact of life.

Take monetary policy, the Federal Reserve Board's method of influencing the economy's performance by manipulating the money supply. Financial deregulation, of course, has blurred the meaning of the money supply figures. But international capital flows have also made it much more difficult for the central bank to plot the nation's monetary course.

Suppose, for example, that the Fed wants to boost the economy's growth rate. When international capital flows were small, the central bank could stimulate borrowing by pumping up the money supply or cutting the discount rate. But now, lower interest rates will spur investors to move their capital out of dollar-denominated investments. Economists can't even begin to estimate the likely extent of those capital flows. If little capital moves abroad, the lower interest rates will powerfully stimulate the U.S. economy. If, on the other hand, lower rates trigger a massive flight from the dollar, higher import prices will inject a strong dose of inflation into the economy, which would discourage the very business spending the Fed wanted to stimulate. Would faster money growth cut the U.S. trade deficit? Nobody knows.

The direction of the overall change remains undisputed: Increasing the rate of money supply growth will stimulate the economy, and reducing it will retard growth. But the magnitude of the change is now almost unpredictable. There is no doubt that a $108 billion budget slash will cut domestic demand. It will also lower deficits and reduce the government's borrowing from abroad, driving down the dollar. But whether a more favorable exchange rate for exports will boost the economy more than lower government spending retards it is an open question. "We don't know the responsiveness of the economy to a changed deficit," contends economist Mickey D. Levy of Philadelphia's Fidelity Bank. "We don't know the lags." Concurs Rudolph Penner, director of the Congressional Budget Office, "If we had been analyzing that big a change twenty years ago, there wouldn't have been much debate that it would cause a recession." The venerable Keynesian multiplier, which links changes in government spending to predictably larger changes in economic output, can, for all practical purposes, be tossed out the window. Using fiscal policy to reach some desired target in terms of, say, unemployment or Gross National Product is thus far more difficult than in the past.

The use of both fiscal and monetary policy has become even more treacherous as government officials have come to realize that they are not operating in an isolated economy. Indeed, the reactions of other governments can blunt or reverse Washington's initiatives, making economic policy a strategic game, according to a brand new line of economic research. The United States must figure out how other countries will respond to its moves, and determine the degree to which those responses will counteract the effects that American policy makers seek to achieve. "We can't make policy without taking into account what our competitor overseas is doing," contends University of Illinois economist Stephen J. Turnovsky.

One way to deal with diminishing effectiveness of monetary and fiscal policies, says the Joint Economic Committee's Quick, is to examine the economic impact of policies long considered unrelated, such as foreign aid or regulation of international lending. Increasing the industrial nations' contributions to the International Monetary Fund, for example, could help stimulate growth in the developing countries, which in turn would step up their purchases of U.S. exports. This viewpoint is catching on in Washington, where Congress has finally come to understand that the debts of developing countries are a major drag on U.S. growth.

HOLDING A DEBATE

Many students will enjoy participating in a debate on this topic either in class or in an informal study group. After completing both readings and possibly doing some additional research, get three to four volunteers for each side of the debate, choose a moderator if your instructor is not available, and devote about half an hour to opening statements, rebuttals, and summaries.

DISCUSSION

1. If you read both articles, it is time to make a judgment. Do the difficulties of accurate policy making make it better to do nothing? Are there times when even Levinson would agree to an activist policy? Explain your answers.

2. If you read the Heller article, it is important to note that Professor Heller was the chairman of the Council of Economic Advisers under Presidents Kennedy and Johnson and played a major role in shaping the fairly activist macropolicy of that era. Do you think his participation in the policy making made him a better or worse judge of the effectiveness of activist policy? Why?

3. If you read the Levinson article, into what economic "camp" would you group him? Reread the article for evidence that he is a monetarist or a supply-sider or a new classical economist. Why is it unlikely that he is Keynesian?

Creating an Environment for Growth and Prosperity

CHAPTER 16

TRUE OR FALSE

T F

☐ ☐ 1. Growth in a country's real output (real GDP) is necessary for growth in a country's real income.

☐ ☐ 2. Economic growth can be depicted as an outward shift (increase) in a country's production possibilities curve.

☐ ☐ 3. When output grows at a faster rate than population, per capita GDP will fall.

☐ ☐ 4. Higher levels of per capita GDP are generally associated with better living standards and improvements in life expectancy, literacy, and health.

☐ ☐ 5. According to the rule of 70, if a country sustains a 2 percent rate of growth, the size of the country's economy will double approximately every 20 years.

☐ ☐ 6. Trade is a source of economic growth because it helps trading partners achieve larger outputs through division of labor, specialization, and adoption of methods of mass production.

☐ ☐ 7. Technological advancement is the term used to describe the introduction of new techniques or methods that increase output per unit of input.

☐ ☐ 8. To an economist, the term "institutions" refers to the legal, regulatory, and social constraints that affect the security of property rights and enforcement of contracts.

☐ ☐ 9. Because it is so small, an economic reform that increases growth by only one percent will have no long-term impact on an economy.

T   F

☐   ☐   10. A country that protects and enforces the private property rights of its citizens, follows policies of free international trade, and maintains low marginal income tax rates will generally grow faster than a country that does not.

☐   ☐   11. A country that regulates its capital markets and has very unstable monetary policy (and thus high price instability) will generally grow faster than a country that does not.

☐   ☐   12. Abundant natural resources are the most important factor for creating high rates of economic growth.

☐   ☐   13. Countries receiving high levels of foreign aid have faster rates of economic growth.

☐   ☐   14. The poor economic performance of tropical countries is largely a reflection of their poor institutional quality rather than their climate and location.

☐   ☐   15. According to economist William Baumol, the time and talents of individuals are more likely to be devoted to unproductive, wealth-destroying activities when a country's institutions fail to protect property rights.

☐   ☐   16. The large amount of foreign aid directed toward Africa has been extremely successful at bringing Africa out of extreme poverty.

PROBLEMS AND PROJECTS

1. Use the rule of 70 to complete the following table.

COUNTRY	GROWTH RATE	NUMBER OF YEARS FOR INCOME TO DOUBLE
Country A	1%	_____
Country B	2%	_____
Country C	7%	_____
Country D	10%	_____

2. For each of the following, tell whether the policy would tend to increase (+) or decrease (–) a country's long-run rate of economic growth.
   a. Government-imposed price controls that keep food prices low.
   b. A sound monetary policy that results in a low and stable rate of inflation.
   c. A legal system that enforces contracts and property rights.
   d. The imposition of tariffs or quotas to protect domestic industries from foreign competition.
   e. Large subsidies to keep failing businesses (those earning losses) open.
   f. Regulations mandating higher worker wages, benefits, and shorter work weeks.
   g. Low tax rates on productive activities.

MULTIPLE CHOICE

1. When a country's real GDP is increasing at a faster rate than its population,
    a. per capita GDP will be rising.
    b. per capita GDP will be falling.
    c. per capita GDP will remain constant.
    d. none of the above.

2. The rule of 70 is
    a. a formula used to determine the number of years it takes for something to double at a given growth rate.
    b. a theory explaining why countries tended to grow more rapidly during the 1970s.
    c. the principle, that for growth, a country needs government spending of at least 70 percent of GDP.
    d. a formula to compute the change in GDP that will occur as investment rises.

3. A 2 percent growth rate will bring about a doubling of real GDP in about how many years?
    a. 1
    b. 2
    c. 35
    d. 70

4. A 7 percent growth rate will bring about a doubling of real GDP in about how many years?
    a. 1
    b. 7
    c. 10
    d. 70

5. The major sources of economic growth are
    a. gains from trade, entrepreneurial discovery, and investment in physical and human capital.
    b. price controls, heavy regulations, and high inflation.
    c. tariffs to protect domestic industries from foreign competition and budget deficits.
    d. a good climate, high levels of foreign aid, and abundant natural resources.

6. Trade is a source of economic growth and prosperity because it
    a. moves goods, services, and resources from people who value them less to people who value them more.
    b. helps trading partners achieve larger outputs through division of labor, specialization, and adoption of methods of mass production.
    c. serves as a zero-sum game in which the gains to one trading partner are offset by losses to the other trading partner.
    d. both a and b, but not c.

7. Which of the following will be required for a low-income country to move up the income ladder and achieve high-income status?
    a. rapid growth of the money supply to increase inflation and prices
    b. restrictions limiting the import of goods from other nations
    c. high tax rates to support a large government sector
    d. a high rate of sustained economic growth

8. Which of the following will most likely contribute to the growth of a country?
   a. secure property rights and low marginal tax rates
   b. price controls that keep the cost of agricultural products low
   c. rapid monetary growth
   d. exchange rate controls and export restrictions

9. Which of the following is a true statement with regard to competitive markets?
   a. Self-interested individuals do not promote the general welfare in competitive markets, only in regulated markets.
   b. Competition promotes prosperity best when price controls are implemented.
   c. Policies that make it easy to enter and exit business promote competition and economic progress.
   d. All of the above are correct.

10. Which of the following is *not* one of the major sources of economic growth?
    a. a large government sector
    b. investment in physical and human capital
    c. advancements in technology
    d. institutions and policies that improve economic efficiency

11. How do high tariffs and other restraints on international trade affect the prosperity of a nation?
    a. They increase domestic employment and thereby promote the growth of real GDP.
    b. They prevent the nation from fully realizing potential gains from specialization, exchange, and competition, thereby reducing economic growth.
    c. They tend to reduce rent-seeking and lobbying by producers and thereby promote economic growth.
    d. Both a and c are correct.

12. If the political leaders of a country wanted to promote economic growth, which of the following policy alternatives would be most effective?
    a. price controls in order to keep the price of food low
    b. expansionary monetary policies designed to increase the rate of inflation
    c. increasing marginal tax rates in order to increase government subsidies and transfers
    d. elimination of price controls and trade restraints and establishment of a monetary policy consistent with long-run price stability (a low rate of inflation)

13. Which of the following is not a government policy that can enhance economic growth?
    a. having free international trade
    b. keeping marginal tax rates low
    c. adopting regulations fixing interest rates at low levels
    d. protecting and enforcing private property rights and contracts

14. A "stable monetary environment" is used to describe monetary policy consistent with
    a. keeping the money income of citizens constant while population grows.
    b. keeping the rate of inflation low.
    c. minimizing the year-to-year fluctuations in the inflation rate.
    d. both (b) and (c).

15. The most important factor for producing long-run economic growth is
    a. abundant natural resources.
    b. foreign aid.
    c. good policies and institutions.
    d. slow population growth.

16. The poor economic performance of countries located in tropical areas is due to
a.   their hot climate.
b.   poor institutional quality in these countries.
c.   a lack of natural resources.
d.   not enough foreign aid.

17. Individuals are more likely to engage in productive activities when institutions and policies
a.   create a fair and unbiased judicial system.
b.   provide for monetary stability.
c.   restrict the ability of government to transfer wealth through taxation and regulation.
d.   All of the above.

18. (I) When a country's institutions and policies provide secure property rights, a fair and balanced judicial system, monetary stability, and effective limits on government's ability to transfer wealth through taxation and regulation, creative individuals are more likely to engage in product development, investment, and other productive activities. (II) When a country's legal and regulatory environment fails to protect property rights and is often used to favor some at the expense of others, individuals are instead more likely to engage in attempts to manipulate the political and legal process in order to plunder wealth from others.
a.   I is true, II is false.
b.   I is false, II is true.
c.   Both I and II are true.
d.   Both I and II are false.

DISCUSSION QUESTIONS

1.   What are the major sources of economic growth? Give examples of government policy changes that could increase the rate of economic growth in a country.

2.   How do you think the less-developed countries can best help themselves attain more rapid growth rates? How do you think the developed countries can best help them? Is foreign aid the answer?

3.   Are abundant natural resources good or bad for economic growth?

4.   What do economists mean when they refer to a country's "institutions"? What are some examples of good and bad institutional structures? How does the quality of institutions in a country affect the allocation of the time and efforts of the residents of that country?

5.   What role do climate, geography, and population growth play in economic prosperity? Are these the most important factors that determine a country's economic growth rate?

CHAPTER 17

Institutions, Policies, and Cross-country Differences in Income and Growth

TRUE OR FALSE

T   F

☐   ☐   1. Economists generally prefer to use the purchasing power parity (PPP) method when comparing incomes across countries because it results in income comparisons that more accurately reflect real income differences across countries and time periods.

☐   ☐   2. The purchasing power parity (PPP) method calculates the cost of purchasing a specific bundle of goods and services in each country, and uses this measure to convert the incomes of different countries to a common currency.

☐   ☐   3. The per capita incomes in Sierra Leone, Malawi, Ireland, and Niger are among the highest in the world.

☐   ☐   4. Most large European countries, such as Germany, France, and Italy, have income levels higher than the United States.

☐   ☐   5. The per capita GDP of low-income countries tends to be overstated because household production, which is generally substantial in these countries, is double-counted in GDP.

☐   ☐   6. The ten fastest-growing countries in the world during the past quarter of a century were almost all LDCs in 1980.

☐   ☐   7. Most high-income industrial economies experienced annual per capita GDP growth rates of around 10 percent over the past 25 years.

☐   ☐   8. The growth records of LDCs have been mixed. Some have experienced growth rates among the fastest in the world whereas others have experienced very weak (or even negative) growth rates.

T F

☐ ☐ 9. Economic freedom is a method of organizing economic activity characterized by: (1) personal choice, (2) voluntary exchange coordinated by markets, (3) freedom to enter and compete in markets, and (4) protection of persons and their property from aggression by others.

☐ ☐ 10. The Economic Freedom of the World (EFW) index uses 42 separate components to measure the consistency of a nation's institutions and policies with personal choice, freedom of exchange, and protection of private property.

☐ ☐ 11. In order to achieve a high EFW rating, a country must provide secure protection of privately owned property, even-handed enforcement of contracts, and a stable monetary environment. It also must keep taxes low, refrain from creating barriers to both domestic and international trade, and rely more fully on markets rather than governments to allocate goods and resources.

☐ ☐ 12. According to the EFW rating, Hong Kong, Singapore, Switzerland, and the United States are among the countries with the highest levels of economic freedom, whereas the Democratic Republic of Congo, Myanmar, Guinea-Bissau, Syria, Algeria, and Zimbabwe are among the lowest.

☐ ☐ 13. Countries with higher levels of economic freedom have both higher levels of per person income and more rapid rates of economic growth.

☐ ☐ 14. Countries with the lowest economic freedom scores tend to have the highest levels of foreign direct investment because of their low wages and relatively short supply of existing capital.

☐ ☐ 15. In countries with higher levels of economic freedom, investment is channeled to more productive uses and thus has a larger impact on economic growth.

☐ ☐ 16. Uniformly, countries that have undertaken reforms to increase their levels of economic freedom have found that it is a painful process that usually results in negative rates of economic growth persisting for about a decade.

☐ ☐ 17. A country's legal system is not important for economic growth once markets are large enough to be mainly characterized by depersonalized exchange between parties who do not know each other.

☐ ☐ 18. Democracy is a form of political organization where adult citizens are free to participate in the political process (e.g., through voting), elections are free and open, and outcomes are decided mostly by majority voting.

☐ ☐ 19. Democracy tends to best promote economic freedom when there are constitutional checks on the powers of elected officials, constitutional protections of private property, and political decentralization.

☐ ☐ 20. (This question pertains to material in the addendum to the chapter.) Countries with higher levels of economic freedom have higher quality of life as is shown by higher life expectancy, lower infant mortality, lower incidence of tuberculosis, better access to sanitary water, and better environmental quality.

PROBLEMS AND PROJECTS

1. The table below lists the Economic Freedom of the World (EFW) ratings for 1990 and 2007, and economic growth rates for five countries. Use the information in the table to answer the following questions.

Country	EFW RATING 1990	EFW RATING 2007	AVERAGE GROWTH RATE OF PER PERSON INCOME 1995–2007
Ireland	6.7	8.0	5.5%
Venezuela	5.5	4.3	1.0%
Hungary	5.1	7.3	4.1%
Zimbabwe	4.8	2.9	−3.4%
China	4.8	6.5	8.8%

   a. Which countries in this table improved their economic freedom ratings between 1990 and 2007?
   b. Which countries experienced declines in economic freedom over this period?
   c. How did economic growth rates differ between these two groups of countries (those who increased versus those who decreased in economic freedom)?

2. Using either the exhibit in your textbook or the Economic Freedom of the World (EFW) rating website (http://www.freetheworld.com/), for each pair of countries, circle the one that has the higher level of economic freedom.
   a. Ireland or Nigeria
   b. Argentina or Hong Kong
   c. Switzerland or Uganda
   d. Mexico or Canada
   e. Singapore or Zimbabwe
   f. United States or Brazil
   g. Russia or New Zealand
   h. Estonia or Venezuela

3. Name three countries that you personally consider prosperous (or places you might want to visit or live one day), and three countries you would consider relatively poor. Visit the Economic Freedom of the World (EFW) rating website (http://www.freetheworld.com/) and find the rankings of these countries. How large are the differences in economic freedom ratings between these two groups of countries?

MULTIPLE CHOICE

1. To compare income across countries in a common currency, economists generally prefer to use the
   a. purchasing power parity (PPP) method.
   b. production possibilities frontier (PPF) method.
   c. common currency converter (CCC) method.
   d. exchange rate conversion (ERC) method.

2. The purchasing power parity method of comparing income across countries is based on
    a. the exchange rate for each country's currency.
    b. the cost of purchasing a specific bundle of goods and services in each country.
    c. the size of government in each country as a percent of GDP.
    d. none of the above.

3. Which of the following countries has the highest per capita income?
    a. Malawi
    b. Niger
    c. Ireland
    d. Mexico

4. Which of the following countries had the highest growth rate of per capita GDP over the past 27 years?
    a. China
    b. Madagascar
    c. Haiti
    d. United States

5. Which of the following is true regarding the growth record of LDCs over the past 27 years?
    a. All have been growing rapidly.
    b. All have experienced negative growth rates.
    c. Some are among the highest growth countries, whereas others are among the lowest.
    d. None of the above.

6. A country that organizes economic activity in a manner consistent with personal choice, voluntary exchange coordinated by markets, freedom to enter and compete in markets, and protection of persons and their property from aggression by others is said to have a high degree of
    a. central planning.
    b. government regulation.
    c. collective choice.
    d. economic freedom.

7. Which of the following would contribute to a higher Economic Freedom of the World (EFW) rating for a country?
    a. low taxes
    b. rapid inflation
    c. high tariffs on imported goods
    d. government spending being a large share of the economy

8. According to the Economic Freedom of the World (EFW) rating, which of the following countries has the highest level of economic freedom?
    a. Myanmar
    b. Syria
    c. Hong Kong
    d. Mexico

9. According to the Economic Freedom of the World (EFW) rating, which of the following countries has the lowest level of economic freedom?
    a. Switzerland
    b. Singapore
    c. Germany
    d. Zimbabwe

10. Dividing a list of data into quartiles will result in how many groups?
    a. two
    b. four
    c. five
    d. twenty-five

11. Countries with higher levels of economic freedom tend to have
    a. higher rates of economic growth.
    b. higher levels of per person income.
    c. higher levels of investment.
    d. all of the above.

12. Which of the following is true regarding investment?
    a. Investment tends to have a larger impact on economic growth in countries with high levels of economic freedom because it is channeled to more productive uses.
    b. Countries who see large inflows of foreign direct investment tend to have negative rates of economic growth as the foreign companies mainly take profits and resources out of the country.
    c. Investment tends to be larger in countries with low levels of economic freedom because of the low wages present in these countries.
    d. None of the above.

13. Which of the following are examples of countries undertaking economic reforms that have increased economic freedom and resulted in better economic growth records?
    a. Hong Kong and Singapore in the 1960s
    b. China and Chile in the 1970s
    c. Ireland and New Zealand in the 1980s
    d. Estonia and Hungary in the 1990s
    e. All of the above.

14. Which of the following is important in the development of a large economy dominated by trade between parties who do not know each other (depersonalized exchange)?
    a. having few or minimal constitutional rules to avoid preventing the democratic institutions of a country from working to their fullest potential
    b. having a sound legal system that protects property and enforces contracts
    c. the presence of abundant natural resources
    d. heavy government regulation and control of prices so that individuals do not try to take advantage of one another in market exchange

15. Which of the following tends to make a country's political institutions more effective in promoting economic freedom?
    a. checks on the powers of the executive and legislative branches of government
    b. constitutional protections for economic rights such as private ownership of property, freedom to trade, and freedom to hold alternative currencies
    c. political decentralization so citizens can more easily escape from bad governments
    d. All of the above tend to promote political institutions that promote economic freedom.

16. Which of the following is one of the reasons to believe that institutional change is more likely now than in the past?
    a. Previously colonized countries are now in the position to make their own institutional and policy choices.
    b. The prevalence of communism is growing around the world.
    c. Increasing transportation and communication costs have weakened the importance of institutions and policies as there is less worldwide competition for investment.
    d. All of the above.

17. Since the mid-1980s, the overall Economic Freedom of the World (EFW) ratings of most countries have been increasing due to
    a. more stable monetary policies.
    b. lower tax rates.
    c. trade liberalization.
    d. All of the above.

18. (This question pertains to the material in the addendum to the chapter.) Countries with higher levels of economic freedom tend to have
    a. higher life expectancy and lower infant mortality.
    b. better environmental quality.
    c. better access to sanitary water and lower disease rates.
    d. All of the above.

DISCUSSION QUESTIONS

1. What are the key components of economic freedom? Indicate some of the policies that a country must follow to score high in the rankings of economic freedom.

2. What is the relationship between economic freedom and: (a) the level of a country's per person income, (b) the country's rate of economic growth, (c) the country's level and productivity of investment, (d) the quality of life in the country?

3. Through what channels does a country's legal system influence its economic performance? Does the importance of the legal system grow as markets expand and rely more heavily on depersonalized exchange?

4. Is democracy necessary for economic freedom? Why are constitutional constraints on democracy important? What are the most important constraints?

5. Which countries have undertaken major reforms to increase economic freedom over the past few decades and what has been their experience in terms of subsequent economic growth?

Gaining from International Trade

TRUE OR FALSE

T F

☐ ☐ 1. Economic theory suggests that free trade between two countries generally benefits only one country while the other is harmed.

☐ ☐ 2. Economic analysis shows that *every* individual within an economy gains from international free trade whenever it takes place.

☐ ☐ 3. The joint output of countries would be maximized if each country specialized in production of those commodities for which it is the low opportunity-cost producer, exchanging them for other commodities for which it is a high opportunity-cost producer.

☐ ☐ 4. In a sense, tariffs and quotas are identical in that they can be designed to produce the same exact outcome in terms of price and quantity of imports.

☐ ☐ 5. A secondary effect of policies that restrict imports is that they lower the demand for the nation's export products.

☐ ☐ 6. An import quota places a maximum limit on the amount of a product that can be imported during a specific time period.

☐ ☐ 7. A country that is rich in resources and an efficient producer will gain if it refuses to trade, although this action hurts the rest of the world.

☐ ☐ 8. Three popular arguments for imposing trade restrictions are to protect infant industries, to prevent dumping of goods below cost, and to keep in place certain industries essential for a country's national defense.

☐ ☐ 9. If all tariffs were removed in the United States, fewer jobs would be available to U.S. workers because wage rates are high in the United States.

T   F

☐   ☐   10.   The North American Free Trade Agreement (NAFTA) has caused widespread job losses in the United States and a large movement of U.S. companies to Mexico.

☐   ☐   11.   Canada, Japan, China, and Mexico are the major trading partners of the United States.

☐   ☐   12.   U.S. tariffs, in general, are much lower now than they were in 1930.

☐   ☐   13.   Because trade restrictions generate concentrated benefits to special interest groups at the expense of the general public, politicians find them attractive to implement.

PROBLEMS AND PROJECTS

1.   Use Exhibit 1 when answering the following questions.
   a.   In the space provided, plot the production possibilities curves for Lebos and Egap from the data given. Label the points in the graph with the corresponding letters and connect the points.
   b.   Lebos is currently producing at point C (80 units of food and 80 units of clothing) but wishes to expand its production of food to 120 units. What point would Lebos move to? How many units of food has Lebos gained? How many units of clothing has Lebos had to give up to free the extra resources to produce this additional food? Write your answers in equation form such as $xx\,F = xx\,C$ where $xx\,F$ represents the number of units of food gained and $xx\,C$ represents the number of units of clothing given up in your answers above.
   c.   Pick any two points (such as points A and B) for Egap. Between these two points, how many units of food are gained? How many units of clothing are given up? Write this in equation form similar to what you did in part b.
   d.   Take the equations you found above for each country and simplify them in terms of one unit of food. (Hint: As an example, for Lebos divide both sides by 40 to get $1F = 1C$.) These equations now represent the opportunity cost of producing one unit of food in each country in terms of how much clothing must be given up. From these new equations, which country has to give up the least amount of clothing to produce one unit of food? Note that this country has the comparative advantage in food (because it has the lowest opportunity cost of producing food). Now rewrite and simplify each equation in terms of one unit of clothing. Using this, which country has the comparative advantage in clothing?
   e.   For survival, Lebos needs to have 120 units of food and Egap needs 40. If these countries do not trade, how much clothing will the people of Lebos be able to produce and consume given the resources remaining after the required food is produced? Egap? Circle these points in the diagrams.
   f.   Suppose that Lebos and Egap agree to trade with each other at the rate of 1 unit of food for 2 units of clothing ($1F = 2C$). Lebos will specialize in producing all food and Egap all clothing. If Lebos produces only food, how much food can it produce? How many units of food will Lebos have left to trade after keeping 120 units for itself? Given the rate of exchange above, how many units of clothing will they acquire in trade from Egap for these extra units of food?
   g.   Carefully compare the amount of food and clothing Lebos has after specializing and trading with the amount it had when it was self-sufficient in part e. Is Lebos better off?
   h.   After Egap specializes in clothing and trades with Lebos, how much food will it have acquired in trade? How much clothing will it have left after trading for this food? Compare the amount of food and clothing Egap has after trade with the amount it had when it was self-sufficient in part e. Is Egap better off?

EXHIBIT 1

PRODUCTION POSSIBILITIES FOR LEBOS AND EGAP

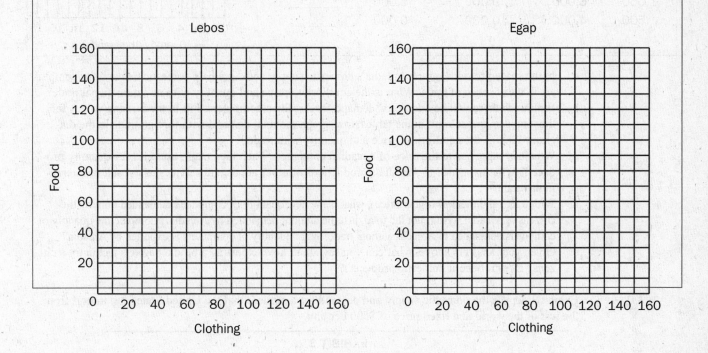

	LEBOS	
	FOOD	CLOTHING
A	0	160
B	40	120
C	80	80
D	120	40
E	160	0

	EGAP	
	FOOD	CLOTHING
A	0	120
B	10	90
C	20	60
D	30	30
E	40	0

Lebos

Egap

2. The country of Arcadia produces and consumes unique computers. Exhibit 2 shows Arcadia's demand and supply curves for their computers along with the demand for Arcadian computers from the rest of the world (ROW). The final column in the table is the total demand for Arcadia's computers from both domestic citizens and foreigners combined.

EXHIBIT 2

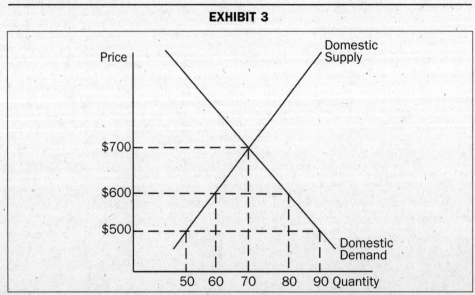

PRICE	ARCADIA'S QUANTITY SUPPLIED	ARCADIA'S QUANTITY DEMANDED	ROW'S QUANTITY DEMANDED	TOTAL QUANTITY DEMANDED
$3,000	14,000	5,000	1,000	6,000
2,500	12,000	6,000	2,000	_____
2,000	10,000	7,000	3,000	_____
1,500	8,000	8,000	4,000	_____
1,000	6,000	9,000	5,000	_____
500	4,000	10,000	6,000	_____

a. In the space provided, graph Arcadia's domestic supply and Arcadia's domestic demand for computers in the absence of trade. What is the equilibrium price and quantity with no international trade?

b. With trade there will be additional demand for Arcadian computers. Fill in the missing values for the total demand column in the table. Now, graph the total demand with foreign trade in the diagram. What is the equilibrium price and quantity with trade?

c. What has happened to the price of Arcadian computers when they begin to trade? the quantity produced? What happened to Arcadia's productions of other goods and services as a result of international trade?

d. With trade (and the new higher price), what is the new quantity of computers demanded only by the citizens of Arcadia? (Hint: not the total, just the amount demanded by Arcadia.) Compare the quantity of computers demanded in Arcadia without trade. What quantity of computers is exported by Arcadia?

e. Given your answers above, what can you say about how exporting a product affects a country's citizens? Does it benefit domestic producers?

3. Exhibit 3 depicts the domestic supply and demand for a product that the United States can import from the rest of the world at a fixed price of $500 per unit.

EXHIBIT 3

a. In the absence of international trade, what would be the price of this product in the United States? What quantities would be demanded and supplied?

b. Suppose this product can be imported into the United States without restriction at a price of $500. Draw a world supply curve in the diagram. (Hint: It is a horizontal line at the world price.) Show in the diagram the new price, quantity demanded, the total quantity supplied, the quantity domestically supplied, and the quantity imported with trade.

c. If a 20 percent tariff is imposed on the importation of the product, the price of the imported products will rise to $600. Show this new world supply with tariff in the diagram as a horizontal line at the new price with the tariff included. How will the price, amount demanded, the amount domestically produced, and the amount imported change as a result of the tariff?

d. Suppose that instead of the tariff of part c, government imposed a quota on imports of 20 units per year. How would the effects of this quota differ from the effects of the tariff on the price, quantity demanded, amount domestically supplied, and amount imported?

4. Consider the following hypothetical information about the United States and South Korea shown in Exhibit 4.

a. Which country has the absolute advantage in steel production? _____

EXHIBIT 4

OUTPUT PER WORKER PER DAY		
	UNITED STATES	SOUTH KOREA
Tons of steel	8	4
Bushels of wheat	80	8

absolute advantage in wheat production? _____
comparative advantage in steel production? _____
comparative advantage in wheat production? _____

b. If these countries trade steel and wheat with each other, which country will export steel and import wheat?

c. Suppose that the United States and South Korea agree to a daily trade of 10 tons of steel for 50 bushels of wheat. One worker in the United States then switches from steel production to wheat production. At the same time, four workers in South Korea switch from wheat production to steel. Complete the following table to show that both countries end up with more steel and more wheat than they had initially.

UNITED STATES	TONS OF STEEL	BUSHELS OF WHEAT
Change in production	−8	+80
Trade	+10	−50
Change in consumption	_____	_____

SOUTH KOREA	TONS OF STEEL	BUSHELS OF WHEAT
Change in production	_____	_____
Trade	_____	_____
Change in consumption	_____	_____

MULTIPLE CHOICE

1. A tariff or quota that limits the entry of foreign goods to the U.S. market will
   a. benefit domestic producers in the protected industries and harm domestic consumers.
   b. increase the nation's real income by protecting domestic jobs from foreign competition.
   c. reduce the demand for U.S. export goods, lowering employment in export industries.
   d. do both a and c.

2. According to the law of comparative advantage, a nation will benefit from international trade when it
   a. imports more than it exports.
   b. exports more than it imports.
   c. imports goods for which it is a high opportunity-cost producer, while exporting goods for which it is a low opportunity-cost producer.
   d. exports goods for which it is a high opportunity-cost producer, while importing those goods for which it is a low opportunity-cost producer.

Exhibit 5 outlines the production possibilities of Italia and Slavia for food and clothing. Use it to answer questions 3 through 6.

EXHIBIT 5

ITALIA		SLAVIA	
FOOD	CLOTHING	FOOD	CLOTHING
0	16	0	8
2	12	2	6
4	8	4	4
6	4	6	2
8	0	8	0

3. Italia is currently producing 4 units of food and 8 units of clothing. If it increases its production of food by 2 units (up to a total of 6 units of food), its clothing production will
   a. fall by 2 units.
   b. fall by 4 units.
   c. increase by 2 units.
   d. increase by 4 units.

4. What is the opportunity cost of producing 1 unit of food in Italia?
   a. one-half of a unit of clothing
   b. 1 unit of clothing
   c. 2 units of clothing
   d. 5 units of clothing

5. Which of the following is true?
   a. Italia has the comparative advantage in producing food.
   b. Italia has the comparative advantage in producing clothing.
   c. Slavia has the comparative advantage in producing clothing.
   d. Slavia is the low opportunity-cost producer of clothing.

6. The law of comparative advantage suggests that
   a. neither country would gain from trade.
   b. only Slavia would gain from trade; Italia would be harmed.
   c. both countries could gain if Italia traded food for Slavia's clothing.
   d. both countries could gain if Slavia traded food for Italia's clothing.

7. If the United States were to adopt a policy of free trade with European countries and Japan, this policy would
   a. help the United States and hurt the other countries because the United States has a larger population.
   b. help all of the countries involved because every country would have a comparative advantage in the production of some good.
   c. hurt the United States and help the other countries involved because job opportunities in the United States would fall while they rose in other countries.
   d. help the United States and hurt the other countries because the United States has more natural resources than the other countries.

8. The theory of comparative advantage suggests that nations should produce a good if they
   a. have the lowest opportunity cost.
   b. have the lowest wages.
   c. have the most resources.
   d. can produce more of the good than any other nation.

9. A tariff differs from a quota in that a tariff is
   a. levied on imports, whereas a quota is imposed on exports.
   b. levied on exports, whereas a quota is imposed on imports.
   c. a tax levied on exports, whereas a quota is a limit on the number of units of a good that can be exported.
   d. a tax imposed on imports, whereas a quota is an absolute limit to the number of units of a good that can be imported.

10. An import quota on a product protects domestic industries by
    a. reducing the foreign supply to the domestic market and thereby raising the domestic price.
    b. increasing the foreign supply to the domestic market and thereby lowering the domestic price.
    c. increasing the domestic demand for the product and thereby increasing its price.
    d. providing the incentive for domestic producers to improve the efficiency of their operation and thereby reduce their per-unit costs of production.

11. Which of the following would be the most likely long-run effect if the United States increased its tariff rates and adopted stricter import quotas?
    a. a decrease in both U.S. imports and exports
    b. an increase in both U.S. imports and exports
    c. a decrease in U.S. imports and an increase in U.S. exports
    d. an increase in U.S. imports and a decrease in U.S. exports

12. Trade restrictions that limit the sale of low-price foreign goods in the U.S. market
    a. increase the real income of Americans.
    b. benefit domestic producers in the protected industries at the expense of consumers and domestic producers in export industries.
    c. help channel more of our resources into producing goods for which we are a low-cost producer.
    d. reduce unemployment and increase the productivity of American workers.

13. A basic flaw in the infant-industry argument is that
    a. most industries need protection when they are mature, not when they are first established.
    b. the amount of the tariff is unlikely to have much impact on the success of an infant industry.
    c. once a tariff is granted, political pressure will likely prevent the withdrawal of the tariff even when the industry matures.
    d. domestic consumers will continue to buy the foreign products anyway, regardless of the tariff.

14. Countries that impose high tariffs, exchange rate controls, and other barriers that restrict international trade have, on average,
    a. high rates of economic growth.
    b. low rates of economic growth.
    c. a large export sector.
    d. a large import sector.

15. If the United States imports low-cost goods produced in low-wage countries instead of producing the goods domestically,
    a. the United States will lose jobs.
    b. the United States will gain and domestic resources will be employed more productively.
    c. dollars that leave the United States will not return to buy goods produced by high-wage American workers.
    d. the availability consumption of goods in the United States will be reduced.

16. Suppose that the United States eliminated its tariff on automobiles, granting foreign-produced automobiles free entry into the U.S. market. Which of the following would be most likely to occur?
    a. The price of automobiles to U.S. consumers would decline, and the demand for U.S. export products would increase.
    b. The price of automobiles to U.S. consumers would increase, and the demand for U.S. export products would decline.
    c. The price of automobiles to U.S. consumers would decline, and the demand for U.S. export products would decline.
    d. The price of automobiles to U.S. consumers would increase, and the demand for U.S. export products would increase.

17. If Japan offered every U.S. citizen a new automobile for a price of only $1,
    a. the action would be considered "dumping."
    b. domestic automobile manufacturers and workers would likely favor imposing tariffs or quotas to restrict this action.
    c. domestic citizens would benefit from this action by Japan.
    d. all of the above are true.

18. Relative to a no-trade situation, what effect will importing a good from foreign nations have on the domestic market for the good?
    a. Equilibrium price will rise and total domestically produced output will fall.
    b. Equilibrium price will rise and total domestically produced output will rise.
    c. Equilibrium price will fall and total domestically produced output will fall.
    d. Equilibrium price will fall and total domestically produced output will rise.

19. Relative to a no-trade situation, what effect will exporting a good to foreign nations have on the domestic market for the good?
    a. Equilibrium price will rise, domestic production will fall, and domestic consumption will fall.
    b. Equilibrium price will rise, domestic production will rise, and domestic consumption will fall.
    c. Equilibrium price will fall, domestic production will fall, and domestic consumption will increase.
    d. Equilibrium price will fall, domestic production will rise, and domestic consumption will increase.

20. If all tariffs (and quotas) between countries on the North American continent were eliminated,
    a. small Central American countries would be hurt because they would be unable to compete with larger nations.
    b. the United States would gain at the expense of the less-developed North American countries.
    c. the combined wealth of the countries would increase because elimination of trade restrictions would permit greater gains from specialization.
    d. wage rates in the United States would decline to the average for the North American continent.

21. Which of the following is not an argument for adopting trade restrictions on imported goods?
    a. antidumping argument
    b. national-defense argument
    c. consumer-protection argument
    d. infant-industry argument

Questions 22 through 25 refer to Exhibit 6, which shows the effect of a country imposing a tariff on an imported product.

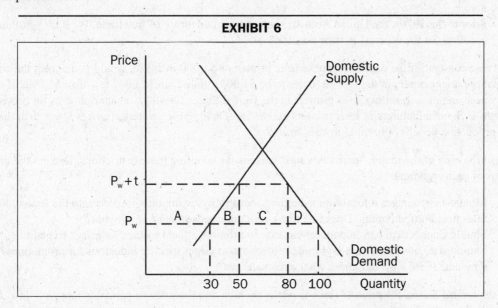

EXHIBIT 6

22. If the world price of this good is P_W and there are no restrictions on imports, domestic suppliers will produce ____ units, domestic demanders will consume ____ units, and total imports will be ____ units. (Fill in the blanks.)
    a. 30; 100; 70
    b. 50; 100; 50
    c. 30; 80; 80
    d. 100; 70; 30

23. Suppose that a tariff of t is imposed upon this good, raising the price to $P_W + t$. As a result,
    a. imports will fall to 30.
    b. domestic production will increase to 50.
    c. domestic consumption will fall to 80.
    d. all of the above are true.

24. Given the tariff described in the question above,
    a. the combined areas $A + B + C + D$ represent the losses to domestic consumers from the tariff.
    b. area C represents the government's revenue from the tariff.
    c. area A represents the gain to domestic suppliers from the tariff.
    d. all of the above are true.

25. The same price and quantity outcomes under the tariff above could have also been produced by the imposition of a quota of
    a. 30 units.
    b. 50 units.
    c. 80 units.
    d. No quota can produce the same price and quantity outcomes.

DISCUSSION QUESTIONS

1. "We are not opposed to competition when it does not destroy jobs. But last year, while many American auto workers were idle, we exported a million jobs to foreigners by importing automobiles that could have been produced by domestic workers. An increase in the tariff on automobiles would strengthen our economy, provide jobs, and improve our standard of living." [Auto Workers' Union official]
   a. Do you agree that higher automobile tariffs would "provide jobs"? Why or why not?
   b. Do you agree that higher automobile tariffs would "improve our standard of living"? Why or why not?
   c. Prior to the 1970s, the United Auto Workers were an advocate of free trade. What do you think accounts for the reversal in their position?

2. All else constant, if the cost of Japanese laser printers is $1,000 in Japan, would you expect the cost of Japanese laser printers in the United States to be $1,000? more than $1,000? less than $1,000? If the Japanese are, in fact, selling laser printers in the United States for $800, what arguments for protection might U.S. manufacturers of laser printers make? Does selling the printers at prices lower than the cost of production benefit or harm U.S. consumers?

3. Describe each of the major, "partially valid" reasons for adopting trade restrictions. Discuss the pros and cons of each argument.

4. a. Montana encourages a local liquor-bottling industry by taxing bulk imports into the state at lower rates than bottled liquors. Does this make economic sense? Why or why not?
   b. Should Connecticut ban imports of bananas to promote a local banana industry? Explain.
   c. Should state governments adopt trade restrictions to target specific industries for promotions? If not, why not? If so, why and under what circumstances?

5. In the United States, the price of labor is relatively high and the price of capital is relatively low. In developing countries, the reverse is true.
   a. Based on these resource market conditions, what types of products would you expect the United States to import from developing countries? to export to them?
   b. Most U.S. trade is with other industrial high-wage nations. In light of the law of comparative advantage, is this surprising? If not, why not? If so, why and how can you account for this aspect of U.S. trade?

PERSPECTIVES IN ECONOMICS

The Economic Case for Free Trade

by Milton and Rose Friedman
[Reprinted with permission from Chapter 2 of *Free to Choose* (New York: Harcourt Brace Jovanovich, 1980) Abridged.]

Today, as always, there is much support for tariffs—euphemistically labeled "protection," a good label for a bad cause. Producers of steel and steelworkers' unions press for restrictions on steel imports from Japan. Producers of TV sets and their workers lobby for "voluntary agreements" to limit imports of TV sets or components from Japan, Taiwan, or Hong Kong. Producers of textiles, shoes, cattle, sugar—they and myriad others complain about "unfair" competition from abroad and demand that government do something to "protect" them. Of

course, no group makes its claim on the basis of naked self-interest. Every group speaks of the "general interest," of the need to preserve jobs or to promote national security.

One voice that is hardly ever raised is the consumer's. The individual consumer's voice is drowned out in the cacophony of the "interested sophistry of merchants and manufacturers" and their employees. The result is a serious distortion of the issue. For example, the supporters of tariffs treat it as self-evident that the creation of jobs is a desirable end, in and of itself, regardless of what the persons employed do. That is clearly wrong. If all we want are jobs, we can create any number—for example, have people dig holes and then fill them up again, or perform other useless tasks. Work is sometimes its own reward. Mostly, however, it is the price we pay to get the things we want. Our real objective is not just jobs but productive jobs—jobs that will mean more goods and services to consume.

Another fallacy seldom contradicted is that exports are good, imports bad. The truth is very different. We cannot eat, wear, or enjoy the goods we send abroad. We eat bananas from Central America, wear Italian shoes, drive German automobiles, and enjoy programs we see on our Japanese TV sets. Our gain from foreign trade is what we import. Exports are the price we pay to get imports. As Adam Smith saw so clearly, the citizens of a nation benefit from getting as large a volume of imports as possible in return for its exports, or equivalently, from exporting as little as possible to pay for its imports.

The misleading terminology we use reflects these errone-ous ideas. "Protection" really means exploiting the consumer. A "favorable balance of trade" really means exporting more than we import, sending abroad goods of greater total value than the goods we get from abroad. In your private household, you would surely prefer to pay less for more rather than the other way around, yet that would be termed an "unfavorable balance of payments" in foreign trade.

The argument in favor of tariffs that has the greatest emotional appeal to the public at large is the alleged need to protect the high standard of living of American workers from the "unfair" competition of workers in Japan or Korea or Hong Kong who are willing to work for a much lower wage. What is wrong with this argument? Don't we want to protect the high standard of living of our people?

The fallacy in this argument is the loose use of the terms "high" wage and "low" wage. What do high and low wages mean? American workers are paid in dollars; Japanese work-ers are paid in yen. How do we compare wages in dollars with wages in yen? How many yen equal a dollar? What determines that exchange rate?

It is simply not true that high-wage American workers are, as a group, threatened by "unfair" competition from low-wage foreign workers. Of course, particular workers may be harmed if a new or improved product is developed abroad, or if for-eign producers become able to produce such products more cheaply. But that is no different from the effect on a particular group of workers of other American firms, developing new or improved products or discovering how to produce at lower costs. That is simply market competition in practice, the major source of the high standard of life of the American worker. If we want to benefit from a vital, dynamic, innovative economic system, we must accept the need for mobility and adjustment. It may be desirable to ease these adjustments, and we have adopted many arrangements, such as unemployment insur-ance, to do so, but we should try to achieve that objective without destroying the flexibility of the system—that would be to kill the goose that has been laying the golden eggs. In any event, whatever we do should be evenhanded with respect to foreign and domestic trade.

What determines the items it pays us to import and to export? An American worker is currently more productive than a Japanese worker. It is hard to determine just how much more productive—estimates differ. But suppose he is one and a half times as productive. Then, on average, the American's wages would buy about one and half times as much as a Japanese worker's wages. It is wasteful to use American workers to do anything at which they are less than one and a half times as efficient as their Japanese counterparts. In the economic jargon coined more than 150 years ago, that is the principle of comparative advantage. Even if we were more efficient than the Japanese at producing everything, it would not pay us to produce everything. We should concentrate on doing those things we do best, those things where our superiority is the greatest.

Another source of "unfair competition" is said to be sub-sidies by foreign governments to their producers that enable them to sell in the United States below cost. Suppose a for-eign government gives such subsidies, as no doubt some do. Who is hurt and who benefits? To pay for the subsidies the foreign government must tax its citizens. They are the ones who pay for the subsidies. U.S. consumers benefit. They get cheap TV sets or automobiles or whatever it is that is subsi-dized. Should we complain about such a program of reverse foreign aid? Was it noble of the United States to send goods and services as gifts to other countries in the form of Marshall Plan aid or, later, foreign aid, but ignoble for foreign countries to send us gifts in the indirect form of goods and services sold to us below cost? The citizens of the foreign government might well complain. They must suffer a lower standard of living for the benefit of American consumers and of some of their fel-low citizens who own or work in the industries that are subsi-dized. No doubt, if such subsidies are introduced suddenly or erratically, that will adversely affect owners and workers in U.S. industries producing the same products. However, that is one of the ordinary risks of doing business. Enterprises never com-plain about unusual or accidental events that confer windfall gains. The free enterprise system is a profit and loss system. As already noted, any measures to ease the adjustment to sudden changes should be applied evenhandedly to domestic and foreign trade.

We are a great nation, the leader of the free world. It ill behooves us to require Hong Kong and Taiwan to impose export quotas on textiles to "protect" our textile industry at the expense of U.S. consumers and of Chinese workers in Hong Kong and Taiwan. We speak glowingly of the virtues of free trade, while we use our political and economic power to induce Japan to restrict exports of steel and TV sets. We should move unilaterally to free trade, not instantaneously, but over a period of, say, five years, at a pace announced in advance.

Few measures that we could take would do more to promote the cause of freedom at home and abroad than complete free trade. Instead of making grants to foreign governments in the name of economic aid—thereby promot-ing socialism—while at the same time imposing restric-tions on the products they produce—thereby hindering free enterprise—we could assume a consistent and principled stance. We could say to the rest of the world: we believe in freedom and intend to practice it. We cannot force you to be free. But we can offer full cooperation on equal terms to all. Our market is open to you without tariffs or other restrictions. Sell here what you can and wish to. Buy whatever you can and wish to. In that way cooperation among individuals can be worldwide and free.

DISCUSSION

1. When a politician speaks out in favor of protectionism against imports, how do you react? Is this debate a question of economic theory against political reality, or are there political and economic arguments on both sides? Explain.

2. As you read the article, you were probably impressed with the superb logic and internal consistency with which the Friedmans write. If you were going to attempt to refute their arguments, where would you start? Are there any major assumptions you could question? Are there secondary effects that they neglect to analyze? Explain.

3. The article points out that the harm done to consumers by restricting trade is usually ignored. Why do you think this is the case? Generally, even people who are "pro-consumer/antibusiness" are in favor of restricting imports, when economic theory tells us that it only helps producers while harming individual consumers. Can you explain this apparent contradiction?

International Finance and the Foreign Exchange Market

CHAPTER 19

TRUE OR FALSE

T F

☐ ☐ 1. Foreign exchange markets enable individuals to exchange the currency of one nation for the currency of another nation.

☐ ☐ 2. A nation's exports generate a demand for the currency of the exporting nation on the foreign exchange market.

☐ ☐ 3. Under a system of fixed exchange rates, a balance-of-payments equilibrium is automatic.

☐ ☐ 4. Under a system of flexible exchange rates, the government must use monetary policy to ensure a balance-of-payments equilibrium.

☐ ☐ 5. The economic analysis of foreign trade is unique in that supply-and-demand relationships do not usually determine equilibrium.

☐ ☐ 6. One problem with a system of flexible exchange rates is that black markets in foreign currencies are more likely to develop than with controlled rates of exchange.

☐ ☐ 7. When a country's balance of trade registers a deficit, both its current and capital accounts will also be in deficit.

☐ ☐ 8. If foreigners suddenly began investing more in the United States, causing the capital account to run a larger surplus, the current account deficit would rise.

☐ ☐ 9. If imports consistently exceeded exports, U.S. consumers would be hurt as a result of an unfavorable balance of trade implied by such a situation.

☐ ☐ 10. If the current exchange rate is one dollar equals three Mexican pesos, the cost of purchasing a 60 peso product in dollars is $20.

T F

☐ ☐ 11. An increase in foreign demand for products made in the United States would cause the dollar to appreciate.

☐ ☐ 12. A depreciation of the U.S. dollar would make U.S. products more expensive to foreigners, thus causing U.S. exports to decline.

☐ ☐ 13. Bilateral trade between countries should be balanced. If other countries are treating us fairly, our exports to them should be approximately equal to our imports from them.

PROBLEMS AND PROJECTS

1. Exhibit 1 shows the exchange rate values of several major world currencies relative to the U.S. dollar as they were on October 23, 2009. The first column shows the number of units of the foreign currency that could be obtained by trading in one U.S. dollar. The second column shows the number of U.S. dollars that could be obtained by trading in one unit of the foreign currency. (Note: These are simply the reciprocals of the data in the first column.)

EXHIBIT 1

FOREIGN CURRENCY	UNITS OF FOREIGN CURRENCY PER U.S. DOLLAR	U.S. DOLLARS PER UNIT OF FOREIGN CURRENCY
English pound	0.611	1.6376
European euro	0.666	1.5020
Canadian dollar	1.052	0.9502
Mexican peso	12.900	0.0775
Japanese yen	91.88	0.0109

a. If a Mexican citizen wished to purchase a Ford automobile costing 30,000 U.S. dollars, how much would it cost in Mexican pesos?

b. If a U.S. citizen wished to purchase a bottle of French wine costing 80 euros, how much would it cost in U.S. dollars?

c. If a Canadian citizen wished to purchase a Japanese automobile costing 2,500,000 Japanese yen, how much would it cost in Canadian dollars? (Hint: With the data given, you must first convert from Japanese yen to U.S. dollars, then convert U.S. dollars to Canadian dollars.)

d. To carry out the transaction in part c, a Canadian citizen could either convert Canadian dollars to U.S. dollars, then U.S. dollars to yen, or she could simply convert Canadian dollars directly to yen. From the data above, what would you expect the exchange rate to be between the Canadian dollar and the yen?

e. In March 2000, one euro was equal to 0.9645 U.S. dollars, one Japanese yen was equal to 0.0093 U.S. dollars, and one Mexican peso was equal to 0.1089 U.S. dollars. Compare these values to the ones in Exhibit 1 and decide whether each of these currencies has either appreciated or depreciated over this period relative to the U.S. dollar.

2. Each of the diagrams below represents the U.S. demand for and supply of foreign exchange, here the English pound. For each of the events described below, diagram how the demand and/or supply of English pounds changes (use +, −, or 0 to show no change). Then fill in the blanks to the right of the diagram, indicating in the last blank whether the English pound has appreciated, depreciated, or undergone an indeterminate change as a result of the event(s). The first question has been answered as an example, and in the diagrams, price (P) is in dollars per English pound.

EVENTS	DIAGRAMS	D	S	CHANGE

a. As a result of recovering from a depression, U.S. incomes rise significantly.

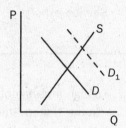

<u> + </u> <u> 0 </u> <u>depreciated</u>

b. The United Kingdom experiences a serious recession, causing a decline in income.

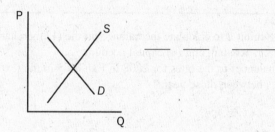

____ ____ _____

c. Restrictive monetary policy in the United States causes U.S. interest rates to rise relative to United Kingdom rates.

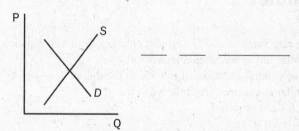

____ ____ _____

d. While the United States experiences stable price, prices in the United Kingdom rise by 15 percent.

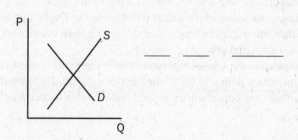

____ ____ _____

e. Both the United States and the United Kingdom experience inflation rates of 20 percent.

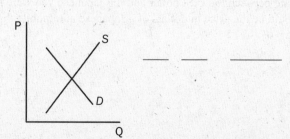

____ ____ _____

3. Exhibit 2 presents balance-of-payment data for the United States for 1980.

EXHIBIT 2

DEBIT		CREDIT	
	(BILLIONS OF DOLLARS)		
CURRENT ACCOUNT			
Merchandise imports	249.3	Merchandise exports	224.0
Service imports	84.6	Service exports	120.7
Net unilateral transfers	7.1		
CAPITAL ACCOUNT			
U.S. investment abroad	18.5	Foreign investment	
Loans to foreigners	58.1	in the United States	10.9
		Loans from foreigners	70.2

a. Use the data in Exhibit 2 to calculate the balance on the (1) merchandise trade account, (2) services account, (3) current account, and (4) capital account.

b. Compare these balances to the ones for 2008 in Exhibit 5 in the text. What happened to U.S. international balances between those years?

MULTIPLE CHOICE

1. If the exchange rate value of one U.S. dollar changes from 120 Japanese yen to 140 yen,
   a. the U.S. dollar has appreciated relative to the yen.
   b. the Japanese yen has depreciated relative to the dollar.
   c. the U.S. dollar has depreciated relative to the yen.
   d. both a and b have occurred.

2. Under a flexible exchange rate system, which of the following will be most likely to cause a depreciation in the exchange rate value of the dollar (relative to the English pound)?
   a. An economic boom occurs in England, inducing English consumers to buy more American-made automobiles, trucks, and computer products.
   b. Real interest rates in the United States fall lower than real interest rates in England.
   c. Restrictive monetary policy in the United States causes inflation to be lower than in England.
   d. Attractive investment opportunities in the United States induce English investors to buy stock in U.S. firms.

3. If the exchange rate between the U.S. dollar and the Japanese yen were such that one U.S. dollar equals 100 yen, what would be the price in dollars of a Japanese automobile that cost 2,000,000 yen?
   a. $100
   b. $20,000
   c. $120,000
   d. $2,000,000

4. Other things constant, which of the following will most likely cause the dollar to appreciate on the exchange rate market?
    a. higher interest rates in the United States
    b. a relatively low rate of inflation in the United States
    c. high rates of income growth in Europe
    d. all of the above

5. If the U.S. dollar depreciates, then U.S. exports become _____ expensive to foreigners and foreign goods become _____ expensive to U.S. citizens. (Fill in the blanks.)
    a. less; less
    b. less; more
    c. more; less
    d. more; more

6. An increase in the dollar price of the Mexican peso (an appreciation of the peso) would cause
    a. Mexico's imports to increase and exports to decline.
    b. Mexico's exports to increase and imports to decline.
    c. both Mexico's imports and exports to decline.
    d. both Mexico's imports and exports to rise.

7. Under a pure flexible exchange rate system, the rate that equates demand and supply in the exchange rate market will also lead to a balance of
    a. merchandise exports and merchandise imports.
    b. current account transactions.
    c. capital account transactions.
    d. current and capital account transactions.

8. If the value of a nation's merchandise imports exceeds merchandise exports, the nation is running a
    a. balance of payments deficit.
    b. balance of payments surplus.
    c. merchandise trade deficit.
    d. merchandise trade surplus.

9. Which one of the following would supply dollars to the foreign exchange market?
    a. the spending of U.S. tourists in Europe
    b. the purchase of U.S. automobiles by Japanese consumers
    c. the sale of U.S. automobiles to European consumers
    d. the purchase of an American electronics factory by a Japanese investor

10. During recent times, the United States has been running a trade deficit (our exports of goods and services have been less than our imports of goods and services). Which of the following is true regarding these trade deficits?
    a. They were primarily caused by rapid economic growth in the United States stimulating imports and also the attractiveness of the United States as a place to invest causing a capital inflow.
    b. These trade deficits put the United States in debt to foreign economies and thus weaken future economic conditions in the United States.
    c. These trade deficits are evidence that other countries practice unfair trade against the United States because under fair trade exports equal imports to another country.
    d. None of the above are true regarding the trade deficits of the United States.

11. (I) The U.S. trade deficit is a financial obligation of the federal government, and if it is not paid off, foreigners will be reluctant to loan money to the U.S. government. (II) When a nation runs a current account deficit due to a merchandise trade deficit, it must also be true that the nation has a surplus on its capital account due to an inflow of foreign capital.
    a.   I is true; II is false.
    b.   I is false; II is true.
    c.   Both I and II are true.
    d.   Both I and II are false.

12. For a country to successfully maintain a fixed exchange rate value of its currency relative to another currency (for example, as is done when currencies are unified or pegged), it must
    a.   maintain a relatively high rate of inflation.
    b.   balance the government budget each year.
    c.   give up the independence of its monetary policy.
    d.   run a trade deficit.

13. An appreciation in the value of the U.S. dollar would
    a.   encourage foreigners to make more investments in the United States.
    b.   encourage U.S. consumers to purchase more foreign-produced goods.
    c.   increase the number of dollars that could be purchased with the euro.
    d.   discourage U.S. consumers from traveling abroad.

14. Which of the following would be likely to cause a nation's currency to depreciate?
    a.   an increase in foreign demand for the nation's products
    b.   a lower domestic rate of inflation than that of the nation's trading partners
    c.   higher domestic interest rates
    d.   higher foreign interest rates

15. Under a system of flexible exchange rates, transactions that increase the supply of the nation's currency to the foreign exchange market will cause the nation's
    a.   currency to depreciate in value.
    b.   currency to appreciate in value.
    c.   trade deficit to increase.
    d.   products to become more expensive to foreigners.

16. With time, a depreciation in the value of a nation's currency in the foreign market will cause the nation's
    a.   imports to increase and exports to decline.
    b.   exports to increase and imports to decline.
    c.   imports and exports to decline.
    d.   imports and exports to rise.

17. "Wine experts are discovering that California wines of several varieties and vintages are comparable to many of the best French wines. The result is an increased demand, here and abroad, for California wines." With regard to the U.S. balance on current account, this trend will
    a.   increase the U.S. deficit because of the rise in the price of California wine.
    b.   decrease the U.S. deficit because of increased shipments of California wines abroad.
    c.   decrease the demand for U.S. dollars.
    d.   increase the U.S. demand for euros.

18. If the value of a country's merchandise exports is less than the value of its merchandise imports, it is said to have a
    a.   trade surplus.
    b.   trade deficit.
    c.   current account surplus.
    d.   capital account deficit.

19. Under a system of flexible exchange rates, which of the following will cause the nation's currency to depreciate in the exchange market?
    a. an increase in foreign incomes
    b. a domestic inflation rate of 10 percent while the nation's trading partners are experiencing stable prices
    c. an increase in domestic interest rates
    d. a reduction in interest rates abroad

20. Which of the following identities regarding the balance of payments must be true?
    a. Current-Account Balance + Capital Account Balance + Official Reserve Balance = 0
    b. Current-Account Balance + Capital Account Balance + Official Reserve Balance = 1
    c. Current-Account Balance + Capital Account Balance + Merchandise Imports = 0
    d. Current-Account Balance + Capital Account Balance + Net Financial Inflow = 0

DISCUSSION QUESTIONS

1. "Exports pay for a nation's imports. Other countries will not continue shipping us their goods if they lose interest in the goods, services, and financial assets we export to them in exchange." Do you agree? Explain.

2. "No patriotic American wants the value of the dollar to fall on the foreign exchange market." Whether or not this quote is true, it is fair to say that Americans seem to like a strong dollar and a trade surplus.
    a. What are the advantages of a strong dollar? the disadvantages?
    b. What are the advantages of a trade surplus? the disadvantages?
    c. Why is it difficult to have both a strong dollar and a trade surplus at the same time?

3. In today's world of flexible exchange rates and mobile financial assets, a country's domestic macroeconomic policies and its foreign sector are closely interrelated. Economists focus especially on the interaction among domestic policies, interest rates, exchange rates, and international capital flows.
    a. How can a budget deficit contribute to capital inflows and an offsetting current account deficit?
    b. With flexible exchange rates, why does trade protection tend to be ineffective as a cure for a current account deficit?
    c. Some economists have recommended that a tax be imposed on international capital flows to reduce their volume. Would you favor such a tax? Why or why not?

4. "A nation's balance of payments must always be in balance." In what sense is this true? What is a "balance-of-payments deficit"? Under a flexible exchange system, will a balance-of-payments deficit automatically be corrected? Explain.

5. "A system of flexible exchange rates is advantageous because it enables a nation to stabilize domestic employment and prices without regard to the foreign sector and insulates a country from the effects of foreign macroeconomic policies." Do you agree or disagree? Explain.

6. Discuss the role of time in balance-of-payments adjustments. Why might the current account of a country with a depreciating currency deteriorate in the short run and improve in the long run? Why would the opposite scenario for the capital account be surprising?

PERSPECTIVES IN ECONOMICS

Don't Worry about the Trade Deficit

by Herbert Stein
[From *The Wall Street Journal,* May 16, 1989. Reprinted with permission from *The Wall Street Journal.* Copyright © Dow Jones & Co., Inc. All Rights Reserved.]

There seems to be a conspiracy against telling even the simplest truth.

This somber thought was brought home to me by an experience on a recent Tuesday afternoon. I'm goofing off, staying at home and watching daytime TV. I have a choice of 16 channels. On 15 of them beautiful women and handsome men are working out the complications of their love-lives, mostly in hospital rooms. I know that at my age I cannot expect any of these complications to be resolved during my lifetime, so I settle for C-SPAN and the U.S. Senate at "work."

I'm hearing a senator carrying on about how terrible it is that other countries insist on selling us more stuff than they buy from us. He demands that we let these countries know in no uncertain terms that we are not going to put up with that kind of thing any longer.

Excuses for Economists. At first I am shocked. Is there no limit to what can be put over the air, even in the daytime when children may be listening? But then I get over it and become more philosophical. I know that this senator has an undergraduate degree from one of our leading liberal arts colleges and another degree from one of our most eminent law schools. He is, however, a senator and may be forgiven for committing nonsense on the public airwaves.

But what about the trained staffs of international financial institutions who write serious reports about the need to correct "imbalances"—which is polite language for eliminating or reducing the U.S. trade deficit? What about the finance ministers from the industrial countries who meet every six months or so to cook up plans for correcting these "imbalances"—again meaning the U.S. trade deficit? And what about my sophisticated economist friends who talk about the need to eliminate the trade deficit? What are they all talking about?

I say to my economist friends that the trade deficit is not hurting the U.S., but, on the contrary, is helping us, and I ask them why we should be concerned about reducing the trade deficit. The more candid among them answer as follows: "We know that the trade deficit is not hurting us. But there are a lot of people out there—including presidents, senators, and congressmen—who think that the trade deficit is a bad thing and as long as it persists they will feel driven to protectionist measures, which would be very bad. In order to restrain the protectionist movement the trade deficit must be reduced."

What this comes down to is an argument for reducing the budget deficit as a way to reduce the trade deficit and thereby head off protectionism, even though we all know that the trade deficit is not hurting us and does not constitute a valid reason for protectionism.

Readers of this page may know that I am more willing than most people to pay more taxes and give up some of my Social Security and Medicare benefits in order to balance the federal budget and run a surplus. There are good reasons for wanting to do that. But I would hate to pay anything in the hope of thereby heading off protectionism.

Some people have good reason to be protectionist; they have immediate interests at stake. No economist, however much devoted to free trade, ever denied that. These "knowing" protectionists will not be dissuaded by seeing the trade deficit disappear. But most people have no good reason to be protectionist. They support or tolerate protectionism out of ignorance. There should be a more efficient way to convert them to the virtues of free trade than by eliminating the trade deficit. Or, to put the case more modestly, it is worth trying to convert them by telling the truth. That is what economists are for. If some more "devious" ways of avoiding protectionism have to be found, let some one else do it.

Let's remember a few simple propositions.

1. The U.S. has a trade deficit because people in the rest of the world invest their savings here. This inflow of capital is voluntary on both sides—foreigners are seeking the best place to put their money and American governments and companies are seeking the best place to obtain money. Foreigners seeking to invest here have to obtain dollars. Their demand for dollars keep the exchange rate of the dollar at a level where U.S. imports exceed U.S. exports.
2. As a result of the capital inflow—and the accompanying trade deficit—over the past eight years, the stock of productive capital in the U.S. is now about $700 billion higher than it would otherwise have been. This fact is commonly misunderstood because people think the capital inflow is financing the budget deficit. It is true that foreigners have bought a large amount of U.S. Treasury securities. But if foreigners had not bought them they would have had to be bought by Americans, who would have had less of their own savings to invest in productive assets.
3. This inflow of capital has been mainly of benefit to American workers, who as a result of it, work with a larger capital stock and have higher productivity and real incomes. It has also increased the U.S. tax base.
4. Large and persistent trade deficits have not prevented an unusually long recovery and the achievement of an unusually high level of total output.
5. Continuation of the capital inflow-trade deficit combination will increase the amount of interest and dividends that American governments and corporations have to pay to foreigners. But it will also increase the amount of capital in this country that would not otherwise be here, and that additional capital will generate the income to pay for foreigners. That income will not come out of income that Americans would otherwise have earned.
6. The inflow of capital and ownership of assets in the U.S. by foreigners is not a cause of dangerous dependence that is a political or security danger to us. What may

be politically dangerous is the effort of governments to manipulate this relationship—an effort to which we are the leaders, unfortunately.

7. The inflow of goods and capital may not go on forever, but it is unlikely to stop so abruptly as to create difficulties for us. The two-sided inflow is an adaptation to basic conditions—propensities to save and investment opportunities at home and abroad—that will change only gradually. The most serious qualification is that government efforts to manage exchange rates may cause such great uncertainties about the future of those rates that international capital flows dry up for a time.

Exchange Rates Everything

8. Protectionist measures imposed by government, ours and others, impair efficiency but do not cause the trade deficit. Trying to eliminate these measures would be worthwhile whether we have a deficit or a surplus, but success would not change the deficit.

9. Having a trade deficit is not a sign of low productivity or economy weakness. Poor, weak countries—like Brazil—can have trade surpluses. Rich, strong countries like us can have trade deficits. Everything depends on prices and exchange rates.

10. Let's forget about the trade deficit. We have plenty of real deficits to worry about—including the education deficit, the defense deficit, the poverty deficit and the investment deficit.

DISCUSSION

1. Do you agree with Stein? Should we worry about the trade deficit? Why or why not?

2. If Stein is right that "rich, strong countries like us can have trade deficits," then why are Congress and the media so concerned with avoiding the current U.S. trade deficit?

3. If the trade deficit isn't hurting the United States but policy makers think it is and are considering protectionist policies that will hurt the country, which would be easier, fixing the trade deficit or educating the policy makers? Explain your reasoning.

Consumer Choice and Elasticity

CHAPTER 20

TRUE OR FALSE

T F

☐ ☐   1. When the demand for a product is unitary elastic, a price change will not affect total revenue (expenditures).

☐ ☐   2. If the price elasticity of demand is equal to one, demand is considered unitary elastic.

☐ ☐   3. The law of diminishing marginal utility suggests that you would value the third milkshake on a given day less than the second.

☐ ☐   4. The market demand curve is a horizontal summation of the demand curves of all individuals in the market.

☐ ☐   5. Economic theory suggests that when deciding whether to buy a $25 shirt, you will consider the value you get from the shirt relative to the value of the other items that you could buy with the $25.

☐ ☐   6. Consumer surplus is generally equal to the price paid for an item.

☐ ☐   7. The income and substitution effects are the two effects leading consumers to change their consumption of a good when its price changes.

☐ ☐   8. If a university faces an elastic demand for enrollment and lowers its tuition (price), the university's total tuition revenue will decrease.

☐ ☐   9. Because income is limited due to scarcity, when consumers use some of their income to purchase goods, they give up the use of that income to purchase other goods.

T F

☐ ☐ 10. Generally, the marginal benefit derived from a good increases with the rate of consumption.

☐ ☐ 11. If a 10 percent increase in price leads to a 20 percent decline in quantity sold, demand is considered inelastic.

☐ ☐ 12. The opportunity cost of time is an important factor in consumer decisions.

☐ ☐ 13. When demand is inelastic, an increase in the price of a good causes total revenue (or total expenditure) to fall. .

☐ ☐ 14. The demand for Ford automobiles is more elastic than the demand for automobiles in general.

☐ ☐ 15. The short-run demand for a good is generally more elastic than the long-run demand.

PROBLEMS AND PROJECTS

1. The following questions relate to the price elasticity of demand.
   a. The most basic version of the price elasticity formula states that the price elasticity of demand is equal to the percentage change in quantity divided by the percentage change in price $[e = \%\Delta Q \div \%\Delta P]$. The law of demand states, however, that whenever price rises (+), quantity demanded falls (–); and whenever price falls (–), quantity demanded rises (+). What does this imply about the true sign of the price elasticity of demand? Is it always negative or positive? If your local clothing store had a 50-percent-off sale (that is, reduced its prices by 50 percent) and as a result it sold 25 percent more shirts, what is the price elasticity of demand?
   b. Economists generally ignore the sign of price elasticity (that is, we generally use the absolute value). The larger the computed elasticity number, the more elastic (or less inelastic) the demand for the product, whereas the smaller the number, the less elastic (or more inelastic) the demand for the product. In addition, we term elasticity as either elastic, inelastic, or unitary elastic depending upon whether the elasticity value is greater than, less than, or equal to one, respectively. If the demand for cigarettes has an elasticity of 0.6, while the demand for oranges has an elasticity of 2.3, how would you classify these demands? If the demand for apples had an elasticity of 2.1, would you say that the demand for apples is more or less elastic than the demand for oranges?
   c. Whenever you are given specific quantities and prices, you will have to find the percentage changes yourself to plug into the elasticity formula. Economists generally use a special "arc" formula for finding these percentage changes. For example, to find the percentage change in quantity, we would take the difference between the two quantities $[Q_2 - Q_1]$ and divide it by the average of (or midpoint between) the two quantities [which can be found as $(Q_1 + Q_2) \div 2$]. The percentage change in price is found in a similar manner by taking the difference in the two prices divided by the average of the two prices. If price falls from $9 to $7, what is the percentage change in price using this formula? If quantity rises from 30 to 50, what is the percentage change in quantity using this formula? Now use these percentage changes to find the elasticity of demand. Is demand elastic or inelastic?

2. The first two columns of Exhibit 1 indicate Keri's marginal benefit she derives from consuming additional pairs of jeans. Remember, marginal benefit is simply Keri's maximum amount that she would be willing to pay for that specific pair of jeans. Use the questions below to fill in the missing information in Exhibit 1.

   a. In the space provided, graph Keri's marginal benefit curve for jeans from the data given in columns (1) and (2). Do Keri's preferences reflect the law of diminishing marginal utility? How can you tell?

   b. Economic theory states that a consumer will purchase all units of a product for which their maximum willingness to pay (that is, their marginal benefit) is greater than or equal to the price of the good. Using the marginal benefit curve you have graphed, fill in the quantity of jeans Keri will purchase in column (4) at the different prices given in column (3).

   c. A demand curve simply shows how many units of a good a person will purchase at different prices. This is the data you now have in columns (3) and (4). If you were to graph Keri's demand curve for jeans, how would it compare to Keri's marginal benefit curve that you drew in part a?

   d. Keri's total spending (total expenditures) on jeans is equal to the number of pairs of jeans she purchases times the price she pays for each pair. Columns (3) and (4) show how many pairs she will buy at different prices. Fill in Keri's total spending in column (5) for each different price and quantity combination along her demand curve.

   e. When the price rises from $10 per pair of jeans to $20 per pair, what happens to Keri's total spending on jeans? For a price increase to cause this to happen to total expenditures, what must Keri's price elasticity of demand be, elastic, inelastic, or unitary elastic?

   f. When the price rises from $20 per pair of jeans to $30 per pair, what happens to Keri's total spending on jeans? For this to happen, what must Keri's price elasticity of demand be, elastic, inelastic, or unitary elastic?

   g. When the price rises from $30 per pair of jeans to $40 per pair, what happens to Keri's total spending on jeans? For this to happen, what must Keri's price elasticity of demand be, elastic, inelastic, or unitary elastic?

   h. Double-check your answers to parts e through g by using the price elasticity formula to calculate Keri's price elasticity of jeans for each price change. Place the results of your calculations in column (6). Do your values correspond to your answers above?

EXHIBIT 1

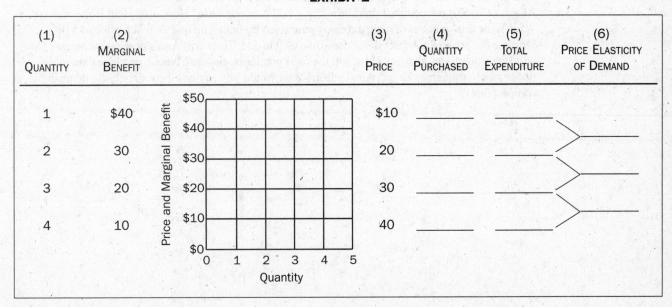

(1) QUANTITY	(2) MARGINAL BENEFIT		(3) PRICE	(4) QUANTITY PURCHASED	(5) TOTAL EXPENDITURE	(6) PRICE ELASTICITY OF DEMAND
1	$40		$10			
2	30		20			
3	20		30			
4	10		40			

3. The table on the left side of Exhibit 2 shows the quantity of compact discs that both Ann and Bob will purchase at different prices. Follow the questions below to fill in the remaining information in the exhibit.

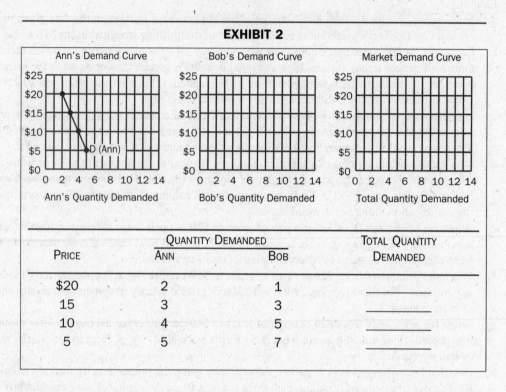

EXHIBIT 2

PRICE	QUANTITY DEMANDED		TOTAL QUANTITY
	ANN	BOB	DEMANDED
$20	2	1	_____
15	3	3	_____
10	4	5	_____
5	5	7	_____

a. Using the data, graph Bob's demand curve for compact discs (Ann's demand curve is already graphed as an example).

b. Assume that the entire market consisted of only Ann and Bob. The total market demand curve can be found by summing up the individual demands in the market. First, fill in the column for the total quantity demanded, then graph the market demand curve in the space provided.

c. At a price of $10 per compact disc, how many will Ann purchase? How many will Bob purchase? What is the total number of compact discs purchased by both Ann and Bob at a price of $10?

d. Suppose the price of compact discs rises from $10 to $15. How will Ann's purchases change? How will Bob's purchases change? How will the total purchases change? Whose purchases are more responsive to the price change, Ann or Bob? Who would you say has the more elastic demand for compact discs?

4. Exhibit 3 shows the quantity of beer sold at Sammy's pub at different prices for beer. Use the data shown to answer the following questions.

EXHIBIT 3

PRICE	QUANTITY OF BEER SOLD	TOTAL REVENUE	ELASTICITY OF DEMAND
$1	600	_____	
2	400	_____	
3	200	_____	

a. Fill in Sammy's total revenue for each price of beer shown.
b. When Sammy raises his price from $1 to $2, what happens to his total revenue? For a price increase to cause this to happen to total revenue, what must be the elasticity of demand, elastic, inelastic, or unitary elastic? Use the formula to calculate the price elasticity of demand to confirm your answer.
c. When Sammy raises his price from $2 to $3, what happens to his total revenue? For a price increase to cause this to happen to total revenue, what must be the elasticity of demand, elastic, inelastic, or unitary elastic? Use the formula to calculate the price elasticity of demand to confirm your answer.
d. As a student in economics, Sammy asks you whether lowering the price of his beer is a good idea to generate more revenue. Is it? Does your answer depend on what price he is currently charging?
e. Generally, customers leave tips for their waiter or waitress as a percent of their total purchase in dollars. If you were the waiter or waitress serving all of these beers, what price would you want Sammy to set in order for you to make the most money in tips? Explain your reasoning.
f. As Sammy raised his price from $2 to $3, his revenue fell from $800 to $600. Suppose the demand for Sammy's beer had been less sensitive to price (that is, more inelastic), so that the price increase would have only caused his beer sales to fall to 300 at a price of $3 instead of 200. Would Sammy's revenue still have fallen when he raised the price?
g. If Sammy lowered his price from $2 to $1, his revenue would fall from $800 to $600. Suppose the demand for Sammy's beer had been more sensitive to price (that is, more elastic), so that the price reduction would have caused his beer sales to rise to 900 at a price of $1 instead of 600. Would Sammy's revenue still have fallen when he lowered price?

5. Exhibit 4 shows the possible demand curves for a product, D_1 and D_2. Use the information in the exhibit to answer the following questions.

EXHIBIT 4

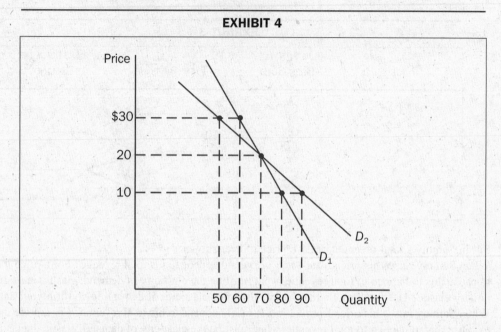

a. If the demand curve for this product was D_1, and price rose from $20 to $30, what would happen to the quantity purchased? If the demand curve for this product was instead D_2, and price rose from $20 to $30, what would happen to the quantity purchased? Given your answers, which demand curve would you consider more elastic? Which demand curve would you consider more inelastic?

b. If the demand curve for this product was D_1, and price fell from $20 to $10, what would happen to the quantity purchased? If the demand curve for this product was instead D_2, and price fell from $20 to $10, what would happen to the quantity purchased? Given your answers, which demand curve would you consider more elastic? Which demand curve would you consider more inelastic?

c. Does your conclusion about which demand curve is more elastic or inelastic depend upon which direction price changed? That is, are your answers to parts a and b the same?

6. John owns a restaurant that serves a lunch buffet. He currently charges $5 for the buffet and has 20 regular customers who come each day. His daily lunch revenue is $100 ($5 per person times 20 people). In an attempt to increase his revenue, he lowers the price to $4. John's regular customers are very happy about the price reduction, as it means they will each be paying less for their lunch each day.

a. How much revenue will John lose from his 20 regular customers as a result of reducing the price from $5 to $4, assuming they all continue to eat there each day?

b. If 3 new customers come each day now that the price is $4, will that be enough new customer revenue to make up for the lost revenue on John's regular customers? By how much will John's total daily lunch revenue change?

c. If, instead, 5 new customers come each day now that the price is $4, will that be enough new customer revenue to make up for the lost revenue on John's regular customers? By how much will his total daily lunch revenue change in this case?

d. If, instead, 10 new customers come each day now that the price is $4, will that be enough new customer revenue to make up for the lost revenue on John's regular customers? By how much will his total daily lunch revenue change in this case?

e. In all three cases presented in b through d, John has lowered price. However, in one case his daily revenue fell, in another it remained unchanged, and in another it increased. Can you relate your answers to parts b through d to the price elasticity of demand?

f. Instead of lowering his price, suppose John raises his price from $5 to $10. For a price increase, the change in his revenue can be decomposed into two parts: (1) the increased revenue on those customers who stay at the higher price and (2) the lost revenue from those customers who leave. Do this for the case where John loses 10 of his 20 regular customers as a result of raising price. Based upon your answer, what do you think would happen to his revenue if only 5 customers left? if 15 customers left? Can you relate these answers for a price increase to the price elasticity of demand?

7. Fill in the missing entries in Exhibit 5 based upon your knowledge about the relationship between demand elasticity, changes in price, and changes in total revenue (or total expenditure).

EXHIBIT 5

PRICE ELASTICITY	CHANGE IN PRICE	CHANGE IN TOTAL REVENUE
0.2	down	_____
3.5	_____	down
1.0	up	_____
0.9	_____	up
_____	down	no change
6.3	down	_____

MULTIPLE CHOICE

1. A 15 percent increase in the price of beef reduces the quantity of beef consumed by 30 percent. Thus, the demand for beef is _____, and total consumer expenditure (or total firm revenue) will _____ as a result of the price increase. (Fill in the blanks.)
    a. elastic; increase
    b. elastic; decrease
    c. inelastic; increase
    d. inelastic; decrease

2. Which of the following is true about marginal benefit?
    a. A consumer's marginal benefit is equal to the height of her demand curve.
    b. Consumers will continue to purchase up until the point where marginal benefit equals price.
    c. Marginal benefit declines as consumption increases because of the law of diminishing marginal utility.
    d. All of the above are true.

3. Jane received a 10 percent increase in her salary and purchased 20 percent more jewelry. For Jane, jewelry
    a. has an income elasticity of two.
    b. is a normal good.
    c. is a luxury good.
    d. is all of the above.

4. An inferior good is distinguished by a
    a. negative price elasticity of demand.
    b. positive price elasticity of demand.
    c. positive income elasticity of demand.
    d. negative income elasticity of demand.

5. If Joe's income increased and as a result he purchased more wine and less fast food,
    a. wine is a normal good and fast food an inferior good for Joe.
    b. wine is an inferior good and fast food a normal good for Joe.
    c. both wine and fast food are inferior goods for Joe.
    d. both wine and fast food are normal goods for Joe.

6. "After eating nothing but fast-food hamburgers on spring break, I was anxious to return home and eat something different." This statement most clearly reflects the law of
    a. the budget constraint.
    b. consumer irrationality.
    c. greater demand elasticity with time.
    d. diminishing marginal utility.

7. If the price elasticity of demand for grapes was 2.5,
    a. the demand for grapes would be considered inelastic.
    b. an increase in the price of grapes would decrease total consumer spending on grapes.
    c. consumer purchases are less sensitive to a change in the price of grapes than to a change in the price of bananas, which have a price elasticity of 1.6.
    d. the income elasticity for grapes must also be 2.5.

8. If a 50 percent increase in the price of hula hoops led to a 10 percent reduction in the quantity of hula hoops purchased, the price elasticity of demand is
    a. 5 and the demand for hula hoops is elastic.
    b. 0.2 and the demand for hula hoops is elastic.
    c. 5 and the demand for hula hoops is inelastic.
    d. 0.2 and the demand for hula hoops is inelastic.

9. "Because of the unseasonably cold weather, Florida orange growers expect (1) fewer bushels of oranges to be harvested, (2) a higher market price for oranges, and (3) larger total revenues from this year's crop." This statement would most likely be correct if the
    a. demand for Florida oranges was elastic.
    b. demand for Florida oranges was unitary elastic.
    c. demand for Florida oranges was inelastic.
    d. income elasticity of Florida oranges was negative.

10. Which of the following statements is true regarding the price elasticity of supply?
    a. The price elasticity of supply is always negative.
    b. The price elasticity of supply is always positive.
    c. The price elasticity of supply will be greater when suppliers have a shorter time to respond to a price change.
    d. None of the above statements are true.

11. Use the diagram below to answer this question.

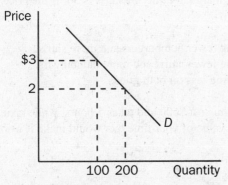

For this demand curve, the price elasticity of demand is
a. more elastic at $3 than at $2.
b. more elastic at $2 than at $3.
c. identical at $2 to that at $3.
d. equal to 1.0 over the range from $3 to $2.

12. A car wash currently sells 30 car washes a day at a price of $5. Total daily revenue is now $150. If they lower their price to $3,
a. total revenue will fall if the number of washes sold only rises to 40.
b. total revenue will remain unchanged if the number of washes sold rises to 50.
c. total revenue will increase if the number of washes sold rises to 60.
d. all of the above are true.

13. Coach Ballford: "To increase our revenue from football games, we need to lower ticket prices." University President Smith: "Coach, that would be counterproductive; a reduction in ticket prices would reduce our revenue, not increase it." Which of the following best explains this disagreement?
a. The coach thinks that demand is elastic, whereas the university president thinks that demand is inelastic.
b. The coach thinks that demand is inelastic, whereas the university president thinks that demand is elastic.
c. The coach believes that lower ticket prices will increase attendance, but the university president must not believe attendance will increase when prices are lowered.
d. Although both the coach and the president believe demand is of unitary elasticity, they disagree about how much attendance will rise.

14. All else equal, if a firm raises its price by 20 percent and the firm's total revenue falls by 20 percent,
a. demand must be elastic.
b. demand must be inelastic.
c. demand must be unit elastic.
d. the price elasticity of demand must be equal to 1.

15. Which of the following is not a fundamental that underlies consumer behavior?
a. Goods can be substituted for one another.
b. Consumers make decisions purposefully based upon past experience and knowledge.
c. The law of diminishing marginal utility applies to all goods.
d. Consumers always make choices with perfect information.

16. Terri currently consumes 10 hamburgers and 2 shirts per month. At her current rates of consumption, her marginal utility of hamburgers is 10 and her marginal utility of shirts is 50. If the price of hamburgers is $2 each, while the price of a shirt is $25, Terri
    a. is maximizing her utility.
    b. could improve her total utility by buying fewer hamburgers and more shirts.
    c. could improve her total utility by buying fewer shirts and more hamburgers.
    d. could improve her total utility by spending less on both goods.

17. If taking an airplane from Pittsburgh to Miami cost $600 and takes 5 hours, while taking a bus would cost $150 and takes 50 hours, the minimum value of your time that would make it worthwhile to fly would be
    a. $1 per hour.
    b. $3 per hour.
    c. $10 per hour.
    d. $12 per hour.

18. Exhibit 6 illustrates two possible demand curves for a product, D_1 and D_2. Which of the following is true regarding these demand curves?

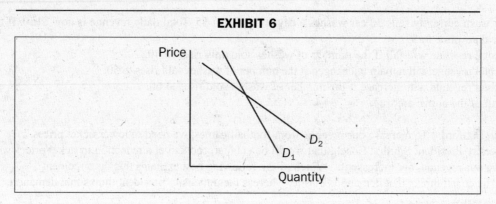

EXHIBIT 6

    a. Demand curve D_1 represents a demand curve that is relatively more elastic than demand curve D_2.
    b. Demand curve D_1 represents a demand curve that is relatively more inelastic than demand curve D_2.
    c. Demand curve D_1 represents a demand curve that shows consumer purchases being more responsive to a change in the price of the good than demand curve D_2.
    d. Both are examples of unitary elastic demand curves.

19. Making drugs, such as cocaine, illegal results in a higher price than would be present if the drugs were legal. All else constant, the higher price results in drug users spending
    a. more on drugs if the demand for drugs is inelastic.
    b. more on drugs if the demand for drugs is elastic.
    c. less on drugs if the demand for drugs is inelastic.
    d. more on drugs if the demand for drugs is unitary elastic.

20. If the price of steak rises from $6 to $10 per pound, and the quantity purchased falls from 90 to 70 pounds, the price elasticity of demand (in absolute value) is
    a. 0.2.
    b. 0.5.
    c. 1.0.
    d. 2.0.

21. When the price elasticity of demand is greater than one, it means that demand is
    a. inelastic and the percent change in quantity is greater than the percent change in price.
    b. inelastic and the percent change in quantity is less than the percent change in price.
    c. elastic and the percent change in quantity is greater than the percent change in price.
    d. elastic and the percent change in quantity is less than the percent change in price.

22. If Russell values a ticket to a rock concert at $100 and is able to purchase it for only $40, he has received _____ in consumer surplus on his purchase. (Fill in the blank.)
    a. $40
    b. $60
    c. $100
    d. $140

23. The market demand for a good is
    a. the horizontal sum of all individual demand curves for the good.
    b. generally upward sloping, unlike individual demand curves.
    c. usually a vertical line at a quantity of one hundred.
    d. the average amount purchased by each individual in the market.

24. Bob goes out to dinner three times per week, usually either to the local steak house or a Chinese restaurant in town. If the steak house were to raise its prices, Bob would probably (1) be less inclined to eat at the steak house and more inclined to eat at the Chinese restaurant when he did go out and (2) eat out fewer times per week because at the higher prices he cannot afford to eat out as much.
    a. Part 1 is an example of the substitution effect, part 2 of the income effect.
    b. Part 1 is an example of the income effect, part 2 of the substitution effect.
    c. Part 1 is an example of the law of diminishing marginal utility, part 2 of the substitution effect.
    d. Part 1 is an example of the proportions hypothesis, part 2 of the income effect.

25. The price elasticity of demand for automobiles measures the responsiveness of
    a. consumer purchases to a change in the price of automobiles.
    b. consumer purchases to a change in the quality of automobiles.
    c. supplier production levels to a change in the price of automobiles.
    d. consumer purchases of automobiles to a change in their income.

26. Which of the following is true regarding the price elasticity of demand?
    a. Demand is generally more elastic in the long run than in the short run.
    b. Along a single demand curve, demand elasticity decreases as you move down the curve (to lower prices).
    c. A demand curve that is flatter (has a less steep slope) is relatively more elastic than a demand curve that has a steeper slope.
    d. All of the above are true.

DISCUSSION QUESTIONS

1. For each of the following pairs of products, indicate which you think will have the lower price elasticity of demand. Explain your reasoning.
    a. salt or tacos
    b. Volkswagens or all automobiles
    c. short-run electricity or long-run electricity
    d. physician services or bus transportation

2. "Rich people spend much of their income on useless items. If consumers limited their purchases to those items they needed, we would have fewer economic problems."
    a. What items do people spend their money on that are not necessary? Do you buy things you do not need? If so, why?
    b. How can you determine if an item is useful or needed? Are demand and usefulness the same thing? How about a need and a want?

3. Why is the price elasticity of demand always negative? Is the income elasticity of demand always negative too? Explain.

4. Goods are classified as having either elastic, inelastic, or unitary elastic demands based upon the value of the price elasticity coefficient. For each of these three cases, explain whether the percent change in quantity is greater than, less than, or equal to the percent change in price. How do these differences relate to the differing effect a price change can have on total revenue (or total expenditure), depending upon the value of price elasticity?

5. When is maximizing revenue the same as maximizing profit for a firm? Can you think of specific real-world situations where this condition is likely to be met? What price should a firm charge if it wishes to maximize revenue?

Costs and the Supply of Goods

TRUE OR FALSE

T F

☐ ☐ 1. It is possible for a firm to be making an accounting profit but an economic loss.

☐ ☐ 2. Economic profit differs from accounting profit because economic profit excludes opportunity costs (such as the opportunity cost of equity capital and forgone wages) from the calculation of profit.

☐ ☐ 3. The corporate form of business organization has two advantages: limited liability and the ease of ownership transfer.

☐ ☐ 4. The short run is a period of time so short that at least one factor of production is fixed.

☐ ☐ 5. A worker's marginal product is the change in total output that results from employing that worker.

☐ ☐ 6. The law of diminishing returns states that eventually each additional unit of a variable input employed with a fixed amount of other inputs will result in less additional output.

☐ ☐ 7. Average fixed costs (AFC) will always decline as output is expanded in the short run.

☐ ☐ 8. The change in total cost resulting from the production of one additional unit is called average variable cost.

☐ ☐ 9. Average total cost (ATC) will always increase when marginal cost (MC) is increasing.

☐ ☐ 10. As a firm expands output in the short run, total variable costs increase, but total fixed costs remain the same.

☐ ☐ 11. A firm is minimizing its per-unit costs of production if it operates where marginal cost (MC) equals average total cost (ATC).

T   F

☐ ☐ 12. A firm's total cost (TC) may be found by subtracting total variable cost (TVC) from total fixed cost (TFC).

☐ ☐ 13. The curve that shows how a firm's per-unit costs change over the long run as plant size is expanded is the LRATC curve.

☐ ☐ 14. When a firm's per-unit costs fall as its plant size increases in the long run, it is said to be experiencing diseconomies of scale.

☐ ☐ 15. A restaurant's average total cost (ATC) curve would shift upward if the price of food ingredients fell.

☐ ☐ 16. A good decision maker will always consider sunk costs in his decisions.

PROBLEMS AND PROJECTS

1. Exhibit 1 represents the annual income statement of Joe's Clothing Store. Joe worked full time in the store and invested $30,000 of his own money to buy the store and stock it with merchandise. He recently turned down an offer of a salaried position paying $10,000 per year to manage another store. He did not pay himself a salary during the year. According to Exhibit 1,
    a. what were Joe's accounting profits?
    b. what major items did he exclude from his costs from an economic standpoint?
    c. if Joe could have earned 10 percent interest on his $30,000 by keeping it in the bank, how much interest is he losing per year by keeping the money invested in the store?
    d. recalculate Joe's total costs in light of your answers to b and c.
    e. what was the economic profit or loss of Joe's Clothing Store?

EXHIBIT 1

REVENUES		COSTS	
Sales	$57,000	Wholesale clothing	$30,000
		Equipment	2,000
		Labor	15,000
		Utilities and insurance	1,000
Total revenues	$57,000	Total costs	$48,000

2. Exhibit 2 shows how a firm's total product, TP (which is the same as the firm's total output), changes as additional units of labor (L) are employed with a fixed amount of other resources in the short run.
    a. Fill in the missing data in the table for marginal product (MP) and average product (AP).
    b. Plot this firm's MP and AP curves in the space provided.
    c. At what level of labor usage does this firm begin to experience diminishing returns?

EXHIBIT 2

UNITS OF LABOR L	TOTAL PRODUCT (TOTAL OUTPUT) TP	MARGINAL PRODUCT MP	AVERAGE PRODUCT AP
1	8	_____	_____
2	24	_____	_____
3	36	_____	_____
4	44	_____	_____
5	50	_____	_____
6	54	_____	_____
7	56	_____	_____
8	56	_____	_____

3. Susan owns a small shop and produces dining room sets. Exhibit 3 presents data on her total costs at various output levels.
    a. Complete Exhibit 3 (you will need a calculator for this problem).
    b. At what output level is Susan's average total cost at a minimum?
    c. At what output level do diminishing returns begin for Susan?
    d. Using your own paper, graph Susan's average total cost, average variable cost, and marginal cost curves.

EXHIBIT 3

COSTS AND OUTPUT

OUTPUT (PER WEEK)	TOTAL COST	TOTAL FIXED COST	TOTAL VARIABLE COST	AVERAGE TOTAL COST	AVERAGE VARIABLE COST	MARGINAL COST
1	$100	$50	_____	_____	_____	_____
2	140	_____	_____	_____	_____	_____
3	177	_____	_____	_____	_____	_____
4	216	_____	_____	_____	_____	_____
5	265	_____	_____	_____	_____	_____
6	324	_____	_____	_____	_____	_____
7	399	_____	_____	_____	_____	_____
8	496	_____	_____	_____	_____	_____

4. Exhibit 4 shows a firm's costs of production in the short run. First, complete the table shown beside the exhibit. This can be done by simply reading the numbers given in the graph. Use your knowledge of the relationships between the costs to answer the remaining questions.

a. For an output level of 3 units, what is the total cost of production? What are the total variable costs and total fixed costs when the firm produces 3 units?

b. For an output level of 6 units, what is the total cost of production? What are the total variable costs and total fixed costs when the firm produces 6 units?

c. You know the total cost of producing 6 units and also the marginal cost of producing the sixth unit. Can you find the total cost of producing 5 units? (Hint: Remember the definition of marginal cost.)

d. What would this firm's total fixed costs be at an output level of 10 units? 15 units?

e. Find the average fixed cost (AFC) for output levels of 3 and 6 units. Are there two ways you can get these numbers? Do they produce identical results?

f. In Exhibit 4, shade in the rectangular area that represents the total cost of producing 3 units. Which part of this area represents total variable costs? Which part represents total fixed costs?

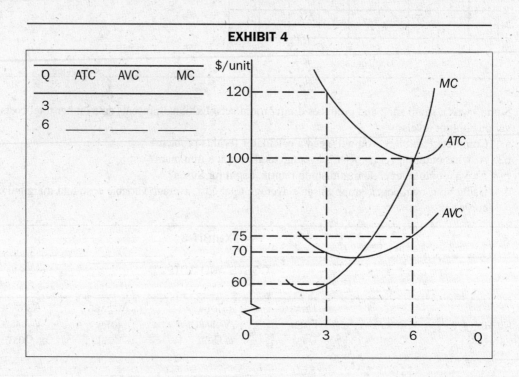

EXHIBIT 4

Q	ATC	AVC	MC
3	___	___	___
6	___	___	___

5. Below is a list of problems to help you learn the relationship between the costs and productivity measures in this chapter. Each problem is independent. That is, answer each question separately because it does not depend on the other answers.

a. If a restaurant can serve 30 tables with 3 waiters and 35 tables with 4 waiters, the marginal product of the fourth waiter is _____.

b. If a garbage collection company employs 2 workers on a garbage truck and they pick up 300 cans of trash, the average product of labor is _____.

c. If a firm's total fixed cost (*TFC*) is $100 and its total variable cost (*TVC*) is $200 when it produces 30 units, its average total cost (*ATC*) is _____.

d. If *ATC* is $5 and *AVC* is $2, then *AFC* is _____.

e. If average variable cost (*AVC*) is $5 when a firm produces 20 units, its total variable cost is _____.

f. If the total cost (*TC*) of producing 10 units is $40 and the total cost of producing 11 units is $45, the marginal cost (*MC*) of producing the eleventh unit is _____.

g. If a firm's total fixed cost (*TFC*) is $350 when it produces 4 units, its total fixed cost when it produces 5 units is _____.

h.   If a firm's total fixed cost (*TFC*) is $200 when it produces 50 units, its average fixed cost (*AFC*) is
_____.

i.   If a firm's average variable cost (*AVC*) is $100 when it produces 5 units and its total fixed cost
(*TFC*) is $200, the firm's total cost (*TC*) is _____.

j.   If a local fast-food restaurant sells 25 hamburgers and its total costs are $50, its per-hamburger cost
is _____.

k.   If a university's total variable cost (*TVC*), such as professors' salaries and chalk, is $5,000,000 when
it has 1,000 students and the total fixed costs (*TFC*), such as buildings, is $1,000,000, the per-stu-
dent total cost is _____.

MULTIPLE CHOICE

1.   The law of diminishing returns indicates why
   a.   beyond some point, the extra utility derived from additional units of a product will yield the consumer smaller and smaller amounts of additional satisfaction.
   b.   the firm's total fixed costs do not change with output in the short run.
   c.   a firm's long-run average total cost curve is U-shaped.
   d.   a firm's marginal costs will eventually increase as the firm expands output in the short run.

2.   The short run is a time period of insufficient length for the firm to change its
   a.   output.
   b.   amount of labor employed.
   c.   plant size and heavy equipment.
   d.   price.

3.   Sunk or "historical" costs are costs
   a.   associated with current operational decisions.
   b.   that have already been incurred as the result of past decisions.
   c.   that add to the firm's marginal costs.
   d.   that form the major component of the firm's variable costs.

4.   Advantages of the corporate form of business organization include
   a.   the ease of transferring ownership in a corporation.
   b.   the limited liability concept that protects the stockholder from potential debts incurred by the
corporation.
   c.   the lack of employee shirking that occurs in corporations.
   d.   both a and b.

5.   The average variable cost curve and average total cost curve become closer together as output increases
because
   a.   the marginal cost curve intersects the average total cost curve at its minimum.
   b.   average fixed cost remains constant as output rises.
   c.   average fixed cost, which is the difference between them, declines with output.
   d.   output is rising more rapidly than inputs are being increased.

6.   Which of the following factors would not shift the cost curves of an automobile company upward?
   a.   a regulation requiring all automobiles be equipped with improved safety equipment
   b.   an increase in the price of steel used to make automobiles
   c.   an increase in the property tax on buildings and equipment used by the automobile company
   d.   An employee develops a new method of installing doors on the cars that requires half as many
workers as before.

7.   The firm's average total costs will be a minimum at the output level where the
   a.   firm just begins to confront diminishing returns to the variable factors.
   b.   marginal costs are a minimum.
   c.   firm's average fixed costs are at their minimum.
   d.   marginal cost curve crosses the firm's average total cost curve.

8.   The law of diminishing returns states that
   a.   as we continually add variable factors to a fixed amount of other resources, output eventually increases at a decreasing rate.
   b.   as we increase plant size, costs must diminish.
   c.   the additional output generated by the employment of additional units of a variable input eventually decline.
   d.   both a and c are correct.

Questions 9 through 15 refer to the following cost curves for one very small firm in a large market.

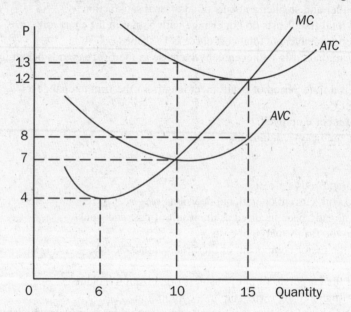

9.   If the firm produces 10 units of output, its average total cost is
   a.   6.
   b.   7.
   c.   12.
   d.   13.

10.   If the firm produces 15 units of output, its average fixed cost is
   a.   4.
   b.   5.
   c.   6.
   d.   60.

11.   If the firm produces 10 units of output, its total cost is
   a.   7.
   b.   13.
   c.   70.
   d.   130.

12. If the firm produces 10 units of output, its total fixed cost is
    a. 6.
    b. 60.
    c. 70.
    d. 130.

13. The marginal cost of producing the tenth unit is
    a. 7.
    b. 13.
    c. 70.
    d. 130.

14. This firm minimizes its per-unit costs of production at an output level of
    a. $Q = 6$.
    b. $Q = 10$.
    c. $Q = 15$.
    d. none of the above.

15. Diminishing returns to the variable factor of production for this firm set in at
    a. $Q = 6$.
    b. $Q = 10$.
    c. $Q = 15$.
    d. none of the above.

16. A homeowner will be away from her house for six months. The monthly mortgage payment on the house is $300. The utilities, to be paid by the owner, cost $100 per month if the house is occupied; otherwise zero. If the owner wishes to minimize her losses from the house, she should rent the house for as much as the market will bear, as long as monthly rent is greater than which of the following? (Assume wear and tear to be zero regardless of whether the house is occupied.) (Hint: Remember the concept of sunk cost.)
    a. $0
    b. $100
    c. $200
    d. $400

17. Suppose you value watching a movie at $5. You rent it from your local movie rental store for $3.50 for one night. You do not get a chance to watch it, so you decide to keep it an extra day and pay a late fee of $2. Your decision is
    a. incorrect; you paid $5.50 to watch a movie you valued at only $5. You should have taken the movie back.
    b. incorrect; you should have returned the movie and rented it later.
    c. correct; the $3.50 paid for the first night is a sunk cost and is not relevant in your decision to keep it an additional night.
    d. correct; you value watching the movie at $5 per night, so keeping it an extra day increases your value of the movie to $10.

18. Which of the following factors is most likely to shift the cost curves of an Iowa corn farmer downward?
    a. an increase in the price of fertilizer
    b. an increase in the tax on diesel fuel, which is used by the farmer
    c. the development of a new, more efficient corn harvester
    d. the adoption of a regulation requiring farmers to treat their crops with three new pesticides.

19. Which of the following is true?
    a. Economic profits are generally lower than accounting profits.
    b. Economic profits are generally greater than accounting profits.
    c. Economic profits are generally equal to accounting profits.
    d. Economic profits plus accounting profits must equal zero.

20. When a firm increases its plant size in the long run and its per-unit costs fall, this is called
    a. diminishing returns and is shown by the downward-sloping portion of the MP curve (or the upward-sloping portion of the MC curve).
    b. constant returns to scale and is shown by the flat portion of the LRATC curve.
    c. diseconomies of scale and is shown by the upward-sloping portion of the LRATC curve.
    d. economies of scale and is shown by the downward-sloping portion of the LRATC curve.

21. When the owner of a business invests his or her own money in the business, they give up the interest this money could be earning in the bank. This forgone interest is called
    a. the marginal cost of diminishing financial services.
    b. the opportunity cost of equity capital.
    c. the opportunity cost of labor services.
    d. interest expense and is included as a cost in the accounting statements of the business.

22. Ron works for Betty at Betty's Pizza Palace. Betty has many work rules, and Ron believes if there were fewer rules and more flexibility, he could do a better job. Betty probably has the rules because
    a. Ron, like her other employees, is a residual claimant.
    b. due to the principal-agent problem, some employees are likely to shirk when the owner is absent.
    c. she is maximizing sales rather than profits.
    d. with regard to their jobs, employees seldom know what is best.

23. Which of the following is true?
    a. Under the partnership form of business organization, the owners are not personally liable for the debts of the business.
    b. When employees are paid by the hour, their incentive to shirk is removed.
    c. The limited liability of stockholders under the corporate business structure makes it easier to raise equity capital.
    d. Under the corporate form of business organization, the owners of the firm are personally liable for its debts.

24. Mary owns her own business and works full time in the store without paying herself a salary. She has $20,000 of her own money invested in the store that she withdrew from her savings account, which earned 10 percent interest. She was offered a job last year making $28,000 per year but turned it down. If Mary's accounting statements show revenues of $100,000 and accounting costs of $60,000, then Mary's
    a. accounting profit is $20,000 and her economic profit is zero.
    b. accounting profit is $40,000 and she is making an economic loss of $8,000.
    c. accounting profit is $40,000 and her economic profit is $10,000.
    d. accounting and economic profit is $40,000.

25. When an economist says a firm is earning zero economic profit, this implies that the firm
    a. will be forced out of business in the near future unless market conditions change.
    b. is earning a zero rate of return on its assets.
    c. is earning as high a rate of return now as could be earned in other industries.
    d. has an accounting profit of zero.

26. The long run is a period of
    a. at least one year.
    b. sufficient length to allow a firm to expand output by hiring additional workers.
    c. sufficient length to allow a firm to alter its plant size and capacity and all other factors of production.
    d. sufficient length to allow a firm to transform economic losses into economic profits.

27. As output is expanded, if *MC* is more than *ATC*,
    a. *ATC* must be at its minimum.
    b. *ATC* must be at its maximum.
    c. *ATC* must be increasing.
    d. *ATC* must be constant.

28. Mr. Hudson notes that if he produces 10 pairs of shoes per day, his average fixed cost (*AFC*) is $14 and his marginal cost $8; if he produces 20 pairs of shoes per day, his MC is $15. What is his *AFC* when output is 20 pairs of shoes per day?
    a. $5
    b. $7
    c. $8
    d. $15

29. Bill lives in Montana and likes to grow zucchini. He applies fertilizer to his crop twice during the growing season and notices that the second layer of fertilizer increases his crop but not as much as the first layer. What economic concept best explains this observation?
    a. the law of diminishing marginal utility
    b. the law of diminishing returns
    c. return equalization principle
    d. the principal-agent problem

30. Larger firms will often have lower minimum per-unit costs than smaller firms because
    a. employee shirking is less of a problem.
    b. large-scale output allows greater specialization for both labor and machines in the production process.
    c. mass production techniques, with high setup and development costs, are appropriate only when a small output is planned.
    d. all of the above are correct.

DISCUSSION QUESTIONS

1. a. What are the reasons that economic profit differs from accounting profit?
    b. In the real world, which reason do you think is the most significant?
    c. Could it make economic sense for a firm to leave an industry when the firm's accounting profits are positive? when its economic profits are positive? Explain both answers.

2. a. Suppose you compute the average weight of the students present at the start of class. Then a student weighing 175 pounds shows up late, and your computed average rises. If another student weighing only 145 pounds shows up, could your computed average rise again, even though the second late student weighs less than the first?
    b. Suppose you are part way through a course, and then your course grade falls because you do poorly on an assignment. Will your course grade necessarily rise back up again if you do better on the next assignment than you did on the last one?
    c. Decide whether the following is true or false and explain: If average cost is falling (rising), then we can conclude that marginal cost is also falling (rising).

3. What are the main reasons that per-unit production costs are often lower for larger firms than for small firms in the same industry? Why don't the small firms go bankrupt because of their higher production costs?

4. How would each of the following influence the cost of producing new housing?
    a. an increase in the price of lumber
    b. the development of a new lighter brick that reduced labor requirements without increasing the costs of material
    c. a reduction in the price of cement
    d. a new "occupational safety" regulation that required all construction workers to wear safety glasses, aluminum hats, and steel-toed shoes
    e. passage of state legislation requiring all contractors to pay a $10,000 licensing fee

5. a. Suppose some friends of yours buy a trailer. After some time, you ask them if they are glad they bought the trailer and they respond, "No, we wouldn't buy one again, but we spent so much on it that we do travel more now." Does their reasoning make sense? If so, why? If not, why not, and why do you think they do travel more now?
    b. Decide whether you agree or disagree with the following and explain: "In deciding whether to produce more of an item, a firm should consider total cost in the long run, but only variable cost in the short run."

6. What are the advantages of corporations compared to proprietorships? the disadvantages?

7. Consider the following three statements:
    (1) "I have to keep driving my old car in order to make up for the loss that I took when the transmission went out." (Hint: Remember the relevance of sunk costs.)
    (2) "It does not make sense to keep operating an old machine when new machines can produce more efficiently."
    (3) "Accounting costs yield valuable information, but they are not the relevant cost consideration when making business decisions."
    a. How would an economist assess the above statements? What economic principles would be used to assess them?
    b. Do you agree or disagree with the economist's assessment? Does the economic way of thinking overlook important real-world considerations?

8. In 1911, Thomas Edison wrote in *The Wall Street Journal:*

    Thirty years ago my balance sheet showed me that I was not making much money. My manufacturing plant was not running to its full capacity. I couldn't find a market for my products. Then I suggested that we undertake to run our plant on full capacity and sell the surplus products in foreign markets at less than the cost of production. Every one of my associates opposed me. I had my experts figure out how much it would add to the cost of operating the plant if we increased this production 25 percent. The figures showed that we could increase the production 25 percent at an increased cost of only about 2 percent. On this basis I sent a man to Europe who sold lamps there at a price less than the cost of production in Europe.

    a. When Edison suggested that he would sell in foreign markets "at less than the cost of production," of what cost was he speaking?
    b. What was happening to Edison's marginal cost as he expanded output by 25 percent?
    c. Edison's pricing idea was opposed by his associates. Assuming that he was motivated by profit, who was right—Edison or his associates? Explain.

9. a. What is the nature of the principle agent problem? How does the principle agent problem affect the cost efficiency of large corporations in the market sector? Can you think of factors that limit the ability of corporate managers to follow policies that are inconsistent with economic efficiency (cost effectiveness)?

    b. Use your answers to part a to discuss the phenomenon of extremely high salaries for corporate managers, who often have "golden parachute" clauses in their contracts that guarantee them large payments if they are forced to leave the corporation.

PERSPECTIVES IN ECONOMICS

Marginal-Cost Policy Making and the Guy Next Door

by Thomas L. Wyrick
[From *The Wall Street Journal*, April 12, 1984, abridged. Reprinted with permission of Thomas L. Wyrick, Southwest Missouri State University.]

Imagine yourself in a supermarket when the manager announces that for the next five minutes bottles of your favorite soft drinks will be sold two for $1 rather than the regular price of $1 each. "Buy one, get one free."

Back at home, a half-hour later, a neighbor with unexpected company calls to ask if you would sell him a bottle of the same soda. You agree, but before he gets there you must decide how much to charge him. Three possibilities come to mind—$1, 50 cents, or nothing—but there doesn't seem to be any way of knowing which is appropriate.

It doesn't take long to narrow your choices to two. Only the most altruistic would figure that the neighbor was getting the free bottle anyway, and shouldn't have to pay for it.

If you concentrate on the average price per bottle, then 50 cents will seem correct. After all, it is impossible to say which bottle was purchased and which one was "free," so it may appear reasonable to split the difference and charge your neighbor 50 cents.

But before the neighbor arrives, you have two bottles of soda. Once he leaves you will have one bottle and 50 cents, if you charge according to average cost. Since the two-for-one sale was only a one-time thing, it will be necessary to spend an additional 50 cents of your own money to replace the bottle once it is gone.

So averaging costs to set a price reduces your wealth by the difference between replacement cost for soda and its average cost to you.

Now, you may charge the neighbor 50 cents just to prevent hard feelings in case he later learns about the two-for-one special. But that is the consequence of placing friendship above economic considerations. If the deal is purely an economic one, then it is proper to charge the neighbor $1. This represents the soda's replacement cost, or the marginal cost incurred by you when selling the soda.

Sound simple? That's because it is. Unfortunately, however, government officials often have difficulty translating such ideas into policy.

Our nation's energy policies have usually been based on the naive view that firms set prices according to their average costs of doing business. Instead, profit-seeking firms use marginal-cost pricing. Thus policies can (and often do) have consequences opposite to those intended.

Recall the experience with oil price controls in the 1970s. The price of domestic crude oil was held down to artificially low levels to try to lower the costs of producing gasoline. As everyone knows, though, gasoline prices have declined (rather than increased) since President Reagan abolished controls in early 1981. This is contrary to what price controllers had expected, so they generally explain the (three-year) decline as temporary.

But a different explanation emerges from the marginal-cost pricing perspective. Oil refiners produce gasoline (and other products) from crude oil purchased from both domestic and foreign sources. Controls held the price of U.S. oil to $2 or $3 a barrel while foreign suppliers charged $36 or more in 1979. Refiners rationally bought all of the U.S. crude available, and turned to OPEC members only as a last resort.

Like a person selling soda to his neighbor, however, refiners charge customers a price based on their marginal costs of selling oil. That is, because Exxon or Texaco had only a limited amount of $2 oil available, a sale of that oil meant they had to rely on OPEC sources to replenish their inventories. Since that meant an additional (marginal) outlay of $36 a barrel, then the price of gasoline had to be high enough to reflect this cost rather than the lower controlled price.

So price controls on oil allowed refiners to pay less than a market price on some of their inputs, while they charged a market price on all of their output. Thanks to Congress, refiners' profits were at an all-time high during the price-control years. Of course, U.S. landowners and others who sold crude to refiners were harmed in proportion to the latter's gain.

The 1981 removal of price controls gave domestic owners of oil reserves more incentive to find and sell crude, and they responded in kind. As new domestic supplies came into competition with foreign oil, OPEC and others were forced to lower their prices to the current range of $28 to $29. This lowered refiners' marginal costs of doing business, and allowed them to lower the price of gasoline.

Meanwhile, because of the average cost-marginal cost confusion, Congress remains unwilling to remove price controls from certain categories of natural gas. Doing so, it is thought, would result in price increases for consumers perhaps by 50 percent or more within a few months.

In reality, however, controls cause owners of artificially low-priced gas to hold down production, so pipeline companies must turn to more expensive (uncontrolled) sources to satisfy customer demands. That drives up the costs to utility companies, and pushes up prices to consumers.

Decontrol would allow all natural gas to sell for the same price. The owners of decontrolled gas would increase production to profit from higher prices, and the now familiar dynamic would be seen again. Lessened demand for higher-priced gas on the margin would bring down the market price of gas. And lower marginal costs for pipelines would ultimately help reduce the heating bills of consumers.

The lesson to be learned is that market participants respond to marginal costs, not average costs. If a firm's costs rise by X dollars when it produces and sells one more unit of output, then price will tend toward X dollars regardless of the firm's costs averaged over all units of output.

Policy makers intent on helping consumers, borrowers and others would do well to stop trying to control the various components of production costs. Such efforts usually end up reducing the total supply of the good or service in question, and customers pay higher retail prices as a result. Public officials should spend more effort understanding how the private economy works; then they wouldn't waste so much energy trying to fix it.

DISCUSSION

1. How much would you have charged your neighbor for the bottle of soda? Why?

2. Wyrick seems to be arguing that getting rid of price controls on crude oil actually helped reduce the retail price of gasoline. How is this possible? Why is the role of marginal cost crucial in all of this?

3. Do you agree with Wyrick's predication that removing price controls from natural gas would decrease natural gas prices rather than increase them (even though an increase is what most people seem to expect)? Why or why not?

Price Takers and the Competitive Process

chapter 22

TRUE OR FALSE

T   F

☐ ☐   1. In a price-taker market, all firms produce an identical product and each firm comprises only a very small portion of the total market.

☐ ☐   2. If a price-taker firm wants to sell its output, it must accept the market price, but it can sell as much output as it wishes at that market price.

☐ ☐   3. For a price-taker firm, its marginal revenue from the sale of an additional unit is generally less than the market price.

☐ ☐   4. A profit-maximizing, price-taking firm will expand output to the point where marginal cost equals the market price.

☐ ☐   5. In a price-taker market, each individual firm confronts a perfectly elastic demand curve that is a horizontal line at the market price.

☐ ☐   6. A price-taker firm's short-run supply curve is equal to the firm's average total cost curve.

☐ ☐   7. The short-run market supply curve for a price-taker market is equal to the horizontal summation of the marginal cost curves (above AVC) for all firms in the industry.

☐ ☐   8. In the short run, price-taker firms will expand their output and earn higher profits when the market price increases.

☐ ☐   9. Whenever short-run economic profits are present in a price-taker market, new firms will enter and the market price will fall until all firms earn only zero economic profit in the long run.

☐ ☐   10. Price takers always produce at the level of output at which average total costs are a minimum in both the short and long run.

T F

☐ ☐ 11. Economic losses cause firms to exit from an industry in the long run, and the market supply declines until zero economic profits are restored.

☐ ☐ 12. A price-taking firm earning zero economic profit will generally go out of business unless it expects to earn positive economic profits in the long run.

☐ ☐ 13. In a constant cost industry, an increase in demand will cause price to rise in the long run because the long-run market supply curve is upward sloping.

☐ ☐ 14. When a firm shuts down in the short run, its total cost will fall to zero.

☐ ☐ 15. If price currently is less than ATC but above AVC, the firm should remain open in the short run but shut down in the long run.

PROBLEMS AND PROJECTS

1. Exhibit 1 shows the total cost schedule for a firm in a price-taker market.

EXHIBIT 1

OUTPUT	TOTAL REVENUE	MARGINAL REVENUE	TOTAL COST	MARGINAL COST	PROFIT
0	$ 0	x	$20	x	−$20
1	25	$25	30	$10	− 5
2	50	25	35	5	+ 15
3	_____	_____	45	_____	_____
4	_____	_____	65	_____	_____
5	_____	_____	95	_____	_____
6	_____	_____	135	_____	_____

a. If the market price is $25, the firm's total revenue is the number of units sold times the market price. Fill in the missing values for the firm's total revenue.
b. Marginal revenue is the change in total revenue that results from producing and selling one additional unit. Fill in the missing values for the firm's marginal revenue. Because this is a price-taker firm, what is marginal revenue equal to?
c. Marginal cost is the change in total cost that results from producing and selling one additional unit. Fill in the missing values for the firm's marginal cost.
d. The firm's profit is equal to total revenue minus total cost. Fill in the missing values for the firm's profit.
e. The profit-maximization rule is that a firm should produce and sell all units up until the point where marginal cost equals marginal revenue (MC = MR). Given your answer to part b above, how can this rule be restated for a price-taker firm?
f. It will not be true in every case that there will be a specific unit for which MC exactly equals MR. Thus, the profit-maximization rule more appropriately stated is that a firm should produce all units

for which marginal revenue (or price, for a price-taker firm) exceeds marginal cost. The logic of this rule is that when a unit is produced that adds more to revenue than it adds to cost, the result will be an increase in profit. Looking at the table in Exhibit 1, is it true that when a unit's marginal revenue exceeds marginal cost, producing and selling the unit results in higher total profit? What happens when units are produced for which marginal revenue is less than marginal cost?

g. Looking at the total profit column, what level of output maximizes this firm's profit? Using the marginal-cost/marginal-revenue rule, what level of output maximizes this firm's profit? Do they yield the same answer?

h. Suppose the market price rose to $40. What new level of output would maximize this firm's profit? (Hint: You can either recalculate the total revenue and total profit columns to find this answer or [easier] use the marginal-cost/marginal-revenue rule.)

i. When there is a specific unit for which MC = MR, how does producing this last unit change the firm's profit? Check your answer by computing the total profit at a price of $40 for output levels of 5 and 6 units.

2. Exhibit 2 depicts a ziwi fruit farm that has a river running along the west side of the property boundary. Because ziwi fruit grows better near water, each row planted further away from the river costs more to grow because of the additional fertilizer and watering needed. Shown in the exhibit are the costs for each row. The first row of fruit planted next to the river costs $10, the second row out costs $20, the third row costs $30, and so forth. Further assume that each row planted results in one ton of ziwi fruit.

a. If the farmer wishes to produce one ton of output, he will plant only row one. His total cost will be $10. If the farmer wishes to produce two tons of output, he will plant both rows one and two, for a total cost of $30 ($10 + $20). Fill in the remaining spaces in the table for total cost.

b. Fill in the remaining spaces in the table for marginal cost. Now in the space provided, graph the ziwi fruit farm's marginal cost curve with the data in the table.

c. If the market price of ziwi this year is $30, draw in the figure the demand curve facing this ziwi fruit farm. What level of output should be produced to maximize profits?

d. At the profit-maximizing level of output, what is the firm's total cost? What is the firm's average total cost per ton? Given that they are receiving a price of $30 per ton, how much profit are they earning per ton?

e. Multiply the per-ton profit by the number of units sold to calculate the firm's total profit. Now calculate the firm's total revenue and compare it to their total cost to find total profit. Are your answers the same?

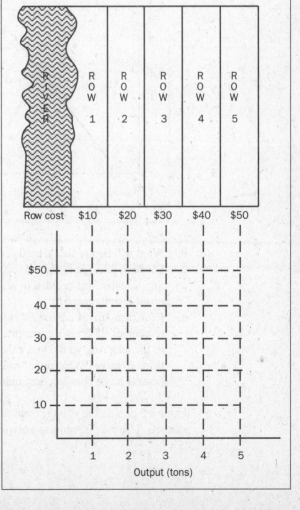

EXHIBIT 2

OUTPUT (TONS)	TOTAL COST	MARGINAL COST
0	$0	x
1	$10	$10
2	$30	$20
3	___	___
4	___	___
5	___	___

3. Exhibit 3 presents selected information relating to a single firm in a price-taker market.

EXHIBIT 3

Price	$8
Total Revenue	8,000
Output	_____
Average Total Cost	8
Total Cost	_____
Marginal Revenue	_____
Marginal Cost	_____
Total Profit	_____

   a. Complete the missing information in Exhibit 3 assuming the firm is currently maximizing profits.
   b. Is this firm in long-run equilibrium?
   c. If this firm is representative of all firms in the industry, what would you expect to happen to the number of firms in this industry in the long run? Would it increase, decrease, or stay the same? (Hint: Remember the exhibit shows economic profit, not accounting profit.)

4. Exhibit 4 shows a firm in a price-taker market. Use the diagrams to answer the following questions
   a. If this firm wants to maximize its profits, how many units should it produce?

EXHIBIT 4

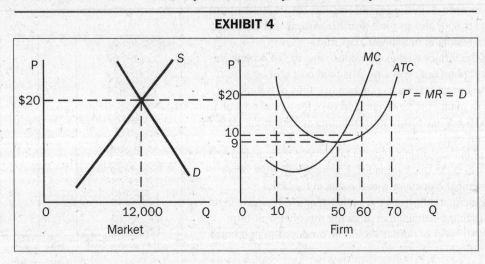

   b. What will be the firm's total revenue at this level of output? total cost? profit?
   c. Shade in the area in the exhibit corresponding to the economic profit of this firm.
   d. Suppose the firm decided to produce 50 units. How much profit would it earn? Is this more or less profit than in part b?
   e. How many firms are in this industry? (Hint: Compare total market output to this firm's output and remember all firms are identical.)
   f. In the long run, would you expect more firms to enter this industry or would you expect some firms to leave? What price would you expect to be present in this market in the long run? (You may assume it is a constant cost industry.)

5. Exhibit 5 depicts the market conditions experienced by representative firms in three different price-taker markets. Use the diagrams to answer the following questions.

EXHIBIT 5

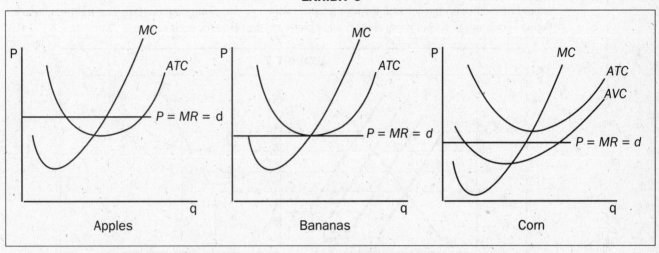

a. Is the representative firm in the apple industry earning an economic profit, an economic loss, or earning zero economic profit? What would you expect to happen to the number of firms in this industry in the long run? Indicate in the diagram the profit-maximizing level of output and shade in the area corresponding to the firm's economic profit or loss.

b. Is the representative firm in the banana industry earning an economic profit, an economic loss, or earning zero economic profit? What would you expect to happen to the number of firms in this industry in the long run? Indicate in the diagram the profit-maximizing level of output.

c. Is the representative firm in the corn industry earning an economic profit, an economic loss, or earning zero economic profit? What would you expect to happen to the number of firms in this industry in the long run? Indicate in the diagram the profit-maximizing level of output and shade in the area corresponding to the firm's economic profit or loss. Should the firm shut down or remain open in the short run?

6. Exhibit 6 shows a firm in a price-taker market. Use the diagrams to answer the following questions.

EXHIBIT 6

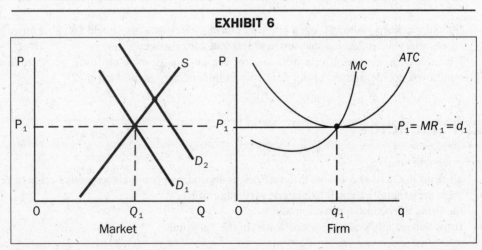

a. The current market demand is given by D_1. Suppose market demand increases to D_2. Indicate the new market price and draw the new demand curve for this firm.

b. What has happened to the profitability of this firm? Will it increase or decrease its level of output? Indicate in the graph the new level of output the firm should produce to maximize profit.

c. What would you expect to happen to the number of firms in this industry in the long run?

7. Suppose you own a small hotel near a ski resort. The left-hand panel of Exhibit 7 depicts the market supply of rooms and the demand for rooms in the winter, spring, summer, and fall. The right-hand panel depicts your unit costs per room rented; these costs are the same for each season.

EXHIBIT 7

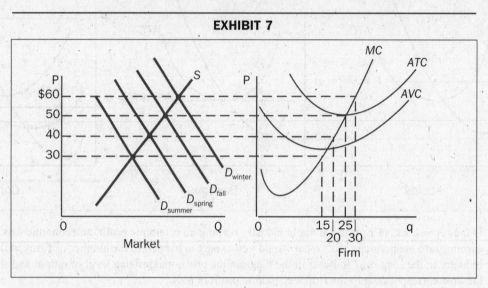

a. Use the diagrams in Exhibit 7 to help you complete the following table. For the profit column, simply indicate whether your profits for the season are positive (+), negative (−), or zero (0).

SEASON	PRICE	NUMBER OF ROOMS RENTED	PROFITS
Winter			
Spring			
Summer			
Fall			

b. Should you keep your hotel open all year? During which seasons should you shut down? How many rooms will you rent during the summer? Explain your reasoning.

c. Given that you earn negative profits in some seasons and positive profits in other seasons, how would you decide whether or not to remain in this industry in the long run?

MULTIPLE CHOICE

1. In a price-taker market,
   a. all firms in the market charge different prices depending upon their respective costs of production.
   b. there are generally a small number of very large firms.
   c. the firms all produce identical products.
   d. firms will usually make economic losses in the long run.

2. A firm that must sell its output at a market-determined price is called a
   a. price-taker firm.
   b. price-searcher firm.
   c. price-setter firm.
   d. price-maker firm.

3. For a firm in a price-taker market, the firm's demand curve is
    a. a horizontal line at the market price that is equal to the firm's marginal revenue curve.
    b. an upward-sloping line that is equal to the firm's marginal cost above AVC.
    c. a downward-sloping line that lies below the firm's marginal revenue curve.
    d. undefined because it cannot determine the price it charges for its output.

4. To maximize profits, a firm should always produce the level of output where
    a. marginal cost equals average total cost.
    b. average total cost equals price.
    c. marginal cost equals marginal revenue.
    d. marginal revenue equals price.

5. If you were the owner of a price-taker firm operating at an output level where the marginal cost of producing another unit was $5, and the market price was $7, then you
    a. could increase your profit by expanding output.
    b. could increase your profit by decreasing output.
    c. are maximizing your profit at your current output level.
    d. will be able to earn positive economic profits in the long run.

6. A price-taker firm is currently producing 50 units of output at an average total cost of $3 per unit. If the market price is $7, then the firm's total economic profit is
    a. $4.
    b. $150.
    c. $200.
    d. $350.

7. For a price-taker firm, marginal revenue is
    a. equal to price.
    b. equal to zero when the market is in long-run equilibrium.
    c. equal to the change in total revenue divided by the change in output.
    d. both a and c.

8. If a firm in a price-taker market is earning zero economic profit, it
    a. will shut down in the long run but not the short run.
    b. will also be earning zero accounting profit.
    c. is doing as well as typical firms in other markets.
    d. will shut down in the short run.

9. If marginal revenue exceeds marginal cost at the current level of output, profit will increase when output is expanded because
    a. other firms in the industry will shut down as the firm expands output.
    b. the market price will rise as the firm expands output.
    c. producing and selling an additional unit will add more to total revenue than it adds to total cost.
    d. marginal cost will decline as output is expanded.

10. Historically, most economists have referred to markets where firms are price takers as
    a. purely competitive markets.
    b. monopoly markets.
    c. open-door markets.
    d. price-searcher markets.

11. Which of the following is true?
    a. When firms in a price-taker market are earning zero economic profit, they will shut down.
    b. When firms in a price-taker market are earning positive economic profits, new firms will enter the industry causing the market price to fall until the firms in the industry are earning only zero economic profit.
    c. When firms in a price-taker market are earning economic losses, some firms will exit the industry causing the market price to rise until the remaining firms are earning zero economic profit.
    d. Both b and c are true.

12. Beginning from a point of long-run equilibrium, an increase in the market demand for wheat would result in
    a. an increase in the market price of wheat.
    b. existing wheat producers increasing output in the short run and earning positive economic profits.
    c. new firms entering the wheat industry in the long run.
    d. all of the above.

13. If the market price in a price-taking industry was currently above the average total cost of production for firms in the industry,
    a. firms in the industry would earn short-run economic profits that would be offset by long-run economic losses.
    b. new firms would enter the industry, which would drive price down to the average total cost of production in the long run.
    c. firms in the industry would earn positive economic profits in the long run.
    d. most firms in the industry would shut down in the long run.

14. Which of the following statements is correct?
    a. In order to maximize profits in the short run, a price taker should always produce at the output level where marginal cost is equal to price.
    b. In long-run equilibrium, a price taker will produce at an output level where average total cost is at its minimum.
    c. A price taker will remain open in the short run, even if it is earning an economic loss, so long as price is sufficient to cover average variable cost.
    d. All of the above are true.

15. When consumer demand for a good produced in a price-taker market decreases,
    a. firms in the industry will continue to produce at the same output levels as before.
    b. total market output will generally rise, but each individual firm will reduce its output.
    c. the market price of the good will rise, causing additional resources to flow into the industry in the long run.
    d. some firms will shut down in the long run, making their resources available for the production of other goods.

16. (I) A firm's short-run supply curve is equal to its average variable cost curve above marginal revenue. (II) The short-run supply curve for a price-taker market is the horizontal sum of the supply curves of all firms in the industry.
    a. I is true; II is false.
    b. I is false; II is true.
    c. Both I and II are true.
    d. Both I and II are false.

17. The long-run supply curve is
    a. a horizontal line for a constant-cost industry.
    b. upward sloping for a decreasing-cost industry.
    c. downward sloping for an increasing-cost industry.
    d. all of the above.

18. If the demand for a product increases in an increasing-cost industry, as the market adjusts in the long run, production costs for all firms will
    a. rise as new firms enter the industry.
    b. fall as new firms enter the industry.
    c. remain unchanged.
    d. fall as firms exit the industry.

19. If firms in a price-taker industry were forced to install antipollution devices that increased their production costs, we should expect
    a. the cost curves for the firms in this industry to shift downward.
    b. the market price of the product to decrease.
    c. that the firms in the industry would suffer long-run economic losses.
    d. that the firms in the industry would earn normal economic profits in the long run, as the higher production costs were passed along to consumers in the form of higher prices.

20. A price-taker market tends toward a state of long-run equilibrium in which firms earn only a normal rate of return (zero economic profits) because
    a. firms will keep their prices low under fear of government regulation.
    b. with firms able to enter and leave the industry freely, competition will drive prices down to the level of production costs.
    c. by definition, production costs always rise to equal the market price.
    d. mismanagement on the part of owners generally results in the firms not equating marginal revenue and marginal cost.

21. Which portion of the marginal cost curve is used to create a firm's short-run supply curve?
    a. the entire marginal cost curve
    b. the marginal cost curve above its intersection with the average variable cost curve because below this price, firms will shut down in the short run
    c. the marginal cost curve above its intersection with the marginal revenue (demand) curve
    d. the marginal cost curve above its intersection with the average total cost curve because below this price, firms will shut down in the short run

22. You are the owner of an ice cream shop that earns a profit most of the year except during the cold winter months. During the month of December, your rent and other fixed costs amount to a total of $200. If you remain open, your total variable costs (workers, ice cream cones, etc.) will amount to $300. If you would be able to sell 100 ice cream cones at $4 each during December, then
    a. to maximize profits, you should remain open in December.
    b. to maximize profits, you should shut down in December.
    c. you will be able to avoid making a loss by shutting down in December.
    d. you should go out of business in the long run if there is any single month in which you do not earn a profit.

23. FYI Sanitation is currently eight months into a year-long lease contract on a garbage truck at a cost that averages $500 per month. Other variable costs (fuel, workers, etc.) for operating the truck amount to $300 per month. If the monthly revenue from operating the truck is $400, and these conditions are expected to continue into the future, to maximize its profit, FYI Sanitation should
    a. stop operating the truck immediately and not renew the lease for next year.
    b. continue operating the truck indefinitely.
    c. continue operating the truck until the lease expires, then not renew the lease for next year.
    d. stop operating the truck now but renew the lease and begin operating the truck again next year.

24. "I have been making furniture for 27 years. I have never heard of either marginal cost or marginal revenue. Fancy economic theories mean nothing to me. I just know how to do well in business. Whenever I can sell something for more than it cost me to produce it, I make it, and whenever I can't sell it for enough to cover my cost, I don't. That's how I stay in business and earn income for my family. Common sense and watching the market are good enough for me." For producers like this, economic models
    a. accurately describe their behavior and allow predictions to be made as to how they will respond to changes in market conditions.
    b. indicate nothing about the behavior of such producers.
    c. will generally only apply if the person has a college education.
    d. do not apply because the producers do not understand the terminology.

25. If consumers suddenly began desiring more apples and fewer oranges,
    a. the market price of apples would rise, creating short-run economic profits in the apple industry. Current firms will expand output and new firms will enter the industry.
    b. the market price of oranges would fall, creating short-run economic losses in the orange industry. Current firms will reduce output and some will go out of business in the long run.
    c. neither a nor b are correct.
    d. both a and b are correct.

26. The schedule of total cost for a firm in a price-taker market is given in Exhibit 8. If the market price for this product is $50, which of the following output levels should this firm produce if it wants to maximize its profit?
    a. 1
    b. 2
    c. 3
    d. 4

EXHIBIT 8

Output	Total Cost
0	$ 25
1	65
2	95
3	140
4	195
5	255

Exhibit 9 depicts a firm in a price-taker market. Use this exhibit to answer questions 27 through 29.

EXHIBIT 9

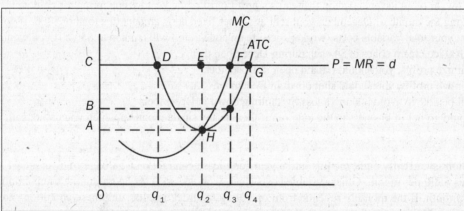

27. To maximize profit, the firm should produce an output level of
    a. q_1.
    b. q_2.
    c. q_3.
    d. q_4.

28. At the profit-maximizing level of output, the firm will earn an economic (Hint: Areas in the exhibit are referenced by the four letters on the corners of the respective area.)
    a. profit of AHEC.
    b. profit of BIFC.
    c. loss of AHEC.
    d. loss of BIFC.

29. Given the current market conditions, in the long run,
    a. new firms will enter the industry and market price will fall.
    b. firms will exit the industry and market price will rise.
    c. firms will neither enter nor exit because the market is in long-run equilibrium.
    d. firms will maintain their current level of economic profit.

30. Exhibit 10 shows a representative firm in a price-taker market. Which of the following is true regarding the situation depicted in the exhibit?
    a. This firm shown is earning zero economic profit.
    b. The industry is in long-run equilibrium.
    c. Firms will neither enter nor exit the market.
    d. All of the above are true.

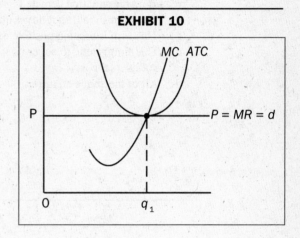

EXHIBIT 10

Exhibit 11 depicts a firm in a price-taker market. Use this exhibit to answer questions 31 through 33.

EXHIBIT 11

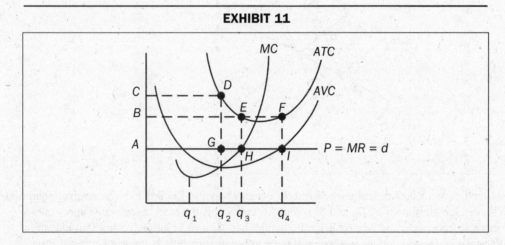

31. To maximize profit, the firm should produce an output level of
    a. zero; the firm should shut down immediately.
    b. q_2.
    c. q_3.
    d. q_4.

32. At the profit-maximizing level of output, the firm will earn an economic
    a. profit of AHEB.
    b. loss of AGDC.
    c. loss of AHEB.
    d. loss of AIFB.

33. Given the current market conditions, in the long run,
    a. new firms will enter the industry and market price will fall.
    b. firms will exit the industry and market price will rise.
    c. firms will neither enter nor exit because the market is in long-run equilibrium.
    d. firms will continue to suffer economic losses.

34. Exhibit 12 shows a representative firm in a price-taker market. Which of the following is true regarding the situation depicted in the exhibit?
    a. This firm should shut down immediately.
    b. This firm is earning positive economic profit.
    c. This firm is able to cover its variable cost but not its total cost.
    d. All of the above are true.

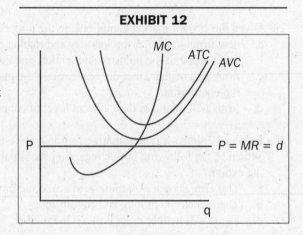

EXHIBIT 12

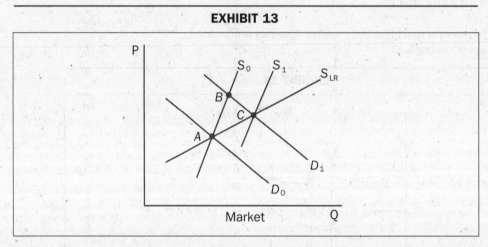

EXHIBIT 13

35. Which of the following best describes the series of events shown in Exhibit 13? The original conditions prior to the change are shown by D_0 and S_0 (point A), and S_{LR} is the market long-run supply curve.
    a. an increase in demand and an expansion in the number of firms in an increasing cost industry
    b. an increase in demand and an expansion in the number of firms in a decreasing cost industry
    c. an increase in demand and an expansion in the number of firms in a constant cost industry
    d. none of the above

DISCUSSION QUESTIONS

1. Why don't price-taker firms have more control over the price they charge for their output? Can you think of several real-world industries that are price-taker markets?

2. Do you think most real-world firms attempt to maximize their profit? How do you think a nonprofit firm (and industry) would respond to changes in the price of the product produced? Would the response be any different? How can you reconcile the fact that most business people probably do not know these economic models, but yet the models are very accurate predictors of their behavior?

3. How does the dynamic process of competition increase prosperity? What important variables are omitted from the simple economic model of a price-taker market?

4. Use the price-taker model to explain fully how a reduction in demand for shrimp would affect (a) the economic profit or loss of shrimp producers and (b) the market price and output in both the short and long run. Use diagrams relating the adjustments of the producers (firms) to the market in explaining your answer.

5. Use the price-taker model to explain fully how an increase in demand for eggs would affect (a) the economic profit or loss of egg producers and (b) the market price and output in both the short and long run. Use diagrams relating the adjustments of the producers (firms) to the market in explaining your answer.

6. Our economy is in a continuous process of change: New firms start up and many existing firms go out of business.
   a. When a firm goes out of business, does it increase or decrease efficiency?
   b. Who loses when a firm goes out of business? Who gains?
   c. If a firm is producing a good or service at a loss, how is it affecting national wealth? Explain.
   d. The government occasionally rescues bankrupt firms, such as Chrysler and many savings and loan associations. Do you approve of these bailouts? Why or why not?

Price-Searcher Markets with Low Entry Barriers

TRUE OR FALSE

T   F

☐ ☐ 1. Unlike price takers, price searchers do not maximize profits by producing at the point where marginal revenue is equal to marginal cost.

☐ ☐ 2. Entry and exit of firms drive economic profits to zero in the long run in competitive price-searcher markets.

☐ ☐ 3. Price discrimination is the term used to describe a situation where a firm is charging the same price to all of its customers.

☐ ☐ 4. The marginal revenue curve for a price searcher is equal to the firm's downward-sloping demand curve.

☐ ☐ 5. Economic models of profit maximization do not fully capture the role played by entrepreneurs.

☐ ☐ 6. Monopolistic competition is a term that has historically been used when referring to competitive price-searcher markets.

☐ ☐ 7. Competition provides firms with a strong incentive to develop improved products and discover lower-cost methods of production.

☐ ☐ 8. The entry of firms into a competitive price-searcher market generally does not affect the demand curve for firms already operating in that market.

☐ ☐ 9. In the long run, a firm in a competitive price-searcher market produces at the point where price is equal to average total cost.

☐ ☐ 10. Competitive price searchers often emphasize quality, location, and advertising as competitive weapons (in addition to price competition).

T F

☐ ☐ 11. A market is said to be contestable when barriers to entry and exit are high.

☐ ☐ 12. To effectively price discriminate, a firm must be able to prevent resale among its customers.

☐ ☐ 13. A competitive price searcher will charge a price equal to marginal cost.

☐ ☐ 14. For a firm with a downward-sloping demand curve, marginal revenue is less than price because to sell additional units, price must be reduced on other units that could have been sold at a higher price.

☐ ☐ 15. A firm currently sells three units at a price of $5. If the firm must lower its price to $4 to sell four units, the marginal revenue derived from producing and selling the fourth unit is $4.

☐ ☐ 16. The benefit of business failure is that those resources are then freed up to move into other, more productive, areas.

☐ ☐ 17. In real-world markets, the most cost-effective structure, size, and scope of businesses are found through entrepreneurial trial and error.

PROBLEMS AND PROJECTS

1. Suppose that you produce and sell tables in a localized market. Past experience permits you to estimate your demand and marginal cost schedules. This information is presented in Exhibit 1.
   a. Fill in the missing values for revenue, cost, and profit.
   b. If you wanted to maximize your profit, what price should you charge? How many tables would you sell at that price?
   c. At the profit-maximizing level of output, what is the relationship between the price you are charging and the marginal cost of producing the last table?
   d. If all the firms in the market for tables face similar costs, what would you expect to happen to your demand in the long run?

EXHIBIT 1

Price	Quantity Demanded	Total Revenue	Marginal Revenue	Total Cost	Marginal Cost	Profit
$65	0	_____	xxx	$ 40	xxx	_____
60	1	_____	_____	90	_____	_____
55	2	_____	_____	110	_____	_____
50	3	_____	_____	135	_____	_____
45	4	_____	_____	164	_____	_____
40	5	_____	_____	204	_____	_____
35	6	_____	_____	254	_____	_____

2. Exhibit 2 indicates the demand and cost conditions facing a firm.
   a. Is this firm a price taker or a price searcher? Explain how you can tell the difference.
   b. Illustrate the firm's profit-maximizing price and output on the diagram.
   c. If the firm produces at the output you indicated in part b, will the firm be making a profit or a loss? Show the area that represents this profit or loss in the diagram.

EXHIBIT 2

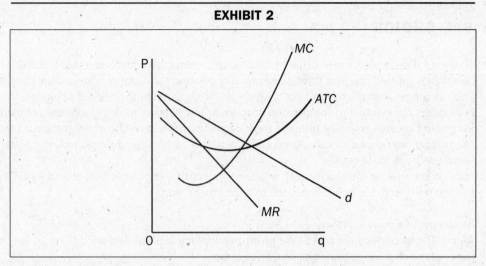

d. If this firm is in a contestable market (one with low barriers to entry), what would you expect to happen to the firm in the long run? Illustrate the long-run equilibrium for this firm in Exhibit 2. (Assume the firm is in a constant cost industry.)

3. Exhibit 3 indicates the demand and cost conditions facing a firm in a competitive price-searcher market.
    a. Illustrate the firm's profit-maximizing price and output on the diagram.

EXHIBIT 3

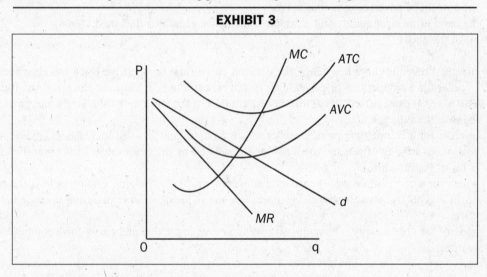

b. If the firm produces at the output you indicated in part a, will the firm be making a profit or a loss? Show the area that represents this profit or loss in the diagram.
c. If this firm is in a contestable market (one with low barriers to entry), what would you expect to happen to the firm in the long run? Illustrate the long-run equilibrium for this firm in the diagram above. (Assume the firm is in a constant cost industry.)

4. When a seller can effectively separate his or her total market into two segments, the theory of price discrimination indicates that a higher product price will be charged in the market segment with the lower elasticity of demand. For each of the markets below, indicate in the blank which segment, (1) or (2), you think will be charged the lower price and be ready to explain why you think that segment has a higher elasticity of demand.
    _____ a. sales of football tickets to (1) students and (2) alumni
    _____ b.   sales of airline tickets to (1) business travelers and (2) vacationers (leisure travelers)
    _____ c.   sales of new cars to (1) those who presently own a car and (2) those who do not
    _____ d.   sales of cosmetic surgery to (1) the poor and (2) the rich

MULTIPLE CHOICE

1. Which of the following is a major difference between a competitive price searcher and a price taker?
    a. Price takers need to compete through advertising because they cannot choose their own price, whereas competitive price searchers compete primarily through their pricing policies.
    b. Price takers are exposed to competition because of low barriers to entry, whereas competitive price searchers are somewhat immune from competition due to relatively high barriers to entry.
    c. Price takers can never earn economic profits, whereas competitive price searchers can earn economic profits in the short run.
    d. Price takers produce identical goods, whereas competitive price searchers produce goods that are differentiated from the goods produced by their competitors.

2. For the competitive price searcher,
    a. price will exceed marginal cost at the profit-maximizing level of output.
    b. price will equal average total cost in the long run.
    c. economic profit will be driven to zero in the long run by the entry and exit of firms.
    d. all of the above are correct.

3. Only undertaking an activity when it adds more to revenue than to cost is the decision rule a profit-maximizing firm will use when deciding upon
    a. the level of output to produce.
    b. the amount of advertising to undertake.
    c. the level of product quality (for example, how many years it is designed to last).
    d. all of the above.

4. The marginal revenue curve lies below the demand curve for a competitive price searcher because
    a. in order for a competitive price searcher to sell an extra unit, it must cut the price on all units. The lowered price offsets the additional revenue from the extra unit sold, so the marginal revenue is lower than the price.
    b. in order for a competitive price searcher to sell an extra unit, it must increase its advertising. The cost of advertising offsets the extra revenue generated by the extra sales, so the marginal revenue is lower than the price.
    c. whenever a competitive price searcher discovers a profit-maximizing pricing policy, the economic profit it generates attracts new competitors into the industry, driving marginal revenue below the price.
    d. none of the above apply. The marginal revenue curve is the demand curve for a competitive price searcher.

5. Suppose you were asked to determine whether a firm was a price taker or a competitive price searcher by looking at a graph of the firm's cost and revenue curves. The key is that for the competitive price searcher,
    a. the firm's marginal revenue curve lies above and to the right of the demand curve, not below and to the left.
    b. there are only total costs, not variable costs, on the graph.
    c. the firm's demand curve is downward sloping, not a horizontal line.
    d. all of the above are true.

6. A competitive price-searcher market is characterized by firms
   a. being able to choose their price and no barriers preventing firms from entering or leaving the market.
   b. being able to choose their price and high barriers preventing firms from entering or leaving the market.
   c. being able to accept the market price for their product and high barriers preventing firms from entering or leaving the market.
   d. having to accept the market price for their product and no barriers preventing firms from entering or leaving the market.

7. If a price-searcher firm can sell 4 units at a price of $6 or it can sell 5 units at a price of $5, the marginal revenue from the fifth unit is
   a. $1.
   b. $5.
   c. $6.
   d. $25.

8. The fact that barriers to entry are low in competitive price-searcher markets means that if current firms are making economic losses,
   a. these losses will remain in the long run because firms will not exit the market.
   b. some current firms will exit the market, causing the demand curves that face the remaining firms to increase.
   c. new firms will enter the market, causing the demand curves that face the existing firms to decrease.
   d. new firms will enter the market, causing no change in the demand curves that face the existing firms in the market.

9. Which of the following is true when *long-run* equilibrium conditions are present in price-taker and competitive price-searcher markets?
   a. MR = MC in both price-taker and competitive price-searcher markets
   b. P = ATC in both price-taker and competitive price-searcher markets
   c. P = MC in both price-taker and competitive price-searcher markets
   d. Both a and b, but not c are true.

10. A market in which the costs of entry and exit are low is called a
    a. regulated market.
    b. monopoly market.
    c. market with high barriers to entry.
    d. contestable market.

11. In both price-taker and competitive price-searcher markets, short-run economic profits will lead to
    a. firms being able to sustain those economic profits into the long run.
    b. the exit of firms from the market and the eventual restoration of zero long-run economic profits.
    c. the entry of additional firms into the market and the eventual restoration of zero long-run economic profits.
    d. none of the above.

12. In order for a firm to be able to engage in price discrimination, it must be able to
    a. identify and separate groups with different price elasticities of demand.
    b. prevent resale of the product between customer groups.
    c. maximize profits at the point where average total cost is minimized.
    d. do both a and b, but not c.

13. Some economists have argued that competitive price-searcher industries are allocatively inefficient relative to price-taker industries because
    a. unlike price takers, price searchers fail to produce at the point where marginal revenue is equal to marginal cost.
    b. competition forces price takers to find the most efficient method of production, whereas product differentiation allows competitive price searchers to stay in business even when their methods of production are inefficient.
    c. unlike price takers, price searchers do not produce at the minimum of their average total cost curves.
    d. price searchers need to pay higher salaries to their managers because of the greater amount of entrepreneurship required in price-searcher industries.

14. Other economists have argued that the allocative inefficiency of competitive price searchers apparent in mechanical models is misleading. They argue that such mechanical models fail to account for
    a. the entry and exit of firms in the long run, which drives economic profits to zero, thereby eliminating any short-run, allocative inefficiencies in competitive price-searcher industries.
    b. the possibility that the higher prices paid by consumers in competitive price-searcher industries are compensated by greater choice of goods or locations than would be present in an allocatively "efficient" industry.
    c. the spillover effects on the advertising industry, which would shrink substantially if competitive price searchers did not need to advertise so much.
    d. the fact that most competitive price-searcher industries are contestable markets, so competitive price searchers react to competitive pressures whether or not numerous competitors actually operate in the market.

15. If economic profits were present in a competitive price-searcher industry,
    a. production inefficiency would develop, causing costs to increase until the profits had been eliminated.
    b. firms would operate in the short run, but they would be forced out of business in the long run as competition eliminated the economic profit.
    c. competition from new entrants would occur until the economic profits had been eliminated.
    d. the firms would eventually find these profits offset by long-run economic losses.

16. The practice of price discrimination has which of the following effects?
    a. Groups with the higher elasticity of demand will pay higher prices.
    b. Groups with the lower elasticity of demand will pay higher prices.
    c. With price discrimination, total output and allocative efficiency will fall.
    d. Groups will pay identical prices that are exactly equal to the firm's marginal cost.

17. Neither price takers nor competitive price searchers will be able to earn long-run economic profit because
    a. with low entry barriers, the entry and exit of firms result in prices that are equal to per-unit costs in the long run.
    b. competition from new firms will result in higher prices in the market, which offset any economic losses they earn.
    c. in both markets, firms charge a price equal to marginal cost.
    d. in both markets, firms produce products that are identical to the products produced by their competitors.

Questions 18 through 20 refer to Exhibit 4, which depicts the demand, marginal revenue, and cost curves facing a firm in a competitive price-searcher industry.

EXHIBIT 4

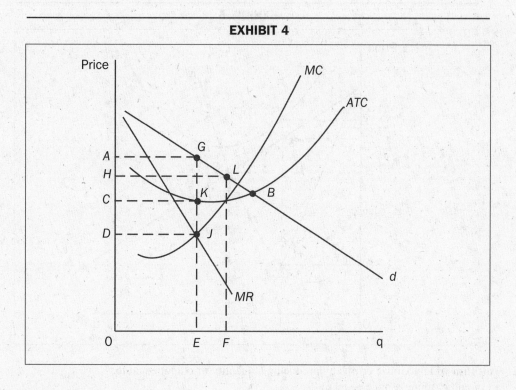

18. This firm will maximize profits by producing a quantity of output equal to
    a. *E* and charging a price equal to *A*.
    b. *E* and charging a price equal to *D*.
    c. *F* and charging a price equal to *H*.
    d. *F* and charging a price equal to *C*.

19. The firm is currently earning an economic
    a. profit equal to the area *CKGA*.
    b. profit equal to the area *DJGA*.
    c. loss equal to the area *CKGA*.
    d. loss equal to the area *DJGA*.

20. In the long run, we would expect the firm's
    a. ATC curve to fall as firms enter the industry, forcing the firm to increase its efficiency.
    b. demand curve to decrease as firms enter the industry due to the presence of positive economic profits.
    c. demand curve to increase as firms exit the industry due to the presence of economic losses.
    d. demand curve to shift such that marginal revenue and marginal cost intersect at quantity F—the point where average total cost is at a minimum.

Questions 21 through 23 refer to Exhibit 5, which depicts the demand, marginal revenue, and cost curves facing a firm in a competitive price-searcher industry.

EXHIBIT 5

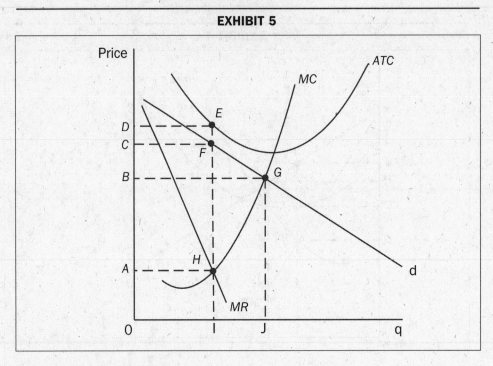

21. This firm will maximize profits by producing a quantity of output equal to
   a. *I* and charging a price equal to *A*.
   b. *I* and charging a price equal to *C*.
   c. *I* and charging a price equal to *D*.
   d. *J* and charging a price equal to *B*.

22. The firm is currently earning an economic
   a. profit equal to the area *AHFC*.
   b. profit equal to the area *CFED*.
   c. loss equal to the area *AHED*.
   d. loss equal to the area *CFED*.

23. In the long run, we would expect
   a. more firms to enter this industry until zero economic profits are restored.
   b. firms to exit this industry until zero economic profits are restored.
   c. the number of firms to remain constant and existing firms will continue to suffer economic losses in the long run.
   d. the number of firms to remain constant and existing firms will continue to earn economic profits in the long run.

24. Given the data shown in Exhibit 6, what price and output level would a profit-maximizing price searcher choose?
   a. price of $8, output of 3 units
   b. price of $7, output of 4 units
   c. price of $6, output of 5 units
   d. price of $5, output of 6 units

EXHIBIT 6

OUTPUT	PRICE	TOTAL COST
1	$10	$10
2	9	11
3	8	13
4	7	16
5	6	20
6	5	25

25. The idea that business failure is a positive force for progress in a market economy is often summarized by the term "creative destruction." Which of the following best states the central idea of this principle?
    a. When a business fails, the assets and resources from that business become unemployed, resulting in higher government subsidies.
    b. Business failure allows the assets and resources from that business to move into other areas where those resources are now more productive and highly valued.
    c. Only through frequent business failure will it be possible to avoid income being concentrated in a few rich entrepreneurs.
    d. The new, rival businesses that drive out old competitors tend to be less efficient and less creative than the older established businesses.

26. (I) The entrepreneurial discovery and development of improved products and production processes is a central element of economic progress. (II) Traditional economic models of the firm accurately capture the role of the entrepreneur.
    a. I is true; II is false.
    b. I is false; II is true.
    c. Both I and II are true.
    d. Both I and II are false.

DISCUSSION QUESTIONS

1. Do you think the town where you live has "too many" gas stations or quick-stop mini food stores? Is this duplication and competitiveness wasteful? Does it result in higher prices than those that would prevail under alternative arrangements? Explain why you think that competitive price-searcher industries are either
    a. wasteful and inefficient, or
    b. consistent with efficiency and a consumer-directed economy.

2. a. List some real-world examples of price discrimination.
    b. Do you think price discrimination is more or less common in the sale of services than in the sale of physical goods? Why might this be the case?
    c. Phone prices are generally lower on weekends than on weekdays. Do you think this is price discrimination? Explain.

3. What is meant by competition? How does competition in price-taker industries differ from the competition that occurs in competitive price-searcher industries? Why is competition important if markets are to work efficiently? Can competition protect the consumer from sellers who sell differentiated products?

4. List five industries or markets that you think are characterized by competitive price searching. Pick two of them and describe the form of competition in those industries. Do these firms compete through price-cutting, advertising, location, or quality differences? Do you think that competition in these industries delivers good-quality products for good prices? Why or why not?

5. Is advertising wasteful or productive? To what extent do commercials like those produced for the soft drink industry provide information to the customer? Why is such advertising effective? Make a list of advertising campaigns that you regard as useful because of the information they provide. Make a list of advertising campaigns that you regard as socially wasteful.

6. What is a contestable market? If there was only one firm presently in an industry, but there were no barriers preventing other firms from entering, would you expect this firm to price its products as if it were in competition with other firms? Explain your reasoning.

7. Discuss the role of entrepreneurship in a market economy. In your answer, address what important aspects of business size, scope, and structure are found through entrepreneurial trial and error and what is meant by the term "creative destruction."

Price-Searcher Markets with High Entry Barriers

TRUE OR FALSE

T F

☐ ☐ 1. Government licensing, patent laws, economies of scale, and control over an essential resource are four potential sources of high entry barriers in a market.

☐ ☐ 2. In the long run, the profits of a monopolist will be eliminated by the entry of new competitors.

☐ ☐ 3. Unlike other firms, a profit-maximizing monopolist will not produce the level of output where MC = MR.

☐ ☐ 4. Because an unregulated monopolist is assured of economic profit, there is little incentive for such a firm to produce efficiently.

☐ ☐ 5. Patent laws result in higher prices to consumers, but they also encourage more investment in research and development.

☐ ☐ 6. The level of output produced by a monopolist will exceed the level of output produced if the industry was instead comprised of many competitive firms.

☐ ☐ 7. An oligopoly is an industry dominated by a small number of rival sellers.

☐ ☐ 8. Collusion is likely to be more successful if barriers to entry are high and the number of producers in the industry is small.

☐ ☐ 9. A cartel is an organization of sellers attempting to act as a single monopolist.

☐ ☐ 10. A competitive firm has more market power than a monopolist because it competes with a larger number of rival sellers.

T F

☐ ☐ 11. Theoretically, price regulation could improve efficiency and resource allocation by forcing a monopolist to charge a price equal to her average (or marginal) cost of production.

☐ ☐ 12. Practically speaking, the advantages of government regulation are greatly limited because of imperfect information about cost and demand conditions.

☐ ☐ 13. Historically, regulatory agencies have sometimes been used as vehicles to maintain high prices and limit competition.

☐ ☐ 14. Reducing artificial barriers to entry (eliminating licensing requirements, for example) would reduce some of the inefficiencies associated with monopolies and oligopolies in industries currently protected by such barriers.

PROBLEMS AND PROJECTS

1. Exhibit 1 indicates the demand and long-run cost conditions in an industry.
   a. Explain why the industry is likely to be monopolized. (Hint: Look at the shape of the LRATC curve.)
   b. Indicate the monopolist's profit-maximizing output level and label it Q.
   c. Indicate the price that a profit-maximizing monopolist would charge and label it P.
   d. Indicate the area representing the profits of the monopolist.

EXHIBIT 1

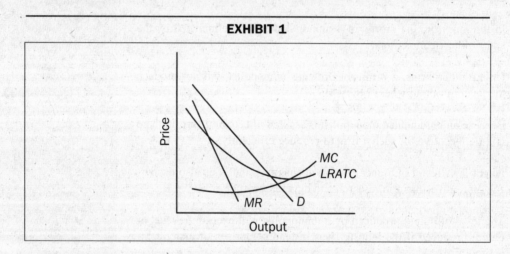

2. The food service at many university campuses is operated by a single firm. Suppose that Exhibit 2 indicates the monthly demand for meals and total operating costs for the food service firm on your campus.
   a. Fill in the firm's TR, MR, and MC schedules.
   b. What price (of those shown) would a profit-maximizing monopolist choose?
   c. Is the monopolist making economic profits? If so, how large per month?
   d. Suppose that the university competitively auctioned the food service rights to the highest bidder. What is the maximum amount this firm would be willing to pay for this license for one year? Who would reap the monopoly profits under this arrangement?

EXHIBIT 2

SALES (IN 1,000s)	PRICE (PER MEAL)	TR	MR (PER 1,000)	TOTAL COST	MC (PER 1,000)
4	$1.60	_____	xx	$6,000	xx
5	1.40	_____	_____	6,400	_____
6	1.30	_____	_____	6,800	_____
7	1.20	_____	_____	7,300	_____
8	1.10	_____	_____	8,000	_____
9	1.00	_____	_____	9,000	_____
10	0.90	_____	_____	10,200	_____

3. Exhibit 3 indicates the demand, marginal revenue, marginal cost, and average cost curves for a monopolist.
   a. To maximize profits, what price would the monopolist set? What is the profit-maximizing level of output? Shade in the area that represents the monopolist's profit or loss.
   b. What are the socially ideal levels of price and output in this market (as might be obtained if the market were a competitive price-taker market)?

EXHIBIT 3

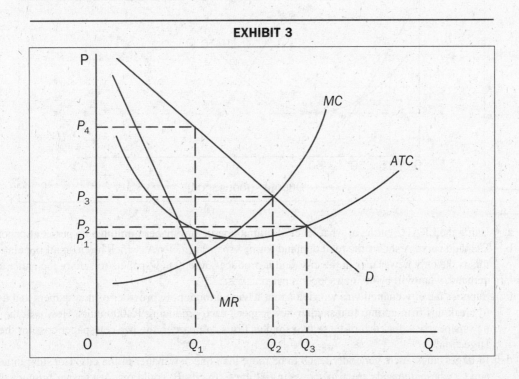

4. Suppose the diagram in Exhibit 4 depicts the demand and cost conditions in an oligopoly market.

EXHIBIT 4

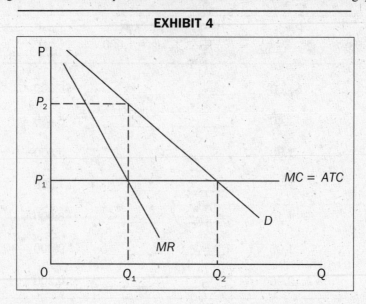

a. If the firms in this industry were to compete, what would be the resulting market price and quantity?
b. If the firms in this industry were to successfully collude, what would be the resulting market price and quantity?

5. Exhibit 5 shows the long-run, per-unit costs (LRATC) for producing newspapers for a single firm. Use the information in the exhibit to answer the following questions.

EXHIBIT 5

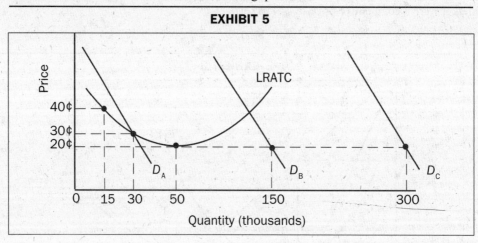

a. Using the LRATC curve, at what level of output does a newspaper minimize its per-newspaper cost?
b. Demand curve A shows the total demand for newspapers in city A, which has a small population. If this is the only newspaper in the city, and it produces 30,000 newspapers to satisfy the entire city's demand, what will be the newspaper's per-unit cost?
c. Suppose the city council was worried about having a monopoly provider of newspapers and decided to break this firm up into two smaller newspapers, each producing 15,000 units. How will the per-newspaper costs for each of these two smaller firms compare to the per-newspaper cost for the one large firm?
d. In larger cities, there generally tends to be more than one newspaper in the city. Consider cities B and C, whose demands are also shown in Exhibit 5. In city B, could one newspaper produce the entire market output at a lower cost than several smaller firms? How many different newspaper firms might we expect to be present in city B? city C?

6. Consider a university town in which two stores sell textbooks, Tom's Texts and Bob's Books. Both stores purchase textbooks from distributors at a cost of $20 per textbook and are considering whether to set their price at either $30 or $40. Because the quantity sold at each store will depend upon not only the price they set but also on the price set by the rival firm, Exhibit 6 shows the quantity of textbooks (Q) sold by each store for all four possible combinations of prices. Use the information in the exhibit to answer the following questions.

    a. The case where Tom's Texts sets its price at $30 while Bob's Books sets its price at $40 is given in the lower left. In this case, Tom's Texts will sell 900 books and Bob's Books will sell 100 books. Profits for each firm will be equal to the number of units sold times the profit earned on each book. Tom's Texts earns $10 profit on each book ($30 price minus cost per book of $20) and sells 900 books, for a total profit of $9,000. Bob's Books earns $20 profit on each book ($40 price minus cost per book of $20) and sells 100 books, for a total profit of $2,000. These values for profit are indicated in the table. For each of the other cases, find profit for both stores and put your answers in the spaces provided in the table.

    b. Suppose that Tom's Texts was almost certain that Bob's Books was going to set their price at $30. Given a $30 price at Bob's Books, what price should Tom's Texts set to maximize their profits?

    c. Instead, suppose that Tom's Texts was almost certain that Bob's Books was going to set their price at $40. Given a $40 price at Bob's Books, what price should Tom's Texts set to maximize their profits?

    d. Given your answers to parts b and c, does the profit-maximizing price for Tom's Texts depend upon the price set by Bob's Books?

    e. Now, view this problem from the standpoint of Bob's Books. What is the price Bob's Books should charge to maximize their profit? Does it depend upon what price they expect Tom's Texts to set?

    f. As the previous questions have uncovered, both stores will choose to set their textbook price at $30 regardless of what the other firm does. How much profit does each firm make in this case? Suppose that the owners of both stores secretly met and agreed to collude, both raising prices to $40. Would both stores earn more profit if they collude?

    g. Do you think this collusive agreement would be stable? Does Tom's Texts have an incentive to cheat on the agreement and lower price? does Bob's Books?

EXHIBIT 6

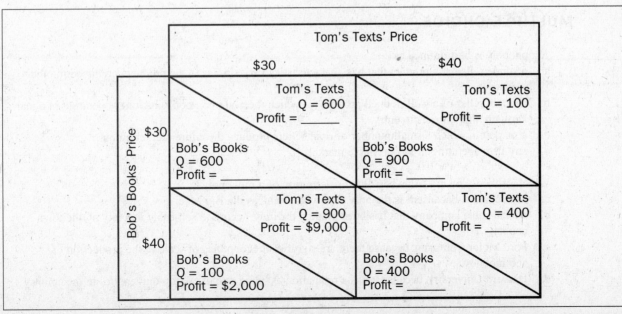

Tom's Texts' Price

	$30	$40
$30	Tom's Texts Q = 600 Profit = _____ / Bob's Books Q = 600 Profit = _____	Tom's Texts Q = 100 Profit = _____ / Bob's Books Q = 900 Profit = _____
$40	Tom's Texts Q = 900 Profit = $9,000 / Bob's Books Q = 100 Profit = $2,000	Tom's Texts Q = 400 Profit = _____ / Bob's Books Q = 400 Profit = _____

Bob's Books' Price

7. Exhibit 7 indicates the demand, marginal revenue, marginal cost, and average cost curves for a monopolist. Use the exhibit to answer the following questions regarding government price regulation of a monopolist.

EXHIBIT 7

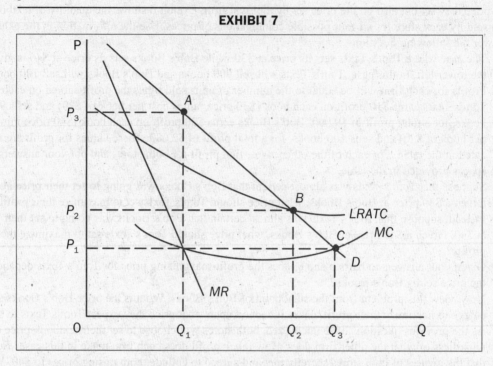

a. In the absence of regulation, what price would the monopolist set to maximize profits? What is the profit-maximizing level of output? Is the monopolist making an economic profit?
b. If a regulatory agency wanted to use average cost pricing to regulate the monopolist, what price would it set? What level of output would the monopolist produce at that price? What level of economic profit would the monopolist earn at this regulated outcome?
c. If a regulatory agency wanted to use marginal cost pricing to regulate the monopolist, what price would it set? What level of economic profit would the monopolist earn at this regulated outcome? What level of output would the monopolist produce at that price in the long run?

MULTIPLE CHOICE

1. A monopoly is best defined as
    a. a single seller of a product that has characteristics very similar to the products produced in other industries.
    b. a single seller of a well-defined product for which there are no good substitutes operating in a market with high barriers to entry.
    c. a market in which a small number of rival sellers produce the entire market output.
    d. any firm operating in a contestable market.

2. Which of the following firms best fits the definition of a monopoly?
    a. McDonald's, because it is the only firm who produces the Big Mac
    b. a local cable company that has been granted the only license to sell cable in a city by the town council
    c. Ford Motor Company, because there are significant economies of scale in the production of automobiles
    d. Harvard University, because it has a reputation as being one of the top universities in the country

3. Which of the following is not a barrier that limits the entry of potential competitors into a market?
   a. government licensing
   b. control over an essential resource
   c. an elastic demand for a product
   d. patent rights

4. When significant economies of scale are present in the production process, an industry will tend naturally toward monopoly because
   a. one firm will be able to produce the entire market output at a lower cost than several smaller firms.
   b. marginal revenue will be less than market price, giving firms the incentive to equate marginal cost with price instead of equating marginal cost and marginal revenue.
   c. economies of scale can only be present when firms produce identical products and there is no reason to have more than one firm producing the same exact product.
   d. consumers will be unwilling to compare the prices charged by several different firms.

5. How will the price and output of an unregulated monopolist compare with the ideal levels that might be reached if the market was competitive?
   a. The output of the monopolist will be larger and the price lower.
   b. The output of the monopolist will be larger and the price higher.
   c. The output of the monopolist will be smaller and the price lower.
   d. The output of the monopolist will be smaller and the price higher.

6. Allowing firms to receive patents on new inventions
   a. increases the price consumers pay for patented products.
   b. gives firms a greater incentive to conduct research and development to invent new products.
   c. results in much lower prices than would be present if other firms were allowed to compete.
   d. does both a and b, but not c.

7. Which of the following is true?
   a. A monopolist is always guaranteed to earn positive economic profits regardless of their cost of production or the price they charge.
   b. A monopolist will charge the highest price possible for their product because no matter what price they charge, people will still have to buy it.
   c. A monopolist has no incentive to find more cost-efficient methods of production because they are protected from competition from other sellers.
   d. None of the above are correct.

8. Which of the following statements accurately describes a difference between a firm that is a monopolist and one that is in a competitive, open price-taker market?
   a. Marginal revenue and price are equal for a price taker but not a monopolist.
   b. Monopolists can earn economic profits in the long run, but price takers cannot.
   c. A price taker sells its output at a price equal to marginal cost, while a monopolist sells its output at a price higher than marginal cost.
   d. All of the above are true.

9. To maximize profit, the monopolist, whose cost and demand conditions are shown in Exhibit 8, should charge a price of
   a. $4.
   b. $5.
   c. $6.
   d. $7.

EXHIBIT 8

PRICE	OUTPUT	TOTAL COST
$7	1	$7
6	2	8
5	3	10
4	4	13
3	5	17

10. Which of the following statements accurately describes a difference between a firm that is a monopolist and one that is in a competitive price-searcher market?
   a. A competitive price searcher produces at the output level where marginal cost equals marginal revenue; a monopolist does not.
   b. A monopolist faces a downward-sloping demand curve; a competitive price searcher does not.
   c. A monopolist charges a price higher than marginal cost; a competitive price searcher does not.
   d. In the long run, a competitive price searcher will earn zero economic profit because of low entry barriers, while a monopolist may earn positive economic profits in the long run.

11. To maximize profits, the monopolist shown in Exhibit 9 would produce output of
   a. Q_1 and charge a price of P_1.
   b. Q_1 and charge a price of P_2.
   c. Q_2 and charge a price of P_3.
   d. Q_1 and charge a price of P_4.

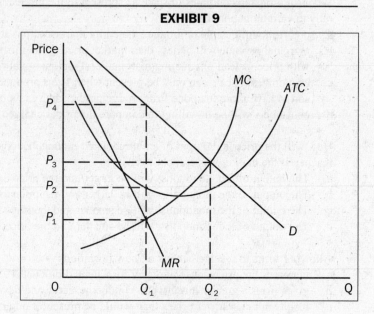

EXHIBIT 9

12. The profit-maximizing monopolist shown in Exhibit 10 would
   a. charge a price equal to C and earn an economic profit of *AFDC*.
   b. charge a price equal to C and earn an economic profit of *AFEB*.
   c. charge a price equal to C and earn an economic profit of *BEDC*.
   d. charge a price equal to A and earn an economic profit of *AFDC*.

13. A market situation in which only a small number of mutually interdependent, rival sellers exists is known as a(n)
   a. oligopoly market.
   b. monopoly market.
   c. open price-taker market.
   d. competitive price-searcher market.

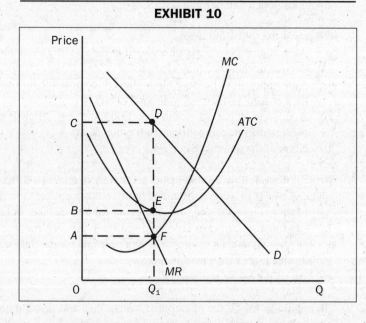

EXHIBIT 10

14. In general, an organization of sellers designed to coordinate supply decisions so that the joint profits of the members is maximized is called a(n) _____. If they are successful, the total market output and price will most closely approximate the output and price in a(n) _____ market. (Fill in the blanks.)
    a. cooperative; open price-taker
    b. cartel; monopoly
    c. cartel; open price-taker
    d. OPEC; competitive price-searcher

15. To increase joint profits, a cartel will attempt to
    a. restrict output in order to increase the market price of the good produced.
    b. restrict output in order to decrease the market price of the good produced.
    c. expand output in order to increase the market price of the good produced.
    d. expand output in order to decrease the market price of the good produced.

16. The oil industry is dominated by a cartel known as OPEC, and the cocaine industry is dominated by the Columbian cocaine cartel. If these cartels are being successful,
    a. the price of oil is higher than if the cartel did not exist, but the price of cocaine is lower.
    b. the price of cocaine is higher than if the cartel did not exist, but the price of oil is lower.
    c. both goods have higher prices than if the cartels did not exist, and both have lower levels of total output.
    d. both goods have higher prices than if the cartels did not exist, and both also have higher levels of total output.

17. Laws designed to prevent monopoly and promote competition are known as
    a. antitrust laws.
    b. statutory amendments.
    c. fair-pricing legislation.
    d. breakup bills.

18. Which of the following would increase the likelihood that firms in an industry could successfully collude?
    a. a large number of firms in the industry
    b. unstable demand conditions in the industry
    c. high barriers to entry in the industry
    d. product characteristics that make it difficult for firms to detect other firms that cheat on the agreement

19. (I) Oligopolistic firms have an incentive to collude to increase profits. (II) Oligopolistic firms have an incentive to cheat on collusive agreements to increase profits.
    a. I is true; II is false.
    b. I is false; II is true.
    c. Both I and II are false.
    d. Both I and II are true.

20. If a local government began licensing funeral homes in the area, effectively making them into a cartel, we would expect
    a. the price of funeral services to rise, and the number of funerals performed in the area to fall.
    b. the price of funeral services to rise, and the number of funerals performed in the area to increase as well.
    c. the price of funeral services to fall, and the number of funerals performed in the area to increase.
    d. the price of funeral services to fall, and the number of funerals performed in the area to fall as well.

21. A major problem with regulatory agencies is that they
    a. have no real legal power over the industries they are supposed to regulate.
    b. tend to be too tough on the firms they are regulating, forcing them into a loss position.
    c. often underestimate the firm's cost of production and consequently force regulated firms into a loss position.
    d. often come to represent the interests of established firms in the industry and use their power to limit competition.

22. An expansion in the number of plumbers in a local area has resulted in lower profits. The local plumbing contractors have called a meeting to discuss ways to improve their long-run profitability. Of the four plans being discussed seriously, which would most likely increase their long-run profits?
    a. passage of legislation requiring new contractors to be licensed, which would require passing a stiff licensing exam and paying a $5,000 fee
    b. an "off-the-record" agreement that each plumbing contractor would increase his or her prices by an average of 7 percent
    c. passage of legislation requiring the local government to share the cost of installing all private sewage systems
    d. repeal of the current tax on installations of plumbing units

23. For which of the following reasons do regulatory agencies sometimes fail to bring the price and output of a natural monopoly to the ideal level?
    a. The regulatory agency does not have all the information concerning a firm's true costs.
    b. Monopolists may conceal profits by inflating the costs of production by spending money to achieve personal objectives (a very nice office building, for example).
    c. Regulatory agencies often come to reflect the views of the industries they are supposed to regulate.
    d. All of the above are reasons.

24. Economic theory suggests that government-operated monopolies will
    a. be highly efficient and follow policies that are in the consumers' interest.
    b. be dominated by persons who, while seeking to serve the public interest, are not hard-nosed enough to run a business efficiently.
    c. be inefficient because of poor incentives for operational efficiency.
    d. favor the consumer at the expense of special interest groups in and out of government.

DISCUSSION QUESTIONS

1. In a famous antitrust case, the government charged the DuPont Company with attempting to monopolize the cellophane industry. The company argued that, while it was the major producer of cellophane, it was competing in the broader market of "flexible packaging," a very competitive industry. Waxed paper, glass-ine, and aluminum foil all had sizable shares of the flexible packaging market. Would you consider DuPont a monopolist? How might you go about determining whether, in fact, DuPont was competing in the flexible wrap industry?

2. What are the advantages of regulating the activities of a monopolist? the major problems? Why does regulation, over time, tend to become a source of economic inefficiency?

3. What are the major sources of monopoly? Can a monopolized industry sometimes be transformed into a competitive industry? Why may it sometimes be costly to break up a monopoly into several smaller independent firms? Explain.

4. Use economic analysis to evaluate the government-operated firm as an alternative to a private-sector monopoly. What factors will influence the price, output, and operational efficiency of the public sector firm? Explain.

5. Explain why firms in an oligopolistic industry have an incentive to collude, but yet also have an incentive to cheat on collusive agreements.

6. What are the main similarities and differences in the economic outcomes between the major market structures we have covered (open price-taker markets, competitive price-searcher markets, oligopoly, and monopoly)? Address in your answer
    a. the price a firm will charge,
    b. the level of output produced,
    c. the role of profits and losses in both the short and long run,
    d. the types of products and different types of competition among firms, and
    e. the number of firms in each market.

PERSPECTIVES IN ECONOMICS

The Parable of the Parking Lots

by Henry G. Manne

[From *Public Interest*, No. 23 (Spring 1971), pp. 10–15, Copyright © by National Affairs Inc., 1971. Reprinted by permission.]

In a city not far away there was a large football stadium. It was used from time to time for various events, but the principal use was for football games played Saturday afternoons by the local college team. The games were tremendously popular and people drove hundreds of miles to watch them. Parking was done in the usual way. People who arrived early were able to park free on the streets, and late comers had to pay to park in regular improvised lots.

There were, at distances ranging from 5 to 12 blocks from the stadium, approximately 25 commercial parking lots all of which received some business from Saturday afternoon football games. The lots closer to the stadium naturally received more football business than those further away, and some of the very close lots actually raised their price on Saturday afternoons. But they did not raise the price much, and most did not change prices at all. The reason was not hard to find.

For something else happened on football afternoons. A lot of people who during the week were students, lawyers, school teachers, plumbers, factory workers, and even stock brokers went into the parking lot business. It was not a difficult thing to do. Typically a young boy would put up a crude, homemade sign saying "Parking $3." He would direct a couple of cars into his parent's driveway, tell the driver to take the key, and collect the three dollars. If the driveway was larger or there was yard space

to park in, an older brother, an uncle, or the head of the household would direct the operation, sometimes asking drivers to leave their keys so that shifts could be made if necessary.

Some part-time parking lot operators who lived very close to the stadium charged as much as $5.00 to park in their driveways. But as the residences-turned-parking-lots were located further from the stadium (and incidentally closer to the commercial parking lots), the price charged at game time declined. In fact houses at some distance from the stadium charged less than the adjacent commercial lots. The whole system seemed to work fairly smoothly, and though traffic just after a big game was terrible, there were no significant delays parking cars or retrieving parked cars.

But one day the owner of a chain of parking lots called a meeting of all the commercial parking lot owners in the general vicinity of the stadium. They formed an organization known as Association of Professional Parking Lot Employers, or APPLE. And they were very concerned about the Saturday parking business. One man who owned four parking lots pointed out that honest parking lot owners had heavy capital investments in their businesses, that they paid taxes, and that they employed individuals who supported families. There was no reason, he alleged, why these lots should not handle all the cars coming into the area for special events like football games. "It is unethical," he said, "to engage in cutthroat competition with irresponsible fender benders. After all, parking cars is a profession, not a business." The last remark drew loud applause.

Thus emboldened he continued, stating that commercial parking lot owners recognize their responsibility to serve the public's needs. Ethical car parkers, he said, understand their obligations not to dent fenders, to employ only trustworthy car parkers, to pay decent wages, and generally to care for the customers' automobiles as they would the corpus of a trust. His statement was hailed by others attending the meeting as being very statesmanlike.

Others at the meeting related various tales of horror about nonprofessional car parkers. One homeowner, it was said, actually allowed his fifteen-year-old son to move other peoples' cars around. Another said that he had seen an $8,000 Cadillac parked on a dirt lawn where it would have become mired in mud had it rained that day. Still another pointed out that a great deal of the problem came on the side of the stadium with the lower-priced houses, where there were more driveways per block than on the wealthier side of the stadium. He pointed out that these poor people would rarely be able to afford to pay for damage to other peoples' automobiles or to pay insurance premiums to cover such losses. He felt that a professional group such as APPLE had a duty to protect the public from their folly in using those parking spaces.

Finally another speaker reminded the audience that these "marginal, fly-by-night" parking lot operators generally parked a string of cars in the driveways so that a driver had to wait until all cars behind his had been removed before he could get out. This, he pointed out, was quite unlike the situation in commercial lots where, during a normal business day, people had to be assured of ready access to their automobiles at any time. The commercial parking lots either had to hire more attendants to shift cars around, or they had to park them so that any car was always accessible, even though this meant that fewer cars could park than the total space would actually hold. "Clearly," he said, "driveway parking constitutes unfair competition."

Emotions ran high at this meeting, and every member of APPLE pledged $1 per parking space for something mysteriously called a "slush fund." It was never made clear exactly whose slush would be bought with these funds, but several months later a resolution was adopted by the city council requiring licensing for anyone in the parking lot business.

The preamble to the new ordinance read like the speeches at the earlier meeting. It said that this measure was designed to protect the public against unscrupulous, unprofessional and undercapitalized parking lot operators. It required, inter alia, that anyone parking cars for a fee must have a minimum capital devoted to the parking lot business of $25,000, liability insurance in an amount not less than $500,000, bonding for each car parker, and a special driving test for these parkers (which incidentally would be designed and administered by APPLE). The ordinance also required, again in the public's interest, that every lot charge a single posted price for parking and that any change in the posted price be approved in advance by the city council. Incidentally, most members were able to raise their fees about 20 percent before the first posting.

Then a funny thing happened to drivers on their way to the stadium for the next big game. They discovered city police in unusually large numbers informing them that it was illegal to pay a non-licensed parking lot operator for the right to park a car. These policemen also reminded parents that if their children were found in violation of this ordinance it could result in a misdemeanor charge being brought against the parents and possible juvenile court proceedings for the children. There were no driveway parking lots that day.

Back at the commercial parking lots, another funny thing occurred. Proceeding from the entrance of each of these parking lots within twelve blocks of the stadium were long lines of cars waiting to park. The line got larger as the lot was closer to the stadium. Many drivers had to wait so long or walk so far that they missed the entire first quarter of the big game.

At the end of the game it was even worse. The confusion was massive. The lot attendants could not cope with the jam up, and some cars were actually not retrieved until the next day. It was even rumored about town that some automobiles had been lost forever and that considerable liabilities might result for some operators. Industry spokesmen denied this, however.

Naturally there was a lot of grumbling, but there was no argument on what had caused the difficulty. At first everyone said there were merely some "bugs" in the new system that would have to be ironed out. But the only "bug" ironed out was a Volkswagen that was flattened by a careless lot attendant in a Cadillac Eldorado.

The situation did not improve at subsequent games. The members of APPLE did not hire additional employees to park cars, and operators near the stadium were not careful to follow their previous practice of parking cars in such a way as to have them immediately accessible. Employees seemed to become more surly, and a number of dented-fender claims mounted rapidly.

Little by little, too, cars began appearing in residential driveways again. For instance, one enterprising youth regularly went into the car wash business on football afternoons, promising that his wash job would take at least two hours. He charged five dollars, and got it—even on rainy days—in fact, especially on rainy days. Another homeowner offered to take cars on consignment for three hours to sell them at prices fixed by the owner. He charged $4.00 for this "service," but his subterfuge was quickly squelched by the authorities. The parking situation remained "critical."

Political pressures on the city council began to mount to "do something" about the inordinate delays in parking and retrieving cars on football afternoons. The city council sent out a stern note of warning to APPLE, and the local university's computer science department to look into the matter. This group reported that the managerial and administrative machinery in the parking lot business was archaic. What was needed, the study group said, was less goose quills and stand-up desks and more computers and conveyor belts. It was also suggested that all members of APPLE be hooked into one computer so that cars could be readily shifted to the most accessible spaces.

Spokesmen for the industry took up the cry of administrative modernization. Subtle warnings appeared in the local papers suggesting that if the industry did not get its own house in order, heavy-handed regulation could be anticipated. The city council asked for reports on failures to deliver cars and decreed that this would include any failure to put a driver in his car within five minutes of demand without a new dent.

Some of the professional operators actually installed computer equipment to handle their ticketing and parking logistics problems. And some added second stories to their parking lots. Others bought up additional space, thereby raising the value of vacant lots in the area, but many simply added a few additional car parkers and hoped that the problem would go away without a substantial investment of capital.

The commercial operators also began arguing that they needed higher parking fees because of their higher operating costs. Everyone agreed that costs for operating a parking lot were certainly higher than before the licensing ordinance. So the city council granted a request for an across-the-board ten percent hike in fees. The local newspaper editorially hoped that this would ease the problem without still higher fees being necessary. In a way, it did. A lot of people stopped driving. They began using city buses, or they chartered private buses for the game. Some stayed home and watched the game on TV. A new study group on fees was appointed.

Just about then, several other blows fell on the parking lot business. But transportation to the area near the stadium was improved with a federal subsidy to the municipal bus company. And several new suburban shopping centers caused a loss of automobile traffic in the older area of town. But most dramatic of all, the local university, under severe pressure from its students and faculty, dropped intercollegiate football altogether and converted the stadium into a park for underprivileged children.

The impact of these events on the commercial parking lots was swift. Income declined drastically. The companies that had borrowed money to finance the expansion everyone wanted earlier were hardest hit. Two declared bankruptcy, and many had to be absorbed by financially stronger companies. Layoffs among car parkers were enormous, and APPLE actually petitioned the city council to guarantee the premiums on their liability insurance policies so that people would not be afraid to park commercially. This idea was suggested to APPLE by recent congressional legislation creating an insurance program for stock brokers.

A spokesman for APPLE made the following public statement: "New organizations or arrangements may be necessary to straighten out this problem. There has been a failure in both the structure of the industry and the regulatory scheme. New and better regulation is clearly demanded. A sound parking lot business is necessary for a healthy urban economy." The statement was hailed by the industry as being very statesmanlike, though everyone speculated about what he really meant.

Others in the industry demanded that the city bus service be curtailed during the emergency. The city council granted every rate increase the lots requested. There were no requests for rate decreases, but the weaker lots began offering prizes and other subtle or covert rebates to private bus companies who would park with them. In fact, this problem became so serious and uncontrollable that one owner of a large chain proclaimed that old-fashioned price competition for this business would be desirable. This again was hailed as statesmanlike, but everyone assumed that he really meant something else. No one proposed repeal of the licensing ordinance.

One other thing happened. Under pressure from APPLE, the city council decreed that henceforth no parking would be allowed on any streets in the downtown area of town. The local merchants were extremely unhappy about this, however, and the council rescinded the ordinance at the next meeting, citing a computer error as the basis for the earlier restriction.

The ultimate resolution of the "new" parking problem is not in sight. The parking lot industry in this town not very far from here is now said to be a depressed business, even a sick one. Everyone looks to the city council for a solution, but things will probably limp along as they are for quite a while, picking up with an occasional professional football game and dropping low with bad weather.

MORAL. If you risk your lot under an apple tree, you may get hit in the head.

DISCUSSION

1. In this fable, who was protected by the regulations? from what? at what cost?

2. Do you see similar situations in regulated businesses in your own area? in state or federally regulated industries? How are they similar? How do they differ? Who gains, and at what cost?

3. In this article, businesses that lobbied to protect themselves from competition ended up hurting themselves in the long run. Do you think that this is a typical result? Explain your answer.

The Supply of and Demand for Productive Resources

CHAPTER 25

TRUE OR FALSE

T F

☐ ☐ 1. Physical capital and human capital cannot be substituted for each other.

☐ ☐ 2. Attending college is an example of an investment in human capital.

☐ ☐ 3. The demand for a resource will be negatively related to its price partly because producers will substitute other factors of production for the resource as it increases in price.

☐ ☐ 4. If consumer demand for automobiles increases, the demand for resources used to produce automobiles will fall to offset the increase.

☐ ☐ 5. Marginal revenue product (MRP) is the change in the total revenue of a firm that results from the employment of one additional unit of a resource. It is equal to the marginal product (MP) of the resource multiplied by the firm's marginal revenue (MR).

☐ ☐ 6. The value of marginal product (VMP) is equal to marginal revenue product (MRP) for a price-searcher firm because for these firms, price (P) equals marginal revenue (MR).

☐ ☐ 7. The demand curve for a resource is equal to the MRP curve for the resource.

☐ ☐ 8. An employer will hire workers as long as their marginal revenue product is positive.

☐ ☐ 9. When multiple resources are employed, a firm will minimize its costs by equating marginal revenue product divided by the price for each resource (in other words, $MRP_A \div P_A = MRP_B \div P_B$).

T   F

☐ ☐ 10. The supply of a resource in the long run will generally be more inelastic than its supply in the short run.

☐ ☐ 11. The marginal products—and therefore wage rates—of employees will be positively influenced by the amount of physical capital per worker in a firm.

☐ ☐ 12. In a market economy, resource prices help to allocate a country's resources among the alternative industries in which they could be employed.

☐ ☐ 13. Because of the law of diminishing marginal returns, a worker's marginal revenue product eventually declines as more workers are hired in a given plant.

☐ ☐ 14. The demand for a resource strongly depends upon the demand for the final good that the resource helps to produce. This is why the demand for a resource is called a derived demand.

PROBLEMS AND PROJECTS

1. Nicole sells building materials in a price-taker industry. Her firm receives $100 for each unit of material sold. Exhibit 1 shows how Nicole's total output changes as additional units of labor are hired.

EXHIBIT 1

UNITS OF LABOR	TOTAL OUTPUT (PER WEEK)	MARGINAL PRODUCT (PER WEEK)	PRODUCT PRICE	TOTAL REVENUE	MARGINAL REVENUE PRODUCT (PER WEEK)
1	5	5	$100	$500	$500
2	9	_____	100	_____	_____
3	12	_____	100	_____	_____
4	14	_____	100	_____	_____
5	15	_____	100	_____	_____

a. Fill in the marginal product, total revenue, and marginal revenue product columns.
b. If she wants to maximize her profits, how many employees should Nicole hire if the market wage rate is $250 per week?
c. How many employees should Nicole hire if the wage rate goes up to $350 per week?
d. The supply-and-demand conditions in the building materials market are represented in Exhibit 2. Suppose that the demand for building materials increases as indicated by D', and Nicole can now sell her output for $150. Using the original wage rate of $250 per week from part b, what will happen to the number of employees Nicole hires?

EXHIBIT 2

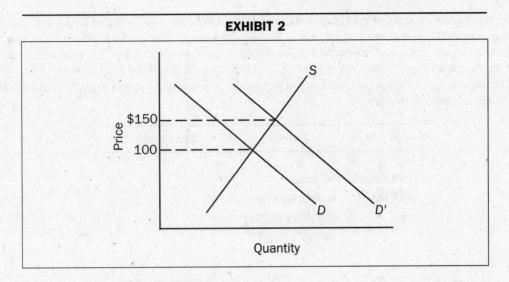

2. Magic Carpet, Inc., produces and sells handmade Oriental rugs in a price-taker industry. The firm receives $100 per square meter for each rug produced. Exhibit 3 shows how total output (in square meters) changes as additional units of skilled labor are hired.
   a. Complete the table.
   b. Given the equilibrium wage rate as $200 per week, indicate how many workers the firm would hire if it wanted to maximize profits.
   c. How many workers would Magic Carpet hire if the market wage increased to $300 per week?

EXHIBIT 3

UNITS OF SKILLED LABOR	TOTAL OUTPUT (SQUARE METERS PER WEEK)	MP	PRICE PER SQUARE METER	TR	MRP
1	5	5	$100	$500	$500
2	12	_____	100	_____	_____
3	18	_____	100	_____	_____
4	21.5	_____	100	_____	_____
5	24	_____	100	_____	_____
6	25	_____	100	_____	_____

3. Use the diagrams to indicate the changes in demand (D), supply (S), equilibrium price (P), and equilibrium quantity (Q) in response to the events in the resource markets. First, show in the diagrams how the described event or events affect demand and/or supply of the resource, and then fill in the table to the right of the diagrams using + to indicate an increase, – to indicate a decrease, and 0 to indicate no effect. (Hint: The diagrams are of the resource markets themselves; for example, the diagram in part a is of the market for high school math teachers.)

RESOURCE MARKET	EVENTS	DIAGRAMS	D	S	P	Q
a. High school math teachers	Wages for mathematicians employed in private industry rise.		___	___	___	___
b. Computers	Technological change raises the speed of computer calculations.		___	___	___	___
c. Computer technicians	The cost of obtaining computer technician training falls.		___	___	___	___
d. Welders	Technological change lowers the cost of robots used to weld auto parts on auto assembly lines.		___	___	___	___
e. Agricultural land in Southern California	A vitamin C fad raises the price of oranges.		___	___	___	___

4. In the growing of corn, a farmer uses two fertilizers: Vitacorn and Cornpower. The farmer has estimated that at the current rate of usage of the two fertilizers, the marginal (physical) product of one ton of Vitacorn is 200 bushels per acre and the marginal product of one ton of Cornpower is 400 bushels per acre. The best price quotations the farmer has been able to get are $800/ton for Vitacorn and $1,200/ton for Cornpower.
    a. From the above information, does the farmer's current usage of the two fertilizers meet the "condition for cost minimization when multiple resources are employed"?
    b. Suppose the farmer used one more ton of Cornpower and two fewer tons of Vitacorn. How would total output change? How would total cost change? Would this substitution be consistent with the goal of profit maximization?
    c. If the farmer continued to substitute Cornpower for Vitacorn, assume that the marginal product of Cornpower would fall. Would these changes lead toward fulfillment of the condition for cost minimization you discussed in part a? How?

5. XYZ Corporation is considering moving its plant from the United States to Mexico to cut its labor costs. Wage rates for labor are $10 per hour in the United States and $6 per hour in Mexico. Suppose the firm's current U.S. workers have a marginal product of 60, whereas Mexican workers would have a marginal product of 30.
    a. Find the ratio of marginal product to price (MP/P) for both U.S. and Mexican labor.
    b. For a given level of output, would the firm's costs be lower or higher if it were to produce in Mexico?
    c. How low would the wage rate have to be in Mexico to make the move profitable for the company?

MULTIPLE CHOICE

1. The short-run supply of a human resource will be more elastic the
    a. more elastic the demand for the product to be produced.
    b. more inelastic the demand for the product to be produced.
    c. lower the skill level necessary to perform the job.
    d. harder it is to acquire the skill and knowledge necessary to provide the resource.

2. A decrease in the demand for a final product will cause
    a. a decrease in demand for the resources used to produce the good.
    b. an increase in demand for the resources used to produce the good.
    c. firms to expand production of the good.
    d. an increase in the supply of resources used to produce the good.

3. The more elastic the demand for a final product,
    a. the more elastic will be the demand for the productive resources used.
    b. the less elastic the supply of resources used in producing the product.
    c. the less firms will reduce their usage of resources when the price of the resources increases.
    d. the higher the MRP of the resources used to produce the product.

4. Which of the following expresses the correct decision-making rule for a profit-maximizing firm hiring units of labor?
    a. If the MRP was rising, less labor would be employed as time passed.
    b. The firm should continue to hire workers as long as their MRP is greater than the wage rate.
    c. The firm should continue to hire workers until the total costs of all workers equals the total revenue from the output of the workers.
    d. The firm should continue to hire workers until the wage rate equals the price of the product.

5. Because the demand for a resource is highly dependent upon the demand for the final goods that the resource helps produce, the demand for a resource is called a(n)
    a.   derived demand.
    b.   independent demand.
    c.   declining proportions demand.
    d.   elastic demand.

6. Compared to the short-run demand, the long-run demand for a resource is
    a.   less elastic.
    b.   more elastic.
    c.   equally elastic.
    d.   either more or less elastic; we cannot predict which.

7. In a price-taker industry, the marginal revenue derived from the sale of an additional unit of the product is equal to the market price of the product. In these circumstances,
    a.   value of marginal product is less than marginal revenue product.
    b.   value of marginal product is greater than marginal revenue product.
    c.   value of marginal product equals marginal revenue product.
    d.   marginal product equals marginal cost.

8. If the cost of using skilled labor was twice the cost of using unskilled labor, and both were used by a profit-maximizing firm, the firm would adjust the quantity of each type of labor until
    a.   the marginal product of each was the same.
    b.   twice as much unskilled labor was used.
    c.   half as much unskilled labor was used.
    d.   the marginal product of skilled labor was twice that of unskilled labor.

9. If a firm used only two factors of production, labor (L) and capital (K), which of the following conditions would be present if the firm was minimizing its cost of production?
    a. $MP_L \div P_L = MP_K \div P_K$
    b. $MP_L \times P_L = MP_K \times P_K$
    c. $MRP_L = MRP_K$
    d. $MP_L = MP_K$

10. A change in the demand for a resource can be caused by which of the following?
    a.   a change in the demand for the final product that uses the resource as a factor of production
    b.   a change in the productivity of the resource
    c.   a change in the price of other resources that could be used as substitutes for the resource in question
    d.   all of the above

11. A firm currently employs 80 units of labor and 50 units of capital equipment to produce 3,000 hamster cages. Given the current input levels utilized, the marginal product of labor is 40 and the marginal product of capital is 10. If we assume that labor costs $20 per unit and capital costs $10 per unit,
    a.   the firm is using the appropriate mix of labor and capital to minimize its costs.
    b.   the firm could lower its costs for the same level of output by using more labor and less capital.
    c.   the firm could lower its costs for the same level of output by using more capital and less labor.
    d.   the current MRP of capital exceeds the current MRP of labor.

12. Which of the following would be the most likely result from a new government program that provided significant financial aid for children of low- and middle-income families to attend college?
    a. Starting salaries for new college graduates would rise because of an increase in the number of high-quality graduates.
    b. Starting salaries for college graduates would be unaffected.
    c. The productivity of the labor force would be permanently lower because more young people would choose to be students instead of workers.
    d. Starting salaries of new college graduates would fall as the supply of graduates increased.

13. If a college education did not increase worker productivity,
    a. no one would go to college.
    b. wages would tend to be the same for workers with and without a college education.
    c. wages would still be higher for workers with college degrees because of the cost of going to college.
    d. the total lifetime earnings of workers who go to college and those who do not would tend to be the same.

14. Economists refer to expenditures on training, education, and skill development designed to increase the productivity of an individual as
    a. overhead expenditures.
    b. investments in human capital.
    c. sunk expenditures.
    d. social capital.

15. If steel workers obtain a substantial wage increase, employment in the steel industry will be likely to fall the most if
    a. the demand curve for steel is highly inelastic.
    b. the demand curve for steel is highly elastic.
    c. the demand curve for steel workers is highly inelastic.
    d. there are no good substitutes for steel.

Use the information given in Exhibit 4 to answer questions 16 through 18. Assume the firm hires labor competitively and sells its product in a competitive price-taker market at a price of $2 per unit.

EXHIBIT 4

Units of Labor	Total Output
1	6
2	11
3	15
4	18
5	20
6	21

16. What is the marginal revenue product of the fifth unit of labor?
    a. $2
    b. $4
    c. $20
    d. $100

17. If the market wage rate is $5 per day, how many workers should the firm employ if it wants to maximize profits?
    a. three
    b. four
    c. five
    d. six

18. If the market wage rate rose to $7 per day, how many workers should the firm employ if it wants to maximize profits?
    a. three
    b. four
    c. five
    d. six

19. Jim Smith runs a company that sells encyclopedia sets for $200 each. When he employs 5 workers, they can sell 20 sets per week, whereas only 17 sets are sold when 4 workers are employed. What is the weekly marginal revenue product of the fifth worker?
    a. $3
    b. $200
    c. $600
    d. $4,000

20. Firms should hire additional units of a resource as long as the
    a. marginal product of the resource exceeds the price of the resource multiplied by the quantity of output produced.
    b. marginal product of the resource is less than the price of the resource.
    c. price of the output produced is positive.
    d. marginal revenue product of the resource exceeds the cost of employing an additional unit of the resource.

21. The marginal revenue product of a resource is best described as the
    a. selling price of the last unit of output produced.
    b. increment of total cost resulting from the use of an additional unit of the resource.
    c. marginal product of the resource divided by the unit price of the good produced.
    d. change in total revenue resulting from employing an additional unit of the resource.

22. For a price searcher, marginal revenue product (*MRP*) differs from the value of marginal product (*VMP*) because
    a. *MRP* equals *MP* times product price (*P*), while *VMP* equals *MP* times marginal revenue (*MR*).
    b. *VMP* equals *MP* times product price (*P*), while *MRP* equals *MP* times marginal revenue (*MR*).
    c. *VMP* equals *MP* times marginal cost (*MC*), while *MRP* equals *MP* times marginal revenue (*MR*).
    d. They do not differ; they are the same for every firm.

23. An increase in the demand for a resource
    a. will cause the price of that resource to fall.
    b. may be the result of a decrease in the demand for products utilizing this resource.
    c. will cause the price of the resource to fall by a smaller amount in the short run than in the long run.
    d. will increase the price of the resource and thereby increase the incentive of potential suppliers to provide the resource in the future.

24. Generally, the supply of a resource in the short run will be
    a. more elastic than in the long run.
    b. less elastic than in the long run.
    c. equally elastic as the supply of the resource in the long run.
    d. directly related to the elasticity of demand for the product that the resource helps produce.

25. A convenience store is considering renting a surveillance camera from a security company that would prevent $100 in shoplifting per year. The yearly rental rate for the camera is $150. To maximize profits, the firm should
    a. rent the camera because the firm wants to completely eliminate shoplifting.
    b. not rent the camera because the rental rate exceeds the value of shoplifting prevented.
    c. rent the camera if *VMP* exceeds *MRP*, but not rent the camera if *VMP* is less than *MRP*.
    d. Without knowing the rate of diminishing marginal returns, there is not enough information to answer the question.

DISCUSSION QUESTIONS

1. In recent years, the computer industry has grown quite rapidly as a result of technological advances. Suppose that the application of computers in the workplace continues at an accelerated rate.
   a. What would happen to the supply of computer technicians in the short run? in the long run?
   b. What would happen to the earnings of computer technicians in the short run? in the long run?
   c. What would happen in the long run to the supply and earnings of workers in industries that compete for the type of workers who become computer technicians?
   d. What would happen to the demand for inputs (for example, bookkeepers and clerks) for which computers are substitutes?

2. Is human labor really a "thing" that can be bought and sold like any other productive resource? What about the feelings of the human beings involved? Although we can buy a person's time, we cannot buy his or her enthusiasm or loyalty so easily. What sort of advantages and disadvantages does the "human element" in purchasing labor inputs have?

3. a. Why is the amount demanded of a productive resource negatively related to the price of the resource? Why is the demand likely to be more elastic when buyers have more time to respond?
   b. If the price of unskilled labor rises, what will tend to happen to the demand for substitute resources? for complementary resources?
   c. Will the demand for unskilled labor be more or less elastic as a result of the demand change described in part b for substitute resources? for complementary resources?

4. Some have argued that if wages really equal the marginal revenue product of the worker, the wage is "fair." Define marginal revenue product in your own words. Does the marginal revenue product of a worker reflect her or his contribution to output? What are the factors that raise marginal revenue products? Is it fair that those with the highest marginal revenue products also receive the highest wages? Why or why not?

CHAPTER 26

Earnings, Productivity, and the Job Market

TRUE OR FALSE

T F

☐ ☐ 1. If all workers had identical levels of education, all workers would have equal earnings.

☐ ☐ 2. Immobility of labor can be a source of wage differentials.

☐ ☐ 3. Higher productivity generally leads to higher wages.

☐ ☐ 4. There is a strong negative relationship between earnings and education level.

☐ ☐ 5. Under a tournament pay system, the top performer receives a wage less than his or her marginal revenue product.

☐ ☐ 6. Employment discrimination can also be caused by discriminatory preferences on the part of a firm's customers or its employees.

☐ ☐ 7. Working conditions and other nonwage job characteristics are called nonpecuniary job characteristics.

☐ ☐ 8. Other things constant, the more dangerous a job, the lower the wage rate it will have. This is known as a compensating wage differential.

☐ ☐ 9. The average wage rate in the United States is high in comparison with that of other countries largely because of the large amount of physical and human capital with which the average American works.

☐ ☐ 10. If employers can hire equally productive minority employees at a lower wage than other workers (because other firms are discriminating against them), the profit motive gives them a strong incentive to do so.

T F

☐ ☐ 11. When comparing wage differences across gender and racial groups, it is important to adjust for differences between the groups in education, experience, and other productivity-related factors.

☐ ☐ 12. When deciding whether to employ a worker, the employer will consider the total cost of the compensation (money wages plus fringe benefits) relative to the worker's marginal revenue product.

☐ ☐ 13. Fringe benefits are the part of a worker's compensation package that includes items like medical insurance, paid vacation days, and retirement benefits.

☐ ☐ 14. Automation is a major source of unemployment.

☐ ☐ 15. Economists believe that the faster rate of productivity growth that has been experienced over the last decade is in large part due to the computer revolution and related technological innovations.

PROBLEMS AND PROJECTS

1. For each of the following, decide whether the factor is likely to increase (+) or decrease (−) the *money* wages paid for the job relative to an identical job without that factor.
    _____ a. A job offers a very generous health-care plan that includes dental coverage.
    _____ b. A job requires the operation of very dangerous equipment.
    _____ c. A job is located in a very undesirable place to live.
    _____ d. A job comes with a company car for the employee to use.
    _____ e. A job is very insecure and is subject to frequent layoffs.
    _____ f. The employer matches all employee contributions to retirement funds for its workers.

2. Jane currently works for a company that pays her compensation all in the form of money wages (in other words, no fringe benefits). Bob works for another company in an identical job that also has fringe benefits like a health-care plan and free child care during working hours, but the job pays $5,000 less per year in money wages.
    a. Who earns the highest *money wages* per year?
    b. Who has the highest *total compensation* per year?
    c. If Bob had children and Jane did not, would this explain why Jane has chosen one job while Bob has chosen the other?
    d. If Jane were offered a job at Bob's company, would she take it? What would she need to consider?

3. Exhibit 1 is a hypothetical, demand-and-supply schedule for sophisticated pocket calculators in a price-taker industry.
    a. What will be the equilibrium quantity and price in this market? (Hint: You may use the graph lined area to plot the demand and supply to figure this out, or you can simply figure it by looking at the numbers.)
    b. Suppose that a new labor-saving technology is developed, resulting in an increase of 2,000 in quantity supplied at every price. What will happen to the equilibrium quantity and price?
    c. If the new technology reduces the quantity of labor used from 50 workers per thousand calculators produced to 40 workers per thousand calculators produced, what will happen to total employment in the industry?

EXHIBIT 1

QUANTITY DEMANDED PER MONTH	PRICE	QUANTITY SUPPLIED PER MONTH
0	$600	6,000
1,000	500	5,000
2,000	400	4,000
3,000	300	3,000
4,000	200	2,000
5,000	100	1,000
6,000	0	0

Price / Quantity (thousands) graph grid, Price axis from 100 to 700, Quantity axis from 0 to 9.

d. Owing to the new technology, the computer industry substituted more machines for labor. Using your understanding of the answer to part c, refute or support the following statement: "If we continue to allow machines to replace workers, we will run out of jobs. Automation is a major cause of unemployment."

4. The text describes the following determinants of earnings differentials:
    a. differences in workers
        A1: worker productivity and specialized skills
        A2: worker preferences
        A3: race and gender discrimination
    b. differences in jobs
        B1: location of jobs
        B2: working conditions
        B3: opportunities for training and experience
    c. immobility of labor
        C1: temporary disequilibrium
        C2: institutional restrictions, such as licensing and unions

Indicate the main reason from the list above for each of the following wage differentials:
    ___ a. College graduates earn more than high school graduates.
    ___ b. Wages in Alaska are higher than in Florida in identical jobs.
    ___ c. Police officers in metropolitan areas with high violent crime rates earn higher wages than police officers elsewhere.
    ___ d. Graduate students teach classes at universities for much less money than they could earn at a regular job.

MULTIPLE CHOICE

1. Evidence suggests that education raises the earnings of the workforce mainly by
    a. increasing the marginal productivity of labor.
    b. keeping young people out of the labor force, thereby reducing the supply of labor.
    c. teaching workers how to demand more pay.
    d. teaching people to read and write, although education beyond this point does not seem to increase worker productivity.

2. Within an occupation, when a given job provides steadier work (fewer layoffs), the hourly wage tends to be
    a. lower than wage rates in jobs that are otherwise similar.
    b. higher than wage rates in jobs that are otherwise similar.
    c. no different from wage rates in jobs that are otherwise similar.
    d. determined by factors other than supply and demand.

3. Which of the following is most likely to decrease the market wage rate in a job category?
    a. The employer provides a generous pension plan.
    b. The work is widely viewed as safe and not stressful.
    c. The job is widely viewed as interesting and prestigious.
    d. all of the above

4. The fact that some people will work hard to earn a lot of money while others will be content with much less income indicates that
    a. worker preferences are an important source of earning differentials.
    b. economics ranks one set of worker preferences as more desirable than another.
    c. some people can be paid less for doing hard work while others have to be paid a premium for doing a similar task.
    d. skill levels of laborers are a minor consideration in wage rate determination.

5. A compensation structure that generates much higher pay rates for the top performers, while those whose productivity is only a little lower receive substantially less compensation is called
    a. tournament pay.
    b. competing differentials.
    c. dueling executives.
    d. winner take all.

6. Assume that empirical evidence shows a difference in mean earnings between two groups, say, majority and minority workers. What conclusion may be drawn?
    a. The group with the lower earnings is being discriminated against.
    b. The group with the lower earnings is less productive.
    c. The group with the higher earnings has a larger quantity of human capital.
    d. Any of the above statements could, either partially or entirely, explain the difference in the mean earnings.

7. If a firm refuses to hire any minorities due to a personal prejudice, its profits will
    a. increase markedly.
    b. decrease.
    c. not be affected.
    d. increase slightly.

8. (I) Productivity growth in the United States since 1996 has been more rapid than it was during the previous two decades. (II) Economists believe that the more rapid productivity growth since 1996 is in large part due to the computer revolution and related technological innovations.
   a. Both I and II are true.
   b. I is true; II is false.
   c. I is false; II is true.
   d. Both I and II are false.

9. Economic theory suggests that the standard of living of American workers would rise if
   a. the minimum wage were doubled.
   b. automation was outlawed.
   c. the amount of physical capital increased.
   d. technological setbacks lowered output per worker hour.

10. (I) Differences in worker productivity are one major reason why individual earnings differ. (II) Even if all workers were identical, differences in the desirability of jobs would still cause earnings differentials.
    a. Both I and II are true.
    b. I is true; II is false.
    c. I is false; II is true.
    d. Both I and II are false.

11. Which of the following *best* states the relationship between machinery and the earnings of labor?
    a. Machines tend to reduce the demand for labor, thereby reducing the earnings rate of labor.
    b. Production of machinery creates jobs, thereby increasing the demand for (and wages of) labor.
    c. High productivity per worker hour is a necessary ingredient for the attainment of high real earnings, and adoption of labor-saving machinery enhances the ability of labor to attain such high productivity.
    d. Output and real earnings can always be increased whenever a machine can be substituted for a function previously performed by labor.

12. If large numbers of young Americans thought the life of a cowhand was great (despite the hardships), we would expect
    a. an increase in the wages of cowhands.
    b. a decrease in the wages of cowhands because supply would be enlarged.
    c. no impact on wages, which are determined by supply and demand, not preferences.
    d. a decrease in the wages of cowhands because demand would be reduced.

13. If customers are racist but employers are not, then employment discrimination will be
    a. less profitable than nondiscrimination.
    b. more profitable than nondiscrimination.
    c. equally profitable as nondiscrimination.
    d. easier to eliminate than if employers were racist but customers were not.

14. Under a tournament pay scheme, the pay gap between a few "winners" (those who receive big promotions) and other employees exceeds the productivity differences between these two groups. The reason firms might use such a scheme is that they
    a. overestimate the productivity of those who receive big promotions and inadvertently pay them "too much."
    b. gain tax advantages by paying a few workers large salaries and using fringe benefits to compensate the rest of the employees.
    c. hope to raise the productivity of those who receive big promotions because marginal productivity adjusts to equal wages.
    d. hope to raise the productivity of all other workers, who will work harder trying to gain a big promotion.

15. Sue: "I much prefer eating at the El Grande Mexican Restaurant to the others in town because all of their employees are Mexican and speak Spanish. It gives the place a real 'authentic' feel." Which of the following is true about the above statement?
    a. This is an example of customer-based discrimination for one group of employees over another.
    b. Despite customer preferences, we would expect the restaurants in town to hire equally from all racial and ethnic groups.
    c. If many customers felt the same way Sue does, there would be pressure for firms to satisfy this consumer preference in their hiring.
    d. Both a and c are correct.

DISCUSSION QUESTIONS

1. Suppose that a new invention cuts the cost of making automobiles in half.
    a. What will happen to output in the auto industry?
    b. What will happen to auto-industry employment if demand for automobiles is elastic? inelastic?
    c. What will happen to output and employment elsewhere in the economy if the auto demand is elastic? inelastic?
    d. Is it more likely for the new invention to make auto-industry employment rise in the short run and fall in the long run or fall in the short run and rise in the long run? Explain.

2. Substantial differences, sometimes up to 150 percent, in wage rates for essentially the same kind of labor (for example, semiskilled labor) prevail between different industries even in the same locality.
    a. What are some of the causes of interindustry wage differentials? List an industry that illustrates each cause.
    b. Which kinds of industries are likely to be at the top of the wage scale? at the bottom?

3. If you owned a firm, how would you expect the wages and racial composition of your employees to compare with your competitors' employees if
    a. firms in general practice employment discrimination, but you do not?
    b. firms in general do not practice employment discrimination, but you do?
    c. Explain both answers.

4. A recent issue of importance has been that of illegal immigration from one country to another. Analyze the impact of such illegal immigration on (1) the immigrants, (2) the new employers of the immigrants, (3) workers who remained in the home country of the immigrants, and (4) workers in the country to which the immigrants came. Given this analysis, attempt to develop a solution for the issue of illegal immigration.

5. Sewer workers face extremely unpleasant working conditions. They work in sewage; have daily encounters with millions of cockroaches, thousands of rats, and other unpleasant vermin; and are forced to take very long hot showers at the end of every working day. In addition, the occupation is extremely hazardous. Sewer workers are often asphyxiated by toxic gases. (We will leave it to your imagination to determine the nature of those toxic gases.) In Los Angeles, the median salary (not the starting salary) for sewer workers is $25,000. The city of Los Angeles has no difficulty filling vacant sewer worker positions. How much would someone have to pay you to compensate you for the disamenities of being a sewer worker? By that estimate, how much would low-skilled workers in reasonably pleasant jobs earn? How much do you (reasonably) hope to earn after graduating from college? What is the wage differential between what you hope to earn and what low-skilled workers appear to be able to earn? Why do you suppose more low-skilled workers do not gain the skills necessary to improve their earnings potential?

6. How has productivity growth in the United States changed over the last thirty years? What are the causes of these changes in productivity growth? Do you think productivity growth will be more or less rapid in the near future?

PERSPECTIVES IN ECONOMICS

The Shrinking Pay Gap

by June Ellenoff O'Neill

[From *The Wall Street Journal,* October 7, 1994,
p. A12. Reprinted with permission from *The
Wall Street Journal.* Copyright © Dow Jones
& Co., Inc., 1994. All rights reserved.]

"Fifty-nine cents," the popular button said, a symbol of the stubborn fact that throughout the post-World War II period, women's wages hovered at around 60% of men's, despite an increasing proportion of women working outside the home. This gender gap did not decline through the 1960s and the 1970s despite the rise of the feminist movement, equal pay and employment legislation, and affirmative action.

But starting in the Reagan years, the gender gap in wages began to decline dramatically. By some measures the ratio of women's earnings to men's rose to nearly 80%; and even this number, I believe, overstates the gender gap between men and women with similar skills and training. Why did this dramatic narrowing in relative wages happen?

The answer has less to do with politics or protests than with the realities of the labor market. Although basic skills are acquired in school, it is in the labor market where specialized skills are developed that bring higher wages. During the three decades following World War II women entered the labor market in record numbers. But many of the new entrants had been out of the labor force for considerable periods of time, raising their children. These women diluted the skill level of the rapidly expanding group of employed women. This was the main reason why the gender gap in pay did not narrow during the postwar years.

More Nearly Equal. Today's working women, particularly those younger than 40, are much more nearly equal to men in work experience than were their mothers. Through delayed marriage, low fertility, and an increasing tendency for mothers of young children to work, women have acquired many more years of continuous work experience than was true in the past. (Close to 60% of married women with children under age six are now in the labor force; in 1960, the proportion was only 19%.)

And the work experience gained by these younger women is likely to have an even greater impact on their future earnings because their work experience has been more correctly anticipated. Many investment choices affecting careers are made at younger ages: years of schooling, subjects in school, other professional training. In the past, women were much less likely than men to invest in lengthy training because they assumed they would not be working enough years to justify it.

In fact, the National Longitudinal Surveys found that even in the late 1960s less than 30% of young women anticipated that they would be working at age 35, yet when this group actually reached 35, more than 70% of them were in the labor force. Their underestimation of future work activity surely influenced their early career preparations (or lack thereof). More recent survey data show a dramatic change in expectations. The vast majority of young women now report an intention to work at age 35.

Those changing work expectations are reflected in rising female enrollments in higher education. In 1960, women received 35% of all bachelor's degrees in the U.S.; by the 1980s, they received somewhat more than half of them. In 1968, women received 8% of the medical degrees, 3% of the MBAs and 4% of the law degrees granted that year. In 1986, they received 31% of the medical degrees and MBAs and 39% of the law degrees. This recent trend in schooling is likely to reinforce the rise in work experience and contribute to continuing increases in the relative earnings of women workers.

By 1980 the stage was set for the gender pay gap to narrow. It had already begun to narrow among younger women and men in the 1970s, and as the baby boomers became the dominant age group their experience and earnings began to influence the overall earnings statistics.

In a systematic analysis of the factors accounting for the narrowing of the gender gap, Solomon Polachek (professor of economics at SUNY Binghamton) and I found that the increase in women's years of work experience relative to men's could account for about 25% to 30% of the approximate 1% per year narrowing of the wage gap since the late 1970s. In addition, on-the-job training appears to have increased more for women than for men, so that women's earnings now rose more rapidly with experience than was once the case; this accounts for an added 35% to 40% of the convergence. That women's college and graduate attainment increased faster than men's also contributed significantly to the shrinking of the gap.

The gains women have made since 1980 are particularly striking considering that the past 10 to 15 years have been years of little growth in the overall wage level and a widening pay difference between skilled and unskilled workers. Low-skill male occupations, which are largely blue-collar, have experienced significant wage declines. Since relatively few women have entered these occupations, they avoided this particular downward drag on wages. The much greater concentration of men in blue-collar occupations accounted for about 20% of the overall wage convergence.

Despite the advances of the past decade, women still earn less than men. The hourly earnings of women were 74% of the earnings of men in 1992 when ages 25 to 64 are considered, up from 62% in 1979. At ages 25 to 34, where women's skills have increased the most, the ratio is 87%.

Economist Barbara Bergmann and others attribute the pay gap to "widespread, severe, ongoing discrimination by employers and fellow workers." But discrimination cannot be directly measured. Instead, researchers estimate the extent to which differences in productivity appear to explain the gap and then attribute the rest to discrimination. Such a conclusion is premature, however, when productivity differences are not accurately measured, which is usually the case.

For example, data are seldom available on lifetime patterns of work experience, and even less material is available on factors bearing on work expectations and the intensity and nature of work investments. As these are still the key sources of skill differences between men and women, there is considerable room for interpretation and disagreement.

When earnings comparisons are restricted to men and women more similar in their experience and life situations, the measured earnings differentials are typically quite small. For example, among people 27 to 33 who have never had a child, the earnings of women in the National Longitudinal Survey of Youth are close to 98% of men's. Among college graduates in the same survey, a differential of 11% narrowed to 6% after adjusting for gender differences in work experience, field of study and math test scores. In special Census surveys of people with science or engineering backgrounds, women's earnings are much closer to men's than in the general population.

In the past, women who chose careers were likely to find their paths filled with obstacles erected to preserve women's role in the home. But even then, these discriminatory barriers were probably not the major cause of pay differences between men and women. Rather, women's decisions about work were rooted in real economic forces affecting the family, particularly gender differences in the priority placed on market work vs. child care responsibilities.

The care of children is the household activity for which market alternatives may be least easily substituted, although increasingly child care has been shifted to the market through earlier school starting ages and greater use of group day-care arrangements. The time demands have been reduced, too, through declining fertility. The decline in fertility is likely to have been in part a response to rising wage rates and the rising labor force participation of women. But modern contraceptives also played a role.

Comparative Advantage. What is more, over the years women's comparative advantage in the labor market has increased as the service sector has expanded, providing jobs that required mental acuity and social skills rather than physical strength. As the costs of denying employment to women have mounted, prejudices have diminished.

It is true that women and men still do not have the same earnings. But I believe that the differential is largely due to continuing gender differences in the priority placed on market work vs. family responsibilities. Until family roles are more equal, women are not likely to have the same pattern of market work and earnings as men. Technology has reduced the burden of housework, but child care remains a responsibility that is harder to shift to the market.

DISCUSSION

1. Which number is more relevant, the ratio of women's earnings to men's earnings for all workers or the ratio of women's earnings to men's earnings for individuals of similar backgrounds and jobs? Explain your answer. (Be careful, this question may be harder than you think it is.)

2. O'Neill attributes the decrease in the pay gap to increases in the work experience of women and other market factors. Do you agree? Do protests and demands for fair treatment have no impact on discrimination? Explain.

3. What is your own personal experience? Have you observed that women get paid less than men for similar work or that women are forced into lower-paying jobs by societal pressures or expectations? Do you agree with O'Neill that any such differences are decreasing? Why or why not?

Investment, the Capital Market, and the Wealth of Nations

27

TRUE OR FALSE

T   F

☐ ☐ 1. If an economy is to achieve a higher level of investment, an increase in personal saving will be required.

☐ ☐ 2. To expand the availability of capital requires reducing current consumption.

☐ ☐ 3. People generally have a positive rate of time preference—they value goods obtained sooner more highly than goods obtained later.

☐ ☐ 4. To a lender, the interest rate is the reward earned from delaying consumption, whereas to a borrower, it is the price paid for earlier availability.

☐ ☐ 5. The net present value of a payment to be received one year from now will fall if the interest rate falls.

☐ ☐ 6. An increase in the positive rate of time preference would raise the real interest rate in the economy.

☐ ☐ 7. If there were an increase in the demand for loans, the interest rate would increase, encouraging people to expand their savings so as to make more money available for loans.

☐ ☐ 8. The inflation premium represents the true real cost of borrowing money.

☐ ☐ 9. Higher risk usually lowers the interest rate agreed to by business decision makers.

T F

☐ ☐ 10. The interest rate charged by a lender has three components: the inflationary premium, the risk premium, and the pure money interest rate component.

☐ ☐ 11. Changes in a corporation's stock price happen too slowly to give corporate officers much feedback on how market investors evaluate their investment decisions.

☐ ☐ 12. The value of an asset is equal to the present value of the expected net revenue that can be earned by the asset.

☐ ☐ 13. Approximately four-fifths of national income in the United States represents a return to human capital, whereas the other one-fifth represents returns to physical capital.

☐ ☐ 14. Properly functioning capital markets are essential to economic prosperity because they make it relatively easy for individual entrepreneurs to try new innovated ideas but also make it difficult for them to remain in business if the idea is a bad one.

PROBLEMS AND PROJECTS

1. For each of the following pairs of countries, decide which would tend to have the higher rate of interest, assuming all else is equal except for the factor listed in the problem.
    ___ a. Country A has a higher rate of inflation than Country B.
    ___ b. Citizens in Country C have a higher positive rate of time preference than in Country D.
    ___ c. Citizens in Country E tend to save a higher proportion of their income than citizens in Country F.
    ___ d. In Country G, a much higher proportion of borrowers default on their loans than in Country H.

2. The owner of a small forest in Florida is raising trees as a cash crop. A forester friend mentions that a certain treatment applied to the trees, costing $500 now, will yield an extra 10,000 board feet of timber when the forest is harvested in 30 years. Harvesting and other costs will not change significantly.
    a. In the first case, assume that the owner expects the price per board foot to be $2 when the crop is harvested. Is this a worthwhile investment for the grower if the interest rate is 5 percent? 10 percent? 15 percent?
    b. Now assume the interest rate is 15 percent, but the uncertainty is over the future price of the timber. At a 15 percent interest rate, is this a worthwhile investment for the grower if the expected price is $1 per board foot? $2 per board foot? $4 per board foot?

3. It was noted in the text that the price of an asset that earns a given payment each year forever is

    Asset price = annual earnings ÷ interest rate.

    The following formula can also be used to assess the present value of any fixed payments that will be earned each year forever.

    Present value = fixed annual payment ÷ interest rate

    Even when the payments do not last forever, this formula can be used to approximate present value whenever the payments last for a "fairly long" period of time. Try the following examples to see how well this simple formula works as an approximation.

a. Recently, Life Cereal held a "Life Cereal Lifetime Allowance Sweepstakes." Each grand-prize winner was promised $2,000 per year for life. With a combined state and federal income tax rate of 50 percent, and an interest rate of 8 percent, what would be the approximate present value of the grand prize after taxes?

b. A few years ago, households across the country received a letter from Ed McMahon (formerly of *The Tonight Show*) urging them to enter the American Family Publishers sweepstakes, which offered America's "first TEN MILLION DOLLAR prize!" The winner of the prize was promised $333,333 per year for 30 years. At 7 percent interest, what is the approximate present value of this stream of receipts? (You may ignore taxes in this problem.)

c. Suppose you or your parents borrow $150,000 to buy a new home. If the interest rate is 10 percent, what is the approximate size of the mortgage payments each year? (Hint: It will be necessary to rearrange the terms in the formula to find this answer.)

4. Use the appropriate discounting method to find the present value of each of the following cases. For all, assume an interest rate of 10 percent. (Hint: Use the formula for an asset price given above to approximate the cases when the payments last for a long time.)

a. a college education, which generally increases a person's average annual earnings by $15,000 for the rest of his or her life

b. a license to be the monopoly provider of cable service in a local area that is expected to generate $5 million in profit per year

c. the current value of a 30-year U.S. Treasury savings bond given to you five years ago by your grandmother—it will mature in another 25 years at a face value of $500

d. a machine that will last three years and generate net revenue of $5,000 at the end of each year

e. a rental property that generates net rental income of $300 per month (that is, $3,600 per year)

MULTIPLE CHOICE

1. The development and construction of machines that enhance our ability to produce goods and services in the future requires
   a. devoting more resources toward investment.
   b. devoting fewer resources toward current consumption.
   c. a negative rate of time preference.
   d. both a and b.

2. A positive rate of time preference implies that a person would value
   a. receiving $100 today more than receiving $100 one year from now.
   b. receiving $100 today less than receiving $100 one year from now.
   c. receiving $100 today equally to receiving $100 one year from now.
   d. any amount, no matter how small, today more than receiving $100 one year from now.

3. The net present value of $100, delivered one year from now, would
   a. fall if the rate of interest increased.
   b. fall if the rate of interest decreased.
   c. rise if the rate of interest increased.
   d. not change if the interest rate changed.

4. If the interest rate was 6 percent, the net present value of $100 to be received one year from now would be
   a. $94.34.
   b. $98.04.
   c. $100.00.
   d. $106.00.

5. If the interest rate was 6 percent, the net present value of $100 to be received two years from now would be
    a. $89.00.
    b. $94.34.
    c. $100.00.
    d. $112.00.

6. If the interest rate was 6 percent, the combined net present value of *two* payments of $100, one to be received one year from now and the other two years from now, would be
    a. $89.00.
    b. $94.34.
    c. $183.34.
    d. $200.00.

7. If the interest rate was 6 percent, the net present value of a contract or asset that generated a repeating payment of $100 each year forever would be
    a. $100.00.
    b. $666.67.
    c. $1,000.00.
    d. $1,666.67.

8. The net present value of $100 to be received one year from now will
    a. increase if the interest rate rises.
    b. increase if the payment is delayed until two years from now.
    c. be greater than the net present value of $95 to be received one year from now.
    d. be greater than the value of having $95 now if the interest rate is 10 percent.

9. (I) Discounting procedures apply to decisions to invest in physical capital but are not relevant to human capital investment decisions. (II) Nonmonetary considerations are usually more important in human capital investment decisions than in nonhuman capital investment decisions.
    a. I is true; II is false.
    b. I is false; II is true.
    c. Both I and II are true.
    d. Both I and II are false.

10. Some governments enact usury laws, which hold the interest rate below its equilibrium level. Economic analysis indicates that under such laws,
    a. saving would increase.
    b. borrowers would demand less from the loanable funds market.
    c. anyone who wanted to borrow would be happy with the lower interest rate.
    d. there would be a shortage of loanable funds, necessitating rationing by some means other than the price (interest rate).

11. A company that mines coal on federally owned land is about to be told by the federal government that, beginning in five years, it must abandon the mine it expected to operate for another twenty years. This will mean a reduction in accounting profits beginning in five years. If the announcement of this ruling was made tomorrow, the price of the firm's stock would fall
    a. in about five years, just before the reduction in accounting profits was to begin.
    b. gradually, as the reduction in the firm's accounting profit drew near.
    c. immediately by the full amount of the discounted value of the decrease in future profit.
    d. immediately because some investors would panic irrationally, whereas smart investors would put the same value on the stock as before, up to the time of the decline in accounting profit.

12. (I) Countries with high rates of investment also tend to have high rates of growth. (II) A country with a high rate of investment but a poorly functioning capital market will tend to have a lower rate of growth than a country with a comparable rate of investment but a capital market that functions well.
    a. I is true; II is false.
    b. I is false; II is true.
    c. Both I and II are true.
    d. Both I and II are false.

13. Which of these are the major sources of economic profit?
    a. uncertainty, entrepreneurial alertness, and barriers to entry
    b. competition, perfect information, and elasticity of market demand
    c. size of firm, economies of scale, and freedom from unionism
    d. externalities, inflation, and size of firm

14. Which of the following would reduce the net present value of your college education?
    a. higher interest rates
    b. earlier retirement age
    c. higher wages for high school graduates
    d. all of the above

15. Economists refer to the desire of consumers for goods now rather than in the future as
    a. a positive rate of time preference.
    b. the rational expectations hypothesis.
    c. roundabout methods of production.
    d. the inflationary premium.

16. The real rate of interest is the
    a. money rate of interest plus the inflationary premium.
    b. money rate of interest minus the inflationary premium.
    c. yield one can expect to receive on loanable funds without taking significant risk.
    d. risk component associated with the ownership of real assets.

17. If the money rate of interest is 10 percent and the real rate of interest is 7 percent, the inflationary premium is
    a. 3 percent.
    b. 7 percent.
    c. 10 percent.
    d. 17 percent.

18. The yield that one can expect to receive on loanable funds without taking significant risk is called the
    a. risk premium.
    b. pure interest yield.
    c. inflationary premium.
    d. nominal interest yield.

19. If the interest rate was 5 percent and an investment project was expected to yield net revenue of $3,000 per year (to be received at year-end) for each of the next three years, profit-maximizing decision makers would undertake the investment only as long as it cost less than
    a. $7,461.
    b. $8,170.
    c. $8,652.
    d. $9,000.

20. If an investment project costing $2,700 was expected to yield $1,000 (to be received at year end) for each of the next three years, a profit-maximizing entrepreneur would
    a. definitely undertake the project.
    b. never undertake the project.
    c. undertake the project if the interest rate exceeded 12 percent.
    d. undertake the project if the interest rate was 5 percent or less.

21. You are considering buying a business that currently earns $15,000 per year in after-tax profit. If these conditions are expected to continue into the future, and the interest rate is currently 10 percent, the current market value of this business is
    a. $1,500.
    b. $15,000.
    c. $150,000.
    d. $1,500,000.

DISCUSSION QUESTIONS

1. U.S. government bonds are considered risk-free in the sense that there is a negligible chance of default.
    a. What uncertainty is still involved in purchasing government bonds?
    b. How can you earn a profit from the purchase and resale of government bonds? How can you suffer a loss?

2. a. What are the components of the money interest rate? the real interest rate?
    b. Are risk premiums efficient because the result is that different borrowers pay different interest rates? Explain.
    c. From the self-interested viewpoint of a future generation responsible for interest payments, is it beneficial to use a positive, market-clearing interest rate for rationing loanable funds among competing investment opportunities? Why or why not?

3. If you were going to lend someone money, would the following events cause you to increase, decrease, or leave unchanged the nominal interest rate you were thinking of asking for?
    a. You hear a news report that causes you to increase the inflation rate you expect to exist over the life of the loan.
    b. You discover documents that cause you to think there is a reasonable chance that the loan might not be completely repaid. (Assume that you still want to loan the money.)
    c. You read in the newspaper that most major banks have lowered the interest rate they charge their prime customers.

4. "When a firm's total costs are less than its sales, the firm has increased the value of the resources it has used. Such firms will be rewarded with profits. In contrast, losses indicate that the resources used to produce a good were more valuable than the good that was produced. Profits are evidence of the wise utilization of resources, whereas losses are indicative of waste and inefficiency." Are these statements always true, never true, or sometimes true? Explain your answer.

5. A smoothly functioning capital market is necessary in order to channel available funds to their most profitable uses. However, with almost an infinite number of possible investment projects, it is the job of the entrepreneur to find the ones that are most beneficial to the economy. Discuss the role of entrepreneurs in a market economy and the role of uncertainty and profit in the job they perform.

PERSPECTIVES IN ECONOMICS

State's Lottery "Millionaires" Will Be Somewhat Less Than

by Lee Dembart

[From the *Los Angeles Times*, August 16, 1985. Reprinted with permission.]

When the California lottery gets into full swing this fall, it will offer jackpots of $1 million, $2 million and $3 million. The lucky winners, therefore, will be "millionaires," according to common parlance.

Not so fast. There's a rub. "All million-dollar prizes will be awarded as annuities over a 20-year period," said an article in *The Times*. In other words, if you win, say, a million dollars, the Lottery Commission won't hand you a check for a million. It will pay you $50,000 now and promise to pay another $50,000 a year for 19 more years, for a total of $1 million.

Now, $50,000 a year for 20 years is not worth a million dollars by a long shot. In fact, according to Bill Seaton, spokesman for the Lottery Commission, if you win "a million dollars" in the lottery, what they actually will give you is not a million dollars but an annuity worth $400,000 today.

A $400,000 annuity winds up being worth $1 million over 20 years because of the miracle of compound interest. Think about it. Money that is put aside today earns interest and is worth more in the future. The longer the future is, the more it grows.

So if the state promises to pay you $50,000 nineteen years from now—the time of the last payment—how much does it have to put aside in order to have the $50,000 then? It depends, obviously, on the interest rate. The higher the interest rate, the less that has to be set aside initially. If it earns 8%, $11,585.60 will yield $50,000 in 19 years. At a 10% rate, $8,175.40 will grow to $50,000 in 19 years. And at 12%, it would take just $5,805.34 today to produce $50,000 in 2004.

This a well-known bit of straight-forward mathematics, which is called the present-value or present-worth calculation. It involves running the formula for compound interest backward, and it answers the question, "What is the present value of a future sum of money?" Everybody understands that if a person invested $1,000 today at 10% interest it would earn $100 in a year and then be worth $1,100. The question can be asked the other way: If you wind up with $1,100 in a year at 10% interest, how much did you start with? The answer is $1,000, and that is called the present value of $1,100 in a year at 10% interest.

Occasionally, when athletes sign multiyear, multimillion-dollar contracts, someone points out an owner who promises to pay $2 million 30 years from now can do it with much less than $2 million today.

How does the lottery figure the present value of $1 million doled out in 20-year installments of $50,000 a year? The same calculation is done for year 19—the last year—can also be done for years 18, 17, 16 and so on to determine the amount of money that must be set aside today to pay the $50,000 in each of the subsequent years. Then those present values can be added to yield the total present value of the state's "million dollar lottery." The following is a table showing the present values of 20 once-a-year payments of $50,000 each, assuming earnings of 12.8%:

Year	Payment	Present value
0	$50,000	$50,000.00
1	50,000	44,326.24
2	50,000	39,296.31
3	50,000	34,837.16
4	50,000	30,884.00
5	50,000	27,379.44
6	50,000	24,272.55
7	50,000	21,518.22
8	50,000	19,076.43
9	50,000	16,911.73
10	50,000	14,992.67
11	50,000	13,291.38
12	50,000	11,783.13
13	50,000	10,446.04
14	50,000	9,260.67
15	50,000	8,209.82
16	50,000	7,278.21
17	50,000	6,452.31
18	50,000	5,720.13
19	50,000	5,071.04

The total present value of $1 million handed out in $50,000 chunks over 20 years is $401,007.48.

So it is at least misleading to call $50,000 a year for 20 years "a million dollars." (This analysis ignores income tax, inflation, life expectancy and all other factors related to the question of which is a better deal, $400,000 today or $50,000 a year for 20 years.)

The Lottery Commission says further that, based on the same calculation, a winner of a $2-million jackpot will receive an $800,000 annuity. In addition, the commission says, the odds against winning a $2-million pot are 25 million to 1.

So a person who buys a $1 ticket will have a 25 million-to-1 shot at winning a "$2-million prize." That sounds like bad odds to begin with. The odds are made worse by the fact that the $2-million prize is really only $800,000.

DISCUSSION

1. After reading the article, a friend says, "It seems to me that a million dollars is a million dollars. As long as you get the money eventually, it's still worth the same amount!" How would you convince your friend that it matters quite a bit when you get the money? Be specific.

2. The article ignores the taxes that will be due on the prize winnings. Assuming a 50 percent tax rate (combined federal and state on prize winnings), what is the true after-tax present value of winning this advertised $2-million jackpot?

3. The present values in the article were calculated assuming earnings of 12.8 percent, but this might seem a bit high for today. Calculate the present value of $50,000 a year for 20 years if the interest rate (earnings) were only 6 percent a year. Does the total go up or down? Why?

4. How ethical is it of the state of California to advertise a $2-million prize when it knows the actual value is less than half of that? What could be done to change the lottery (or at least its advertising) to make the truth obvious? Many people have claimed that a private firm could not get away with this kind of deception in its advertising. Do you agree?

Income Inequality and Poverty

TRUE OR FALSE

T F

☐ ☐ 1. Differences in the number of persons working per family are an important source of income inequality among families in the United States.

☐ ☐ 2. Income inequality in the United States increased in recent decades.

☐ ☐ 3. Most millionaires in the United States inherited their wealth.

☐ ☐ 4. Income mobility refers to the movement of individuals and families up and down the income distribution rankings.

☐ ☐ 5. Income and wealth are not a "fixed-size economic pie" to be divided among individuals but rather are created by individuals.

☐ ☐ 6. Families headed by workers in their prime working years (ages 35 to 64) tend to have more income than families headed by either younger or older persons.

☐ ☐ 7. Households headed by either a single parent or an elderly person are more likely to be in poverty.

☐ ☐ 8. Unlike other transfer programs, the eligibility for means-tested income transfer programs does not depend upon income status.

☐ ☐ 9. The increasing gap between the wages earned by college graduates and those with less education has contributed to the rise in income inequality in the United States.

☐ ☐ 10. When deciding whether a family is officially counted in poverty, the value of all transfer and welfare benefits are counted in the family's income.

☐ ☐ 11. The Samaritan's dilemma refers to how transfer programs also create a stronger incentive to avoid choices leading to poverty.

T F

☐ ☐ 12. When transfer programs have high take-back rates (implicit marginal tax rates), they reduce the incentive for poor families to work and earn.

☐ ☐ 13. The experience from the last several decades shows that increased spending on transfer programs produces substantial reductions in poverty and income inequality.

☐ ☐ 14. Because large transfer programs lead to higher tax rates for taxpayers and also higher implicit tax rates for recipients, they tend to lower an economy's productivity and output.

☐ ☐ 15. Opponents of government action to correct income inequality argue that the pattern of economic outcomes (such as the observed distribution of income) is not nearly as important as the fairness of the process that generates the outcome.

☐ ☐ 16. Government actions to reduce poverty and income inequality generally have harmful secondary effects (such as the creation of adverse incentives) that can either partially or fully offset the intended outcome of the actions taken.

PROBLEMS AND PROJECTS

1. When transfer programs have high implicit marginal tax rates (or "take-back rates"), it lowers the incentive for those receiving the transfer to work. Exhibit 1 shows data from a study prepared for the U.S. House of Representatives on how a family's disposable (spendable) income changed with earned income from work in 1983. This data is for a single mother with two children living in Pennsylvania.
   a. Disposable income is equal to earned income from work minus any taxes that must be paid on this income plus any transfer (welfare) benefits received. For the three levels of earned income shown, compute this family's disposable income.
   b. Suppose this mother is currently not working (earned income is zero), but she has been offered a part-time job earning $6,000 per year. If she accepts the job, how many dollars worth of transfer benefits will she lose? Considering both the reduction in benefits and the taxes she will owe on this earned income, what will happen to her disposable income if she accepts the job?
   c. Alternatively, suppose this nonworking mother has been offered a full-time job earning $10,000 per year. Taking the job will mean having to pay for transportation to and from work that totals $200 per year and for child care that will total $1,800 per year. After subtracting the expenses for transportation and child care, will the family have more or less spendable income if she accepts the job?

EXHIBIT 1

	MINUS	PLUS	EQUALS
GROSS EARNINGS FROM WORK	INCOME AND EMPLOYMENT TAXES DUE	TRANSFER BENEFITS RECEIVED	DISPOSABLE INCOME
$ 0	$ 0	$7,568	_____
6,000	611	2,059	_____
10,000	1,469	698	_____

Between 1983 and 1994, welfare programs were changed to reduce the high implicit marginal tax rates faced by welfare recipients. Exhibit 2 compares the disposable income from 1983 (from Exhibit 1) to the disposable income at these same earned income levels in 1994.

d. In 1983, how much extra disposable income would the family have if the mother earned $6,000 per year instead of not working? How had this changed by 1994?

e. In 1983, how much extra disposable income would the family have if the mother earned $10,000 per year instead of not working? How had this changed by 1994?

f. How do you think the changes between 1983 and 1994 would have affected the incentive of this mother to take a job?

EXHIBIT 2

Gross Earnings from Work	1983 Disposable Income	1994 Disposable Income
$ 0	$7,568	$7,548
6,000	7,448	9,657
10,000	9,229	10,937

2. For each of the following pairs of countries, decide which country would tend to have the higher degree of income inequality among families as measured by traditional statistics.

____ a. In country A, all husbands work and all wives stay at home. In country B, all husbands work and half of the wives work as well.

____ b. In country C, half the population is college educated and half has only a high school education. In country D, all persons have only a high school education.

____ c. In country E, all families have two parents. In country F, there is a substantial fraction of single-parent families.

____ d. In country G, everyone is the same age. In country H, people differ in their ages.

____ e. In country I, the poor stay poor and the rich stay rich, whereas in country J, there is substantial income mobility from year to year.

EXHIBIT 3

INCOME MOBILITY—INCOME RANKING, 1994 AND 2004

PERCENT DISTRIBUTION BY INCOME STATUS OF FAMILY IN 2004

INCOME STATUS OF HOUSEHOLD IN 1994	HIGHEST QUINTILE	NEXT-HIGHEST-QUINTILE	MIDDLE QUINTILE	NEXT-LOWEST-QUINTILE	LOWEST QUINTILE
Highest Quintile	53.0	25.0	12.0	5.5	4.5
Next-Highest Quintile	23.0	32.5	24.0	14.0	6.5
Middle Quintile	14.0	22.5	28.0	24.0	12.0
Next-Lowest Quintile	5.5	12.5	25.5	33.5	23.5
Lowest Quintile	5.0	7.5	10.0	24.5	53.5

3. Income mobility refers to the degree to which individuals move up and down within the income distribution through time. Exhibit 3 shows data regarding family income mobility in the United States between 1994 and 2004.

   a. The data show that for the richest 20 percent of families in 1994 (the top paid quintile), only 53 percent remained among the richest 20 percent of families by 2004. Reading across the first row shows that 25.0 percent of these richest families in 1994 had fallen to the second highest quintile by 2004. What percent of these richest families in 1994 had fallen into the poorest 20 percent of families by 2004? On average, was it more likely that a family in the highest quintile in 1994 remained there or that they moved down the income distribution?

   b. Consider the poorest 20 percent of families in 1994 (the lowest quintile). What percent of these families remained in the poorest 20 percent by 2004? What percent had risen to the richest group by 2004? On average, was it more likely that a family in the lowest quintile in 1994 remained there or that they moved up the income distribution?

   c. For the middle quintile in 1994, what percent remained there by 2004? What total percent had risen up in the income distribution by 2004? What total percent had fallen down in the income distribution by 2004?

   d. An alternative way to look at these data is to see where families in a given quintile in 2004 came from with respect to their position in 1994 (by reading down the columns, instead of across the rows). What percent of the top quintile of families in 2004 came from the lowest two quintiles in 1994 combined? What percent of the lowest quintile in 2004 came from the top two quintiles in 1994 combined?

   e. Let's consider the top two quintiles the "top half" of the income distribution and the bottom two quintiles the "bottom half" of the income distribution. What percent of those in the bottom half of the income distribution in 2004 came from the top half of the income distribution in 1994? What percent of those in the top half of the income distribution in 2004 came from the bottom half of the income distribution in 1994?

4. Exhibit 4 shows data on the income distribution in a three-person economy. Before working the following questions, calculate the percent of total income earned by each individual in the economy for cases two, three, and four. Case one is already done as an example.

   a. Compare the percent of income earned by the richest person and the poorest person in each case. Which case would you say has the most unequal distribution of income? Which case has the most equal distribution of income?

   b. Suppose through time this economy originally began with case one and moved to case two. Has the distribution of income become more or less equal or has it stayed the same? Who is better or worse off in case two relative to case one in terms of the money income they have?

EXHIBIT 4

PERSON	CASE 1 INCOME	PERCENT OF TOTAL INCOME	CASE 2 INCOME	PERCENT OF TOTAL INCOME	CASE 3 INCOME	PERCENT OF TOTAL INCOME	CASE 4 INCOME	PERCENT OF TOTAL INCOME
Ann Rich	$100	50%	$200	_____	$45	_____	$330	_____
Mike Middle	60	30	120	_____	30	_____	180	_____
Rob Low	40	20	80	_____	25	_____	90	_____
Totals	$200	100%	$400	100%	$100	100%	$600	100%

c. Suppose instead that the economy moved from case one to case three. Here, has the distribution of income become more or less equal or has it stayed the same? Who is better or worse off in case three relative to case one in terms of the money income they have?

d. Suppose instead that the economy moved from case one to case four. Here, has the distribution of income become more or less equal or has it stayed the same? Who is better or worse off in case three relative to case one in terms of the money income they have?

e. Finally, assume that beginning from case one, these individuals could choose between which government policy they would prefer, one leading to case two, one leading to case three, and the other to case four. Which do you think Ann would prefer? Mike? Rob?

f. Over the past 30 years, average real income in the United States has doubled, but at the same time, the distribution of income has become more unequal. Based upon your answers above, has this increase in inequality necessarily made someone worse off?

MULTIPLE CHOICE

1. Over the past several decades, family incomes in the United States have
    a. become less equal.
    b. become more equal.
    c. maintained the same level of inequality.
    d. declined substantially for all families.

2. Which of the following is false about data on the inequality of annual family (or household) incomes?
    a. The degree of inequality is reduced when transfers and taxes are considered.
    b. The inequality in annual income data understates the true degree of inequality in lifetime income.
    c. Differences in age and family characteristics contribute to the degree of inequality.
    d. The inequality in consumption spending across households is smaller than the inequality in annual income.

3. Because the United States has a progressive tax system, the distribution of income after taking into account the effects of taxes and transfers is
    a. less equal than the distribution of before-tax income.
    b. more equal than the distribution of before-tax income.
    c. exactly the same as the distribution of before-tax income.
    d. none of the above.

4. Which of the following has contributed to the rising income inequality in the United States?
    a. The proportion of single-parent families has increased.
    b. The proportion of dual-earner families has increased.
    c. Earnings differentials between skilled and less-skilled workers have increased.
    d. all of the above

5. Use the following two statements to answer this question. (I) In a market system, resource prices both provide incentives for the efficient allocation of resources *and* determine income distribution. (II) Income and wealth are neither created nor destroyed, they are just fixed-sized pies to be allocated among individuals.
    a. Both I and II are true.
    b. Both I and II are false.
    c. I is true; II is false.
    d. I is false; II is true.

6. (I) High implicit marginal tax rates reduce the incentive of the poor to earn. (II) The Samaritan's dilemma is that transfer programs lower the opportunity cost of activities that lead to poverty.
    a. Both I and II are true.
    b. Both I and II are false.
    c. I is true; II is false.
    d. II is true; I is false.

7. Even if lifetime incomes were equal, there still might be substantial inequality in annual income data because
    a. wage rates might differ substantially.
    b. some might have inherited their wealth.
    c. some might have retired, whereas others are prime-age earners.
    d. educational levels might differ substantially.

8. When deciding whether to classify a family as in poverty, official figures
    a. count all transfer and welfare benefits received by the family as income.
    b. do not count in-kind benefits in the calculation of the family's income.
    c. do not count cash benefits in the calculation of the family's income.
    d. do not count any transfer or welfare benefits as income.

9. (I) In 2009, a family of four making $22,050 would be considered living in poverty. (II) The poverty threshold level of income is adjusted for family size and for inflation (price level changes) through time.
    a. Both I and II are true.
    b. Both I and II are false.
    c. I is true; II is false.
    d. II is true; I is false.

10. Imagine two countries, Lebos and Egap, that have identical average annual incomes. In Lebos, the poorest families one year almost always end up as the richest families the next year and become middle-income families the year after that. In Egap, however, the poor remain poor and rich remain rich. Which of the following is true about the two countries?
    a. The measured distribution of annual income in any given year is more equal in Lebos than in Egap.
    b. The measured distribution of annual income in any given year is more equal in Egap than in Lebos.
    c. The measured distribution of annual income in any given year will be the same in Lebos and Egap.
    d. The distribution of lifetime income is more equal in Egap than in Lebos.

11. In a market economy,
    a. there is not a fixed economic pie to be divided among individuals, but rather income is created by the individuals who earn it.
    b. differences in incomes provide individuals with an incentive to supply resources that are highly valued by others.
    c. a person's income is determined by the quantity and value of the resources that they supply to the market.
    d. all of the above are true.

12. Compared to low-income families, high-income families tend to
    a. have smaller family sizes (fewer persons per family).
    b. have more workers per family.
    c. be headed by a person who has not completed high school.
    d. supply fewer weeks of work per year.

13. Since 1970, income inequality in the United States has
    a. decreased.
    b. increased.
    c. remained the same.
    d. increased throughout the 1970s and 1980s but fell during the 1990s.

14. Which of the following is true?
    a. The distribution of income after taxes and transfers is considered more equal than when they are excluded.
    b. The distribution of lifetime income tends to be more unequal than the distribution of annual income.
    c. The distribution of income has become more equal in recent years.
    d. Developed, industrialized countries generally tend to have higher income inequality than less-developed countries.

15. Data on income inequality in the United States indicate that
    a. rich families stay rich and poor families stay poor through time.
    b. there is substantial movement among income groupings in the United States through time.
    c. most poor families never significantly rise above the poverty level, but rich families tend to become less wealthy over time.
    d. most rich families remain rich, but most poor families move up in the income distribution through time.

16. Which of the following is accurate regarding income statistics?
    a. Current annual income is also an accurate indicator of relative economic status over a longer period, such as a decade or lifetime.
    b. Inequalities of income observed at one point in time with annual income data overstate the degree of true income inequality in lifetime income.
    c. Recent studies indicate that the relative income position of a family generally determines the relative income position of their children and grandchildren.
    d. High-income earners generally maintain their status year after year, whereas those with low current incomes tend to stay poor year after year.

17. Transfers that are limited to persons or families with an income below a certain cut-off point are referred to as
    a. means-tested income transfers.
    b. poverty transfers.
    c. Social Security transfers.
    d. cash income transfers.

18. How do the high implicit marginal tax rates that often occur when transfer payments are inversely linked to earnings affect the incentive of poor people to work and earn?
    a.   A poor person's incentive to earn is increased.
    b.   A poor person's incentive to earn is reduced.
    c.   The incentive of the poor to earn is unaffected.
    d.   The incentive of the poor to earn reported income is increased, but the incentive to earn unreported income is reduced.

19. If a family earned an additional $6,000 of income from work and as a result their welfare benefits were reduced by $3,000, the implicit marginal tax rate for this family would be
    a.   zero.
    b.   30 percent.
    c.   50 percent.
    d.   100 percent.

20. The idea that transfer benefits to the poor encourage behavior that increases the risk of poverty is known as the
    a.   Samaritan's dilemma.
    b.   rule of inverse benefits.
    c.   implicit marginal tax law.
    d.   Smith paradox.

21. Data suggest that the large increase in government spending on income transfers over the past three decades has been accompanied by
    a.   a reduced poverty rate for the nonelderly.
    b.   a more equal distribution of income.
    c.   fewer single-parent families because a married couple receives benefits twice as large.
    d.   none of the above.

22. (I) Opponents to government action to reduce income inequality argue that the pattern of economic outcomes is more important than the process that generates the outcomes. (II) Opponents of government action to reduce income inequality argue that the proposed solutions will retard economic growth.
    a.   Both I and II are true.
    b.   Both I and II are false.
    c.   I is true; II is false.
    d.   I is false; II is true.

DISCUSSION QUESTIONS

1. Some people blamed the rising income inequality in the 1980s on "bad" economic policies. However, income inequality continued to increase in the 1990s. What do you think are the major factors contributing to rising income inequality in the United States in recent decades?

2. "The average poor person in the United States has three times as much annual income as the average middle-class person in most other countries in the world. If we really cared about helping the poor and reducing income inequality, we would be sending our money to other countries rather than giving it to people in the United States." Evaluate this statement. Does giving our welfare dollars to a "richer" person in the United States rather than a "poorer" person in another country imply that our main concern is not with helping the poor in general?

3. "When the government engages in large-scale redistribution from the rich to the poor, it results in a smaller total economic pie, reducing the income of all." Evaluate this statement. How does the tax rate on taxpayer income and the implicit tax rate on transfer programs alter the incentive to work and earn

income for each group? What is the Samaritan's dilemma, and what does it imply about the validity of this statement?

4. What are some of the problems with annual income data at a given time as a measure of one's economic well-being? Do you think that, across individuals, lifetime earnings are more or less unequal than annual earnings? In the United States, is it typical for the vast majority of poor to remain poor and the rich to remain rich over long periods of time? Explain.

5. In a free market economy, a person's income is linked to their contribution to the nation's output. The traditional Marxist view is that a person's income should be determined by their need, while everyone should put forth maximum work effort regardless of the personal reward they get from working.
   a. Economist Milton Friedman has argued that a perfectly equal income distribution would thoroughly undermine our incentives to be productive. Do you agree or disagree?
   b. Is it fair that someone who produces more output receives more income independent of their needs? What, or who, determines exactly what a person's "needs" are?

6. Do you think the official poverty statistics in the United States are misleading? If so, in what ways? How would you change the way poverty is measured? In your answer, be sure to address how transfer benefits are considered in the calculations.

7. "If I were to take a job, my welfare benefits would fall by more than the amount of income I would earn. It is not that I do not want to work, but rather that I care about best supporting my family." Evaluate this statement. How do the implicit marginal tax rates of welfare programs affect the incentive of recipients to work?

8. Outcome: Joe has $1,000,000 and Steve has $200 of annual income this year. Below are several possible cases of how this outcome arose (the "process" that generated this outcome). In each case, judge whether you think the outcome and/or process is fair. Does your judgment about the fairness of the outcome depend upon how fair you consider the process?
   a. Process: Joe and Steve both used to have $201 and both spent $1 on a lottery ticket. Joe won the lottery.
   b. Process: Steve owns his own business and made $1,000,200, but Joe came in and robbed the business at gunpoint and took $1,000,000.
   c. Process: Joe owns his own business and made $1,000,200, but Steve came in and robbed the business at gunpoint and took $200.
   d. Process: Joe made the money from his new business that he purchased from Steve in exchange for a house and a yacht. Steve is now sailing the oceans on his new boat and made $200 of interest income this year on the little money he left in his savings account back home.
   e. Process: Joe and Steve are both retirees who invested their money in the stock market. Joe did well this year, but Steve did not.
   f. Process: Joe owns his own business and made $1,000,200, but he had to pay $200 in taxes to the government, which were then paid out to Steve in the form of welfare benefits.

9. Do you believe that rising income inequality is a serious problem? Why or why not? Do you believe that our economic process, the market system, is "fair"? Why or why not? How do you define "fair"?

Government Spending and Taxation

TRUE OR FALSE

T F

☐ ☐ 1. At the federal level, the personal income tax accounts for almost half of all revenue.

☐ ☐ 2. The federal government accounts for approximately three-fifths of all government spending in the United States.

☐ ☐ 3. Federal spending on national parks, highways, education, and law enforcement together account for over 50 percent of the federal budget.

☐ ☐ 4. All 50 U.S. states have both a state personal income tax and a state sales tax.

☐ ☐ 5. Sales taxes, income taxes, property taxes, and grants from higher levels of government are the major sources of state and local revenue in the United States.

☐ ☐ 6. Federal government spending in real per capita terms has grown rapidly throughout the entire history of the United States.

☐ ☐ 7. Corrected for inflation, the average person today pays more federal taxes in one week than the average person in 1900 paid in an entire year.

☐ ☐ 8. Over the past 40 years, national defense expenditures as a share of the federal budget have risen while transfer payments as a share of the federal budget have fallen.

T F

☐ ☐ 9. Including both the excess burden and administration, enforcement, and compliance costs of taxes in the United States, $1 in taxes to the government imposes a cost of somewhere between $1.20 and $1.30 on the economy. Thus, the cost of a $100 million government program financed with taxes is really somewhere between $120 million and $130 million.

☐ ☐ 10. The top 10 percent of income recipients paid 70.8 percent of the personal income tax in 2006.

☐ ☐ 11. In 2006, 32 percent of those filing an income tax return either had zero tax liability or actually received funds from the IRS as the result of the Earned Income Tax Credit, a provision in the tax code that provides a credit or rebate to persons with low earnings.

☐ ☐ 12. The share of the personal income tax paid by high-income Americans has fallen dramatically over the past 30 years, while the share paid by low-income Americans has risen.

☐ ☐ 13. While earners in the top quintile paid 25.5 percent of their income in federal taxes in 2005, the average tax rate in the bottom quintile is 4.3 percent, illustrating the highly progressive nature of the federal tax system.

☐ ☐ 14. Under the progressive income tax system in the United States, a larger and larger share of income is taxed at higher rates as real incomes rise.

☐ ☐ 15. There is substantial variation in the size of government across countries. The relative size of government in most other high-income industrial countries is greater than that of the United States.

☐ ☐ 16. When the size of a country's government grows to a large share of GDP, it will result in slower economic growth.

PROBLEMS AND PROJECTS

1. Exhibit 1 provides data on the federal government budget in fiscal years 1960 and 2000. Use the data provided to answer the following questions.
    a. Fill in the missing numbers for fiscal year 1960.
    b. Fill in the missing numbers for fiscal year 2000.
    c. What has happened to national defense expenditures as a percent of federal spending between 1960 and 2000?
    d. What has happened to Social Security expenditures as a percent of federal spending between 1960 and 2000?
    e. What has happened to payments for interest on the debt as a percent of federal spending between 1960 and 2000?
    f. What has happened to health and Medicare spending as a percent of federal spending between 1960 and 2000?
    g. What has happened to welfare spending as a percent of federal spending between 1960 and 2000?
    h. What was the single largest expenditure category in 1960? in 2000?
    i. What has happened to corporate income taxes as a percent of revenue between 1960 and 2000? Does this mean businesses are paying less of the tax burden in 2000 than in 1960?
    j. What was the single largest revenue source in 1960? in 2000?
    k. Given the nature of the data presented, why is it better to make comparisons using the percentages of the budget rather than using the dollar amounts?

EXHIBIT 1

FEDERAL GOVERNMENT FINANCES FOR FISCAL YEARS 1960 AND 2000

	FISCAL YEAR 1960		FISCAL YEAR 2000	
	AMOUNT (IN BILLIONS)	PERCENT OF TOTAL	AMOUNT (IN BILLIONS)	PERCENT OF TOTAL
Total Receipts (Revenues)	$549.5	100.0%	$1,883.0	100.0%
Individual income taxes	241.8	44.0	899.7	47.8
Corporate income taxes	127.7	_____	189.4	10.1
Social Security revenue	87.3	15.9	636.5	_____
Other revenue	92.7	16.9	157.4	8.4
Total Outlays (Expenditures)	$547.7	100.0%	$1,765.7	100.0%
National defense	285.8	_____	274.1	_____
Health and Medicare	4.8	0.9	368.9	20.9
Income security (welfare)	44.0	8.0	258.0	_____
Social Security	68.9	_____	408.6	23.1
Net interest on the debt	41.0	7.5	215.2	_____
Other expenditures	103.2	18.8	240.9	13.6

2. Exhibit 2 provides data from the Internal Revenue Service on the amount of federal income tax paid by different income groups in 2007. Use the data provided to answer the following questions.
    a. Fill in the missing blanks for the percent of income tax paid by group.
    b. In 1980, the top 1 percent paid 19.10 percent of the federal income tax. What has happened to the share of income tax paid by this group since 1980?
    c. In 1980, the bottom 50 percent paid 7.00 percent of the federal income tax. What has happened to the share of income tax paid by this group since 1980?
    d. Based on this data, would you say the rich pay their fair share of taxes in the United States?

EXHIBIT 2

FEDERAL INCOME TAX PAID BY INCOME GROUP IN 2007

INCOME GROUP	TOTAL FEDERAL INCOME TAX PAID BY GROUP (IN MILLIONS)	PERCENT OF TOTAL FEDERAL INCOME TAX PAID BY GROUP
Top 1%	$450,926	_____
Top 5%	676,293	60.63
Top 10%	794,432	_____
Top 25%	965,875	_____
Top 50%	1,083,243	_____
Bottom 50%	32,261	2.89
Total all groups	1,115,504	100.00

MULTIPLE CHOICE

1. At the federal level, which of the following accounts for almost half of all revenue?
    a. corporate income taxes
    b. retail sales taxes
    c. personal income taxes
    d. cigarette taxes

2. (I) Sales taxes, income taxes, property taxes, and grants from higher levels of government are the major sources of state and local revenue in the United States. (II) Including both the excess burden and administration, enforcement, and compliance costs of taxes in the United States, $1 in taxes to the government imposes a cost of somewhere between $1.20 and $1.30 on the economy.
    a. Both I and II are true.
    b. I is true; II is false.
    c. I is false; II is true.
    d. Both I and II are false.

3. Under the progressive income tax system in the United States, as real incomes rise,
    a. a smaller share of income is taxed at higher rates.
    b. there is no change in the share of income taxed at higher rates.
    c. a larger share of income is taxed at higher rates.
    d. none of the above are true.

4. For the first time in almost a century,
    a. the rapid growth of federal spending stopped during the 1990s.
    b. the slow growth of federal spending began to increase during the 1990s.
    c. state and local governments spent more than the federal government during the 1990s.
    d. national defense became the largest category of federal spending in the 1990s.

5. Which of the following is true regarding U.S. federal government expenditures?
    a. National defense has fallen from 52.2 percent of the federal budget in 1960 to 21.0 percent in 2008.
    b. Federal expenditures on income transfers and health care have risen from 21.5 percent of the budget in 1960 to 57.7 percent in 2008.
    c. Corrected for inflation, the average person today pays more federal taxes in one week than the average person in 1900 paid in an entire year.
    d. All of the above are true.

6. One dollar of tax revenue ends up costing citizens in the economy
    a. less than one dollar.
    b. exactly one dollar.
    c. more than one dollar.
    d. nothing.

7. In 2006, the income tax payments of the richest 1 percent of Americans accounted for approximately what percent of all federal income tax revenue?
    a. 1 percent
    b. 20 percent
    c. 40 percent
    d. 60 percent

8. In 2006, the income tax payments of the poorest 50 percent of Americans accounted for approximately what percent of all federal income tax revenue?
    a. 3 percent
    b. 25 percent
    c. 50 percent
    d. 76 percent

9. Estimates from the U.S. Treasury Department suggest that the typical family in the highest income quintile pays approximately what percent of their total income in federal taxes?
    a. 4 percent
    b. 25 percent
    c. 50 percent
    d. 76 percent

10. Estimates from the U.S. Treasury Department suggest that the typical family in the lowest income quintile pays approximately what percent of their total income in federal taxes?
    a. 4 percent
    b. 25 percent
    c. 50 percent
    d. 76 percent

11. Based on estimates from the U.S. Treasury Department, the federal tax structure is
    a. highly regressive.
    b. roughly proportional.
    c. highly progressive.
    d. regressive at lower incomes and progressive at higher incomes.

12. Because of which provision in the tax code did more than one-third of all taxpayers either have a zero tax liability or actually receive money from the IRS in 2004?
    a. Earned Income Tax Credit
    b. Standard Deduction
    c. Marginal Tax Rate
    d. Families with Low Income Credit

13. Government expenditures as a percent of GDP in the United States
    a. are very high in comparison to the rest of the world.
    b. are smaller than for most other high-income industrial countries.
    c. are much smaller today than they were a century ago.
    d. are none of the above.

14. Which of the following most clearly distinguishes government from a private business?
    a. the power to tax
    b. the hiring of educated employees
    c. the production of goods and services
    d. the need to make managerial decisions

15. Which of the following correctly expresses the relationship between the size of government and economic growth?
    a. Because it is the private sector in which growth occurs, the size of government is generally unrelated to the rate of economic growth.
    b. When government is small, an increase in its size may increase economic growth, but beyond some point, further increases in the size of government will reduce economic growth.
    c. When government is small, an increase in its size may initially lower economic growth, but when it becomes large enough, expansions in government generally increase the rate of economic growth.
    d. The rate of economic growth appears to be increasing with the size of government for the levels of government that we observe in most major industrialized countries.

DISCUSSION QUESTIONS

1. Discuss the trends in the size of the U.S. federal government over its history. Was the growth rate of real per capita federal expenditures similar in the 1800s and the 1900s?

2. What are the major expenditure areas and revenue sources of the U.S. federal government and how has this changed over the past several decades?

3. How progressive is the U.S. federal tax system? How heavy is the burden of the federal income tax on the rich?

4. How do the types of expenditure programs and sources of revenue differ between the federal government and state and local governments in the United States?

5. How does the size of a country's government influence its growth rate? Does it matter whether the government sector is small or large? Does the evidence indicate that reducing the size of government would increase or reduce economic growth in the United States?

The Internet: How Is It Changing the Economy?

TRUE OR FALSE

T   F

- ☐ ☐ 1. On-line sales of goods and services to consumers totaled $228 billion in 2008.

- ☐ ☐ 2. In 2008, there were over 100 million Web sites.

- ☐ ☐ 3. Approximately 25 percent of the U.S. population uses the Internet.

- ☐ ☐ 4. People in Africa, Latin America, and the Middle East account for a relatively small proportion of all Internet users.

- ☐ ☐ 5. The Internet is beneficial because it lowers transaction costs in the economy, makes markets more competitive, and increases networking opportunities.

- ☐ ☐ 6. On-line sales account for a larger percentage of computer hardware and software sales than for automobile sales.

- ☐ ☐ 7. The Internet generally makes it more difficult for consumers to obtain access to some goods, particularly specialty products and customized goods with unique characteristics.

- ☐ ☐ 8. The Internet has generally benefited consumers but has been of little use in fostering transactions between business firms.

- ☐ ☐ 9. The Internet has rapidly become an important part of the job search process and helps to match job seekers with potential employers.

- ☐ ☐ 10. By helping to lower search time and improve the quality of the matching between potential employees and potential jobs, the Internet has created economic benefits in the labor market.

PROBLEMS AND PROJECTS

1. A lot can be learned by looking at the most popular search terms on the Internet and how they change from week to week. One such list for the Web site Yahoo! can be found at http://buzz.yahoo.com. Look at this Web page as you do this problem and answer the following questions.
    a. What are the top five search terms this week?
    b. Which search terms gained the most and which fell by the most from last week? Can you explain why?
    c. Which search terms have been in the top 20 list for the longest number of weeks?
    d. Of the search terms currently in the top 20, which do you expect will stay on the list for the longest number of weeks into the future?

2. Go to the Amazon.com Web site (http://www.amazon.com) and search in "Popular Music" for your favorite CD (or the one you listen to the most). Answer the following questions while you look at the Web page for your favorite CD.
    a. How much does this CD cost from Amazon.com? How does this compare to the price you paid for it? How would shipping and handling costs affect this comparison?
    b. Further down the Web page you will see a section titled "Customers who bought this title also bought:." These are the CDs most frequently purchased by other shoppers who also purchased your favorite CD. Do you like and/or own these CDs as well? If there is one you don't know about, or haven't heard, go to the page for it and listen to some of the song samples to see if you like it.
    c. Read the reviews at the bottom of the Web page for your favorite CD. Do you agree or disagree with them? Readers can rank the "helpfulness" of each review, and the average "helpfulness" is indicated by the number of stars colored orange out of the total of five stars. Do the reviews you agree with the most tend to have the highest number of stars?

3. Many students complain about the low prices they get when they go to sell their used textbooks. Because the Internet lowers transaction costs, it should be making it easier for students to buy and sell textbooks from one another without the use of a bookstore as a middleman.
    a. Visit the Student Book Exchange Web site (http://www.stubex.com). How much are the textbooks you are using this semester selling for used on this Web site? Do you think you will sell your textbooks on-line or will you sell them back to your local college bookstore? How much more would you have to get for your textbook on-line to be willing to sell it there instead of back to your local student bookstore? What does this say about the value your student bookstore provides?
    b. At the University of Iowa there is a Web site devoted to helping students trade used textbooks (http://uiowa.collegetextbookexchange.com). How do the resale prices at this Web site compare to the prices at the Student Book Exchange for your textbooks?

MULTIPLE CHOICE

1. By 2008, there were over how many Web sites?
    a. 10 million
    b. 50 million
    c. 100 million
    d. 500 million

2. The Internet produces economic gains because it
    a. lowers transaction costs.
    b. makes markets more competitive.
    c. increases the ability of people to network.
    d. does all of the above.

3. What percent of households were paying bills on-line in 2007?
    a. 1 percent
    b. 39 percent
    c. 59 percent
    d. 99 percent

4. For which of the following products or services does on-line sales account for the largest percentage of total sales?
    a. computer hardware and software
    b. travel
    c. music and videos
    d. automobiles

5. For which of the following products or services does on-line sales account for the smallest percentage of total sales?
    a. computer hardware and software
    b. travel
    c. music and videos
    d. automobiles

6. On-line retail firms may have lower costs than traditional retail firms because
    a. it will often not be necessary for on-line firms to unpack or display products.
    b. there are fewer losses due to shoplifting for on-line retailers.
    c. on-line retailers can use low-cost warehouses rather than expensive stores to house their products.
    d. all of the above.

7. A major drawback with purchasing goods on-line is that
    a. consumers can't touch, taste, smell, or try the goods on before purchasing them.
    b. it is generally more difficult to find specialty products or customized goods.
    c. they generally cost more than goods available at local retail stores because on-line retail firms have to pay higher inventory costs.
    d. most major retailers do not have Internet sites.

8. Which of the following is true regarding job-posting Web sites?
    a. Job-posting Web sites contain more job openings and are easier to search than traditional newspaper help-wanted ads.
    b. Job openings posted on Web sites tend to be more current and updated than ones in traditional print sources, and they are also less costly for the advertiser.
    c. It is generally possible for job seekers to advertise their skills to employers on job-posting Web sites as well as the reverse.
    d. All of the above are true.

9. Which of the following economic benefits result from the use of the Internet in the job search process?
    a. Job seekers will obtain employment more quickly and thus the unemployment rate will be lower.
    b. On-line screening of candidates may contribute to a faster and higher quality of match between workers and employers, which should increase productivity in the economy.
    c. Job turnover will be lower because employed workers generally do not browse employment ads on the Internet.
    d. Both a and b are true, but not c.

10. In 2008, approximately how many workers provided part or all of their work at home or other locations through the use of the Internet?
    a. 5 million
    b. 19 million
    c. 39 million
    d. 69 million

11. The use of the Internet to work from home or another location is called
    a. Internetting.
    b. telecommuting.
    c. spiderwebbing.
    d. surfing.

DISCUSSION QUESTIONS

1. Some people claim that Internet sites such as eBay do not create meaningful economic value because people are simply trading their old "junk" for higher prices than it is worth. Evaluate this position from an economic standpoint; do you agree or disagree?

2. What cost advantages do on-line retailers have over traditional retail stores? What are some disadvantages to buying things on-line compared to buying from a traditional retail store?

3. How has the Internet changed the job search process? What potential economic gains are there from the use of the Internet in the labor market?

4. Does the Internet make markets more or less competitive? In what ways has the Internet changed the nature of retail competition?

The Economics of Social Security

TRUE OR FALSE

T F

☐ ☐ 1. The Social Security program in the United States takes the taxes collected from present workers and saves this money for their retirement.

☐ ☐ 2. When a current worker pays Social Security taxes, the majority of that money is directly paid out to current retirees rather than being saved.

☐ ☐ 3. The downward trend in the number of workers per retiree requires that higher Social Security tax rates be used just to maintain a constant level of benefits for retirees.

☐ ☐ 4. In terms of benefits received relative to taxes paid, today's workers will fare much better than workers have in the past.

☐ ☐ 5. For a worker aged 40 or younger, the rate of return they will receive on their Social Security contributions exceeds what could have been earned if they had invested the money personally.

☐ ☐ 6. The share of the population aged 70 or over will continue to rise as the baby boom generation ages.

☐ ☐ 7. Essentially, the surplus of the Social Security system exists only on paper. The federal government used this money to finance current government spending by issuing U.S. Treasury bonds.

☐ ☐ 8. For Social Security to spend its trust fund, it will require the federal government to either raise taxes or cut other spending to repay the trust fund money it has borrowed.

T F

☐ ☐ 9. Because lower income persons tend to belong to demographic groups with a lower life expectancy, they will on average receive less benefits from Social Security than higher income persons who generally live longer.

☐ ☐ 10. Because of the shorter life expectancy for whites, the Social Security system adversely affects their economic welfare when compared to blacks.

☐ ☐ 11. Most married women who work will receive virtually no additional benefits relative to if they had not worked (and not paid Social Security taxes) at all.

☐ ☐ 12. An unfunded liability is a shortfall of tax revenues at current rates relative to promised benefits for a government program.

☐ ☐ 13. A personal retirement account is owned personally by an individual and can be passed along to the person's heirs.

PROBLEMS AND PROJECTS

1. Social Security is a "pay-as-you-go" system, so the money paid out in benefits to current retirees comes from tax collections on current workers. One of the main problems facing Social Security is the declining number of workers per retiree in the United States. Suppose that Social Security wishes to pay benefits of $15,000 per year to each retiree. If there were ten workers per retiree, this would mean each current worker would have to pay, on average, $1,500 in taxes per year to support this level of benefits for each retired person.
    a. In the 1950s, there were approximately fifteen workers per retiree. How much would each worker in the 1950s have to pay in taxes each year to support a level of benefits equal to $15,000 per year per retiree?
    b. By 2000, this ratio had fallen such that there were approximately three workers per retiree. How much would each worker in 2000 have to pay in taxes each year to support a level of benefits equal to $15,000 per year per retiree?
    c. By 2030, this ratio will fall to approximately two workers per retiree. How much will each worker in 2030 have to pay in taxes each year to support a level of benefits equal to $15,000 per year per retiree?
    d. As this ratio falls in the future, the alternative to increasing taxes is to cut benefits. If the amount of taxes per worker is held constant between 2000 and 2030, by how much will benefits to each retiree have to be reduced?

2. Suppose you have been saving for a new boat by putting cash in an old shoe box in your house. So far you have saved $5,000. Your spouse, however, has been running a "deficit" and has borrowed all of the money and left IOUs (notes promising to repay the money) in the box.
    a. Technically do you have $5,000 saved for your boat?
    b. If you went to buy the boat and needed the money, what would it require your spouse do?
    c. How does this example differ from the Social Security trust fund, which has been "invested" in U.S. Treasury bonds?

3. Workers born between 1945 and 1964 will earn a real rate of return of about 1.8 percent from their Social Security contributions. This same money, if invested in the stock market, would have given approximately a 7 percent rate of return. A frequently used tool in finance is the "rule of 72," which states that the number of years it will take for an investment to double (with compound interest) is equal to 72 divided by the rate of return. With a rate of return of 1.8 percent, this implies that a given amount of money invested would double every 40 years. On the other hand, at a rate of return of 7 percent, the money would double almost every 10 years.

a. Using these values, if you placed $20,000 in a retirement account invested in the stock market at age 25, it would grow to $40,000 by the time you were 35, to $80,000 by the time you were 45, to $160,000 by the time you were 55, and to $320,000 by the time you retired at age 65. How does this compare to the amount you would have at age 65 had you earned the 1.8 percent offered by the Social Security program?

b. If a worker selected a private retirement plan that was safer than the stock market and so only earned a 3.6 percent rate of return, how much additional money would they have at age 65 than at the 1.8 percent rate?

c. Because Social Security pays current tax revenue out to current recipients ("pay-as-you-go" system), there is no real savings involved in the program. Many economists believe that the structure of the system has lowered the savings rate in our economy, which in turn lowers investment and economic growth. The system is approximately 72 years old. Suppose that it has lowered our rate of economic growth by 1 percentage point per year. If these numbers were accurate, how much larger would our economy be today if Social Security had not been adopted?

d. You may have heard that it is much better to save a little bit when you are younger than to save a lot when you are older. Use a 7.2 percent rate of return (so the money doubles every 10 years) to figure out the following amounts. If you placed $10,000 in an account when you were 25, how much would you have in the account when you turned 65? How much would you have at age 65 if you had put $15,000 in when you were 25? Suppose you waited until age 35 to put money in an account. How much would you have to deposit at age 35 to have the same amount at age 65 as if you placed $10,000 in when you were 25? if you waited until age 45?

MULTIPLE CHOICE

1. Social Security
    a. collects taxes from current workers and invests this money to repay the workers when they retire.
    b. is based on the same principles as private insurance programs.
    c. is an intergenerational transfer program that takes money from current workers and transfers it to current retirees.
    d. is designed so that administrative decisions can be made independent of political concerns.

2. Which of the following best explains why the Social Security system is expected to face financial difficulties in the near future?
    a. Too much Social Security revenue was invested in the private sector rather than in government bonds.
    b. The federal government does not pay interest on the money it borrows from the Social Security system.
    c. The funds in the Social Security trust fund were invested in high-risk ventures that failed to pay off.
    d. The number of workers paying into the system is expected to decline relative to the number of retirees collecting benefits.

3. When the Social Security system enters its deficit years and the bonds held in the trust funds are drawn down,
    a. overall taxes will be reduced as the trust funds are used to pay benefits to retirees.
    b. the payroll taxes used to finance Social Security benefits can be reduced because the trust funds will be sufficient to pay the retirement benefits of the baby boom generation.
    c. income and other federal taxes will have to be raised (or additional funds will have to be borrowed) in order to redeem the bonds held by the trust fund.
    d. income taxes will have to be reduced in order to keep the revenues and expenditures of the Social Security system in balance.

4. In approximately what year will Social Security outlays begin to exceed revenues?
   a. 2008
   b. 2016
   c. 2050
   d. 3030

5. A shortfall of tax revenues at current rates relative to promised benefits for a government program is called a(n)
   a. personal retirement account.
   b. expected equity.
   c. promissory note.
   d. unfunded liability.

6. (I) Current Social Security retirees typically receive real benefits that are equal to three or four times the amount of their contributions into the system. (II) Current young workers can expect to receive real benefits less than their contributions into the system.
   a. I is true; II is false.
   b. I is false; II is true.
   c. Both I and II are false.
   d. Both I and II are true.

7. The surplus in the Social Security retirement system is currently held in the form of
   a. U.S. Treasury bonds.
   b. gold.
   c. U.S. corporate stock.
   d. cash reserves in major U.S. banks.

8. The Social Security system is currently generating tax revenues that exceed the benefits paid to recipients. This surplus is
   a. being invested in foreign bonds, which will provide Americans with a source of income when the baby boom generation retires.
   b. being invested in government bonds, which will require an increase in general tax revenues when the bonds come due.
   c. separated from other government revenue so politicians will not spend the money during the current period.
   d. being channeled into earmarked private savings accounts.

9. As the baby boom generation retires in the future, Social Security will have to
   a. reduce benefits to retirees.
   b. increase taxes on workers.
   c. borrow money.
   d. utilize some combination of a, b, and c.

10. In 2009, the Social Security payroll tax did not apply to annual income above
    a. $15,000.
    b. $32,000.
    c. $106,800.
    d. $145,900.

11. Based on average life expectancy, which of the following groups would you expect to collect Social Security benefits for the greatest number of years?
    a. college graduates
    b. blacks
    c. persons with AIDS
    d. single males

12. Most married women who choose to work can expect to receive
    a. substantially higher Social Security benefits than if they had not worked and thus not paid into the system.
    b. substantially lower Social Security benefits than if they had not worked and thus not paid into the system.
    c. approximately the same Social Security benefits than if they had not worked and thus not paid into the system.
    d. benefits based on their husbands' salary plus 50 percent of their own salary.

13. (I) Because married women are permitted to receive benefits based on either their own earnings or 50 percent of the benefits earned by their spouse, whichever is greater, the payroll tax takes a big chunk of the earnings of many working women without providing any significant additional benefits to them. (II) Because blacks have a shorter life expectancy, they are economically disadvantaged by Social Security relative to whites and Hispanics.
    a. I is true; II is false.
    b. I is false; II is true.
    c. Both I and II are false.
    d. Both I and II are true.

14. Which of the following countries has not taken steps to privatize its Social Security system?
    a. United States
    b. Mexico
    c. United Kingdom
    d. Chile

DISCUSSION QUESTIONS

1. If given a choice between remaining in the government Social Security program or switching to a private investment fund, which would you choose? What factors would be the most important in your decision?

2. The most popular reform option for Social Security involves using personal savings accounts. What do you see as the major advantages and disadvantages of switching to a system of personal savings accounts?

3. What is the difference between a "fully funded" system and a "pay-as-you-go" Social Security system? How would the problems facing the Social Security system have been different if the system had been fully funded from the beginning?

4. Discuss how the differing life expectancies by race, gender, and education impact the Social Security benefits received by different groups. In addition, how does the calculation of benefits for married women affect their return from Social Security contributions?

The Stock Market: Its Function, Performance, and Potential as an Investment Opportunity

TRUE OR FALSE

T F

☐ ☐ 1. During the 1980s and 1990s, the real returns from stock market investment have been far worse than the long-term average of 7 percent.

☐ ☐ 2. An investor may lower the risk of his or her portfolio by holding shares of many different firms in unconnected industries.

☐ ☐ 3. Although the stock market may vary substantially from day to day, if stocks are held over long periods of time, the variation in return is relatively small.

☐ ☐ 4. About one-half of all households in the United States now own stock either directly or through investment in a mutual fund.

☐ ☐ 5. Periods of low interest rates will generally be accompanied by a poorly performing stock market.

☐ ☐ 6. The random walk theory of the stock market suggests that current stock prices already reflect the best-known information about the future values of stocks.

☐ ☐ 7. A corporation can tie the compensation of top executives to stock performance through the use of stock options.

☐ ☐ 8. Mutual funds allow small investors with limited investment budgets to obtain lower risk and more diversity in their portfolios than if the investors had to purchase individual stocks.

T F

☐ ☐ 9. When a corporation originally issues stock, this is done in the primary market. The more familiar secondary markets are where investors trade the ownership rights embodied in stocks that were previously issued.

☐ ☐ 10. When a person purchases a stock, they are effectively lending a corporation money, which will be repaid to the stockholder at a future date.

☐ ☐ 11. The price of a firm's stock will tend to fall when investors believe that the management of a firm has made a business decision that will result in a decrease in the firm's earnings in the future.

☐ ☐ 12. The Standard and Poor's 500 index provides a measure of the rate of return received by investors in the form of both dividends and changes in share prices.

☐ ☐ 13. A stock market bubble refers to a situation in which high stock prices cannot be maintained into the future because they are out of line with the future earning prospects of business firms.

☐ ☐ 14. The operating costs of indexed mutual funds is substantially higher than the operating costs of managed mutual funds.

☐ ☐ 15. The mutual funds most likely to do well in the future are the ones that have been the best performers in the recent past.

PROBLEMS AND PROJECTS

1. Underlying the current price of a firm's stock is the present value of the firm's expected future net earnings or profit. For each of the following, indicate whether the change would result in an increase or decrease in the present value of a firm's future net earnings.
   _____ a. The interest rate increases.
   _____ b. There is an increase in the annual dividend the corporation is expected to pay.
   _____ c. The corporation withholds this year's dividend and uses the money to make an investment that is expected to be extremely profitable in the future.

2. Use the present value formula in the text to compute the current value of each of the following streams of future income.
   a. a payment of $100 one year from now and a payment of $100 two years from now, when the interest rate is 10 percent
   b. a payment of $100 one year from now and a payment of $100 two years from now, when the interest rate is 5 percent
   c. a payment of $150 one year from now and a payment of $50 two years from now, when the interest rate is 10 percent
   d. a payment of $100 one year from now and a payment of $150 two years from now, when the interest rate is 10 percent
   e. a payment of $150 one year from now and a payment of $150 two years from now, when the interest rate is 10 percent

MULTIPLE CHOICE

1. Investors can make their investments in corporate stocks less risky by
   a. purchasing shares of a mutual fund, which holds the stocks of many diverse corporations.
   b. buying stocks and holding them each for only for short periods of time.
   c. investing in firms that are in the same, rather than different, industries.
   d. none of the above.

2. Which of the following would reduce the risk of an investment in the stock market?
   a. investing in a portfolio of diverse firms
   b. holding the investment for a long period of time
   c. both a and b
   d. neither a nor b

3. Historically, when a diverse set of stocks are held over a lengthy time period, stocks have yielded a
   _____ rate of return and the variation in the rate of return has been _____. (Fill in the blanks.)
   a. low; low
   b. low; high
   c. high; low
   d. high; high

4. (I) The market for new issues of stock is called the primary market. (II) The New York Stock Exchange
   is an example of a secondary market in which previously issued shares are traded between investors.
   a. I is true; II is false.
   b. I is false; II is true.
   c. Both I and II are true.
   d. Both I and II are false.

5. Which of the following types of mutual funds best describes one in which an "expert" seeks to pick the
   stock holdings in a way that maximizes the rate of return?
   a. indexed equity mutual fund
   b. managed equity mutual fund
   c. supervised equity mutual fund
   d. marked equity mutual fund

6. Which of the following is true?
   a. The P/E ratio provides information on the price of a stock relative to its current earnings.
   b. The P/E ratio provides information on the price of a stock relative to its future earnings.
   c. The P/E ratio provides information on the price of a stock relative to its past earnings.
   d. The P/E ratio average from 1950–2004 was 26.

7. A lower interest rate will increase the present value of future income and thereby
   a. decrease the market value of stocks.
   b. increase the market value of stocks.
   c. have no effect on the market value of stocks.
   d. decrease the discounted market value of stocks.

8. According to the random walk theory, which of the following is true?
   a. Stock prices reflect all available information about factors that affect stock prices.
   b. Future movements of stock prices are unpredictable.
   c. Changes in stock prices are driven by surprise occurrences.
   d. All of the above are true.

9. Which of the following represents a method for a firm to obtain funds for growth and product development?
   a. use of retained earnings
   b. borrowing money
   c. selling stock
   d. all of the above

10. The current market value of a stock option contract to purchase 1,000 shares of IBM stock at a price of $100 that can be exercised five years from now would
    a. increase if the expected future price of IBM stock rose.
    b. increase if the expected future price of IBM stock fell.
    c. decrease if the expected future price of IBM stock rose.
    d. remain unchanged regardless of the expected future price of IBM stock.

DISCUSSION QUESTIONS

1. A friend of yours just inherited $100,000 and asks your opinion on the best way to invest the money for her retirement. She wants to earn the highest return possible but also wants to have a relatively low-risk investment. What advice would you give her? Would your advice depend on her current age?

2. What factors have contributed to the relatively high performance of the stock market over the past 20 years? Based upon what might happen to these same factors in the future, how do you expect the stock market to perform in the near future?

3. The random walk theory holds that all available information is already reflected in stock prices. Therefore, stock prices change due to new, surprise information. The result is that stock prices move in a random, unpredictable fashion. What does this theory imply about
    a. how well a person who picks stocks by throwing darts at the newspaper will do relative to someone who spends hours picking their stocks based upon detailed research?
    b. how well someone will do who holds on to one portfolio of stocks for many years relative to someone who buys and sells stocks frequently?
    c. the current price of the stock of XYZ corporation relative to the price of ABC corporation stock if XYZ is expected to earn more profits in the future than ABC?

4. How much has the stock market fallen in the past few years? Is now a good or bad time to invest in the stock market? Explain your reasoning.

The Crisis of 2008: Causes and Lessons for the Future

TRUE OR FALSE

T F

☐ ☐ 1. Fannie Mae and Freddy Mac were both government-sponsored enterprises that were able to borrow funds cheaper than private lenders could because it was widely perceived that the government would back Fannie and Freddy's bonds if they ever ran into financial trouble.

☐ ☐ 2. A sub-prime loan is a loan with an extremely low interest rate made to someone with an outstanding documented credit history.

☐ ☐ 3. Adjustable-rate mortgages offer borrowers a low interest rate that varies with the inflation rate so that monthly payments on the loan will remain fixed.

☐ ☐ 4. Malinvestment is investment made in a malicious attempt to undercut the competition.

☐ ☐ 5. According to the scale used by security rating firms, a triple-A rating is supposed to indicate a security where the risk of default is low.

☐ ☐ 6. In 2008, household debt as a share of disposable income was more than double its level in the mid 1980s.

☐ ☐ 7. Throughout history, the Fed has been able to appropriately use discretionary monetary policy to stabilize the economy.

☐ ☐ 8. Both history and economic theory indicate that additional regulations will be an effective way to prevent a future financial crisis.

☐ ☐ 9. The main focus of the Fed should be monetary and price stability.

☐ ☐ 10. The expansionary monetary policy pursued by the Fed in the period following the recession of 2001 is at least partly responsible for the financial crisis of 2008.

PROBLEMS AND PROJECTS

1. Many factors affect the interest rate you pay when financing a house, including your FICO credit score and the size of your down payment relative to the price of the house. However, Fed policy is the main factor that drives overall interest rates in the economy. This question requires you to predict the impact that Fed policy had on the decisions of borrowers over the past decade. For reference, between 2002 and 2004, the Fed kept short-term interest rates at historic lows, then subsequently increased interest rates. Please use a + (increase) or a – (decrease) to indicate what you think happened to the following in response to the Fed's recent actions:

   ___ a. The demand for interest-sensitive goods like automobiles and houses during the period of low interest rates.

   ___ b. The size and, subsequently, the total purchase price of the houses that people chose to buy during the period of low interest rates.

   ___ c. The number of loans made to riskier borrowers (those with lower credit scores).

   ___ d. The monthly payments on houses *after* interest rates were increased from their historically low levels.

   ___ e. The number of people who were unable to make their monthly house payments *after* interest rates were increased.

2. This chapter includes a number of financial terms that may be unfamiliar to you. In an effort to improve your understanding of these various terms, try to match the term with the definition by writing the number associated with the term in the space provided.

   1. Sub-prime Loan

   2. FICO Score

   3. Adjustable Rate Mortgage

   4. Malinvestment

   5. Leverage Ratios

   6. Security Rating

   7. Mortgage-backed Securities

   8. Basis Point

   ___ a. One one-hundredth of a percentage point.

   ___ b. A score measuring a borrower's ability to repay a loan.

   ___ c. A home loan in which the interest rate is tied to a short-term rate.

   ___ d. A loan made to a borrower with blemished credit or one who provides only limited documentation of indicators of creditworthiness.

   ___ e. A rating indicating the risk of default on a security.

   ___ f. The ratios of loans and other investments to firms' capital assets.

   ___ g. Investment caused when the Fed holds interest rates artificially low, encouraging too much borrowing.

   ___ h. Securities issued for the financing of large pools of mortgages.

MULTIPLE CHOICE

1. Fannie Mae and Freddie Mac held a competitive advantage over other mortgage lenders primarily because
   a. they were established as nonprofit entities and thus did not need to show that they were profitable.
   b. they could borrow funds cheaper than other lenders because their bonds were perceived to be backed by the federal government.
   c. they were allowed to institute higher loan standards than other banks and mortgage lenders.
   d. they were exempt from federal regulations monitoring lending practices.

2. The 1995 modifications to the Community Reinvestment Act
    a. imposed numeric goals for loans extended to low-income and minority groups that were difficult for many banks to meet without reducing loan standards.
    b. reduced the incentive of banks to extend loans to low-income and minority groups.
    c. encouraged low-income and minority housing purchasers to make larger down payments so they would have more equity in their houses.
    d. made it more difficult for low-income and minority groups to obtain conventional loans.

3. Since the mid-1990s, the percentage of new mortgages categorized as sub-prime or Alt-A loans has
    a. remained steady at about 5 percent of all loans.
    b. decreased to about one-third of all loans, while conventional loans have increased to about two-thirds.
    c. increased to about one-third of all loans, while conventional loans have decreased to about one-third as well.
    d. decreased as a result of regulations designed to tighten loan standards.

4. The Fed's low short-term interest rate policy of 2002 to 2004 made it highly attractive for buyers to purchase a house
    a. with a large down payment and a 30-year, fixed-rate mortgage.
    b. with a large down payment and an adjustable rate mortgage.
    c. with a small down payment and an adjustable rate mortgage.
    d. quickly before housing prices began to decline in 2006.

5. Beginning in 2002, Federal Reserve policy
    a. switched from its focus on price stability to stimulating real GDP and reducing unemployment.
    b. kept interest rates artificially high, driving housing prices upward.
    c. kept interest rates artificially low, driving housing prices downward.
    d. switched its focus from stimulating real GDP and reducing unemployment to price stability.

6. During 2006–2008, the housing foreclosure rate rose sharply
    a. for fixed interest rate loans, but it was virtually unchanged for adjustable rate loans.
    b. for adjustable rate loans to both subprime and prime borrowers, but there was little change in the foreclosure rate on fixed interest rate loans.
    c. for adjustable rate loans to subprime borrowers, but the foreclosure rate on these loans to prime borrowers was virtually unchanged.
    d. for adjustable rate loans to prime borrowers, but the foreclosure rate on these loans to subprime borrowers was virtually unchanged.

7. An SEC rule change allowing investment banks to increase the leverage of their investment capital prompted many investment banks to
    a. increase the amount of assets held in relation to mortgage-backed securities being issued.
    b. decrease the amount of assets held in relation to mortgage-backed securities being issued.
    c. decrease the amount of mortgage-backed securities being offered.
    d. reduce the ratio of mortgage loans to equity capital of the investment bank.

8. The mortgage-backed securities issued by investment banks caused many investment banks to fail when
    a. stock prices declined by approximately 40 percent in 2008.
    b. housing prices increased rapidly beginning in 2002.
    c. federal regulators required investment banks to maintain more capital against their residential housing loans than was true for commercial business loans.
    d. the default rates of the mortgages financed by the securities increased sharply.

9. Which of the following is an example of how incentive structures contributed to the collapse of investment banks?
    a. The bonus structure of most executives was tied to long-term profitability.
    b. The ratings agencies were paid attractive fees by investment banks seeking high ratings for their securities.
    c. Mortgage-backed securities were closely scrutinized in order to minimize risk and obtain higher ratings.
    d. Despite SEC regulations, investment banks kept leverage ratios low in order to increase profits.

10. Compared to the 1980s, household debt as a share of income in 2007 has
    a. increased at a steady rate over time.
    b. remained about the same.
    c. more than doubled.
    a. decreased slowly over time.

11. When interest payments on home mortgages and home equity loans are tax deductible,
    a. households will keep other forms of debt separate from their home mortgage.
    b. households will shift other forms of debt to their home mortgage.
    c. households are likely to increase the amount of equity in their home.
    d. the overall amount of household debt is likely to decrease in relation to household income.

12. Which of the following makes it difficult for monetary policymakers to institute policy changes in a manner that will promote economic stability?
    a. Monetary policymakers do not have sufficient tools to alter the supply of money.
    b. The time lags between changes in monetary policy and when the changes exert an impact on output and prices are long and variable.
    c. Monetary policy is unable to alter short-term interest rates.
    d. Even though monetary policy can alter interest rates, there is little evidence that interest rates influence the demand for and prices of housing.

13. Are new regulations likely to prevent a future financial crisis?
    a. Yes, regulatory agencies have been effective at anticipating the secondary effects of new regulations.
    b. Yes, industries that were highly regulated were unaffected by the Crisis of 2008.
    c. No, regulators have a poor record with regard to foreseeing future problems.
    d. No, current regulations could have prevented the Crisis of 2008, but were largely ignored.

14. The primary objective of the monetary policy of the Fed should be
    a. low rates of unemployment.
    b. the growth rate of real GDP.
    c. the achievement of price stability.
    d. the regulation of financial institutions.

DISCUSSION QUESTIONS

1. In the period immediately following the recession of 2001, the Fed reduced short-term interest rates and held them at historic lows. What do you think the Fed was trying to do at the time? What were the secondary effects of this low-interest rate policy in terms of setting the stage for the recent financial crisis?

2. If the recent financial crisis can be blamed partially on the expansionary monetary policy the Fed followed after the 2001 recession, do you think the Fed should continue to engage in discretionary monetary policy? Why or Why not?

Lessons from the Great Depression

TRUE OR FALSE

T F

☐ ☐ 1. The Great Depression was caused by the stock market crash of 1929.

☐ ☐ 2. The government lowered personal income taxes during the time period that marked the Great Depression in an effort to help stimulate the economy.

☐ ☐ 3. The stock market had nearly rebounded back to its original level in less than a year following the crash in October of 1929, before it started to steadily decline in response to the passage of the Smoot-Hawley tariff.

☐ ☐ 4. The government appropriately used expansionary monetary policy in an effort to increase the money supply throughout the Great Depression.

☐ ☐ 5. During the Great Depression, the government passed the National Industrial Recovery ACT (NIRA), which essentially organized businesses into government-sponsored cartels in an effort to keep prices high.

☐ ☐ 6. During the Great Depression, the government passed the Agricultural Adjustment Act (AAA), which paid farmers to destroy their products and make them unfit for human consumption.

☐ ☐ 7. Under the Agricultural Adjustment Act (AAA), the government sponsored the slaughter of six million baby pigs in 1933.

☐ ☐ 8. The introduction of massive new programs and regulations during the Great Depression created an unstable economic environment where people were reluctant to undertake business ventures and investments because the government was constantly changing the rules.

☐ ☐ 9. During recessions, the government is generally slow to make any changes out of fear of making the situation worse.

☐ ☐ 10. The New Deal policies instituted by the government during the Great Depression is what finally caused the economy to rebound and bring the Great Depression to an end.

PROBLEMS AND PROJECTS

1. Listed below is a series of economic policies that indicate possible responses by the government to an economic recession.
    a. For each policy, fill in the blank with the letter E if the policy is in accordance with economic theory regarding the appropriate government response to a recession, the letter G if the policy resembles what the government actually did during the Great Depression, or the letter B if the policy is both, appropriate according to economic theory and what the government actually did during the great depression.

    ____   Lower taxes

    ____   Reduce the discount rate to increase money supply

    ____   Aggressively sell bonds to decrease the money supply

    ____   Allow businesses to compete so that they operate efficiently

    ____   Drastically raise personal income taxes and impose a heavy tax on international trade

    ____   Impose regulations such as the National Industrial Recovery Act designed to keep prices high and limit competition.

    ____   Buy bonds to increase the money supply

    ____   Make constant drastic structural changes that lead to an unstable economic environment where people are reluctant to invest and undertake new business ventures

    ____   Increase the discount rate to reduce money supply

    ____   Promote a stable economic environment conducive to investment and growth.

    b. Did you mark any policies with the letter B? In other words, did the government incorporate any policies during the Great Depression that were supported by sound economic theory?
    c. Given your answer to part (b), what can you say about the government's actions and the length and severity of the Great Depression?
    d. Why do you think the government failed to use the appropriate policies according to economic theory at this important time?

MULTIPLE CHOICE

1. Which of the following about the Great Depression is correct?
    a. The 1929 stock market crash explains the lengthy duration of the Great Depression.
    b. The severity of the economic downturn, if not its onset, was the result of perverse monetary and fiscal policies.
    c. The sharp decreases in tariff rates and tax rates cushioned the downturn and limited it to three years.
    d. The Great Depression indicates that monetary policy affects prices but exerts little impact on output.

2. An analysis of stock market prices during 1929 to 1930 indicates that
    a. the stock market crash of October 1929 was the cause of the Great Depression of the 1930s.
    b. the stock market was not able to recover to its previous levels following the crash of October 1929.
    c. after recovering most of its value from the crash of October 1929, stock prices again declined steadily after the passage of the Smoot-Hawley trade bill.
    d. after the crash of October 1929, the Smoot-Hawley trade bill marked the beginning of a steady recovery of the stock market.

3. Monetary policy from 1929 to 1933, and again in 1937 to 1938, was characterized by
    a. monetary expansion, which led to deflation.
    b. monetary contraction, which led to deflation.
    c. monetary expansion, which led to inflation.
    d. monetary contraction, which led to inflation.

4. How do high tariffs and other restraints on international trade affect a nation's prosperity?
    a. They increase employment and thereby promote the growth of GDP.
    b. They prevent a nation from fully realizing the potential gains from specialization, exchange, and competition.
    c. They protect domestic producers and thereby promote economic growth.
    d. Both a and c are correct.

5. As a result of the Smoot-Hawley trade bill of 1930,
    a. both the volume of U.S. trade and the tariff revenues derived from trade increased substantially.
    b. the volume of U.S. trade decreased, but the tariff revenues derived from trade increased.
    c. the volume of U.S. trade increased, but the tariff revenues derived from trade decreased.
    d. both the volume of U.S. trade and the tariff revenues derived from trade decreased substantially.

6. Which of the following contributed to the severity of the Great Depression in the 1930s?
    a. large increases in taxes designed to balance the budget in the early 1930s
    b. large increases in the money supply during the early 1930s
    c. a reduction in tariffs protecting many U.S. industries
    d. a substantial tax rate reduction, which led to large deficits and high interest rates during the early 1930s

7. During the Great Depression, fiscal policy focused primarily on
    a. keeping taxes low.
    b. raising taxes during an economic expansion and lowering taxes during a recession.
    c. a balanced federal budget.
    d. running budget deficits in order to stimulate real output and GDP.

8. The National Industrial Recovery Act, passed in 1933, was a New Deal effort to
    a. remove trade barriers so that U.S. corporations could be more competitive.
    b. fix prices, wages, and quotas in an effort to keep prices high.
    c. lower corporate taxes in order to stimulate real output.
    d. stimulate demand for agricultural products through tax incentives.

9. Which of the following factors contributed to a breakdown of the economy during the Great Depression?
    a. a sharp increase in tax rates in 1932
    b. a sharp decline in the money supply during 1929 through 1933
    c. a sharp increase in tariff rates during 1930
    d. all of the above

10. The New Deal policies of the Great Depression resulted in
    a. a reduction in unemployment and an increase in real output.
    b. a stable economic environment and an increase in investment.
    c. economic uncertainty and prolonged unemployment.
    d. a quick end to the depression once the policies had taken effect.

11. Which of the following is an indication that fiscal policy failed to exert an impact on the economy during the Great Depression?
    a. Government spending as a share of GDP increased significantly, and budget deficits were large.
    b. Government spending as a share of GDP decreased significantly, and budget deficits were large.
    c. Government spending as a share of GDP increased significantly, and budget deficits were small.
    d. Government spending as a share of GDP changed little, and budget deficits were small.

12. The Great Depression illustrates that monetary policy is
    a. effective against inflation but incapable of dealing with a decline in output.
    b. a source of economic instability if utilized inappropriately.
    c. incapable of reversing an economic downturn when the money supply is increasing at a constant rate.
    d. incapable of reversing a major downturn unless the recession stems from inflation.

13. The Great Depression demonstrates that the appropriate fiscal and monetary policy to combat a recession would be
    a. an increase in taxes and a contraction in the money supply.
    b. a decrease in taxes and a contraction in the money supply.
    c. a decrease in taxes and an expansion in the money supply.
    d. an increase in taxes and an expansion in the money supply.

DISCUSSION QUESTIONS

1. Times of severe economic hardship give politicians the incentive to institute new programs and enact changes because it is often perceived that doing something is better than nothing. What were some of the policy changes the government made during the Great Depression? Do you see any similarities between what the government did during the Great Depression and what the government did in response to the financial crisis of 2008?

2. Traditional economic theory says that lowering taxes is the proper response for combating an economic downturn. However, during the Great Depression, the government drastically increased personal income taxes and imposed the Smoot-Hawley tariff, which severely increased the tax on foreign goods. Why do you think the government raised taxes at this time? What was the result?

Lessons from the Japanese Experience

TRUE OR FALSE

T F

☐ ☐ 1. Japan's growth rate went from over 6.2 percent to about 1 percent during its recession in the 1990s.

☐ ☐ 2. Japan has a much more dynamic business environment with higher labor mobility than the United States has.

☐ ☐ 3. During the recession of the 1990s, the Japanese government increased spending by adopting at least seven different stimulus packages designed to increase aggregate demand and stimulate economic growth.

☐ ☐ 4. Data indicate that fiscal policy was highly restrictive in Japan during the 1990s following the asset price meltdown.

☐ ☐ 5. Monetary policy in Japan was highly restrictive during the economic downturn of the 1990s.

☐ ☐ 6. Younger workers are usually more productive and make higher wages than prime age workers (ages 35 to 59) because they are more highly educated and highly skilled.

☐ ☐ 7. As the share of a nation's population age 65 and older expands, economic growth will be slowed by lower productivity and increased government expenditures on health care and retirement benefits financed through higher taxes.

☐ ☐ 8. The United States tends to have a higher savings rate than Japan, and so it can more easily finance the increases in government debt that occur during recessions.

☐ ☐ 9. There are a number of similarities between the conditions surrounding Japan's recession in the 1990s and the financial crisis experienced by the United States in 2008.

☐ ☐ 10. The United States practiced restrictive monetary policy during the 2008 recession just like Japan did in their recession during the 1990s.

PROBLEMS AND PROJECTS

1. Please fill in the blank with a J if the statement is related to the Japanese experience during its recession of the 1990s, a U if the statement is related to the U.S. experience during its financial crisis of 2008, or a B if the statement is related to both the Japanese recession and the United States financial crisis.

    ____ a. Prior to the recession, expansionary monetary policy pushed interest rates to low levels that contributed to rising asset prices

    ____ b. A collapse in asset prices has plummeted the country into a recession

    ____ c. The government responded to the recession with increased spending leading to larger budget deficits.

    ____ d. The country instituted expansionary monetary policy *during* the recession

    ____ e. The country instituted restrictive monetary policy *during* the recession

    ____ f. The country has an aging population that will lead to lower productivity, increased government spending, and a longer adjustment period for the economy.

    ____ g. The country has a high savings rate that could help finance the government debt that was run up during the recession

    ____ h. The economy has a dynamic and flexible labor market that could speed up the adjustment process that is necessary due to dislocations caused by the recession.

MULTIPLE CHOICE

1. Which of the following describes the relationship between the decline in asset prices and the recession for both Japan in the 1990s and the United States in 2008–2009?
   a. A recession was responsible for the decline in stock market and real estate prices.
   b. The decline in stock market and real estate prices preceded the recession and was a major cause of an economic downturn.
   c. Both the decrease in real estate prices and an economic recession were the result of a stock market crash.
   d. The decline in stock market and real estate prices and the economic recession were separate events, and there was no relationship between the two.

2. When the Bank of Japan reduced the discount rate from 5 percent to 2.5 percent in 1987,
   a. both the demand for real estate and asset prices decreased dramatically.
   b. the demand for real estate increased, but asset prices decreased.
   c. the demand for real estate decreased, but asset prices increased.
   d. both the demand for real estate and asset prices increased dramatically.

3. Following World War II, Japan's GDP grew at an annual rate of about _____, but in the decade following the stock market crash in 1990, Japan's GDP grew at an annual rate of about _____. (Fill in the blanks.)
   a. 1 percent; 6 percent
   b. 6 percent; 1 percent
   c. 5 percent; –5 percent
   d. 3 percent; 10 percent

4. Japan's response to the recession of the 1990s of increased government spending and borrowing is characteristic of which policy?
   a. Keynesian economics
   b. supply-side economics
   c. U.S. policy during the Great Depression
   d. Japan's policy before the recession of the 1990s

5. Which of the following is indicative of Japan's expansionary fiscal policy during the 1990s?
   a. a shift from budget deficits to budget surpluses during the 1990s
   b. a decrease in government spending as a share of GDP during the 1990s
   c. an increase in tax rates during the 1990s
   d. a shift from budget surpluses to budget deficits during the 1990s

6. What is the relationship between monetary policy and interest rates?
   a. Expansionary monetary policy will always result in an increase in interest rates.
   b. Restrictive monetary policy will tend to push interest rates up, unless people expect deflation to occur, in which case interest rates would remain low.
   c. Expansionary monetary policy will tend to push interest rates up, unless people expect inflation to occur, in which case interest rates would remain low.
   d. Restrictive monetary policy will always result in a decrease in interest rates.

7. Which of the following is a similarity between Japan's response to the recession of the 1990s and the U.S. response to the Great Depression?
   a. Both countries increased government spending as a percentage of GDP significantly in response to the recessions.
   b. Both countries were able to utilize fiscal policy to significantly reduce unemployment during the recessions.
   c. Both countries followed a restrictive monetary policy during the recessions.
   d. Both countries tried to stimulate real output and aggregate demand through an expansionary monetary policy.

8. If Japan thought that both fiscal and monetary policy could promote a recovery from the 1990s recession, which combination would be expected?
   a. a decrease in government spending, combined with expansionary monetary policy
   b. an increase in government spending, combined with restrictive monetary policy
   c. both an increase in government spending and expansionary monetary policy
   d. both a decrease in government spending and restrictive monetary policy

9. As the share of a nation's population age 65 and older expands
   a. the tax burden on current workers will decrease.
   b. government expenditures on this population will increase.
   c. economic growth of the nation will increase.
   d. government expenditures on this population will decrease.

10. Which of the following is a similarity between Japan's experience of the 1990s and the U.S. recovery from the recession of 2008–2009?
   a. Aging populations have the potential to slow an economic recovery.
   b. Balancing the budget remained the goal of fiscal policy.
   c. Both countries followed a restrictive monetary policy during the recessions.
   d. Neither country increased government expenditures in order to stimulate aggregate demand.

11. One advantage that the United States holds during the recession in 2008–2009, over the Japanese recession of the 1990s, is in its
    a. fiscal policy response.
    b. rate of saving.
    c. aging of the labor force.
    d. flexibility of the labor market.

12. Based on the Japanese experience of the 1990s, the U.S. could cautiously expect that
    a. asset prices will quickly return to their pre-recession levels.
    b. fiscal stimulus is likely to promote a quick, sustainable recovery.
    c. housing and stock market prices are unlikely to rebound quickly.
    d. expansionary monetary policy will result in a period of deflation.

DISCUSSION QUESTIONS

1. Given the similarities between the causes and characteristics of the respective economic recessions experienced by Japan and the United States, and the similarities between the demographics of the two economies, do you expect United States' recovery to resemble that of Japan? What, if any, differences by the two countries in their response to their respective economic declines might account for the United States undergoing a different recovery experience.

2. How do you think the economic downturn of Japan in the 1990s affected the United States? How do you think the economic downturn of the United States in 2008 affected Japan? Given how global and integrated our economy has become, is it ever in the best interest of a country to see another country experience severe economic hardships? Please explain.

3. It has often been quoted that "there is no substitute for experience," which may be why younger workers tend to not be as productive as prime age workers (age 35 to 59) even if they are highly educated and highly skilled. However, as workers continue to age and enter into retirement, their productivity and earnings will decrease. Describe the different stages of growth a country can expect to experience as its general population continues to get older.

The Federal Budget and the National Debt

TRUE OR FALSE

T   F

☐ ☐ 1. When the government runs a budget deficit, it increases the national debt.

☐ ☐ 2. Approximately 39 percent of the national debt is held by agencies of the federal government.

☐ ☐ 3. Financing current government expenditures by borrowing pushes the opportunity cost of the resources used onto future generations.

☐ ☐ 4. The larger the stock of physical capital available to future generations, the lower wages they will earn.

☐ ☐ 5. The traditional (or crowding-out) view holds that government borrowing increases interest rates, lowering investment and the future capital stock.

☐ ☐ 6. Privately held government debt is the term used to refer to the debt held by the citizens of foreign nations.

☐ ☐ 7. To understand how government debt influences future generations, its impact on capital formation must be determined.

☐ ☐ 8. According to the new classical view of government deficits, deficit and tax financing of government expenditures have equivalent macroeconomic effects.

☐ ☐ 9. The harm done to future generations by government borrowing is larger under the new classical view than under the traditional (or crowding-out) view.

T F

☐ ☐ 10. As a share of GDP, the United States has a larger debt than any other country in the world.

☐ ☐ 11. The current inclusion of Social Security receipts and expenditures in the budget calculation makes the deficit appear smaller (or the surplus larger) than would otherwise be the case.

☐ ☐ 12. More than half of the federal debt is now held by foreigners, including foreign central banks.

PROBLEMS AND PROJECTS

1. Exhibit 1 shows the first six years of annual budget data for the government of Grak, a country that recently gained its independence. Fill in the missing information.

EXHIBIT 1

	TOTAL REVENUE	TOTAL EXPENDITURE	SURPLUS (+) OR DEFICIT (−)	TOTAL DEBT (END OF YEAR)
Year 1	$150	_____	$ 0	$ 0
Year 2	_____	200	−50	50
Year 3	200	180	_____	30
Year 4	240	250	_____	_____
Year 5	250	280	−30	_____
Year 6	260	_____	_____	0

2. Exhibit 2 presents data for the U.S. federal government's receipts (revenue) and outlays (expenditures) for 1997 and 1998. In the exhibit is also shown the reported surplus or deficit for each year.
    a. To examine the effect of the Social Security system on the reported figures, calculate total receipts and outlays each excluding Social Security and fill in this data in the space provided.
    b. With these revised figures for receipts and outlays, calculate the budget surplus or deficit excluding Social Security.
    c. How do your results compare to the reported surplus or deficit figures?

EXHIBIT 2

	FISCAL YEAR	
	1997	1998
Receipts		
Income Taxes	$919.7	$1,017.3
Social Security Revenue	539.4	571.8
Other Revenue	120.2	132.7
Total Receipts	$1,579.3	$1,721.8
Outlays		
National Defense	$270.5	$268.5
Social Security	365.3	379.2
Other Spending	965.4	1,004.9
Total Outlays	$1,601.2	$1,652.6
Surplus (+) or Deficit (–)	–$21.9	+$69.2
Excluding Social Security		
Total Receipts	_____	_____
Total Outlays	_____	_____
Surplus (+) or Deficit (–)	_____	_____

MULTIPLE CHOICE

1. Which of the following is a true statement about the federal deficit and the national debt?
   a. Both are "flow" concepts.
   b. The deficit is a "flow" concept and the debt is a "stock" concept.
   c. The deficit is a "stock" concept and the debt is a "flow" concept.
   d. Both are "stock" concepts.

2. The external debt is the portion of the national debt
   a. owned by foreigners.
   b. owned by the public instead of the Fed.
   c. owned by any party other than the Treasury Department.
   d. attributable to off-budget federal programs.

3. Privately held government debt is
   a. the portion of the national debt held by government agencies.
   b. the portion of the national debt that imposes a net interest burden on the federal government.
   c. the portion of the national debt held by foreign citizens.
   d. equal to the federal government debt minus any state and local government surpluses.

4. Domestically financed deficit spending shifts the cost of government spending to future generations by
   a. causing a higher future tax liability with no offsetting gains.
   b. shifting the opportunity cost of the resources used by government onto future generations.
   c. reducing the capital stock, lowering productivity and wages.
   d. all of the above.

5. According to the traditional view of deficit financing, an increase in debt-financed government expenditure
   a. causes interest rates to rise, private investment to fall, net exports to fall, and an inflow of foreign capital.
   b. causes interest rates to rise, private investment to fall, net exports to fall, and an outflow of domestic capital.
   c. causes interest rates to fall, private investment to rise, net exports to increase, and an inflow of foreign capital.
   d. causes interest rates to rise, private investment to fall, net exports to fall, and an outflow of domestic capital.

6. Since 1970, the federal debt has expanded rapidly because
   a. revenues have gone down, while expenditures have gone up.
   b. expenditures have risen faster than revenues.
   c. expenditures have increased slightly, while revenues have remained about the same.
   d. revenues have fallen faster than expenditures.

7. The difference between the federal budget deficit and the national debt is that the
   a. national debt is the cumulative effect of all prior surpluses and deficits.
   b. budget deficit is the cumulative effect of all prior debts and surpluses.
   c. debt includes all outstanding bonds, while the deficit excludes bonds held by government agencies.
   d. There is no difference.

8. Widespread acceptance of the Keynesian theory of fiscal policy
   a. caused most economists to reject the public choice view of budget deficits.
   b. relaxed the political pressure to balance the budget and hence paved the way for the continual budget deficits of recent decades.
   c. was based on the view that continual budget deficits would help stabilize the economy.
   d. increased the pressure for a constitutional amendment mandating that the federal government balance its budget.

The table below shows the revenues and expenditures for a new country during its first three years of existence. Use this data to answer questions 9 through 11.

YEAR	GOVERNMENT REVENUES	GOVERNMENT EXPENDITURES
First	$100	$110
Second	$150	$120
Third	$200	$250

9. In the first year, this country
   a. ran a deficit of $210.
   b. had a surplus of $10.
   c. ran a deficit of $10.
   d. had a surplus of $210.

10. In the second year, this country
    a. ran a surplus of $20.
    b. ran a surplus of $30.
    c. had a deficit of $20.
    d. had a deficit of $30.

11. Which of the following is correct regarding this government?
    a. In the third year, it had a $50 national debt and ran a $30 deficit.
    b. In the third year, it ran a $50 deficit and its national debt after the third year was $60.
    c. In the third year, it ran a $50 surplus and its national debt after the third year was $30.
    d. In the third year, it ran a $50 deficit and its national debt after the third year was $30.

12. Why are the bonds held by the Fed and government agencies excluded from the privately held debt figures?
    a. The U.S. Treasury does not have to pay off these bonds.
    b. These bonds were not issued by the Treasury.
    c. These bonds do not represent a net-interest obligation of the government.
    d. These bonds are not interest-bearing bonds.

13. In 2009, the *privately held* federal debt was approximately what percent of GDP?
    a. 19 percent
    b. 49 percent
    c. 79 percent
    d. 100 percent

14. The idea that a large public debt is "mortgaging the future of our children and grandchildren" is misleading because
    a. it is the Federal Reserve that will be responsible for making interest payments on the debt.
    b. future generations will have to bear the opportunity costs of the resources that are used today.
    c. future generations will not owe any interest obligations on the debt.
    d. future generations will inherit interest payments along with interest obligations.

15. Deficit spending and a large national debt can have important effects on future generations because they
    a. allow generations to pass the opportunity costs of government spending onto future generations.
    b. can significantly impact spending on capital formation.
    c. pass costs onto future generations with no corresponding benefits.
    d. will cause the government to go bankrupt.

16. Currently, the Social Security trust fund is running a
    a. deficit, which reduces the apparent size of the budget deficit.
    b. surplus, which reduces the apparent size of the budget deficit.
    c. surplus, which increases the apparent size of the budget deficit.
    d. deficit, which increases the apparent size of the budget deficit.

17. If the revenues and expenditures of the Social Security trust fund were *not* included when calculating the budget deficit, the recalculated deficit would
    a. be larger.
    b. be smaller.
    c. be unchanged.
    d. actually be a surplus.

DISCUSSION QUESTIONS

1. Do you favor or oppose each of the following proposals for reducing the budget deficit? Why?
   a. a balanced-budget amendment
   b. a presidential line-item veto
   c. an aggregate spending constraint adopted prior to the start of each fiscal year
   d. inversely linking congressional salaries to the size of the deficit

2. a. How is a budget deficit financed by selling bonds to the Fed different from selling the bonds to another government agency?
   b. How is a budget deficit financed by selling bonds to the Fed or another government agency different from selling the bonds to the public?
   c. How is a budget deficit financed by selling bonds to a domestic resident different from selling bonds to a resident of a foreign country?

3. Do you think the budget deficit "problem" is overstated? Why or why not?

4. Do you prefer the traditional view of budget deficits or the new classical view? Which is most logically appealing to you? What evidence is there in support of each view?

5. "Debt financing is a way to make future generations pay for today's government spending. We are mortgaging our children's future." What is wrong with the economic thinking reflected in the quotation? What are some of the true costs of the national debt?

SPECIAL TOPIC

9

The Economics of Health Care

TRUE OR FALSE

T F

☐ ☐ 1. Health-care expenditures in the United States have remained fairly constant over the past few decades.

☐ ☐ 2. Approximately 86 percent of health-care spending is paid for by a third party, either the taxpayer or a private insurance company.

☐ ☐ 3. The unfunded liability of Medicare is nearly five times larger than the unfunded liability of the Social Security system.

☐ ☐ 4. Employee compensation in the form of health insurance is not subject to taxation, making it attractive for people to purchase health insurance through their employer rather than privately and also to demand policies with small co-payment rates and low deductibles.

☐ ☐ 5. The decrease in the share of health-care payments made out-of-pocket by consumers has resulted in a decrease in the price of medical services.

☐ ☐ 6. Since 1960, medical-care prices have risen, on average, twice as rapidly as consumer prices in general.

☐ ☐ 7. Economic theory suggests that controlling health-care costs through rules and regulations imposed by the government or another third party is generally more effective than using competition and the choices of consumers spending their own money to control costs.

☐ ☐ 8. The growth rates of health-care prices and expenditures are expected to slow in the future because the baby boomers will move into the retirement phase of life during the years following 2015.

☐ ☐ 9. The main reason why health care costs so much is that consumers pay for so little of it directly out-of-pocket.

T F

☐ ☐ 10. Allowing health savings accounts to have similar tax treatment as employer-provided health insurance and reducing the regulatory restrictions on their use could help to improve the situation in the health-care industry.

☐ ☐ 11. One way to improve the operation of health-care markets would be to encourage the purchase of catastrophic health insurance and discourage the purchase of policies with first-dollar coverage and small co-payments.

☐ ☐ 12. Many new medical schools have been established in the United States over the last two decades.

PROBLEMS AND PROJECTS

1. Using a demand and supply diagram, illustrate how each of the following would affect the price and quantity of medical services.
    a. an increase in the proportion of the population over age 65
    b. a new law requiring all medical insurance plans to have a zero co-payment rate and a low deductible
    c. the imposition of government price ceilings on medical-care services that legally holds prices below equilibrium
    d. a government subsidy program that encourages the creation of many new medical schools
    e. a reform that reduces medical malpractice insurance costs for doctors

2. Erin, a program assistant at a major state university, wants to purchase health insurance. She can purchase exactly the plan she wants directly from an insurance company (outside of her employer) for $6,000 per year. If she does so, she will have to pay for it out of her after-tax net pay. Her employer also offers the same exact plan that she can purchase on a pre-tax basis through the university. She would prefer to purchase the insurance outside of her employer so she does not lose her insurance if she changes jobs. The current tax rates Erin faces on her income are a 15.3 percent payroll tax, a 28 percent federal income tax, and a 6 percent state income tax.
    a. If she purchases this $6,000 plan through her employer, by how much will her after-tax net pay fall?
    b. How much cheaper is it for her to purchase the plan through her employer than outside of her employer?
    c. Do you think that this price differential is large enough to encourage Erin to purchase the insurance through her employer even though she would prefer to purchase it outside of her employer so she does not lose it if she changes jobs?
    d. Erin also has an auto insurance policy that costs $4,000 per year that she currently purchases outside of her employer. Why do you think that Erin, as well as most other people, purchase automobile insurance outside of their employer whereas they purchase health insurance through their employer (in other words, why do you think it is that most employers offer health insurance plans to their employees but not automobile insurance plans)?

MULTIPLE CHOICE

1. In countries such as Canada that have socialized health care, the government operates hospitals, and health-care services are financed through tax revenue. In these countries,
   a. the government is able to provide as much health care, free of charge, as citizens would like.
   b. methods other than price, such as political rules and waiting lists, must be utilized to allocate health-care services.
   c. a large number of services, such as MRIs, that involve expensive equipment are performed.
   d. citizens are usually so satisfied with their health-care system that they never travel to other countries to purchase health-care services.

2. In 2007, health-care expenditures were approximately what percent of GDP?
   a. 6 percent
   b. 16 percent
   c. 26 percent
   d. 36 percent

3. (I) The Medicare program is financed by general tax revenue and provides low-income families with access to health care either free or at a low cost. (II) The Medicaid program covers the bulk of the health-care costs of the elderly and is financed mostly through a tax on the wages and salaries of current workers.
   a. I is true; II is false.
   b. I is false; II is true.
   c. Both I and II are true.
   d. Both I and II are false.

4. Which of the following is true regarding employer-provided health insurance?
   a. About two-thirds of nonelderly adults have health insurance through group plans offered by their employers.
   b. Employee compensation in the form of health insurance is not subject to taxation, which makes it particularly attractive for people to purchase it through their employers rather than privately, and also to demand policies with small co-payment rates and a low deductible.
   c. The linking of health insurance to employment reduces employee mobility and creates a situation where employees lose their health insurance when they lose their job or change jobs.
   d. All of the above are true.

5. In 2007, third-party payments accounted for approximately what percent of medical-care expenditures in the United States?
   a. 26 percent
   b. 46 percent
   c. 66 percent
   d. 86 percent

6. The growth of third-party payments has resulted in higher prices for health-care services because
   a. the lower out-of-pocket cost for consumers has increased the demand for health-care services.
   b. consumers have less of an incentive to economize and shop for low-cost services when they pay a lower share of their bill.
   c. producers have less of an incentive to provide health-care services at a low price when consumers are not as cost conscious.
   d. All of the above are true.

7. Relative to the general index of consumer prices, medical-care prices have
   a. fallen quite substantially since the beginning of the Medicare and Medicaid programs in 1965.
   b. risen quite substantially since the beginning of the Medicare and Medicaid programs in 1965.
   c. remained roughly constant since the beginning of the Medicare and Medicaid programs in 1965.
   d. fallen, but only slightly, since the beginning of the Medicare and Medicaid programs in 1965.

8. Economic theory suggests that controlling health-care costs through rules and regulations imposed by the government or another third party is generally
   a. more effective than using competition and the choices of consumers spending their own money to control costs.
   b. less effective than using competition and the choices of consumers spending their own money to control costs.
   c. only workable if the entire health-care sector is socialized (operated by the government).
   d. possible to implement successfully because these rules and regulations tend to be in harmony with the interests of both consumers and health-care providers.

9. The growth rate of the elderly population will accelerate in the future as the baby boomers move into the retirement phase of life during the years following 2010. Unless structural changes are undertaken, this increase in the growth rate of the elderly population
   a. will cause future health-care prices and expenditures to increase even more rapidly than in the past.
   b. will cause future health-care prices and expenditures to decrease rapidly.
   c. will cause the rate of technological advance in medicine to slow significantly.
   d. is generally expected to have no significant impact on the health-care industry.

10. By promoting third-party payment of health-care expenses and the purchase of health insurance through employers, health-care policy has
    a. eroded the incentive of health-care consumers and providers to economize.
    b. undermined the smooth operation of health-care markets.
    c. made it more costly for persons without a job to obtain health insurance.
    d. done all of the above.

11. Special savings accounts that individuals could pay into directly and then use to pay medical bills or purchase a catastrophic health insurance plan are known as
    a. flexible benefit accounts.
    b. health savings accounts.
    c. health-care savings bonds.
    d. HMOs.

12. Which of the following reforms could help to improve the operation and efficiency of health-care markets?
    a. equalizing the tax treatment of out-of-pocket medical expenses and the direct purchase of health insurance with that of health insurance purchased through an employer
    b. encouraging consumer use of health savings accounts and the direct payment of medical bills from the accounts
    c. encouraging the purchase of catastrophic health insurance and discourage the purchase of policies with first-dollar coverage and small co-payments
    d. All of the reforms listed above could help to improve the situation.

13. Which of the following reforms could help to improve the operation and efficiency of health-care markets?
    a. shifting Medicare at least partially from a reimbursement service to a defined-benefit plan
    b. placing more emphasis on the demand side of the health-care market
    c. encouraging the purchase of health insurance policies with first-dollar coverage and small co-payments
    d. All of the reforms listed above could help to improve the situation.

DISCUSSION QUESTIONS

1. One of the frequently cited problems in health care in the United States is that people lose their health insurance when they lose their job or change jobs. Why is it that people generally purchase health insurance through their employer but not automobile insurance? Do you think the preferential tax treatment of health insurance financed through an employer contributes to this problem?

2. What has happened to health-care prices and expenditures in the United States over the past few decades? What do you think has contributed to these changes? What is predicted to happen to health-care prices and expenditures in the future?

3. Only about 14 percent of payments for medical care are made by consumers out-of-pocket; the remaining 86 percent are made by third parties. What incentives change when a good is financed to such a large degree by third-party payments? What impact does this have on health-care markets?

4. What are some possible reforms that could be undertaken to improve the operation and efficiency of health-care markets? Of the five listed in the text, which do you think would help the most and which do you think would help the least?

School Choice: Can It Improve the Quality of Education in America?

TRUE OR FALSE

T   F

☐   ☐   1. Average achievement (SAT) scores of high school graduates are higher today than they were 35 years ago.

☐   ☐   2. International comparisons show that U.S. students are way ahead of students in most other developed countries.

☐   ☐   3. After correcting for inflation, spending per pupil in public elementary and secondary schools in the United States has more than doubled during the last three decades.

☐   ☐   4. In 2005, the United States spent approximately $10,585 per pupil for public elementary and secondary education, ranking it among the highest in the world.

☐   ☐   5. Lack of sufficient spending explains the lower performance of U.S. students when compared to students from other countries and explains why achievement scores have been falling in the United States over the past three decades.

☐   ☐   6. When the government both provides education and covers its costs through taxation, parents are in a weak position to either discipline poorly performing schools or alter the quantity or quality of schooling provided.

☐   ☐   7. In the U.S. higher educational system, students and parents have choices as to which college or university the student attends and generally must finance part of it from personal funds. The U.S. higher educational system is among the best in the world.

T F

☐ ☐ 8. A voucher system is one in which parents receive a certificate equal to the current value of educational expenditures per pupil at their school, and the parents may then use this voucher to finance their child's education at any school (public or private) of their choice.

☐ ☐ 9. A modified voucher system targeted toward low- and middle-income families would overcome many of the objections typically raised about switching to a voucher system.

☐ ☐ 10. Religious schools are allowed to be charter schools.

☐ ☐ 11. Most parents of students in charter schools and voucher programs indicate that they are highly satisfied with their children's schools.

☐ ☐ 12. Evidence suggests that voucher programs appear to decrease the achievement scores of African-American students and tend to increase racial segregation among schools.

PROBLEMS AND PROJECTS

1. For each of the following indicate whether you think it would increase (+), decrease (−), or the change would be uncertain (?) under a voucher system as compared to the current public school system.
   _____ a. wage rate of good teachers
   _____ b. wage rate of bad teachers
   _____ c. enrollment at good schools
   _____ d. enrollment at bad schools
   _____ e. educational attainment of students in families with above average income
   _____ f. educational attainment of students in families with below average income
   _____ g. amount of diversity in program offerings at schools
   _____ h. degree of racial segregation among schools
   _____ i. average cost per pupil

2. Exhibit 1 presents data for public and private elementary and secondary schools in the United States in 1998. Use the data to answer the following questions.
   a. Calculate the average number of students per teacher for public schools and for private schools. How do they compare?
   b. Calculate the average number of students per school for public schools and for private schools. How do they compare?
   c. Calculate the average expenditures per student for public schools and for private schools. How do they compare?
   d. The average tuition charged by private schools is $3,116 (less than the expenditures per pupil because they also raise money in other ways). If a voucher program were to be instituted, approximately what percent of the average public school student's expenditures would need to be given to the parents in the form of a voucher for them to afford the average private school?
   e. How do the average proficiency test scores compare for students in public and private schools?
   f. Given this data, what can you say about the relative cost effectiveness and quality of education in private and public schools?

EXHIBIT 1

DATA ON ELEMENTARY AND SECONDARY SCHOOLS, 1998

	PUBLIC SCHOOLS	PRIVATE SCHOOLS
Number of students (total enrollment)	46,535,000	5,924,000
Number of teachers	2,826,000	391,000
Average number of students per teacher	_____	_____
Number of schools	89,508	27,402
Average number of students per school	_____	_____
Average math and science proficiency test score (9 year olds)	229.5	240.5
Average writing and reading proficiency test score (9 year olds)	208.0	221.9
Total Expenditures	$320,998,430,000	$27,700,624,000
Expenditures per student	_____	_____

MULTIPLE CHOICE

1. Which of the following is true regarding the average achievement (SAT) scores of high school graduates in the United States?
   a. The average achievement (SAT) scores of high school graduates fell during the 1970s.
   b. The average achievement (SAT) scores of high school graduates is lower today than it was 35 years ago.
   c. The average achievement (SAT) scores of high school graduates rose slightly during the 1990s.
   d. All of the above are true.

2. When compared to the achievement scores of students in other nations, U.S. students are
   a. well-below average.
   b. well-above average.
   c. about average.
   d. above average in mathematics, but below average in science.

3. After correcting for inflation, spending per pupil in public elementary and secondary schools in the United States over the last three decades has
   a. more than doubled.
   b. fallen dramatically.
   c. remained roughly constant.
   d. increased, but only slightly.

4. In 2005, average spending per pupil in public elementary and secondary schools in the United States was approximately
   a. $4,585.
   b. $6,585.
   c. $8,585.
   d. $10,585.

5. Relative to other countries, U.S. spending per pupil for public elementary and secondary education is
   a. among the lowest in the world.
   b. roughly average when compared with other countries.
   c. among the highest in the world.
   d. higher than in most other developed countries but less than in developing countries.

6. Spending per pupil is higher in the United States than in
   a. Japan.
   b. Australia.
   c. Belgium.
   d. all of the above.

7. If elementary and secondary schooling were produced entirely by private firms and purchased by parents with their own money,
   a. parents would have a strong incentive to search out those schools offering their children the best education at the best value.
   b. schools would better cater to the desires of parents and supply education more efficiently.
   c. schools would face much stronger competition from one another that would tend to increase the quality of schooling.
   d. all of the above would occur.

8. When the government both provides education and covers its costs through taxation,
   a. public schools have a strong incentive to supply a high quality education at a low cost.
   b. parents are in a weak position to either discipline poorly performing schools or alter the quantity or quality of schooling provided.
   c. competition between schools is greatly enhanced relative to a system of privately produced and funded education.
   d. public school administrators are driven to care more about pleasing parents than about pleasing teachers' unions.

9. The incentive of schools to provide a high quality education at a low cost and the incentive of parents and students to shop around for the best schools will be weakest when education is produced
   a. privately but paid for by taxpayers and provided free of charge.
   b. by public schools and the cost of education is covered by taxes.
   c. privately and parents must purchase it with their own money.
   d. by public schools and parents purchase it with their own money.

10. In the U.S. higher educational system, students and parents have choices as to which college or university the student attends and generally must finance part of it from personal funds. As a result of this different incentive structure, the U.S. higher educational system is
    a. one of the best in the world.
    b. one of the worst in the world.
    c. about average when compared to other higher educational systems.
    d. relatively worse in international rankings than U.S. elementary and secondary education.

11. Which of the following is true about a voucher system?
    a. A voucher system is one in which parents receive a certificate equal to the current value of educational expenditures per pupil at their school, and the parents may then use this voucher to finance their child's education at any school (public or private) of their choice.
    b. Under a voucher system, competition would be greatly increased among schools as they compete for students.
    c. Under a voucher system, the quality of teachers and the diversity of school program offerings would increase.
    d. All of the above are true.

12. In contrast to schools in a voucher system, charter schools are
    a. not allowed to be religious schools.
    b. not allowed to charge tuition.
    c. not exempt from a variety of standards including financial, safety, and educational outcomes.
    d. All of the above apply to charter schools.

13. During the 2008–2009 school year, approximately how many students attended a charter school?
    a. 100,000
    b. 600,000
    c. 1,400,000
    d. 2,400,000

14. In 2009, how many states permitted public school choice in some or all school districts?
    a. 25
    b. 30
    c. 35
    d. 40

15. Which of the following is true?
    a. The achievement scores of African-American students tend to be higher after one or two years in voucher programs.
    b. Most parents of students in charter schools and voucher programs indicate they are highly satisfied with their children's schools.
    c. Targeted voucher programs tend to decrease racial segregation in schools in highly segregated communities.
    d. All of the above are true.

DISCUSSION QUESTIONS

1. How has spending per pupil in public schools changed over the past few decades? How does it currently compare to spending per pupil in other countries? Does there seem to be a close link between spending per pupil and educational outcomes as measured by achievement scores?

2. How does the structure of the U.S. higher education system differ from the structure of the primary and secondary education system? Does the quality of higher education in the United States compare more favorably with other countries than the quality of primary and secondary education?

3. What beneficial incentives would be created by a school voucher program? What are some of the frequently cited objections to voucher programs? Can a modified voucher system targeted at low- and middle-income families overcome many of these objections?

Earnings Differences Between Men and Women

TRUE OR FALSE

T F

☐ ☐ 1. The labor force participation rate of women has risen from 37.6 percent in 1960 to 60.6 percent in 2007.

☐ ☐ 2. The hourly earnings of full-time working women were more than 80 percent of those of their male counterparts in 2007.

☐ ☐ 3. Until recently, more than half of all women were employed in just four occupations—clerical workers, teachers, nurses, and food service workers.

☐ ☐ 4. Women have tended to seek jobs with more flexible hours.

☐ ☐ 5. The male/female earnings differential was just as large between single males and females as between married males and females, strongly suggesting that employment discrimination is responsible for the observed earnings difference.

☐ ☐ 6. By 1968, the majority of females 14 to 24 years of age expected to be working at age 35.

☐ ☐ 7. Since 1970, the proportion of degrees in economics and engineering earned by women has fallen, while the proportion in veterinary medicine and accounting has risen.

☐ ☐ 8. The 1962 equal pay legislation and the 1964 civil rights legislation resulted in a substantial increase in the earnings of females relative to males during the 1960s and 1970s.

T F

☐ ☐ 9. The earnings of women is expected to continue to rise relative to the earnings of men in the near future.

☐ ☐ 10. When employment discrimination results from the personal prejudices of employers, economic theory suggests that employers who discriminate will have higher costs than employers who do not.

PROBLEMS AND PROJECTS

1. Exhibit 1 presents data on the median annual earnings of year-round, full-time workers (age 18 and older) in 2000 by selected characteristics. Use the data in the table to answer the following questions.
   a. Compute the F/M annual earnings ratios for each worker group.

EXHIBIT 1

MEDIAN ANNUAL EARNINGS FOR YEAR-ROUND, FULL-TIME WORKERS, 2000			
	MALES	FEMALES	F/M RATIO
All workers	$39,060	$28,845	_____%
Single (never married)	26,916	26,127	_____
Married	44,695	30,063	_____
White	40,368	29,683	_____
Black	30,907	25,751	_____
High school degree only	32,494	23,721	_____
College (bachelor's) degree	53,508	38,213	_____

   b. How does the F/M earnings ratio differ for single and married workers?
   c. In the textbook, the F/M earnings ratio for all single workers (which includes divorced and widowed workers as single) is given as 81. How does this compare to the F/M ratio among never-married single workers?
   d. How does the F/M earnings ratio differ for white and black workers?
   e. How does the F/M earnings ratio differ for workers with only a high school degree and workers with a college (bachelor's) degree?
   f. For which group is the gender earnings gap the largest? For which group is it the smallest?

2. When comparing the average earnings of males and females, it is important to correct for differences in worker characteristics that could account for part of the difference. Use the following hypothetical data to correct earnings for these differences.

a. Suppose the average male earnings were $50,000 while the average female earnings were $35,000. Compute the F/M earnings ratio.

b. Suppose that the average male worked 2,288 hours per year while the average female worked 1,976 hours. Compute the average hourly wage for both males and females.

c. Suppose the average woman had instead worked the same number of hours as the average man. Using the wage you calculated for females in part b, how much would average annual female earnings have been had females worked as many hours as males? Compute the new F/M earnings ratio adjusting for hours worked using this adjusted female earnings relative to the original male earnings.

d. Suppose that the average years of work experience of males was 17 years whereas the average for females was 13 years. Further suppose it has been estimated that each year of labor market experience adds approximately $1,000 to a person's annual earnings. Had females both worked the same number of hours as males and had the same number of average years of experience, how much would average female earnings have been? Compute the new F/M earnings ratio that now adjusts for both hours worked and experience. How does it compare to the unadjusted F/M ratio in part a?

MULTIPLE CHOICE

1. In 2007, the labor force participation rate of women was
   a. 20.6 percent.
   b. 40.6 percent.
   c. 60.6 percent.
   d. 80.6 percent.

2. The annual earnings of full-time working women were approximately what percent of those of their male counterparts in 2007?
   a. 68 percent
   b. 78 percent
   c. 88 percent
   d. 98 percent

3. The hourly earnings of full-time working women were a little more than what percent of those of their male counterparts in 2007?
   a. 60 percent
   b. 70 percent
   c. 80 percent
   d. 90 percent

4. If the wages of equally qualified women were really 20 percent less than those of men,
   a. profit-seeking employers would have a strong incentive to hire more women, resulting in this differential falling.
   b. profit-seeking employers would generally find that hiring men was still more profitable.
   c. employers would still be reluctant to hire women because they generally care little about their profits.
   d. profit-seeking employers would have a strong incentive to hire fewer women, resulting in this differential rising even further.

5. Given the traditional responsibility for monetary earnings in the family, men were more likely than women to
   a. have continuous labor force participation.
   b. move in order to get a higher-paying job.
   c. accept jobs with long hours, uncertain schedules, and out-of-town travel.
   d. do all of the above.

6. The earnings difference between single men and women is
    a. significantly more than the earnings difference between married men and women.
    b. significantly less than the earnings difference between married men and women.
    c. about the same as the earnings difference between married men and women.
    d. none of the above.

7. The proportion of degrees earned by women in which of the following fields has increased since 1970?
    a. economics
    b. engineering
    c. architecture
    d. all of the above

8. During the decade following the passage of the 1962 equal pay legislation and the 1964 civil rights legislation,
    a. the male/female wage differential became much smaller.
    b. the male/female wage differential became much larger.
    c. there was little change in the earnings of women relative to men.
    d. the educational choices of women and men became less similar.

9. As a result of the educational and career choices of women becoming more like those of men during the last two decades, the earnings of women have
    a. risen toward those of men.
    b. fallen relative to those of men.
    c. remained relatively unchanged relative to those of men.
    d. fallen in clerical occupations, but risen in business careers.

10. In the future, the earnings differential between women and men is expected to
    a. widen.
    b. become smaller.
    c. remain about the same as it is now.
    d. become smaller over the next five years then begin to widen again.

11. Which of the following would tend to cause the observed earnings of women to be lower than the observed earnings of men?
    a. The average woman has fewer years of schooling than the average man.
    b. The average number of hours worked is smaller for women than men.
    c. Women are more likely to prefer jobs that have more flexible hours.
    d. All of the above would be causes.

12. When employment discrimination results from the personal prejudices of employers,
    a. only legal requirements will be able to reduce the amount of employment discrimination.
    b. competitive markets will generally tend to promote discrimination as firms try to lower their costs to increase their profits.
    c. competitive markets will tend to make it costly for employers to discriminate, reducing the amount of discrimination.
    d. none of the above will be true.

DISCUSSION QUESTIONS

1. Is employment discrimination responsible for the earnings difference between men and women? What other factors contribute to the earnings difference?

2. Do competitive markets tend to lessen or increase discrimination? If all employers cared about was profit, would discrimination exist in a competitive marketplace?

3. How have the educational and career choices of women changed over the past 40 years, and how has this affected the earnings differential between men and women?

Do Labor Unions Increase the Wages of Workers?

TRUE OR FALSE

T F

☐ ☐ 1. Union membership as a percentage of the labor force has steadily increased since 1960.

☐ ☐ 2. The bargaining power of a union is limited by competition from other firms selling similar products.

☐ ☐ 3. A right-to-work law prohibits union shop provisions that require employees to join a union as a condition of employment.

☐ ☐ 4. The increased competition and lower prices caused by deregulation in the transportation and communication industries have lowered union strength in these industries.

☐ ☐ 5. A union will be more successful in raising wages when it is able to organize all firms in an industry rather than only one.

☐ ☐ 6. Men and women are about equally represented in union membership.

☐ ☐ 7. Of all sectors of the economy, the service sector tends to be the most unionized.

☐ ☐ 8. The greater the ability of management to substitute machines and nonunion labor for union labor, the weaker the bargaining power of a union.

☐ ☐ 9. Southern states tend to have higher rates of union membership than other parts of the United States.

☐ ☐ 10. Evidence shows that unions have increased the wages of all workers, including nonunion workers.

PROBLEMS AND PROJECTS

1. If the professors at a university form a union and successfully increase their salaries, indicate whether you would expect each of the following to (+) increase or (–) decrease as a result.
    ___ a. the tuition rate charged by the university
    ___ b. the number of students attending the university
    ___ c. the average number of students per class (i.e., the size of classes)
    ___ d. the number of professors employed by the university
    e. Explain how your answers to b and c help explain your answer to d.

2. According to the text, unions can raise wages three ways:

    (1) Supply restrictions on competitive labor.

    (2) Bargaining power (resulting in a wage floor above the equilibrium level).

    (3) Increase in the demand for union workers.

    For each of the following union strategies, list the number given above for the type of effect the strategy illustrates, and indicate whether employment in the unionized industry rises (+) or falls (–) as a result. The first case is completed as an example.

TYPE OF EFFECT	CHANGE IN EMPLOYMENT	UNION STRATEGY
3	+	a. In a practice called featherbedding, railroad unions require that all trains carry firemen, even though modern locomotives pose little fire danger.
___	___	b. The American Medical Association restricts accreditation of medical schools.
___	___	c. Garment workers run an ad campaign with the jingle, "Look for the union label."
___	___	d. Unions commonly bargain for wage increases indexed to inflation plus a negotiated premium.
___	___	e. Auto workers lobby for domestic content legislation stipulating that at least 90 percent of each car sold in the United States be constructed from U.S.-made parts.
___	___	f. To become Certified Public Accountants, candidates must pass an industry-administered exam that over three-fourths of all applicants fail.

MULTIPLE CHOICE

1. Which of the following is true?
   a. The proportion of female workers who are union members is higher than the proportion of male workers.
   b. The proportion of government employees who are union members is higher than the proportion of private sector workers.
   c. The proportion of workers in southern states who are union members is higher than the proportion in northern states.
   d. The proportion of white workers who are union members is higher than the proportion of black workers.

2. Which of the following is *not* a cause of the decline in unionization in the United States?
   a. deregulation in transportation and communication industries
   b. increased foreign competition
   c. growth in the number of smaller firms
   d. an increase in the number of workers wishing to be union members

3. Which of the following is *not* one of the channels through which a union may raise wages?
   a. supply restrictions
   b. increasing the demand for union labor
   c. more competitive product pricing
   d. bargaining power

4. A worker living in a state with a right-to-work law
   a. cannot be employed at a union firm until he has joined the union.
   b. cannot be required to join a union as a condition of employment.
   c. must agree when he is hired never to join a union.
   d. is guaranteed a job in government if he cannot find a private sector job.

5. Because the demand for a broadly defined product line (automobiles, for example) is less elastic than the demand for a more narrow product category (Fords, for example), a union will be better able to raise wages without large unemployment effects when
   a. it has organized an entire industry rather than only one firm.
   b. it organizes only a few firms in each industry.
   c. it bargains with all firms in a narrow product line but ignores the rest of the industry.
   d. only a small part of the industry that makes the broadly defined product is unionized.

6. By raising their wages, unions typically
   a. increase total productivity, which must rise proportionally with the wage rate.
   b. encourage employers to find substitutes for union labor.
   c. raise the wages of nonunion workers as well.
   d. lower the prices consumers pay for the products produced by union firms.

7. In 2008, approximately what percent of the nonagricultural workforce belonged to a union?
   a. 2.5 percent
   b. 12.5 percent
   c. 35.5 percent
   d. 98.5 percent

8. The percent of workers belonging to a union in the United States
   a. has been continuously declining since the 1950s.
   b. has been continuously increasing since the 1950s.
   c. has remained fairly constant since the 1950s.
   d. rose sharply from 1950 to 1970 but has declined since.

9. The experience of the Teamsters in the late 1970s and early 1980s suggests that
    a. there are few restraints on the ability of a strong union to increase the wages of its members.
    b. product market competition with goods made from (or services provided by) nonunion labor significantly limits the ability of a union to get increased wages for its members.
    c. higher wages tend to stimulate aggregate demand, which makes it easier for a union to gain still higher wages.
    d. wages are established by the relative skill of union and management negotiators, independent of market conditions.

10. From 1950 to 2008, union membership has declined from more than 30 percent of the workforce to approximately 12.5 percent. Over this period, the share of national income going to labor
    a. declined substantially.
    b. increased substantially.
    c. remained approximately the same.
    d. initially increased but has fallen recently.

11. A union representing a group of workers will tend to be stronger when
    a. there are no good substitutes for the labor services of the unionized workers.
    b. the domestic producers of the good produced by the unionized workers face intense competition from foreign suppliers of the good.
    c. the cost of employing the unionized workers is a large part of the total cost of the product that they produce.
    d. the demand for the good produced by the unionized workers is highly elastic.

12. Which of the following statements is true for the U.S. economy?
    a. Higher wages in the unionized sectors of the economy push up wages in the nonunion sectors as well.
    b. Inflation tends to accelerate when the proportion of the labor force that is unionized increases.
    c. Union workers currently receive wages that are 21 percent higher, on average, than similar nonunion workers.
    d. When we compare similar union and nonunion workers, we find virtually no difference in the wages they receive.

DISCUSSION QUESTIONS

1. "The wages of union workers are higher than the wages of nonunion workers." Which of the following can we conclude from this observation? Explain your decision in each case.
    a. Unions raise the wage rates of union members.
    b. Unions generally organize high-wage workers.
    c. Unions lower wages for nonunion labor.

2. It is sometimes argued that the largest factor limiting the ability of unions to raise wages is the unwillingness of consumers to pay higher prices for the goods they consume. Evaluate this statement and explain how it relates to the idea that a union will be more successful if it organizes all firms in an industry instead of only one.

3. For each item below, discuss how it affects the ability of unions to raise the wages of their members. Explain your reasoning in each case.
    a. right-to-work laws
    b. competition from foreign firms
    c. organizing only one firm in an industry instead of all firms in the industry

4. Business decision makers can sometimes argue that they cannot make a profit because of the excessive wage demands of unions. Suppose that a strong union in a highly competitive industry obtains for its members a 15 percent increase in wages.
    a. Will the higher wage rates reduce the industry's rate of profit in the short run? in the long run?
    b. How much of the higher wage rates do you think will be passed on to consumers in the long run?

5. "Every union knows that an airline is more vulnerable to strikes than most other businesses. Airlines have high fixed costs regardless of whether their planes are flying. They can neither stockpile seats during a strike nor sell from inventory afterward. Strike losses cannot be recovered. The strong impulse is to avoid a strike, even if that means settling on an unsatisfactory basis." (From an airline newsletter.)
    a. Do you think the airline industry is particularly vulnerable to union demands? Why or why not?
    b. If the airlines are vulnerable, who would pay for an "unsatisfactory" labor settlement in the short run? in the long run? Explain.
    c. Many economists have concluded that, in the absence of regulation, barriers to entry are pretty low in the airline industry. How does this affect your answer to part a?
    d. Do you think unions would favor or oppose a return to government regulation of airlines? Why or why not?

Are We Running Out of Resources?

TRUE OR FALSE

T   F

☐ ☐   1. Evidence suggests that resource scarcity is growing rapidly and that the relative price of most resources is rising as a result.

☐ ☐   2. An increase in the price of a resource will encourage people to conserve on their use of the resource.

☐ ☐   3. An increase in the price of a resource (such as oil) will encourage more effort to be put into finding and using substitute (alternative) resources.

☐ ☐   4. Proved reserves are the verifiable quantity of a resource available at current prices and technology, not the total supply of the resource that will be available in the future.

☐ ☐   5. Proved reserves can be expanded with improvements in technology and increases in prices.

☐ ☐   6. Timber would be an example of a non-renewable resource.

☐ ☐   7. The United States has about the same amount of land devoted to forest as it did in 1920, and far more timber is growing on it.

☐ ☐   8. By raising productivity per acre, technology reduces the amount of land required to produce food and fiber.

☐ ☐   9. When natural resources are not traded, or where markets are not allowed to function efficiently, problems of waste and scarcity are common.

T F

☐ ☐ 10. Water supply problems reflect the fact that in most situations water markets are missing or are incomplete.

☐ ☐ 11. Government subsidies to water consumption help to conserve water and make sure it is efficiently allocated across individuals and areas.

PROBLEMS AND PROJECTS

1. Exhibit 1 shows data on natural gas reserves, consumption, and prices in the United States from 1950 to 2000. Use this data when answering the following questions.

EXHIBIT 1

NATURAL GAS RESERVES, CONSUMPTION, AND PRICE: 1950–2000

YEAR	PROVED RESERVES	ANNUAL CONSUMPTION	PRICE
1950	185.6	6.0	$0.50
1960	246.6	10.3	0.68
1970	291.0	21.1	0.76
1980	199.0	19.9	3.32
1990	169.3	18.7	2.25
2000	167.4	22.7	3.68

Notes: Quantities in trillions of cubic feet. Price in constant 2000 dollars per 1,000 cubic feet.

a. In 1950, the proved reserves of natural gasoline were 185.6 trillion cubic feet and the rate of natural gas consumption was 6.0 trillion cubit feet per year. If the reserve data really reflected the remaining amount of natural gas, and if annual consumption rates continued into the future, how many years worth of natural gas remained in 1950? If someone had presented you with this data in 1950, and had asked you when we were going to run out of natural gas, what year would you have told them based upon your calculation?

b. Given your answer to part a, why have we not run out of natural gas? Between 1950 and 1960 and again between 1960 and 1970, proved reserves of natural gas increased. Does this explain part of the answer? How is it possible for reserves to increase despite continued consumption?

c. Is the trend of increasing reserves you found in part b continuing? Between 1990 and 2000, proved reserves fell by 1.9 trillion cubic feet (from 169.3 to 167.4). However, based upon the data given, we should have consumed about 200 trillion cubic feet over these 10 years (10 years at a usage rate of about 20 trillion cubic feet). What does this suggest about the rate of growth in proved reserves relative to the rate of consumption?

d. What happened to the price of natural gas between 1970 and 1980? How did the annual consumption of natural gasoline change in response? Given that it takes time for consumption to fully adjust, is it surprising that consumption continued to fall between 1980 and 1990?

e. What happened to the price of natural gas between 1990 and 2000? While not shown in the exhibit, most of this increase happened during the year 2000 (in 1999, the price was $2.26, only one cent higher than in 1990). Given this rather large increase during the year 2000, what would you expect to happen to natural gas consumption by 2010?

f. Based upon the proved reserves and rate of consumption in 2000, in what year do you *really* think we will run out of natural gas?

2. Exhibit 2 shows data on the usage of natural gas by residential homes and commercial buildings. These data show how many trillions of BTU were used by homes and businesses depending upon the age of the building (i.e., the year the building was constructed).

EXHIBIT 2

NATURAL GAS USAGE (TRILLIONS BTU PER YEAR)

YEAR BUILT	RESIDENTIAL HOMES	COMMERCIAL BUILDINGS
Prior to 1960	2,820	736
1960s	730	375
1970s	740	393
1980s	560	288
1990s	430	154

---

a. Homes built prior to 1960 use more than twice as much natural gas as homes built since. In addition, while there is only a slight difference between homes constructed in the 1960s and 1970s, homes constructed in the 1980s and 1990s use significantly less natural gas. How well do these changes in usage correspond to changes in the price of natural gas? (Hint: You will need to look back at Exhibit 1 in problem 1 for the price data.)

b. Usage of natural gasoline by homes built in the 1980s and 1990s is very low relative to homes built earlier. While some of the reduction in natural gasoline consumption could be accounted for by rising use of other fuels, overall, household energy consumption for homes built in the 1990s is only one-fourth of the usage of old homes. How can this be explained?

c. How much of the reduced consumption do you think is explained by people becoming aware of energy problems in society versus how much is simply due to a reaction to higher natural gas prices? Which is more effective at creating incentives to conserve?

d. Is the trend for commercial buildings similar to the trend for residential homes?

3. Exhibit 3 shows how a decrease in supply affects the market for gasoline. Included in the diagram is both the short-run and long-run demand curves for gasoline. Use the exhibit to answer the following questions.

a. In the short run, how did the decrease in supply (from S_1 to S_2) affect the price of gasoline and the quantity consumed?

b. In the long run, how did the decrease in supply (from S_1 to S_2) affect the price of gasoline and the quantity consumed relative to its original level? relative to the short-run level?

c. Based upon your answers to a and b, would you say that the conservation that results from higher prices is greater in the short run or in the long run? Why is there a difference?

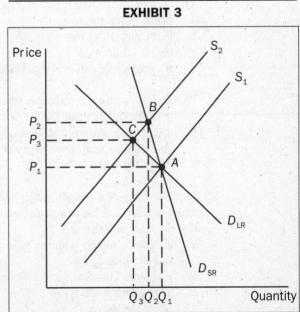

EXHIBIT 3

4. Suppose that the blue-eyed fillow was in danger of extinction because its natural habitat has been declining. The bird is very particular and will only nest in red sipe trees (which require special care and added fertilizer to grow well). For each of the following, decide whether the government regulation or policy stated would increase (+) or decrease (–) your incentive to keep, plant, and have red sipe trees on your property.

_____ a. a law that if a blue-eyed fillow is found nesting on your property, the government will fence off a 50-foot circle around the tree, remove all buildings from the area, and place the property under public control without compensation to you

_____ b. a law that requires each person owning a red sipe tree to purchase a new, very expensive fertilizer that increases growth and longevity and apply it to the trees 10 times a month.

_____ c. a law that provides for a $100 cash payment to any property owner finding a blue-eyed fillow nesting on their property

_____ d. a new tax provision that exempts any property with more than 10 red sipe trees per acre from any local, state, and federal property taxes.

MULTIPLE CHOICE

1. "Doomsday" predictions about the imminent depletion of one or more of our vital natural resources usually are
   a. correct but are not reflected by relative price changes within our market economy.
   b. overstated because of arithmetic calculation mistakes.
   c. overstated because they disregard human responses to relative price changes.
   d. understated because substitutes for such natural resources are also becoming less available.

2. The amount of a resource consumed depends on
   a. the price of the resource.
   b. consumer income.
   c. the price of substitute resources.
   d. all of the above.

3. The concept of "proved reserves" refers to the amount of a resource that can be produced
   a. in one year's time.
   b. in the next 10 years.
   c. before it runs out.
   d. at current levels of expected prices and technology.

4. Predictions that natural resources such as oil will be essentially used up in the next few decades have
   a. been frequently made for the past century, but have always proven to be false.
   b. usually been based on the quantity of proved reserves.
   c. ignored the role of price in governing the quantities demanded and supplied.
   d. All of the above.

5. Suppose that new demands greatly reduce the proved reserves of titanium to unexpectedly low levels, and it appears that the new demands will continue. If the market price is unregulated, we should expect that the price will rise and
   a. increase exploration and encourage more effective recovery methods, resulting in additional new supplies of titanium.
   b. encourage consumers and manufacturers to conserve titanium.
   c. increase the incentive to find and use substitutes for titanium.
   d. All of the above.

6. Empirical evidence suggests that the relative scarcity of most resources is
   a. declining.
   b. increasing slowly.
   c. increasing rapidly.
   d. largely unchanged.

7. Resources that are not created or renewed at a significant rate, and therefore could potentially be used up over time, are called
   a. renewable resources.
   b. nonrenewable resources.
   c. fixed resources.
   d. earthly geographic resources.

8. An example of a renewable resource is
   a. coal.
   b. oil.
   c. timber.
   d. diamonds.

9. Compared with 1920, the United States today has
   a. far less forest land.
   b. far more forest land.
   c. about the same amount of forest land.
   d. far fewer trees growing per acre of forest land.

10. Technological advances in agriculture (such as chemical fertilizers and harvesting equipment) have helped to preserve and grow forest land because they
    a. reduce the amount of land needed to grow food.
    b. result in a larger population.
    c. are made from timber.
    d. None of the above.

11. Water supply problems are generally the result of
    a. missing or incomplete markets for water.
    b. too much trading of water.
    c. too few government subsidies to desalination.
    d. all of the above.

DISCUSSION QUESTIONS

1. "With only a fixed amount of natural resources available, it is impossible for the quantity supplied to increase as price rises." Evaluate this statement.

2. "We are running out of forest land." Evaluate this statement. Be sure to discuss how much forest land exists today relative to the past, and also the role of agricultural technology in your answer.

3. In 2000, natural gas reserves were 168 trillion cubic feet. Given that we currently consume 23 trillion cubic feet per year, we only have a few years of natural gas left. Evaluate and discuss.

4. What are the underlying causes of water supply problems? How would greater use of markets and trading help to solve these problems?

Difficult Environmental Cases and the Role of Government

TRUE OR FALSE

T F

☐ ☐ 1. When there are a large number of polluters, high transaction costs weaken the ability of property rights to solve environmental problems.

☐ ☐ 2. The Kyoto Protocol is a treaty that requires industrial nations to keep the total amount of carbon dioxide emissions to no more than their 1990 level.

☐ ☐ 3. The Kyoto Protocol is not affected by special interest politics and lobbying.

☐ ☐ 4. Studies have now unquestionably concluded that disastrous effects from global warming are inevitable.

☐ ☐ 5. Economic development generally leads to environmental improvements because people with higher incomes are willing to pay more for environmental quality.

☐ ☐ 6. The "cap-and-trade" programs reduce both pollution levels and the overall costs of meeting pollution standards.

☐ ☐ 7. Overfishing in the oceans is a clear example of overexploitation of a resource because it is not privately owned.

☐ ☐ 8. The earth has experienced both warming and cooling trends in the past, and the current warming trend may well be unrelated to the emissions of carbon dioxide and other greenhouse gases into the atmosphere.

☐ ☐ 9. The main focus of government intervention in environmental issues deals with establishing regulations to control pollution.

T F

☐ ☐ 10. When a resource such as a national park is not privately owned, lack of information and incentives often creates the mismanagement of funds.

PROBLEMS AND PROJECTS

1. Consider the animals listed in the following table.

Column 1	Column 2
Cows	African elephants
Pigs	American bison
Chickens	Spotted owl
Cats	Blue whale
Dogs	Bald eagle

a. Which column of animals above is either extinct or is currently threatened with extinction?
b. Which column of animals above is allowed to be privately owned?
c. What, if any, correlation is there between your answers to a and b above?
d. People generally believe that the reason why animals go extinct is because they are killed at a very high rate solely for human consumption. Based upon your best guess, which specific animals listed above do you believe are killed in the highest numbers each year for human consumption? What correlation is there between the ones being killed in the highest numbers and the ones going extinct?
e. Generally, cows are everywhere in the United States; they are far from going extinct. Who owns these cows, the environmental groups or the people who will eventually kill them? Based upon your answer, do you think that African elephants would be doomed for extinction if the private property rights to the animals were given to the ivory poachers in Africa? (Note: Ivory poachers are persons who kill the elephants to get their ivory tusks to sell.)

2. The Audubon Society is a private organization that uses money from contributors to purchase the private property rights to land that they wish to preserve. In several cases, the Audubon Society has sold the mineral rights to allow companies to drill oil on their properties.
a. Explain what incentive there would be for the Audubon Society to sell oil companies the right to drill oil on their property. Are both parties (the oil company and the Audubon Society) made better off by this voluntary transaction?
b. When making a decision as to whether to allow oil drilling, what factors do you think the Audubon Society considers?
c. Rumors have it that the U.S. government allowed a timber company to harvest trees in a government-owned forest and built a government-financed road into the forest for the company to use. However, the money the company received from selling the timber was not even as much as it cost the government to build the road into the forest. If this had been a property of Audubon, and the company would have had to buy the rights and pay for the building of the road themselves, would the timber company have found it profitable to do so?
d. Suppose environmental groups currently spend $35 million each year lobbying to buy the votes of politicians to ensure they do not grant access to a U.S. government-owned forest for drilling oil. If a private oil company owned the forest, and could make $25 million in profit if they drilled, would they be willing to sell the property to the environmental group for $30 million instead? Would the environmental group be better off than under the current system?

MULTIPLE CHOICE

1. Which of the following would illustrate an example that leads to high transaction costs when dealing with pollution?
    a. air quality in New York City
    b. water pollution caused by a large number of firms located near the same river
    c. noise pollution near a busy airport
    d. all of the above

2. Which of the following is an example of a deficiency caused by a regulatory approach to pollution?
    a. ignored information provided by market signals
    b. special interests
    c. lack of accountability
    d. all of the above

3. Higher levels of carbon dioxide may be leading to a
    a. 1.4 degree (F) level of warming of the earth.
    b. 10.4 degree (F) level of warming of the earth.
    c. 1.4 degree (F) level of cooling of the earth.
    d. 10.4 degree (F) level of cooling of the earth.

4. Empirical evidence indicates that
    a. changes in the earth's cloud cover will clearly enhance the warming effects of carbon dioxide.
    b. the increase in carbon dioxide, over thousands of years, is definitely the cause of global warming.
    c. if global warming continues, the sea levels will definitely rise.
    d. none of the above are true.

5. Besides the scientific uncertainties, which of the following has kept most economists from recommending strong regulations to reduce emissions of carbon dioxide?
    a. consumer ignorance
    b. the Kyoto Protocol
    c. the potential for special-interest involvement
    d. The Clean Air Act of 1990

6. (I) Richer people are more willing to make sacrifices to gain greater environmental quality. (II) Poor countries are not as resilient when faced with the threats caused by environmental degradation.
    a. Both I and II are true.
    b. I is true; II is false.
    c. I is false; II is true.
    d. Both I and II are false.

7. Pollution charges will be efficient if
    a. the charge is just equal to the cost borne by others from the pollution.
    b. the charge is greater than the cost borne by others from the pollution.
    c. the charge is less than the cost borne by others from the pollution.
    d. none of the above.

8. The tragedy of the commons refers to a situation in which a resource is overexploited because it is not
    a. a common resource.
    b. privately owned.
    c. a public good.
    d. scarce.

DISCUSSION QUESTIONS

1. Suppose the government installed a monitor in your car that measured the pollutants in the car's exhaust. Further suppose that you received a monthly bill of $1.00 for every pound your car polluted the air. Would you change the amount of your driving because of it? If you were charged only for those pollutants that were emitted during heavy driving times (like rush hour), would you change the times of your driving?

2. "In nearly every case, environmental problems stem from insecure, unenforceable, or nonexistent property rights." Evaluate this statement made by Jane Shaw.

CHAPTER ONE

TRUE OR FALSE

The following are true: 1, 3, 5, 7, 9, 11, 13, 15.

The following are false:

2. The opportunity cost is the value of the next best alternative that you forgo to attend class that day (such as the value of sleeping later or watching television).

4. The value of a good is subjective; it differs across individuals. Some people like liver, while others hate it.

6. The resources devoted to education have alternative uses, thus public education is not free to society. It is a scarce or economic good.

8. Economizing behavior suggests you will purchase whichever is the *least* expensive.

10. *Ceteris paribus* means everything else is held constant.

12. This is a normative statement because it is an opinion.

14. Association is not causation.

PROBLEMS AND PROJECTS

1. a. (6) The lost manufacturing jobs were a secondary effect of the tax.
   b. (3) Incentives matter; as the benefits rise, the incentive to take the time to pick it up does as well. However, one could also relate this to guidepost (4) in a similar manner.
   c. (2) Economizing behavior suggests you will attempt to get the most out of your limited budget.
   d. (5) The deaths are the cost of waiting to acquire more information about the drug.
   e. (7) Value is subjective; the tomato and onion are worth different amounts to the husband and wife. This is what creates the opportunity for trade.
   f. (1) Bill Gates has a very high opportunity cost of his time spent making the wine, thus the wine is very costly to produce.

g. (8) The test of a theory (and its eventual acceptance) is dependent upon its ability to predict real-world events.
   h. (4) The marginal cost of the trip to the beach is lower from the grandmother's house. However, one could also relate this to guidepost (3) in a similar manner.

2. a. (5) Only information worth the cost of acquiring should be collected.
   b. (6) This would cause secondary effects that would harm the poor. For example, those making less than $10,000 per year would have trouble finding someone who would rent housing to them.
   c. (1) While it becomes free to the student, it is still costly to society in terms of other forgone activities (other things that could have been produced with those resources).
   d. (2) You would prefer the one that is the least expensive.
   e. (3) Incentives matter—they predictably influence behavior, even for criminals. (2) "Individuals choose purposefully" would also apply.
   f. (4) The tuition and books are expenses that are not relevant for the current decision to attend class—they are not *marginal* costs.
   g. (7) Value is subjective.
   h. (8) If it predicts well, the theory should be considered accurate.

3. a. (4) What is true for one individual is not necessarily true for the group. In fact, probably no one would play if the top prize was winning your $1 back!
   b. (1) The advent and popularity of computers is an event which is affecting the relationship; we have not held all else constant.
   c. (3) Better students tend to ask more questions. This does not imply that asking more questions will *cause* you to be a better student.
   d. (2) Just because Senator Mackenzie has good intentions does not mean that the policy will have the desired results.

4. b. There is a direct (or positive) relationship.
   c. 1/15 is the slope; the car gets 15 miles per gallon; the slope is 1 divided by miles per gallon.

5. b. Inversely (or negatively) related.
    d. Increase by 200 thousand tons (from 600 to 800).
    e. Decrease by 100 thousand tons (from 800 to 700).

MULTIPLE CHOICE

1. b. Scarcity and poverty are not the same thing.

2. a. Economics is about the choices people make because of scarcity.

3. c. This is the definition of scarcity.

4. d. This is a definition. Economizing behavior extends to a broad range of human activity.

5. a. The statement concerns what the government *ought* to do.

6. c. Choices *a* and *b* are violations of guideposts; choice *d* misunderstands what economists mean by the term scarce.

7. a. Scarcity prompts competitive behavior regardless of what allocation system is adopted.

8. b. Someone must incur the cost of producing a scarce good, regardless of who actually consumes it.

9. d. Goods will always be scarce regardless of whether there is poverty. Scarcity and poverty are not the same.

10. b. There is as much air freely available from nature as we would like to consume.

11. d. This is an example of thinking at the margin.

12. c. All other answers are characteristics of both micro and macro.

13. a. This is the definition of opportunity cost.

14. d. In all three, individuals are acting in accord with the incentives.

15. b. The total cost of 9 gallons plus the car wash is $14.50 (9 × $1.50 = $13.50 for the gas plus $1 for the car wash), while the total for 10 gallons plus the car wash is $15.00 (10 × $1.50 = $15.00 for the gas, and the car wash is free). Thus, buying the extra gallon only adds $0.50 ($15.00 − $14.50) to her total cost.

16. b. Both positive and normative economics deal with costs, benefits, and theory.

17. c. This is a subjective opinion.

18 a. The other answers are counter to the economic way of thinking.

19. c. This is the only statement that could be tested with data.

20. c. This is the definition of *ceteris paribus*.

21. b. This is the definition of utility.

CHAPTER TWO

TRUE OR FALSE

The following are true: 2, 3, 5, 7, 9, 10, 11, 13, 15.

The following are false:

1. Opportunity cost is the value of the highest valued alternative forgone as the result of washing your car (say an afternoon at the movies with friends), not the undesirable non-money aspects of the choice.

4. As long as trade is voluntary, both parties gain from trade.

6. The value of property is determined by how much it is valued by others not by the owner. Thus, private property rights create an incentive for owners to use their property in ways that are most highly valued by others.

8. Middlemen play an important role in coordinating the economic activities of others. By bringing buyers and sellers together, they help create economic value by providing a service.

12. Capitalism is the use of unregulated market prices and the decentralized decisions of private property owners to allocate resources. Socialism uses the political process and government planning to allocate resources.

14. Increased technology increases a country's productive capacity and thus shifts the production possibilities curve outward.

PROBLEMS AND PROJECTS

1. a. Because Susan will have to quit her job, she will forgo earning $20,000 per year, or a total of $80,000 over the four years. This is her opportunity cost of attending college and should be added to the table.
   b. Because room and board and transportation are costs that she will have regardless of whether she keeps working or goes to college, they are not relevant in the decision. They are not marginal costs of college because they do not change with her decision. If the drive to the university was longer than to her current job, her transportation expenses might increase and this is relevant; however, we do not have the information to know this here.
   c. For the per-year amounts, adding $20,000 and subtracting transportation ($557) and room and board ($4,434) yields a new per-year total of $22,743. For four years, this is a total of $90,972 ($22,743 × 4)
   d. Her forgone earnings account for 87.9 percent of her cost of going to college ($20,000 ÷ $22,743).
   e. Because earnings rise with age, the cost of college (the opportunity cost component of forgone earn-

ings) rises with age. College is thus more expensive for older students.

2. a. (1) They are attempting to make the home more attractive to others to increase its market value.
   b. (4) You are held accountable for the damages you cause.
   c. (2) Commonly owned property is not taken care of as well as private property.
   d. (3) Commonly owned property is not conserved as well as private property. It is generally used up much more quickly.
   e. (2) or (3) Cows, pigs, and chicken are privately owned, while whales and elephants are not. Thus, they are better managed and better conserved through breeding to maintain future stocks.
   f. (2) Rented property is given less care because the occupant does not own the property and will not bear the full cost of the reductions in the value of the property from misuse and damage.
   g. (1) The selling value of the automobile is determined by how much others value the car. When Sam does things to his property that are not valued by others, he bears the cost.

3. a. The plane cost $450, the bus $200, so the plane is $250 more than the bus ($450 − $200).
   b. The plane takes 6 hours, the bus 56 hours, so the plane saves 50 hours of Bob's time.
   c. For 50 hours to be worth $250 requires that each hour be valued at $5 per hour ($5 = $250 ÷ 50).
   d. Fly. In fact, if Bob values his time at any rate more than $5 per hour he should fly.

4. b. 4; 3; 1
   c. 10; 8; 2
   d. Larry
   e. Larry's is 1, Sam's is 1/2 (Hint: For Sam, you must divide both sides by two to get this answer from the exhibit which shows that 2 chairs = 1 table.); Sam
   f. If Larry specializes in tables, he produces 4 tables and no chairs. Sam specializes and produces 10 chairs and no tables. Together they have produced 10 chairs and 4 tables, which is one more table and one more chair than if they do not specialize.

5. a. 3
   b. 2
   c. Brazil
   d. United States
   e. The United States should specialize in producing coffee, Brazil in tobacco, and the two countries should trade. As a result, both countries will be better off.

6. a. yes; yes; no
   b. 900 million bushels; 200 million bushels

c. 100 million bushels; 1 bushel of wheat (Hint: 100 corn = 100 wheat, so dividing both sides by 100 gives 1 corn = 1 wheat.)

d. No, point E is unattainable because the country does not have enough resources to simultaneously produce this much of both goods.

7. a. (3)
   b. (1)
   c. (5)
   d. (4)
   e. (2)

8. a. (1) C = 3, I = 5; (2) C = 5, I = 3
   b. Any of the points on the curve between C = 3, I = 5 to C = 5, I = 3 (the portion that includes C = 4, I = 4).

MULTIPLE CHOICE

1. c. Opportunity cost is the value (or utility) of the highest valued forgone alternative (such as, building more interstate highways).

2. c. The opportunity cost of time spent not working is the wage forgone.

3. a. For saving 20 hours of time to be worth $200 requires that each hour be valued at least $10 ($10 = $200/20).

4. a. Specialization by comparative advantage raises available output.

5. d. The rational choice is the alternative that is most highly valued.

6. d. Answers *a* through *c* are the three basic questions listed in the text.

7. b. Private property rights allow an owner to gain when they use their property in ways that others value.

8. a. Ken gains $2,000 ($7,000 − $5,000), and Monica gains $1,000 ($8,000 − $7,000).

9. b. When the political process replaces market forces in allocating resources, political influence will be the primary determinant of allocations.

10. a. Specialization and trade result in gains at all levels from individuals to nations.

11. c. Points inside the curve represent output possibilities when resources are not being fully utilized.

12. c. Transaction costs are the costs of searching out and conducting a transaction.

13. a. Middlemen specialize in providing information and arranging trades, so you will not have to.

14. d. These are simply the three characteristics of private property rights given in the text.

15. b. Only if all resources are currently being used does it require taking resources away from the production of another good to expand production in another area.

16. d. All of these items shift the production possibilities curve outward.

17. b. The alternative to the date is to have $10 worth of other goods and play tennis.

18. d. Point A is efficient because it is on the curve, meaning all resources are employed; point B is inefficient because it is inside the curve, meaning the country is not using all of its resources; while point C is unattainable because the country does not have enough resources to produce this much of both goods.

19. d. The extra cost of driving is = $200 (4 hours × $50 per hour)

20. b. Specialization according to comparative advantage maximizes total output.

21. a. One party of an exchange benefiting does not imply that others lose.

22. c. These are the two important aspects of voluntary exchange given in the text.

23. d. In Lebos, 2F = 2C or equivalently 1F = 1C, while in Slavia 1F = 2C. These numbers are found by taking the differences in the numbers between rows.

24. c. Because the opportunity cost of producing food is lower in Lebos, Lebos has the comparative advantage in food and Slavia has the comparative advantage in clothing.

25. c. This is the definition of creative destruction given in the text.

CHAPTER THREE

TRUE OR FALSE

The following are true: 1, 2, 3, 5, 7, 8, 9, 13.

The following are false:

4. Relatively inelastic refers to when consumer purchases are not very responsive. The correct answer is relatively *elastic*.

6. A decrease in supply results in a higher price.

10. Lower prices for wine will cause a movement along the supply curve (a decrease in quantity supplied), not a shift in the supply curve (a decrease in supply).

11. A change in the cost of production results in a shift in the supply curve, not just a movement along the curve. Thus, it results in a change in supply, not just a change in quantity supplied.

12. The higher lumber prices would cause a decrease in the supply of new housing. This would result in higher prices, but only a reduction in *quantity* demanded, not demand (in other words, the demand curve does not shift).

14. The market is able to coordinate complex economic activity through the use of price signals. This is the "invisible hand."

PROBLEMS AND PROJECTS

1. c. $12
   e. $15
   f. There has been a change (an increase) in demand (a shift to the right of the demand curve), showing that consumers are willing to buy more shoes at all prices.
   g. There has been a change (an increase) in quantity supplied (a movement along the original supply curve) as producers expand output at the higher price.

2. a. 40 cents; 10
   b. 70 cents; 12
   c. Yes, lower bun prices would also cause the demand for hot dogs to increase.

3. a. increase
   b. increase
   c. decrease
   d. increase
   e. increase; increase
   f. increase
   g. increase

4. b. 0; −; +; −
   c. −; 0; −; −
   d. +; 0; +; +
   e. 0; +; −; +

5. a. Quantity will fall by 5 (from 25 to 20) along demand curve D_1.
   b. Quantity will fall by 15 (from 25 to 10) along demand curve D_2.
   c. Demand curve D_2 shows a demand more responsive to price.
   d. Demand curve D_2 is relatively elastic; demand curve D_1 is relatively inelastic.

MULTIPLE CHOICE

1. d. A below-equilibrium price results in an excess of quantity demanded relative to quantity supplied.

2. d. Higher income would increase the demand for automobiles, causing an increase in price.

3. a. Consumer surplus arises when a consumer purchases an item for a price lower than the maximum price they would be willing to pay.

4. a. When cigar prices rise, smokers will substitute cigarettes for cigars.

5. d. If consumers expected the price to fall in the near future, they would hold off their purchases until later, causing the *current* demand to decline.

6. a. Because Budweiser is a substitute for Miller, higher Budweiser prices will cause people to substitute to Miller beer.

7. d. These are true statements of what the height of both the demand and supply curves represent.

8. a. Travelers will substitute bus, train, and air travel for auto travel.

9. b. Lower coffee prices will cause consumers to buy more coffee and, thus, more cream. The demand for cream will increase (shift to the right).

10. b. As price falls toward equilibrium, quantity demanded rises and quantity supplied falls.

11. d. This is the law of supply, which relates to the actions of sellers not buyers.

12. c. He is the seller, so it is producer surplus of the difference between the actual selling price and the minimum price he would accept. Thus, $2,600 − $2,000 = $600.

13. d. This is the definition of economic efficiency along with the second part that no activity generating more cost than benefit be undertaken.

14. c. A shift to the right of the demand curve results in a higher price and a higher quantity.

15. a. The area below the demand curve and above the price is consumer surplus, while the area above the supply curve and below the price is producer surplus.

16. b. Lower consumer income has caused a decrease in the demand for new cars. As a result, the price of new cars has fallen, which has caused a reduction in quantity supplied by producers.

17. c. The tax raises price causing *quantity demanded* (not demand) to fall.

18. c. Response *a* would lower price; *b* lowers quantity; *d* raises quantity but results in little change in the price.

19. c. A decrease in supply results in a higher price (which reduces quantity demanded, not demand).

20. a. Lower cattle feed prices reduce the cost of producing beef, causing an increase in supply and a lower price.

21. c. Flour is a resource used in making donuts, therefore, a decrease in the price of flour will decrease the cost of production, causing an increase in supply. This causes the supply curve to shift to the right.

22. b. The invisible hand shows that markets direct self-interested individuals to pursue activities that are beneficial to society.

23. d. The existing supply of plywood is now not sufficient to meet the increased demand to rebuild homes, so the price rises due to the higher demand.

24. c. An increase in demand results in a higher price and a movement upward along the given supply curve. This is an increase in quantity supplied, not an increase in supply.

25. c. The freeze will reduce the supply of orange juice (higher price, lower quantity) while the study will increase the demand for orange juice (higher price, higher quantity). Both effects work to increase the price, but the quantity impacts work in opposite directions. Whether quantity rises or falls will depend on which effect is bigger, thus the impact on quantity is ambiguous.

CHAPTER FOUR

TRUE OR FALSE

The following are true: 1, 3, 4, 9, 10, 12, 13, 15.

The following are false:

2. Higher demand for housing would increase (not decrease) the demand for lumber.

5. A price ceiling will reduce the incentive for landlords to improve the quality of housing because the price ceiling prevents them from charging rents higher than the mandated price. Landlords will instead allow the quality of rental housing to deteriorate.

6. Because the demand for tobacco is relatively inelastic, tobacco consumers will capture the majority of the benefit from the subsidy.

7. A price ceiling that sets the price below equilibrium causes a shortage, not a surplus.

8. Shortages are caused by prices being set below equilibrium.

11. Because market prices will change, the burden of a tax can be shifted to other parties. The actual burden of a tax, in fact, will not depend on whether the tax is legally imposed on the buyer or seller.

14. A proportional tax is one in which everyone pays the same percent of their income in taxes. A tax that took the same dollar amount from everyone would instead be regressive because it would take a smaller percentage of a rich person's income.

PROBLEMS AND PROJECTS

1. (i). An increase in the supply of accountants (shift to the right of the supply curve) would lower the equilibrium wage and raise equilibrium employment.
    (ii). This would decrease the demand for accountants, lowering the equilibrium wage and equilibrium employment.

2. a. $250; 500
    b. fall to 200, rise to 800, a shortage of 600 units of rental housing
    c. it would fall
    d. it would fall
    e. other non-price factors (such as discrimination) would become more important

3. a. $4; 5,000
    b. rise to 7,000; fall to 3,000
    c. a surplus of labor, a situation also known as unemployment

d. better off as they retain their jobs at a higher wage rate
e. worse off as they are no longer able to find jobs, not only lowering their current income but also reducing job training opportunities, which will reduce their future employment prospects

4. a. $1.50
    b. $2.25, risen by $.75
    c. $1.25 ($2.25 − $1.00), fallen by $.25 from the pretax level of $1.50
    d. Buyers are now paying $.75 more, while sellers receive $.25 less, so buyers bear the larger burden of the tax.
    e. Tax revenue is $200 ($1 × 200) which is the rectangle from $1.25 to $2.25 in price and 0 to 200 in quantity.
    f. Consumption falls by 50 units (250 − 200), and the deadweight loss is the triangular area to the right of the tax revenue box.
    g. Had the tax been imposed on buyers, the price would have fallen to $1.25. Sellers would receive $1.25 from each sale, but buyers would pay $1.25 plus the tax of $1, or $2.25.
    h. The burden is identical to when the tax is imposed on sellers.

5. a. 20 percent ($10,000 ÷ $50,000)
    b. 15 percent ($15,000 ÷ $100,000)
        10 percent [($15,000 − $10,000) ÷ ($100,000 − $50,000) = ($5,000 ÷ $50,000)]
        90 percent [100 percent − MTR = 100 percent − 10 percent]
        regressive because the ATR falls with income (15 percent now versus 20 percent before)
    c. A regressive tax means the average tax rate (the percent of income paid in taxes) falls with income, not that the dollar amount of tax paid falls.
    d. 20 percent ($20,000 ÷ $100,000)
        20 percent [($20,000 − $10,000) ÷ ($100,000 − $50,000) = ($10,000 ÷ $50,000)]
        80 percent [100 percent − MTR = 100 percent −20 percent]
        proportional because the ATR stays the same (still 20 percent)
    e. 35 percent ($35,000 ÷ $100,000)
        50 percent [($35,000 − $10,000) ÷ ($100,000 − $50,000) = ($25,000 ÷ $50,000)]
        50 percent [100 percent − MTR = 100 percent − 50 percent]
        progressive because the ATR rises with income (35 percent now versus 20 percent before)
    f. 60 percent ($60,000 ÷ $100,000)
        100 percent [($60,000 − $10,000) ÷ ($100,000 − $50,000) = ($50,000 ÷ $50,000)]
        0 percent [100 percent − MTR = 100 percent − 100 percent]

progressive because the ATR rises with income (60 percent now versus 20 percent before)

No, she will earn no additional take home pay because taxes take all of her raise.

6. a. $0, 500, 800, 900, 800, 500, 0

   c. $3

   d. lowering the tax to $3 would increase revenue from $500 to $900.

7. a. Because the subsidy shifts the demand curve, it is being statutorily granted (paid) to the buyers in the market, here the students.

   b. The subsidy amount can be found by the vertical distance between the two demand curves, which at a quantity of 900 is clearly seen as $500 (found by taking the difference between $1,250 and $750).

   c. Prior to the subsidy, the average tuition was $1,000. After the subsidy, average tuition rises to $1,250.

   d. The student must now pay $1,250 to attend college but is given a subsidy of $500, reducing the cost of attending college from the old tuition price of $1,000 to the post-subsidy net price of $750.

   e. Because the impact of the subsidy program is to increase the demand for college, and thus increase average tuition, a student who does not qualify for the subsidy will have to pay a higher price for tuition without receiving any subsidy to offset this higher price.

MULTIPLE CHOICE

1. a. The demand for resources will increase when the demand for the product rises.

2. c. The benefit of a subsidy will always be shifted toward the more inelastic side of the market (or away from the more elastic side of the market).

3. c. This is the formula for computing the average tax rate given in the text.

4. a. Markets eliminate shortages by price rising to ration the available gasoline among the consumers desiring it.

5. d. Price floors create a surplus, also known as unemployment in this context.

6. c. This is kind of a trick question. A price ceiling sets a maximum legal price, so when it is set above equilibrium, it has no effect on the market. The market will remain in equilibrium as long as the equilibrium price remains less than the legal maximum. A price ceiling set below the equilibrium price creates a shortage, while a price floor (a minimum legal price) set above equilibrium creates a surplus.

7. d. There will be a reduction in the future supply of rental housing.

8. d. All of the other answers are false statements and show the harmful secondary effects of making a market illegal.

9. c. The price is now $.40 higher to consumers than in the absence of the tax, while sellers are receiving $.05 less from each gallon sold (they now receive $1.20 minus the $.45 tax, or $.75).

10. b. The deadweight loss (or excess burden) is the lost gains from trade when market quantity falls.

11. a. A relatively inelastic demand means that most of the tax will be borne by consumers as the sellers pass the tax along to buyers in the form of higher prices.

12. d. A regressive tax requires that the percentage of income paid in taxes falls with income, not the dollar amount of taxes paid.

13. b. The average tax rate is 10 percent at all income levels shown. Since it remains the same as income rises, the tax is proportional.

14. a. The Laffer curve shows that revenue can rise when high tax rates are reduced.

15. a. When tax rates are high, lowering them will increase revenue, but when tax rates are already low, lowering them further will reduce revenue.

16. d. The marginal tax rate is the change in tax liability ($12,000 − $5,000 = $7,000) divided by the change in income ($30,000 − $20,000 = $10,000), so $7,000 ÷ $10,000 = 70 percent.

17. b. The minimum wage is a minimum legal price, thus a price floor. A price ceiling is a maximum legal price (for example, a cap on the maximum professional sports players' salaries).

18. d. Under both, the quantity traded falls as the quantity traded is determined by the lower of quantity demanded or quantity supplied.

19. a. The tax would increase price and lower the amount purchased.

20. b. The tax is borne less heavily by the elastic side of the market and more heavily by the inelastic side of the market.

CHAPTER FIVE

TRUE OR FALSE

The following are true: 1, 2, 3, 5, 6, 8, 9, 11, 12, 15, 16.

The following are false:

4. Public goods are goods that have two characteristics: joint-in-consumption and nonexcludable. The government provides both public goods and private goods as do private markets. Mail delivery, for example, is a private good provided by government.

7. Poor information is present in many real-world markets.

10. This is an example of a private market providing a solution to the information problem.

13. The free rider problem happens when nonpaying customers *cannot* be excluded.

14. Price controls, tariffs, and quotas decrease the intensity of competition in markets.

PROBLEMS AND PROJECTS

1. a. yes, yes, public
    b. yes, no, private
    c. no, no, private
    d. no, no, private
    e. yes, yes, public
    f. yes, no, private
    g. no, no, private
    h. yes, no, private

2. a. $P = \$120$; $Q = 4,000$ tons/year
    b. $P = \$130$; $Q = 3,000$ tons/year (Hint: Add \$20 to each price and graph the new supply curve. It will appear parallel to the original supply curve but shifted upward by \$20. Find the efficient point at the intersection of the new supply curve and the original demand curve.)
    c. When producers and consumers do not bear the full cost of their actions, they will tend to overproduce (and overconsume) the good relative to what would be efficient.
    d. A tax of \$20 per ton would shift the original supply curve upward (see Chapter 4), and it would match the supply curve reflecting the true social cost of production. The resulting private market equilibrium would match economic efficiency.

3. a. $P = 50$; $Q = 26$
    b. 32
    c. a subsidy of \$24 million to a team locating in the city

d. No, it will result in a number of teams exceeding the efficient amount.

4. a. efficient, rule 1
    b. inefficient, rule 2
    c. efficient, rule 1
    d. inefficient, rule 2
    e. inefficient, rule 2
    f. efficient, rule 1
    g. inefficient, rule 2
    h. inefficient, rule 2
    i. efficient, rule 1

MULTIPLE CHOICE

1. d. Government mandated price ceilings reduce efficiency.

2. b. The inability of private firms to exclude nonpaying customers creates a free rider problem. The firm will not be able to generate enough revenue to produce the good efficiently.

3. d. All three are ways in which the market offers consumers information about potential products and services.

4. b. The four problem cases are public goods, externalities, lack of competition, and poorly informed buyers or sellers.

5. d. Your purchasing a hamburger is not likely to affect other third parties.

6. a. Externalities are costs that you impose on others such as pollution and congestion for which you do not have to pay compensation.

7. a. These are the two rules for efficiency listed in the book.

8. b. National defense is the only one meeting both criterion for a public good.

9. a. When private markets do not fully reflect the social costs, the good or service will be overprovided.

10. c. All externalities are the result of poorly defined or poorly enforced private property rights.

11. d. These are the two characteristics of a good that make it a public good.

12. d. Brand names are one way private markets attempt to overcome information problems.

13. c. Public goods are goods that are both non-excludable and non-rival. Non-excludable means that it is hard to exclude nonpaying customers, and non-rival

means that the good is joint-in-consumption such that one person's use of the good does not diminish anyone else's use of the good.

14. c. The external benefit is the benefit that goes to others in the form of a reduced likelihood of catching the flu.

15. a. National defense is under the protective function.

16. d. Markets underprovide goods that generate external benefits and overprovide goods that generate external costs.

17. a. All externalities are the result of poorly defined or poorly enforced private property rights.

18. b. Nonexcludability gives individuals an incentive to free ride, that is to consume without paying.

19. d. These are the primary functions of government listed in the book.

CHAPTER SIX

TRUE OR FALSE

The following are true: 1, 2, 4, 6, 7, 10, 11, 12, 14, 15, 18.

The following are false:

3. These are methods legislators use to get the special interest issues for their district passed in the legislature by gaining the votes of other members of the legislature.

5. Information is costly to acquire. With little personal benefit from being informed, voters will generally gather little information and be rationally ignorant.

8. The costs to any one individual are small, so they will not devote resources to fighting it.

9. Only one-sixth of all transfer dollars go to programs that are "means-tested," the rest are directed toward people who qualify based on criteria other than poverty. Transfers are directed to those interest groups with the most political power.

13. It is called logrolling. Pork-barrel legislation is combining many separate special interest issues together on a single bill.

16. This is true for private markets, but the public sector breaks this link. Some people get more benefits from government than they pay for in terms of taxes, while others pay more than they receive.

17. There is always an opportunity cost associated with the government use of resources. Scarcity remains as someone must bear the cost of the government-provided goods.

PROBLEMS AND PROJECTS

1. a. A is efficient (benefits of $200 exceed costs of $150); B is inefficient (costs of $120 exceed benefits of $100).

    b. Under the equal tax plan, Adam would vote for proposal A because his benefit is $140 while his tax is only $50. Bob and Cathy would vote against proposal A. So proposal A would fail to gain a majority and would not pass. Proposal B would pass as both Bob and Cathy would vote in favor of it, while Adam votes against it.

    c. No. The efficient proposal A fails, while the inefficient proposal B passes.

    d. Proposal A would now pass unanimously (all three in favor), while proposal B would now fail unanimously (all three against).

    e. Yes. When taxes are divided in proportion to benefits received, all voters will benefit from an efficient project and will all be opposed to an inefficient project.

2. a. Only the new dam for district C is efficient (the total is positive). The totals for the other two are negative (the costs outweigh the benefits), so they are inefficient.

    b. In all three cases, only one representative gains from each project. Thus, each would receive one yes vote and two no votes. All three would fail.

    c. You gain $10 from the road in district A and lose only $5 from paying for B's park. You would be better off ($10 – $5 = +$5). Similarly, the representative from B gains $9 from the park and loses only $6 from your road. B would agree to the trade because $9 – $6 = +$3. With both you and B voting for these projects, they would both pass by a majority (2 to 1).

    d. A bill containing all three would give each representative the total that can be found by summing each row. Representative A would value the total bill at +$3 (+ $10 – $5 – $2), B would value it at +$1 (–$6 + $9 – $2) and C at +$2 (–$6 – $5 + $13). All three would vote unanimously in favor of the pork-barrel bill, and it would pass.

3. a. (2); b. (3); c. (1); d. (3); e. (1)

4. a. Types 1 and 3 where the costs and benefits are either both widespread or are both concentrated. This is the most similar to benefits-received principle of taxation.

    b. Type 2
    c. Type 4
    d. Type 2
    e. Type 4
    f. Type 1
    g. Type 2
    h. Type 4
    i. Type 2
    j. Type 3

MULTIPLE CHOICE

1. d. This is the special interest effect described in this chapter.

2. c. Of these groups, the remainder are large and unorganized.

3. a. The effect says politicians count the current more than the future and are best off for reelection purposes giving easy-to-see current benefits financed by uncertain future costs.

4. c. The costs of gathering information are worthwhile only if there are direct personal benefits.

5. b. Only one-sixth of all transfer dollars go to programs that are "means-tested," the rest are directed toward

people who qualify based on criteria other than poverty. Transfers are directed to those interest groups with the most political power.

6. d. The ability of individuals to move from one local area to another effectively creates competition among localities that leads them to be more efficient.

7. a. Remember only voters from your district get to vote for your reelection.

8. d. Public choice theory applies basic economic principles to the individuals involved in the public sector decision-making process.

9. a. Incentives matter—it is the basic postulate of economics and is the key premise economists use in analyzing the behavior of individuals in the public sector.

10. d. A politician must win votes to get elected.

11. a. This is demonstrated in the problem and projects section in problem number 1.

12. c. In this way it most closely resembles taxes reflecting benefits received.

13. a. The political process has a bias toward adopting projects with concentrated benefits and widespread costs even when they are unproductive.

14. d. This is the definition of pork-barrel legislation.

15. a. This is the definition of logrolling.

16. d. When the government begins giving away more money, more resources will be devoted by individuals to capture this additional money that is now "up for grabs."

17. d. This is the definition of the shortsightedness effect.

18. b. Just like markets, governments can be inefficient. When special interests gain the upper hand in the political process, government action will retard our welfare.

19. a. Competition over scarce resources is present in both sectors.

20. d. Scarcity implies that opportunity costs are always present when a good is produced either in the private or public sectors.

21. c. The ability to legally use coercive force is a unique feature of government.

22. a. This is considered earmarking because it is directed to a specific project in a specific location.

CHAPTER SEVEN

TRUE OR FALSE

The following are true: 1, 2, 4, 5, 9, 11, 12.

The following are false:

3. The motorcycle only counted in the GDP of the year in which it was sold new.

6. Transfers of money are not counted toward GDP to avoid double counting. The money will eventually be counted when it is spent on goods and services by the person who receives it. GDP is a measure of current production, so the money only counts when it is associated with the production of new output.

7. Only the incomes of those living within the boarders of the domestic country are included in GDP. Note, however, this income would be counted in GNP.

8. This is a purely financial transaction and does not count toward GDP, which is a measure of production. Note, however, that any commission paid to a stockbroker for their current services would be counted toward GDP.

10. Nominal GDP reflects changes in both output and prices, whereas real GDP reflects changes in output only and is thus a better measure.

PROBLEMS AND PROJECTS

1. a. $14,265
    b. $14,265
    c. Total output can be measured either by adding up all money spent on purchasing output or by adding up all of the income generated by the money spent on the output. All money spent on output eventually flows to someone as income.
    d. $27
    e. Net exports is exports minus imports, so imports were greater than exports.
    f. $14,398; 12,431; 11,351

2. a. The real values are found by dividing each nominal wage by the price index for the same year then multiplying by 100. So $0.75 × (100 ÷ 29.9) = $2.51, $3.00 × (100 ÷ 90.9) = 3.30, and $6.50 × (100 ÷ 177.1) = 3.67.
    b. Bob had the highest real wage ($3.67) and thus had the most purchasing power with his hourly wage.
    c. $0.75 × (177.1 ÷ 29.9) = $4.44 is the real 2001 equivalent of what Bob's grandfather made in 1961.

3. a. $5,986 for nominal GDP; 91.8 for GDP deflator; 7,066 for real GDP.
    b. 5.6 percent for nominal GDP; 2.4 percent for GDP deflator; and –0.5 percent for real GDP.
    c. Inflation fell for the first three years, then rose slightly in the fourth.
    d. Changes in nominal GDP include both the change in prices and the change in output, while real GDP measures only the change in output. So during a period of inflation, the change in real GDP is smaller than the change in nominal GDP. In fact, a rough approximation for this relationship is percent change in nominal = percent change in prices + percent change in real, which can be seen in the data in the table as being fairly close to the true values.
    e. The negative growth in real GDP shows that the economy was in a recession during 1991. Growth was a positive 3.1 percent in 1992, so the economy was out of the recession and in an expansionary period.

4. a. 0   j. +
    b. +   k. 0
    c. 0   l. +
    d. 0   m. 0
    e. 0   n. +
    f. +   o. +
    g. 0   p. +
    h. 0   q. +
    i. 0

MULTIPLE CHOICE

1. c. Real GDP is what GDP is "really" worth, that is, adjusted for price changes.

2. b. $RealGDP_{00} = NominalGDP_{00} \times (GDPdeflator_{95} \div GDPdeflator_{00}) = \$2,500 \times 1/2 = \$1,250$.

3. d. The sale of the house does not count, but the Realtor's commission does count.

4. b. They measure the cost of purchasing a given bundle of goods in each year.

5. a. See answer 2. Remember, the price index from the same year as the nominal figure goes on the denominator of the fraction, while the year you are converting to goes in the numerator of the fraction.

6. c. The others represent current production of a final good.

7. b. Earnings of citizens are counted in GNP; earnings within a country's borders are counted in GDP.

8. b. Net exports = exports – imports = 40 – 75 = –35.

9. c. GDP = personal consumption expenditures + gross investment + government consumption and gross investment + net exports = 900 + 200 + 300 − 35 = 1,365.

10. a. GDP does count the value in the year it was produced. GDP is a fairly good measure of current production when that production occurs in legal market exchange.

11. a. Comparisons of dollar values through time are wrong and incorrect unless they have been adjusted for inflation first.

12. b. The percentage change in nominal is approximately equal to the sum of the percentage change in prices plus the percentage change in the real value. Thus, prices increased by approximately 3 − 1 = 2 percent.

13. a. Measured GDP would fall as individuals shifted their economic activity towards leisure, household production, and the underground economy to avoid taxation. All of these activities would still be part of "total economic activity," however.

14. c. GDP counts only production within the domestic borders.

15. b. The commission is payment for a service that is being provided during this year, so it is counted toward GDP.

16. b. The improvements to the car are part of this year's production of goods and services and are thus added toward GDP.

17. b. This is the definition of GDP. Remember, only final goods and only domestically produced goods are counted.

18. b. The value of a price index in its base year is always 100.

19. c. The percentage change in the price index is (107 − 100) ÷ 100 = 7 percent.

20. c. Convert the 1929 value into a 2008 value by 0.65 × (215.3 ÷ 17.1) = $8.18.

21. d. Convert the 2000 value into a 2010 value by 3 × (200 ÷ 100) = $6.

22. a. There are three ways to work this problem. First, you could convert the 2009 value to 2008 dollars with $15,600 × (100 ÷ 103) = $15,145.63, then find the percent by which this exceeds his 2008 salary with (15,145.63 − 15,000) ÷ 15,000 = 0.97

percent, which is roughly 1 percent. Alternatively, you could have converted his 2008 salary into 2009 dollars, then found the percentage change (15,600 − 15,450) ÷ 15,450 = 0.97 percent. Finally, the easiest method is to recall that the percentage change in the real value is equal to the percentage change in the nominal value (15,600 − 15,000) ÷ 15,000 = 4 percent minus the percentage change in the price index (103 − 100) ÷ 100 = 3 percent, so 4 percent − 3 percent = 1 percent.

23. d. Household production is considered nonmarket production because there is no money exchanged for the service. Because of the lack of a recorded transaction *measured,* GDP does not include it even though it is current production.

24. c. Its most useful purpose is to inform us about how current output and production compare to recent periods in the past (i.e., compared to last year).

25. b. (165 − 150)/150 = 15/150 = 0.1 = 10 percent.

CHAPTER EIGHT

TRUE OR FALSE

The following are true: 1, 2, 4, 5, 7, 8, 9, 11, 14.

The following are false:

3. Frictional and structural unemployment are present regardless of the state of the economy. They are due to natural phenomenon in labor markets.

6. The remaining 25 persons are either unemployed or are out of the labor force. The unemployment rate would be equal to the number unemployed divided by the labor force.

10. The natural rate is composed of frictional and structural unemployment. Cyclical unemployment is excluded.

12. The inflation rate is the percentage change in the price index, or $(132 - 120) \div 120 = 12 \div 120 = 0.1 = 10$ percent.

13. Inflation is an increase in all prices, including wage rates, so inflation causes consumer prices and worker incomes to rise simultaneously.

15. Actual GDP will exceed potential GDP during an economic boom.

PROBLEMS AND PROJECTS

1. a. F; b. S; c. F; d. C; e. O; f. C; g. O; h. O

2   a. 150, 80, 60 (The labor force is equal to employed plus unemployed.)
    b. 33.3 percent, 5 percent, 10 percent (The unemployment rate is unemployed divided by labor force.)
    c. Bela has the lowest unemployment rate, Abos the highest.
    d. 75 percent, 80 percent, 60 percent (The labor force participation rate is the labor force divided by population.)
    e. 50 percent, 76 percent, 54 percent (The employment to population ratio is employed divided by population.)
    f. The unemployment rate is measured as a percent of the labor force while the employment rate is measured as a percent of the population.

3. a. R; b. R; c. F; d. B

MULTIPLE CHOICE

1. d. Due to the lack of information, it takes time for both employees and employers to find a good match.

2. d. Unemployment is calculated as a percent of the labor force.

3. b. Inflation refers to a process of general rising prices.

4. a. This is the definition of the natural rate.

5. b. It is the labor force (which is employed plus unemployed) divided by the population.

6. c. Structural refers to a mismatch of skills with job openings.

7. b. During a recession, output (GDP) will be less than the full employment or potential level.

8. c. On the contrary, long-term contracts become more uncertain because individuals are uncertain what prices will be in the future. Most individuals avoid uncertainty.

9. b. They are a normal part of dynamic labor markets.

10. a. The economy is contracting between the boom and the recession.

11. a. During an expansion, the economy is growing, so output rises and unemployment falls.

12. d. A mismatch of skills is structural unemployment.

13. d. None of the ones listed are classified as unemployed.

14. c. The labor force is the number employed plus the number unemployed, so $120 + 30 = 150$.

15. b. The unemployment rate is the number unemployed divided by the labor force, so $30 \div 150 = 0.2 = 20$ percent.

16. c. The labor force participation rate is the labor force divided by the population, so $150 \div 200 = 0.75 = 75$ percent.

17. b. The employment/population ratio is the number employed divided by population, so $120 \div 200 = 0.6 = 60$ percent.

18. b. Both can affect the natural rate of unemployment.

19. b. In a boom, output is greater than normal. Both c and d refer to recessions, and a is wrong both because it is a recession and because it is not the natural rate that changes.

20. c. A key term here is sustainable. The economy's maximum sustainable output rate is the full employment, or potential level. When the economy is operating at that level, the actual unemployment rate will equal the natural rate.

CHAPTER NINE

TRUE OR FALSE

The following are true: 2, 5, 8, 9, 11, 12, 13, 14, 17, 18.

The following are false:

1. Being vertical, it shows that real output is the same regardless of the price level in the long run.

3. It is when imports of goods and services are greater than exports.

4. Bond prices will decrease when interest rates rise. They move in opposite directions.

6. It shows the relationship between the aggregate quantity of goods and services demanded and the price level, not the interest rate.

7. The real interest rate equals the money (or nominal) interest rate *minus* inflation, or alternatively, the money interest rate equals the real interest rate plus inflation. It can be written either way by rearranging the terms in the equation.

10. When the dollar appreciates, U.S. goods become more expensive to foreigners (so our exports will fall). On the other hand, foreign goods become less expensive to U.S. citizens (so our imports increase). This is why net exports fall when the dollar appreciates.

15. The aggregate demand curve slopes downward because of the real balance effect, the interest rate effect, and the international substitution effect.

16. Interest rates would fall as the market would need to induce more individuals to borrow the excess money now available for loans.

PROBLEMS AND PROJECTS

1. a. For 2008, AD and SRAS should cross to the left of LRAS; for 1997, they should cross at a point equal to LRAS; and for 2000, they should cross to the right of LRAS. The values for LRAS come from the potential GDP column, while the value where AD crosses SRAS comes from the actual GDP column.
   b. 4.9 percent (Remember, the natural rate is the rate present when the economy's real output equals the full-employment or potential level of GDP.)
   c. 2008, 2008, yes, recession
   d. 2000, 2000, yes, boom
   e. 1997, 1997, yes, "at full employment"

2. a. 1.4 percent; 8.8 percent; 4.1 percent; 1.6 percent; rising; falling
   b. between 1979 and 1982 a decrease, between 2001 and 2004 an increase

3. a. real GDP = 310; P = 120
   b. The LRAS should be a vertical line at output of $330.
   c. A recession; output is below the full employment level.

4. a. 0; the money amount repaid is the same as the money amount loaned.
   b. 5; negative (while he can buy ten pizzas now with the $100, you will only be able to buy five pizzas one year from now with the $100 he returns to you, so you are losing purchasing power meaning a negative real interest rate)
   c. 0; $200 (the original $100 plus $100 of money interest)
   d. You (the lender) are worse off, you will be able to buy eight pizzas with $200 if the price is $25 versus ten pizzas if the price is $20. Your friend (the borrower) is better off because he is having to repay you less in real terms. The real interest rate has fallen and the nominal interest rate is unchanged (it was fixed in the contract).
   e. You might have agreed to a contract where he repays you $250 (enough to buy ten pizzas). Higher expected inflation would increase the nominal interest rate you agree to so that the real interest rate is unaffected.

5. a. $20; saving = income − taxes − consumption ($100 − $10 − $70)
   b. $15; business borrowing = savings − government borrowing ($20 − $5)
   c. $25; total revenue = taxes from households + business taxes + borrowing ($10 + $10 + $5)
   d. $110; GDP = C + I + G + NX ($70 + $15 + $25 + $0)
   e. $100; total inflow = $110 + $15 = $125 and of this, $10 goes for taxes and $15 is spent on business investment leaving $125 − $10 − $15 = $100
   f. Yes. Household income is primarily based on business income from the sale of goods and services to other households (consumption), other businesses (machines and other investment goods), the government, and foreign economies (net exports—not shown). Real income is primarily dependent on real output.

6. a. Either household net saving must increase or business investment must fall (or some of both happens).
   b. Business investment must fall by an offsetting amount. Savings is required for investment. To have higher investment and higher growth requires a higher level of savings. As a politician, to have higher growth you would want to use government

tax and expenditure policy to encourage households to save more.

7. a(i). This would decrease the demand for loanable funds, lowering the equilibrium interest rate and quantity of loanable funds.

a(ii). This would increase the supply of loanable funds, causing the interest rate to fall, and the equilibrium quantity to rise.

b(i). This would increase the demand for the Mexican peso, causing the peso to appreciate (increase in value), and increasing the quantity traded.

b(ii). This would increase the supply of pesos in the foreign exchange market, causing the peso to depreciate (decrease in value) and increasing the quantity traded.

MULTIPLE CHOICE

1. b. Note that d represents the price variable in the aggregate goods and services market.

2. a. The real interest rate represents the burden in terms of the purchasing power of money.

3. c. Current output takes place where $AD = SRAS$. Long-run equilibrium (consistent with being at the natural rate of unemployment) occurs when all three curves intersect.

4. a. Bond prices (their current value) fall as interest rates rise.

5. c. The inflationary premium reflects the expected rate of inflation. When it is zero, the two interest rates are the same using the equation.

6. d. This is the price of loanable funds in the loanable funds market.

7. d. In equilibrium, the net inflow of capital offsets the balance of trade (net exports).

8. a. These are the major markets in the circular flow diagram.

9. c. The purchasing power of any given amount of money falls when prices rise.

10. d. These are the three reasons why the AD curve slopes downward.

11. c. Inflation higher than expected will lower the real interest rate, lowering the burden on buyers and lowering the reward to lenders.

12. d. The money interest rate is the real interest rate plus inflation.

13. a. Your real return will be the nominal interest rate minus what part of it is eaten up by inflation (5 percent – 3 percent = 2 percent).

14. a. The expected rate of inflation equals the nominal interest rate minus the real interest rate.

15. b. When borrowing, you want the lowest *real* interest rate (nominal minus inflation).

16. c. It now takes more U.S. dollars to buy an English pound, so the dollar has fallen in value (it has depreciated). The English will find U.S. goods cheaper for them to buy.

17. b. A depreciation makes domestic goods less expensive for foreigners (increasing exports) and it makes foreign goods more expensive to domestic citizens (lowering imports).

18. c. A trade deficit is when imports exceed exports. It would create a positive net inflow of foreign capital to offset the trade deficit.

19. a. A vertical long-run supply curve shows that in the long run, aggregate supply does not depend on the price level. One reason why is stated in the answer.

20. a. A higher price level will increase output in the short run, but not the long run once resource prices have adjusted to the higher price level.

21. c. The short-run aggregate supply curve intersects the long-run aggregate supply curve when the price level is equal to the expected price level. At higher prices, the economy moves up along the short-run aggregate supply curve expanding output past its long-run capacity.

22. a. These are part of the definition of long-run equilibrium.

23. b. When exports are greater than imports, net exports are positive and there is a trade surplus. To offset this there must be an outflow of capital (a negative net capital flow).

24. a. These are the two basic policies the government can use to alter the macroeconomy.

25. a. A higher demand for loans will increase the interest rate.

CHAPTER TEN

TRUE OR FALSE

The following are true: 1, 3, 4, 6, 8, 10, 11, 14.

The following are false:

2. This would decrease aggregate demand, not short-run aggregate supply.

5. A depreciation of the dollar would increase net exports causing aggregate demand to rise, not fall. The statement would be true if it said an appreciation of the dollar.

7. It would decrease the short-run aggregate supply, not the long-run aggregate supply.

9. Real output would rise, not fall.

12. An economic boom is not sustainable in the long run.

13. There is a large debate among economists as to how rapidly and effectively the self-correcting mechanism works.

PROBLEMS AND PROJECTS

1. a. –, 0, 0, –, –
    b. 0, +, +, –, +
    c. +, 0, 0, +, +
    d. +, –, 0, +, 0 (Expected rate of inflation shifts both AD and SRAS.)
    e. 0, –, 0, +, – (Remember, oil is a resource.)

2. a. Economy a is in a short-run equilibrium but not a long-run equilibrium; the current level of GDP is below the full-employment level; the current rate of unemployment is above the natural rate; the economy is in a recession. Economy b is in both short-run equilibrium and long-run equilibrium; the current level of GDP is equal to the full-employment level; the current rate of unemployment is equal to the natural rate; the economy is neither in a recession nor a boom. Economy c is in a short-run equilibrium but not a long-run equilibrium; the current level of GDP is above the full-employment level; the current rate of unemployment is below the natural rate; the economy is in a boom.
    b. Resource prices will fall, shifting SRAS to the right (an increase in SRAS), restoring full employment at a lower price level (at the point where the AD crosses LRAS in the figure).
    c. Nothing. The economy is currently in a sustainable long-run equilibrium that will remain unless the economy is disturbed by another event.
    d. Resource prices will rise, shifting SRAS to the left (a decrease in SRAS), restoring full employment at a

higher price level (at the point where the AD crosses LRAS in the figure).

3. a. +, +, – (increase in consumption and investment increases AD)
    b. –, –, + (lower real wealth lowers consumption and decreases AD)
    c. +, +, – (increase in exports, reduction in imports, increase in AD)
    d. +, –, + (reduces SRAS)
    e. –, +, – (increases SRAS)
    f. –, +, 0 (increases LRAS and SRAS)
    g. +, 0, 0 (increases AD and decreases SRAS at the same time)
    h. –, –, + (decrease in consumption and investment decreases AD)
    i. –, –, + (lowers exports, thus lowering AD)

4. a. T
    b. T
    c. F (toward B because it would increase AD)
    d. T
    e. F (resource prices would rise, not fall)
    f. F (toward F, not J)
    g. T
    h. T
    i. F (toward F, not J)
    j. F (increase in SRAS, not a decrease)
    k. F (decrease in AD, not SRAS)
    l. T

MULTIPLE CHOICE

1. b. All of the others will increase AD.

2. b. An increase in the LRAS shifts the SRAS curve with it. Increases are shifts to the right.

3. b. During a recession, businesses lower their investment spending, which reduces the real interest rate.

4. c. The market will adjust (i.e., the self-correcting mechanism) to either stimulate or slow the economy to where unemployment equals the natural rate and real GDP equals the full-employment level.

5. c. It would shift SRAS to the right, lowering the price level and increasing real GDP. The actual unemployment rate would fall, and the natural rate does not change.

6. d. The aggregate demand curve shifts to the left, lowering real GDP and increasing unemployment.

7. a. The SRAS curve shifts to the right, real GDP rises, and the price level falls.

8. a. This is the self-correcting mechanism.

9. c. This is a favorable supply shock.

10. d. AD shifts to the right, SRAS to the left, so the price level rises while real GDP stays unchanged.

11. a. Optimism stimulates current investment and consumption.

12. c. This increases our long-run productive capacity, shifting LRAS to the right (an increase). Any shift in LRAS pulls the SRAS with it.

13. b. This would shift AD, not SRAS.

14. d. A shift to the left of AD causes all three.

15. a. If it is fully anticipated, decision makers on the AD side will expect the price level to rise as a result of this event. Thus, the higher expected rate of inflation will cause a simultaneous shift to the right of AD, resulting in a higher price level and no change in real GDP.

16. a. It would reduce net exports of the U.S., causing AD to decline.

17. a. It will increase U.S. net exports, increasing AD. This will result in higher real GDP (which means higher employment or lower unemployment). This will only last until the self-correcting mechanism begins acting to move the economy back to the original output level.

18. a. A shift to the right of AD increases the price level.

19. a. Both *b* and *c* shift SRAS, not LRAS, and *d* causes a decrease in LRAS, not an increase.

20. d. This has permanently increased our productive capacity, increasing LRAS. SRAS always shifts along with LRAS.

21. d. An unanticipated increase in AD will lead to a higher level of output and a lower level of unemployment in the short run. However, this cannot be sustained in the long run and the SRAS curve will shift the economy back to its long-run equilibrium level so that the only lasting result is a higher price level.

22. c. Firms are much less likely to invest in long-term growth during a recession, so the demand for investment funds will decrease, which will cause the real interest rate to decline.

23. b. When the economy is experiencing a recession, falling resource prices and interest rates will automatically cause the SRAS curve to shift to the right until long-run equilibrium is restored.

24. d. All of these factors contributed to the 2008 economic recession in the United States.

CHAPTER ELEVEN

TRUE OR FALSE

The following are true: 1, 3, 5, 6, 8, 11, 12, 14, 15, 17, 18.

The following are false:

2. The full-employment level of output is fixed by resources and technology. General countercyclical fiscal policy cannot alter this. However, one could argue that this statement is true in that changes in marginal tax rates in the supply-side view are an example of fiscal policy that could increase the economy's long-run level of output.

4. Higher interest rates would tend to decrease private consumption and investment.

7. Fiscal policy is subject to severe timing problems, even more so than monetary policy because of the long decision-making time of Congress.

9. Modern views (new classical and crowding-out) suggest that fiscal policy is much less potent than was thought in Keynesian theory.

10. Keynes believed that inflexible wages and prices prevented the economy from automatically restoring full employment.

13. MPC = the change in consumption divided by the change in disposable income.

16. It shows a negative relationship.

PROBLEMS AND PROJECTS

1. a. recession
   b. B (SRAS would shift to the right until it crossed AD along LRAS.)
   c. Lower taxes and/or increase government spending; budget deficit
   d. C (AD would shift to the right until it crossed SRAS along LRAS.)
   e. same output, but at a different price level

2. a. boom
   b. Raise taxes and/or decrease government spending; budget surplus
   c. First, SRAS would shift to the left until it crossed AD along LRAS. Then AD would shift to the left, sending the economy into a recession.
   d. This ends up destabilizing the economy rather than helping it.

3. a. 2/3
   b. 1/1.5 = 2/3

c. 0
d. (4 − 1)/4 = 3/4

4. 3; 3; 1; 4

MULTIPLE CHOICE

1. c. The multiplier is used to derive the total end effect of a change in autonomous expenditure.

2. d. Prior to Keynes, economists thought aggregate demand played no important role in the macroeconomy.

3. a. The multiplier = 1/(1 − MPC) = 1/(1 − 3/4) = 4.

4. c. MPC = additional consumption / additional income = 200/300.

5. c. This was one of Keynes' major challenges to classical thinking.

6. b. The multiplier applies: [1/(1−0.75)] × ($12 million) = $48 million.

7. c. A greater MPC raises the multiplier, which equals 1/(1 − MPC).

8. c. When the federal government runs a budget deficit, the funds to finance this increase in spending comes from additional bonds issued by the U.S. Treasury.

9. a. A surplus is when spending is less than revenue.

10. c. Correct timing is essential for fiscal policy to effectively stabilize the economy. Improper timing could actually make the economy less stable.

11. a. Automatic stabilizers increase spending during recessions and cut spending during booms without any legislative action.

12. c. When the economy enters a recession, automatic stabilizers will cause government spending to increase and the revenue collected to decrease, leading to larger budget deficit.

13. b. The others do affect consumption, but this is the primary determinant.

14. b. It may lead to increased borrowing or less saving currently.

15. d. Inventories will rise, and production will be reduced because total spending is less than total output.

16. a. Spending is not sufficient to purchase all output, so inventories will accumulate.

17. d. When planned expenditures equal output produced.

18. a. If the economy is operating at less than full employment, than Keynesians believe that the government should increase spending and/or reduce taxes, thus creating a budget deficit, in an effort to bring the economy back to full employment.

19. c. If the economy were in a recession, than according to Keynesian theory the government needs to run a budget deficit by increasing spending and/or reducing taxes to stimulate the economy.

20. c. The Keynesian model gained its popularity during the 1930s when the economy was struggling to recover during the Great Depression.

21. d. Keynes argued that the Great Depression was the result of insufficient aggregate spending, which is why he advocated using countercyclical policy to promote increased aggregate spending.

22. b. According to the Keynesian model, an increase in aggregate demand is necessary to restore full employment.

23. b. According to the Keynesian view, running a budget deficit by increasing government spending and/or reducing taxes would help the economy avoid falling into a recession.

24. b. Equilibrium only occurs when total spending is equal to current output in the Keynesian model.

CHAPTER TWELVE

TRUE OR FALSE

The following are true: 2, 3, 4, 5, 7, 9, 11, 12.

The following are false:

1. Crowding out is when high interest rates caused by government borrowing reduce private consumption and investment expenditures.

6. Both Keynesians and non-Keynesians agree that proper timing of fiscal policy is important, but difficult to achieve

8. They have actually come to the agreement that, due to crowding out and the Ricardian equivalence, fiscal policy is much less potent than originally thought.

10. While it is true that the debt caused by expansionary policy in times of a severe recession will lead to higher interest payments and tax rates, these higher interest payments and tax rates will retard growth, rather than spur it.

PROBLEMS AND PROJECTS

1. a. K
   b. CO
   c. NC
   d. NC
   e. CO
   f. SS
   g. SS
   h. K

2. a. +
   b. 0
   c. −
   d. +
   e. +
   f. −
   g. +
   h. + (but by less than in the Keynesian view)
   i. 0

MULTIPLE CHOICE

1. d. All of the choices are theoretically possible, although there is controversy about which is most likely.

2. a. The higher demand for loanable funds increases the real interest rate; private borrowing for consumption and investment fall. With lower investment, there will be a lower capital stock in the future.

3. c. Higher interest rates caused by increased government borrowing will lead to lower consumption and investment which will partially offset the higher level of government spending in the aggregate demand equation.

4. a. The public will have to pay higher taxes later to repay the debt, so they save accordingly now.

5. d. Under the new classical view, fiscal policy has no real effect on AD, the real interest rate, or the economy.

6. d. The new classical view is that fiscal policy has no real effect.

7. d. These are the reasons why supply-siders stress lower marginal tax rates.

8. c. The long-run growth effects take a while to appear.

9. d. Both *b* and *c* are part of the modern consensus view listed in the book, but *a* is not; it is incorrect.

10. c. Deficits cause higher interest rates. An appreciation of the dollar will make our goods more expensive relative to foreign goods, causing a reduction in net exports.

11. a. Keynesians think we should use budget deficits and surpluses to stabilize aggregate demand in the economy.

12. c. The crowding-out view says that it will be at least partially offset by reductions in private investment caused by higher interest rates. The new classical view holds that it will have no effect as it is completely offset by reductions in current consumption (because of higher savings in response to the deficit).

13. c. According to the Keynesian view, when the economy is operating at less than its potential rate of output and exhibiting widespread employment, then it is most appropriate to use expansionary fiscal policy to bring the economy back up to full employment level.

14. b. Keynesian critics would argue that the budget deficit necessary to finance expansionary fiscal policy would lead to higher future interest payments and taxes to pay off the debt.

15. d. An increase in government spending will lead to higher interest rates through increased government borrowing. This will reduce private consumption and investment, which at least partially offsets the increase in government spending.

16. c.   While it is politically popular for the government to institute new programs during a recession, it is unpopular to cut these programs after the economy has recovered. So the increased level of government spending associated with these programs will persist into the future.

17. c.   This increase in savings (and reduction in consumption) will reduce the overall demand for goods and services, causing businesses to reduce output and layoff workers.

18. b.   A high level of savings will lead to additional investment, which is necessary for economic growth.

19. b.   A person's marginal tax rate is equal to the person's change in tax liability divided by the person's change in taxable income. So it indicates how much of a person's additional earning has to be paid in taxes and how much the person actually gets to keep.

20. d.   Lower marginal tax rates mean a person will get to keep more of his or her additional earnings, which creates the incentive to engage in more productive activity.

21. b.   According to the crowding-out view, budget deficits will cause the government to demand more loanable funds, which will drive up interest rates, thus reducing consumption and investment. According the new classical view, budget deficits will lead to higher future taxes, inducing people to spend less now in order to save more. The resulting effect under either view is slower economic growth.

CHAPTER THIRTEEN

TRUE OR FALSE

The following are true: 2, 3, 7, 8, 10, 11.

The following are false:

1. M2 includes even more (such as time deposits) and thus is a broader definition than M1.

4. Fiat money is money that has neither intrinsic value nor is backed by a commodity; our paper money is an example of fiat money.

5. A bank must keep only a percent of the money deposited on reserve. This percent is given by the required reserve ratio.

6. The bank would have to keep 5 percent, or $5 on reserve. It could use the other $95 to make a loan.

9. The value of money is not fixed but is rather determined by supply and demand. Higher prices, for example, lower the value of money because they lower its purchasing power.

12. Extending fewer loans would cause bank reserves to decrease, discourage bank loans, and reduce the money supply. The Federal Reserve would want to extend more loans to increase the money supply.

13. This would reduce the money supply because when the Fed sells bonds, it would receive money from the sale, which is then taken out of circulation.

14. Unlike the Fed, the U.S. Treasury does not change the supply of money by buying (retiring) or selling (issuing) bonds. The treasury will use the money collected from selling bonds to finance current government spending, which keeps it in circulation. The Fed would withdraw this money from circulation.

PROBLEMS AND PROJECTS

1. a. M1
    b. M2
    c. neither
    d. M1
    e. neither
    f. M1
    g. neither
    h. M1
    i. M2
    j. neither

2. a. $1 \div 0.20 = 5$
    b. It should buy (sometimes we say purchase) bonds.
    c. $10 billion (with a multiplier of 5, $10 billion would create $50 billion)
    d. 10; buy; $5 billion; the multiplier rises and the amount to buy falls

3. a. –; 0
    b. 0; +
    c. +; + (note that the Fed is buying these bonds)
    d. 0; 0
    e. –; 0
    f. +; 0
    g. 0; –

4. a. increase the money supply
    b. Round 1: 10,000; 2,000; 8,000
        Round 2: 8,000; 1,600; 6,400
        Round 3: 6,400; 1,280; 5,120
        Round 4: 5,120; 1,024; 4,096
        Total: 50,000; 10,000; 40,000

MULTIPLE CHOICE

1. c. Open market operations refer to the Fed buying and selling U.S. government securities, such as treasury bonds, treasury bills (T-bills), treasury notes, etc. To increase the money supply, it must buy government securities. If you are having trouble with this, just remember that when the Fed sells you a bond, they take your money so there is less money supply, and when they buy your bond, they give you new, freshly printed money.

2. a. The multiplier is $1 \div 0.05 = 20$; so $20 \times \$10$ million = $200 million. If the Fed buys bonds, it will increase the money supply, not decrease it.

3. a. The Fed has this responsibility.

4. d. See the text discussion on ambiguities in measuring the money supply.

5. c. $100 is 20 percent of $500 (figured as $100 ÷ $500).

6. c. Fiat money is money with no backing or intrinsic value.

7. b. It is the most flexible, hence, the most often used.

8. a. Do not confuse this with the discount rate. The federal funds rate is a market-determined interest rate that banks charge each other for loans. The discount rate is set by the Fed and is the rate the Fed charges banks for loans.

9. b. These are the three functions of money listed in the book.

10. a. Choices c and d reduce the money supply; b is not under the control of the Fed who sets only monetary policy, not fiscal policy.

11. b. Potential deposit multiplier = $1 \div$ required reserve ratio.

12. d. Excess reserves and cash held out of the system lower the amount of loans made and thus lower the expansion generated.

13. c. Answer a is the medium of exchange function of money, while d is the store of value function of money.

14. d. The value of money is what it can buy. If prices rise, the same amount of money will buy fewer goods.

15. d. Credit cards do not represent an asset. They are not part of the money supply.

16. d. All of the ones listed are in M2.

17. a. Excess reserves are money the bank has on reserve over and above the amount it needs to meet its reserve requirement. This money can be loaned out if the bank wishes to do so.

18. b. The multiplier is $1 \div 0.20 = 5$.

19. d. The Fed selling bonds lowers the money supply but does not affect the national debt.

20. c. When the U.S. Treasury issues and sells new bonds, it increases the national debt but does not affect the money supply.

21. c. Savings deposits are in M2 but not in M1.

22. a. There was a big increase in the monetary base and excess reserves. The volume of loans did not increase, nor did interest rates.

23. c. If the Fed were to increase the interest rate paid on excess reserves, banks would choose to hold more reserves and thus make fewer loans, causing a reduction in the money supply.

24. c. Prior to 2008, the Fed only used government bonds, but now it also uses corporate bonds, commercial paper, and mortgage-backed securities in the conduct of open-market operations.

CHAPTER FOURTEEN

TRUE OR FALSE

The following are true: 1, 2, 3, 4, 8, 12, 13, 14.

The following are false:

5. The quantity theory of money states that it will cause a proportional change in prices (P) and leave output (Y) unchanged.

6. A vertical supply curve indicates that the quantity of money supplied does not depend on the interest rate but is set by the Fed.

7. According to the Taylor rule, the higher the inflation rate and the larger the current level of output is relative to the potential level of output, the more restrictive the monetary policy needed for the achievement of full employment with price stability.

9. While the decision lag is shorter for the Fed, there are still "long and variable" lags in the time it takes for changes in the money supply to have an impact on the economy.

10. It would be 2 percent. The growth rate version of the equation of exchange states that $\%\Delta M + \%\Delta V = \%\Delta P + \%\Delta Y$, where $\%\Delta$ stands for "percent change." So, the inflation rate [$\%\Delta P$] may be found as $\%\Delta P = \%\Delta M + \%\Delta V - \%\Delta Y$, here this is 2 percent = 5 percent + 0 percent – 3 percent.

11. An expansion in the money supply is "expansionary monetary policy," while a reduction in the money supply is "restrictive (or contractionary) monetary policy."

PROBLEMS AND PROJECTS

1. a. II; 2 (V = nominal GDP ÷ M, so 9,963 ÷ 4,945 = 2.01)
    b. I; 30 ($Y = M \times V \div P$, so 600 × 5 ÷ 100 = 30)
    c. III; 4 percent [$\% \Delta P = \% \Delta M + \% \Delta V - \% \Delta Y$, so 7 percent + 0 percent – 3 percent = 4 percent, note that when velocity is constant, III may be simplified to $\% \Delta P = \% \Delta M - \% \Delta Y$]
    d. III; –2 percent (This is "deflation," a falling price level, of 2 percent, see derivation in part c.)
    e. III; 3 percent (From the derivation in part c above, to get $\% \Delta P = 0$ with constant velocity requires $\% \Delta M = \% \Delta Y$. This is known as the constant growth rate rule favored by the monetarists.)

f. I; 16 (This is the strict quantity theory of money. With constant output and velocity, doubling the money supply doubles the price level.)
g. I; price level rises to 6 in the short run and to 10 in the long run.

2. a. S_1 shifts left (decreases) in both, causing the interest rates to rise.
    b. Higher interest rates reduce consumption and investment, so AD shifts to the left (a decrease in AD). Real GDP falls and the price level falls.

3. a. higher real GDP and a higher price level
    b. No, eventually SRAS will shift to the left restoring output to the full-employment level (Y_f) and moving the economy to an even higher price level.

MULTIPLE CHOICE

1. b. The nominal (money) interest rate represents the price (in terms of opportunity cost) of holding money. A lower price would increase the quantity demanded.

2. c. Using the growth rate version of the equation of exchange, if velocity is constant, inflation will be zero when the growth rate of the money supply equals the growth rate of output.

3. b. Under the strict quantity theory of money, whatever happens to the money supply happens to prices as well (in other words, a "proportional change in prices").

4. b. MV = nominal GDP, so V = nominal GDP ÷ money supply. Do not mix up real GDP, which is Y, with nominal GDP, which is PY.

5. b. $\% \Delta P = \% \Delta M - \% \Delta Y$ when velocity is constant, so 9 percent – 3 percent = 6 percent.

6. a. Answers b and c are stated in reverse (that is, they would be true if the question read "unexpectedly decreases the money supply").

7. b. It would lower the supply of loanable funds, increasing the real interest rate and thus lowering consumption, investment, and aggregate demand and output as well.

8. a. In the short run ("initially"), if it is unanticipated, it will have its impact on real output. The major impact on prices will come in the long run.

9. c. Both are true statements of the impact of monetary policy.

10. d.   Interest rates will fall as the supply of loanable funds rises, and the lower interest rate will stimulate consumption and investment spending.

11. a.   Once the economy returns to long-run equilibrium, prices are higher and output returns to full employment.

12. a.   This is a definition. In the equation, M stands for money supply, V for the velocity of money, P for the price level, and Y for real GDP. Together, PY stands for nominal GDP.

13. c.   Demand curves show the relationship between the price and quantity demanded.

14. c.   This is the quantity theory of money.

15. d.   The unanticipated increase in the money supply will cause real interest rates to fall, and the foreign exchange value of the dollar will depreciate.

16. b.   The Taylor Rule is a tool used to gauge the appropriateness of monetary policy with respect to the targets of price stability and full employment.

17. a.   With the actual federal funds rate lower than the target rate this indicates that monetary policy is more expansionary than it should have been and that a shift toward more restrictive policy is appropriate.

18. a.   The Fed held interest rates very low, causing a high demand for housing and contributing to the dramatic rise in housing prices.

19. b.   The doubling of the monetary base has the potential to lead to high inflation in the future.

20. b.   Time lags make it difficult or impossible to properly time changes in policy so that their impact is felt in the economy at the right time.

21. d.   Movements in shorter-term interest rates are more reflective of monetary policy actions.

CHAPTER FIFTEEN

TRUE OR FALSE

The following are true: 1, 2, 3, 6, 7, 8, 10, 11, 12, 13, 14, 15, 17.

The following are false:

4.   As originally developed, the Phillips curve would predict that higher inflation would cause unemployment to decline.

5.   Forecasting models are wrong on many occasions because most major economic changes are the result of unanticipated shocks to the economy.

9.   According to the modern Phillips curve analysis, unemployment will fall below the natural rate when inflation is greater than expected (underestimated).

16.   When people overestimate inflation, it means that actual inflation was lower than what was expected.

PROBLEMS AND PROJECTS

1.   a.   10 percent, the same as last year
     b.   3 percent (13 percent nominal minus 10 percent inflation)
     c.   9 percent (13 percent nominal minus 4 percent inflation)
     d.   Unhappy; she is paying a real interest rate three times higher than she expected.

2.   a.   *SRAS* would shift to $SRAS_2$ and the economy would move to point B.
     b.   expansionary fiscal policy (tax cuts and/or spending increases) and expansionary monetary policy (increasing the money supply)
     c.   *AD* would shift to AD_2 and the economy would move to point C.
     d.   *SRAS* would have already shifted to $SRAS_2$, moving the economy to point B, so the economy would then experience *AD* moving to AD_2, resulting in point D.

3.   a.   No. After moving to point B, *SRAS* would shift to the left bringing the economy back to Y_f at a higher price level.
     b.   Yes, but the only way the economy could be moved to point B on a sustainable basis would be if the *LRAS* curve shifted right. Increased productivity or economic organization (among other things) could permanently increase our productive capacity, shifting the *LRAS* to the right.

4. a. B
   b. C
   c. C
   d. C
   e. This statement is true. In the long run, both result in point C. The only difference is whether we move directly there in the short run (rational expectations) or whether we move to point B in the short run first (adaptive expectations).

5. a. There should be two distinct Phillips curve lines, one for 1993–1995 and another for 2000–2002.
   b. 0, –1, +2, 0, –1, +2
   c. Yes
   d. 5%

MULTIPLE CHOICE

1. b. It is a composite index used to forecast the future direction of the economy.

2. d. These are the two variables plotted in the diagram.

3. a. This was the prediction of the original Phillips curve.

4. b. Only when inflation is higher than was anticipated (in other words, inflation was underestimated) will employment fall below the natural rate.

5. d. This is the time used up in the decision-making process. It is much shorter for monetary than fiscal policy.

6. d. Answer *b* is the opposite of what is true.

7. a. Adaptive expectations are that the inflation rate will be whatever it has been in the recent past (period 2).

8. c. This is a definition.

9. a. If people can correctly anticipate policy, it becomes ineffective even in the short run.

10. a. In the short run, AD will fall, lowering output. In the long run, SRAS will adjust and output will return to its old level, but inflation (the price level) will be lower.

11. b. Both SRAS and AD shift downward, so output remains unchanged and the price level (inflation) falls.

12. a. When people overestimate inflation, unemployment rises above the natural rate.

13. b. Unemployment will be above the natural rate when people overestimate the inflation rate—that is, the

inflation rate turns out to be lower than was anticipated, or alternatively that people expected inflation to be higher than what actually occurred.

14. b. Unemployment will fall below the natural rate when people underestimate the inflation rate—that is the inflation rate turns out to be higher than was anticipated, or alternatively that people expected inflation to be lower than what actually occurred.

15. c. Under adaptive expectations, people base it on whatever it was in the recent past.

16. c. Under rational expectations, people use all available information when forming their expectations.

17. d. All are true and this summarizes the graphical representation of both viewpoints.

18. b. The abrupt reduction in the rate of inflation will cause actual inflation to fall below the expected rate of inflation, and thus the actual rate of unemployment will rise above the natural rate of unemployment.

19. c. The index of leading indicators has fallen prior to actual recessions as it should, but it has also forecasted recessions that did not occur.

20. a. Falling commodity prices and an appreciating dollar are caused by reductions in the money supply.

21. b. This is one of the areas of agreement among economists listed in the text.

22. c. This is information in the textbook chapter.

23. c. When the Fed shifts policies too much it creates an environment in which people have a hard time forecasting the future. This uncertainty results in economic instability.

CHAPTER SIXTEEN

The following are true: 1, 2, 4, 6, 7, 8, 10, 14, 15.

The following are false:

3. Per capita GDP would increase.

5. The country's economy would double every 35 years (70 divided by 2).

9. Over time, even small differences in growth rates produce large differences in the size of an economy.

11. These policies would reduce the rate of economic growth.

12. Other factors such as a country's institutions and policies tend to matter more than does the abundance of natural resources. In fact, abundant natural resources tend to lead to conflict, instability, and authoritarian political regimes that reduce growth.

13. Countries receiving high levels of foreign aid tend to have low income and slower economic growth.

16. While a great deal of foreign aid has been directed toward Africa, much of the continent still faces extreme poverty because of its poor legal institutions.

PROBLEMS AND PROJECTS

1. 70; 35; 10; 7

2. a. –
    b. +
    c. +
    d. –
    e. –
    f. –
    g. +

MULTIPLE CHOICE

1. a. Per capita GDP will rise when GDP is growing faster than population.

2. a. The rule of 70 is used to determine how long something will take to double at a given growth rate.

3. c. According to the rule of 70, the answer is 35 years (70 divided by 2).

4. c. According to the rule of 70, the answer is 10 years (70 divided by 7).

5. a. These are the three key sources of growth listed in the chapter.

6. d. Answer *c* is not correct because trade benefits both parties; there are no losers.

7. d. The others would retard economic growth.

8. a. The others would retard economic growth.

9. c. Free entry and exit from business leads to improved products and production methods and directs resources toward projects that create more value.

10. a. A large government that goes beyond certain core functions generally reduces economic growth.

11. b. Free trade promotes growth because it allows for specialization by comparative advantage.

12. d. These policies are consistent with the listed keys to economic growth. The others would lower growth.

13. c. This would lower economic growth (because it violates the goal of having free, open, and unregulated capital markets).

14. d. Stable prices mean low inflation, and an important part of this is keeping the variation of inflation from year to year small and predictable.

15. c. Good policies and institutions are most important for economic growth.

16. b. Tropical countries perform poorly because of their weak economic policies and institutions, not because of the other factors listed.

17. d. All of the items listed promote productive activities.

18. c. Both of these statements are true.

CHAPTER SEVENTEEN

The following are true: 1, 2, 6, 8, 9, 10, 11, 12, 13, 15, 18, 19, 20.

The following are false:

3. While Ireland does have one of the highest per capita incomes, the other three countries have per capita incomes ranking among the lowest in the world.

4. The large European countries have lower incomes than the United States does.

5. Household production, such as people making their own clothes or growing their own food, is excluded from GDP. Thus, per capita GDP tends to be understated (not overstated) for low income economies where this type of activity is more prevalent.

7. The growth rates are closely bunched around 2 percent for these countries.

14. Instead, it is the countries with the highest levels of economic freedom that attract the most investment, and these countries also tend to have higher existing wages.

16. All of the countries that have increased economic freedom have seen substantial sustained positive growth after the reforms. Countries that fell dramatically in economic freedom were the ones that experienced negative growth.

17. A country's legal system is a critical component of economic freedom, especially in the development of larger markets with specialization and depersonalized exchange that require sound contract enforcement.

PROBLEMS AND PROJECTS

1. a. Ireland, Hungary, China
   b. Venezuela, Zimbabwe
   c. The three that improved had higher positive growth rates, while the two that fell had lower or even negative growth rates.

2. a. Ireland
   b. Hong Kong
   c. Switzerland
   d. Canada
   e. Singapore
   f. United States
   g. New Zealand
   h. Estonia

3. The answer to this problem would, of course, depend on your selection of countries. Most likely you found that the countries you think of as more prosperous, or more desirable places to visit or live have higher economic freedom ratings.

MULTIPLE CHOICE

1. a. Economists prefer to use the purchasing power parity (PPP) method.

2. b. This method finds the cost of purchasing an identical bundle of goods and services in each country and then uses that information to convert each country's income to a common currency.

3. c. Of this group, Ireland has the highest per capita income.

4. a. China's growth rate of over 9 percent was by far the highest among this group.

5. c. Some have been among the fastest growing, while others have stagnated.

6. d. This is the definition of economic freedom.

7. a. The other three would all reduce economic freedom.

8. c. Hong Kong is one of the most economically free countries in the world.

9. d. Zimbabwe is one of the lowest scoring countries in the EFW rating.

10. b. Quartiles result in four groups each having one-fourth (or one-quarter) of the observations.

11. d. Countries with higher economic freedom have higher income levels and growth rates, and they also have more investment.

12. a. Better economic institutions (as measured by higher economic freedom) tend to increase the productivity of a country's investment dollars. Investment of all types is beneficial to economic growth, and it tends to flow toward those countries with high levels of economic freedom.

13. e. All of these are examples.

14. b. A sound legal system is one of the most critical components of economic freedom and prosperity, particularly in fostering depersonalized exchange.

15. d. All of these tend to make a country's political system work more effectively to promote economic freedom.

16. a. Former colonies are now able to choose their own policies. The prevalence of communism is falling

and lower transportation and communication costs are putting more pressure on governments to adopt sound policies.

17. d. All of these have contributed to the overall upward trend in EFW ratings across the globe over the past few decades.

18. d. Countries with higher EFW ratings do better in all of these quality of life measures.

CHAPTER EIGHTEEN

TRUE OR FALSE

The following are true: 3, 4, 5, 6, 8, 11, 12, 13.

The following are false:

1. Both countries benefit from free trade.

2. Specific domestic producers of goods that are imported may "lose," and domestic consumers of goods that are exported may "lose," but in both cases the gains of the "winners" outweigh the losses to the "losers."

7. Even countries with an absolute advantage in all goods can gain by trading for goods in which they have a comparative disadvantage.

9. Jobs would be lost in the industries that were protected by the tariffs, but they would be more than offset by gains in other industries.

10. NAFTA has resulted in trade expansions that have benefited all three countries involved.

PROBLEMS AND PROJECTS

1. a. For Lebos, a line from 160 food and zero clothing (point E) in the upper left to zero food and 160 clothing (point A) in the lower right. For Egap, a line from 40 food and zero clothing (point E) in the upper left to zero food and 120 clothing (point A) in the lower right.
    b. D; 40 food; 40 clothing; 40F = 40C
    c. 10 food; 30 clothing; 10F = 30C
    d. Lebos: 1F = 1C; Egap: 1F = 3C; Lebos gives up the least clothing to produce one food and thus has a comparative advantage in food. In terms of one clothing, Lebos: 1C = 1F, Egap: 1C = 1/3F, so Egap has the lowest opportunity cost of producing clothing.
    e. 40 clothing (point D) for Lebos; zero clothing (point E) for Egap
    f. 160; 40; 80
    g. Compared with part e, Lebos has the same amount of food (120) but has more clothing (80 versus 40). Lebos is better off.
    h. From part g, Egap has sent Lebos 80 clothing in exchange for 40 food. So, Egap now has 40 clothing left (it produced 120 and traded away 80) and 40 food. Compared with e, Egap has the same amount of food (40) but more clothing (40 versus zero). Egap is better off.

2. a. $1,500 and 8,000 (where Arcadia's quantity demanded equals Arcadia's quantity supplied)

b. Total quantity demanded: 6,000; 8,000; 10,000; 12,000; 14,000; 16,000. New equilibrium $2,000 and 10,000 (where total quantity demanded equals Arcadia's quantity supplied).

c. Price has risen from $1,500 to $2,000; quantity produced has risen from 8,000 to 10,000; quantity of other goods must have fallen (moved along production possibilities curve).

d. At the new price of $2,000, Arcadians demand only 7,000 compared with 8,000 prior to trade and the higher price. With trade, Arcadia exports 3,000 computers (it produces 10,000 and domestic consumers buy 7,000 of them leaving 3,000 for exports).

e. hurts domestic citizens (higher price and lower consumption) and helps domestic producers (higher price and higher sales)

3. a. $700; 70; 70

b. $500 is the new price; 90 is the quantity demanded (consumed); 90 is the total quantity supplied; 50 is supplied by domestic suppliers (found along the domestic supply curve); 40 is imported (the difference between total supply of 90 and domestic supply of 50).

c. Price rises to $600; quantity demanded (and consumed) falls to 80; domestic production expands to 60; amount imported falls to 20.

d. Everything would be identical with a 20-unit quota as it is with the tariff.

4. a. U.S.; U.S.; South Korea; U.S.

b. South Korea

c. U.S. production: −8; +80
U.S. trade: +10; −50
U.S. consumption: +2; +30
S. Korea production: +16; −32
S. Korea trade: −10; +50
S. Korea consumption: +6; +18

MULTIPLE CHOICE

1. d. Restrictions on imports create benefits only to domestic producers in the import competing industries. Consumers and producers in export industries are made worse off. The losses outweigh the gains and the country is worse off.

2. c. Buy goods abroad when they are cheaper than alternative domestic products.

3. b. It will fall by 4 units from a total of 8 to a total of 4.

4. c. From above, 2 food equals 4 clothing. Dividing both sides by 2 gives 1 food equals 2 clothing.

5. b. Slavia has the comparative advantage in food, Italia in clothing. Remember that low opportunity cost producer and comparative advantage mean the same thing.

6. d. Slavia specializes in food, Italia in clothing, and they trade.

7. b. With free trade, all nations that are involved benefit.

8. a. This is a restatement of the law of comparative advantage.

9. d. They are both levied on imports. A tariff is a tax, while a quota is a limit on the quantity.

10. a. With less foreign competition, the price to domestic consumers will rise, which allows the relatively inefficient U.S. firms to stay in business with their higher costs.

11. a. There is a link between a nation's imports and its exports. Imports give foreign countries the money to buy domestic exports. Lower imports mean lower exports.

12. b. They are harmful by wasting our resources in areas where we are relatively unproductive, thus lowering our standard of living. Consumers pay higher prices for goods (and thus cannot afford as many goods to consume), and only domestic producers in the specific industries gain (producers in export industries suffer).

13. c. Many tariffs, originally put in place to protect infant industries, remain in place forever. It is always politically costly to remove the tariff because of the special interest groups involved.

14. b. The evidence shows that these bad economic policies lead to lower levels of income and economic growth in the long run.

15. b. Consumers will benefit from lower prices; our resources will be redirected to more efficient uses.

16. a. Increased competition lowers price; increased imports generate higher exports.

17. d. Domestic producers would want to stop this action even though domestic consumers would gain substantially. Dumping is selling goods at prices below cost.

18. c. Foreign competition lowers price, which lowers domestic quantity supplied.

19. b. Higher demand raises price, lowering domestic consumption but increasing domestic production (the difference is exported).

20. c.   This is the basic lesson of comparative advantage.

21. c.   The other three are listed in the textbook as "partially valid" reasons for adopting trade restrictions. Their validity is hotly debated.

22. a.   Use a horizontal line at P_W to find the answers. Domestic supply is where this line crosses the domestic supply curve, while domestic consumption is where the horizontal line crosses domestic demand. The difference between these values (100 − 30 = 70) is the value of imports.

23. d.   All are correct. Use a horizontal line at $P_W + t$ to find these values as is described in the answer for question 22.

24. d.   All are correct. $A + B + C + D$ represents the loss in consumer surplus, C the revenue to the government, and A the gain in producer surplus (domestic).

25. a.   A quota equal to the new level of imports with the tariff (30 units) would produce the same price and level of imports.

CHAPTER NINETEEN

TRUE OR FALSE

The following are true: 1, 2, 8, 10, 11.

The following are false:

3.   A balance-of-payments equilibrium is automatic under purely *flexible* exchange rates. With fixed exchange rates, central banks must buy and sell foreign currency to maintain balance.

4.   The exchange rate will move to ensure a balance-of-payments equilibrium.

5.   The foreign exchange market is ruled by supply and demand as is any other market.

6.   Black markets in foreign currency arise when the official exchange rate differs substantially from the exchange rate that would be set by the market.

7.   When a country's balance of trade is in deficit, its current account is nearly always in deficit as well. However, the balance of payments must always balance to zero so this implies a capital account surplus.

9.   When the U.S. imports more than it exports, Americans are able to consume more than they otherwise would. The long-term desirability of a trade deficit depends on the underlying causes of the trade deficit.

12.   A depreciation of the dollar would make U.S. products less expensive to foreigners, causing U.S. exports to increase. However, note that it would make foreign products more expensive to U.S. citizens, causing U.S. imports to fall.

13.   There is no more reason to expect bilateral trade to balance between nations than between individuals.

PROBLEMS AND PROJECTS

1.   a.   About 387,000 Mexican pesos [$30,000 × 12.900 or $30,000 ÷ 0.0775]
      b.   About 120 U.S. dollars [80 × 1.5020 or 80 ÷ 0.666]
      c.   About 28,624 Canadian dollars [2,500,000 ÷ 91.88 × 1.052]
      d.   87.34 [91.88 ÷ 1.052] per Canadian dollar or 0.0114 Canadian dollars per yen, which is exactly what the true exchange rate was between these two currencies on this date.
      e.   The euro and the Japanese yen have appreciated relative to the U.S. dollar, while the Mexican peso has depreciated.

2. b. 0, −, depreciate
   c. −, +, appreciate
   d. −, +, appreciate
   e. 0, 0, no change

3. a. (1) −25.3; (2) 36.1; (3) 3.7; (4) 4.5
   b. There has been a rising current account deficit and a rising capital account surplus to offset it.

MULTIPLE CHOICE

1. d. One dollar now buys more yen, and one yen now buys fewer dollars.

2. b. Capital would leave the U.S. and flow toward England, thus an increase in the supply of dollars and an increase in the demand for the pound. The others would cause an appreciation of the dollar.

3. b. Every dollar traded results in obtaining 100 yen, so 20,000 U.S. dollars would exchange for 2,000,000 yen.

4. d. All would either reduce the supply of dollars or increase the demand for dollars, leading to an appreciation of the dollar.

5. b. If the dollar depreciates, it exchanges for fewer units of foreign currency. Foreign goods become more expensive to U.S. citizens, and U.S. goods become less expensive to foreigners.

6. a. When the peso appreciates, foreign goods become less expensive to Mexicans (thus Mexican imports will rise), but Mexican goods become more expensive to foreigners (so Mexican exports will fall).

7. d. Flexible exchange rates make the balance-of-payments accounts automatically balance.

8. c. A trade deficit is when imports exceed exports.

9. a. The others would supply the foreign currency and create a demand for dollars.

10. a. This is a listing of the two main factors responsible for the trade deficits of the United States. The other answers are the two trade balance fallacies discussed in the chapter. They are both incorrect.

11. b. The trade deficit is not an obligation or a government account. It is simply an aggregate number, such as the number of people who migrated out of (or into) your state this year. The balance of payments must balance, so a current account deficit means a capital account surplus.

12. c. Otherwise, the free market value will differ substantially from the official value causing major balance of payments and official reserve problems.

13. b. Cheaper foreign currency means cheaper foreign goods and services.

14. d. Demand for foreign currency will rise and the supply of foreign currency will fall as investors in all countries shift investment to foreign countries. The domestic currency depreciates as a result.

15. a. An increase in supply (of anything) tends to decrease price (cause depreciation).

16. b. Depreciation makes foreign goods more expensive and domestic goods cheaper.

17. b. Increased exports of U.S. wine and fewer imports of French wine would reduce the trade deficit and thus also reduce the current account deficit.

18. b. When the value of merchandise exports is less than the value of merchandise imports, the country has a trade deficit.

19. b. Higher prices raise demand for foreign exchange (imports) and lower supply (exports).

20. a. The sum of the debit and credit items of the balance-of-payments accounts must balance at a value of zero.

CHAPTER TWENTY

TRUE OR FALSE

The following are true: 1, 2, 3, 4, 5, 7, 9, 12, 14.

The following are false:

6. Consumer surplus is the difference between the maximum price a consumer would be willing to pay (their marginal benefit) and the price.

8. If demand is elastic, total revenue will rise when price is decreased.

10. Marginal benefit is a reflection of marginal utility and thus diminishes with the rate of consumption due to the law of diminishing marginal utility.

11. It would be considered elastic because the price elasticity is greater than one (20 divided by 10 equals 2).

13. If demand is inelastic, total revenue will rise when price is increased.

15. Because consumers have more time to adjust and find substitutes, demand in the long run is more elastic.

PROBLEMS AND PROJECTS

1. a. Sign is always negative; 0.5 or 1/2.
    b. Cigarettes inelastic, oranges elastic; apples less elastic than oranges.
    c. Percent change in price is −0.25 or −1/4 [(7 − 9) ÷ ((7 + 9) ÷ 2) = −2 ÷ 8 = −1/4].
        Percent change in quantity is 0.5 or 1/2 [(50 − 30) ÷ ((50 + 30) ÷ 2) = 20 ÷ 40 = 1/2].
        Price elasticity is −2.0 [0.5 ÷ −0.25 or 1/2 ÷ −1/4]; demand is elastic.

2. a. Yes, because *MB* declines with quantity consumed.
    b. 4, 3, 2, 1
    c. They would be identical. Keri's demand curve is her marginal benefit curve.
    d. $40, 60, 60, 40
    e. increases; inelastic
    f. it stays the same; unitary elastic
    g. decreases; elastic
    h. 0.43 (or 3/7); 1; 2.33 (or 7/3); yes

3. b. 3, 6, 9, 12
    c. 4, 5, 9
    d. Ann's purchases will fall from 4 to 3; Bob's purchases will fall from 5 to 3; Bob's purchases are more responsive to price; Bob has the more elastic demand.

4. a. $600, 800, 600
    b. rises; inelastic; 0.6 or 3/5
    c. falls; elastic; 1.67 or 5/3
    d. It depends. If price is currently $3, lowering it to $2 will increase revenue. If price is currently $2, lowering it to $1 will decrease revenue.
    e. A price of $2 maximizes the total dollars spent and thus would maximize total tip revenue as well if tips are given as a percent of sales.
    f. No, revenue would have increased to $900.
    g. No, revenue would have increased to $900.

5. a. Fall from 70 to 60; fall from 70 to 50; D_2; D_1
    b. Rise from 70 to 80; rise from 70 to 90; D_2; D_1
    c. Answers are the same in either direction.

6. a. $20
    b. No; 3 new customers at $4 each is a gain of only $12 in new customer revenue, not enough to make up for the loss of $20 on his regular customers. His total revenue will fall by $8 ($12 − $20) from $100 to $92.
    c. Yes, exactly enough; 5 new customers at $4 each is a gain of $20 in new customer revenue, exactly what he will be losing on his regular customers. His total revenue will remain unchanged at $100.
    d. Yes, more than enough; 10 new customers at $4 each is a gain of $40 in new customer revenue. His total revenue will rise by $20 ($40 − $20) to $120.
    e. Yes; In part *b*, demand was inelastic so total revenue fell; in part *c*, demand was unitary elastic so total revenue remained the same; in part *d*, demand was elastic so total revenue increased as a result of the price reduction.
    f. If John loses 10 regular customers, he loses the $50 they used to spend. However, 10 customers keep coming and they are each paying $5 more (for a total of $50). The gains exactly equal the losses, so John's total revenue will remain unchanged. If only 5 customers left, his revenue would rise (lose $25 on the 5 who leave, gain $75 on the 15 who stay, so the net is $50 more total revenue). If 15 customers left, his revenue would fall (lose $75 on the 15 who leave, gain $25 on the 5 who stay, so the net is a loss of $50 in revenue). When 5 leave, demand is inelastic so revenue rises; when 10 leave, demand is unitary elastic so revenue remains unchanged; when 15 leave, demand is elastic so revenue falls.

7. Price elasticity: 1.0
    Change in price: up; up
    Change in total revenue: down; no change; up

MULTIPLE CHOICE

1. b. Price elasticity is 30 ÷ 15 = 2, which is greater than one, so demand is elastic. If demand is elastic, a

price increase lowers total expenditure (or total revenue).

2. d. All of these are true statements about marginal benefit.

3. d. Income elasticity is +20 percent ÷ +10 percent = +2. This is positive, so jewelry is a normal good (her purchases rise with higher income). It is also greater than one, which means jewelry is a luxury good for Jane.

4. d. An inferior good is one for which purchases fall when *income* (not price) rises and vice versa. This inverse relationship shows up as a negative income elasticity.

5. a. Wine purchases rise with income so wine is a normal good, but fast food purchases fall with income so fast food is an inferior good.

6. d. As the rate of consumption increases, the additional (or marginal) utility derived from additional units falls.

7. b. The demand is elastic because the value is greater than one. It is larger than the value for bananas so it shows more responsiveness. If demand is elastic, an increase in price lowers total expenditures (or total revenue).

8. d. 10 ÷ 50 = 0.2, which is less than one so demand is inelastic.

9. c. For a higher price to increase total revenue, demand must be inelastic.

10. b. The price elasticity of supply is positive because the quantity producers are willing to supply is directly related to price.

11. a. Demand elasticity always increases with price along a linear demand curve.

12. d. This is why lowering price can either lower revenue, leave it unchanged, or raise revenue. In answer *a,* demand is inelastic; in answer *b,* demand is unitary elastic; and in answer *c,* demand is elastic.

13. a. The issue is not *whether* more people will come or not, but *how many* more people will come. This is answered by elasticity. If demand is elastic, revenue will rise when price is lowered. If demand is inelastic, revenue will fall. The previous question (question 12) gives a numerical example to illustrate this point.

14. a. The numbers here are irrelevant. If an increase in price decreases total revenue, demand must be

elastic. Remember, total revenue is *not* the same as quantity so these numbers cannot be directly used in the elasticity formula.

15. d. Consumers generally have incomplete information. This is why we sometimes make mistakes in our purchases, but we learn from these mistakes and make future choices more wisely.

16. c. To maximize utility, she should equate MU/P for both goods. Currently MU/P for hamburgers is 10/2 = 5, while MU/P for shirts is 50/25 = 2. Hamburgers are giving her more utility per dollar than are shirts, so she should buy fewer shirts and more hamburgers to maximize her utility.

17. c. The *marginal* cost of flying is $450 ($600 − $150), while the *marginal* benefit of flying is the 45 hours (50 − 5) of time saved. It is only worth spending the extra $450 to save 45 hours if you value your time at $10 per hour or more.

18. b. A demand curve with a steeper (more negative) slope shows less responsiveness to price so it is relatively more inelastic.

19. a. Total expenditures will be increased by a higher price if demand is inelastic.

20. b. (90 − 70)/((90 + 70)/2) ÷ (10 − 6)/((10 + 6)/2) = 20/80 ÷ 4/8 = 1/4 ÷ 1/2 = 1/2.

21. c. Greater than one is elastic. When a fraction is greater than one, it means the numerator (the percent change in quantity) is greater than the denominator (the percent change in price).

22. b. Consumer surplus is equal to the difference between the maximum a consumer would be willing to pay ($100) and the price actually paid ($40), so $100 − $40 = $60.

23. a. The total amount purchased in the market at a given price is the sum of the amounts purchased by all individuals at that price.

24. a. He *substitutes* away from the place whose prices have risen, and the reduction in his *real income* will cause him to cut back on eating out.

25. a. It measures how the quantity purchased by buyers responds to a price change.

26. d. All of these are true regarding demand elasticity.

CHAPTER TWENTY-ONE

TRUE OR FALSE

The following are true: 1, 3, 4, 5, 6, 7, 10, 11, 13.

The following are false:

2. Economic profit calculations differ because they include opportunity costs. Thus, economic profit calculations generally have higher levels of cost and thus lower levels of profit.

8. It is called marginal cost. Average variable cost is total variable cost divided by output.

9. Average cost will always increase when marginal cost is above average cost. It does not matter whether the marginal cost is increasing, decreasing, or remaining constant.

12. Total cost may be found by adding total variable cost and total fixed cost.

14. It is experiencing economies of scale. Disecono-mies of scale are when per unit costs rise with increased plant size in the long run.

15. It would shift the cost curves downward because the cost of production would decline.

16. A good decision maker ignores sunk costs when making decisions.

PROBLEMS AND PROJECTS

1. a. $9,000
   b. the opportunity cost of his equity capital, which is the forgone interest he could have earned on the $30,000 and the opportunity cost of his labor, which is the forgone wages he could have earned working for someone else (here given as $10,000)
   c. $3,000
   d. His total cost would be $48,000 + $3,000 + $10,000 = $61,000.
   e. He is making an economic loss of $4,000, which shows that he could make more money in his next best alternative. If he shut down, put his money back in the bank, and worked for the other person, he would make $4,000 more income per year. He is making $9,000 in accounting profit now but could make $3,000 of interest income plus $10,000 of regular wage income for a total of $13,000 in his next best alternative.

2. a. MP: 8, 16, 12, 8, 6, 4, 2, 0 (calculated as the change in total product)

   AP: 8, 12, 12, 11, 10, 9, 8, 7 (calculated total product divided by units of labor)
   c. After the second unit of labor, because this is the point after which MP begins to fall. You could say that diminishing returns begins on the third unit of labor, but we generally say that diminishing returns begin after the second unit because some firms can employ fractions of units of inputs (such as pounds of steel).

3. a. TFC: $50, 50, 50, 50, 50, 50, 50 (Remember TFC stays the same at all levels of output.)
   TVC: $50, 90, 127, 166, 215, 274, 349, 446 (equal to TC minus TFC)
   ATC: $100, 70, 59, 54, 53, 54, 57, 62 (equal to TC divided by output)
   AVC: $50, 45, 42.33, 41.50, 43, 45.67, 49.86, 55.75 (equal to TVC divided by output)
   MC: $50, 40, 37, 39, 49, 59, 75, 97 (equal to the change in TC from before; to find MC for the first unit, remember that the total cost of producing zero units of output is equal to total fixed cost [$50] because total variable cost is zero when no units are produced)
   b. 5, because this is the output level where the number in the ATC column is the smallest.
   c. after the third unit, because MC is at its minimum at 3 units of output. See the answer for 2c above about the terminology.

4. ATC: $120, 100; AVC: $70, 75; MC: $60, 100
   a. $360 (equal to ATC times Q), 210 (AVC times Q), and 150 (equal to either AFC times Q or TC minus TVC)
   b. $600, 450, 150
   c. $500 (total cost of six units is $600 and the MC of the sixth unit was $100, so $600 minus $100 was the total cost of five units)
   d. $150 (it is the same at all output levels)
   e. $50, 25 (either TFC divided by output or ATC minus AVC)
   f. Total cost is the rectangle with the corners: 0, $120, the ATC curve at three units, and the quantity 3. This rectangle has a bottom of length three and a side of length $120, so its area is $120 times 3 or $360, which is the total cost of producing 3 units. If the rectangle is divided into upper and lower parts at a value of $70 (by the AVC curve), the upper portion is TFC and the lower portion is TVC.

5. a. 5; (35 − 30)
   b. 150; (300 ÷ 2)
   c. $10; (TC is $100 + $200 = $300, so ATC is $300 ÷ 30)
   d. $3; (5 − 2)
   e. $100; (5 × 20)
   f. $5; (45 − 40)

  g. $350; (TFC same at all levels of output)

  h. $4; (200 ÷ 50)

  i. $700; (TVC is $100 × 5 = $500, so TC is $500 + $200)

  j. $2; (50 ÷ 25)

  k. $6,000; ($5,000,000 + $1,000,000 = $6,000,000 is TC, so ATC is $6,000,000 ÷ 1,000)

MULTIPLE CHOICE

1. d. The marginal cost curve is a reflection of the marginal product curve.

2. c. These are the "fixed" factors of production. They take the most time to change.

3. b. This is the definition of sunk cost.

4. d. Both of these are advantages.

5. c. AFC, which is the difference between ATC and AVC, declines with output.

6. d. This productivity or technological advance would lower costs.

7. d. MC crosses ATC at the minimum of ATC.

8. d. It can be stated either way. They mean the same thing.

9. d. Find 10 on the horizontal (quantity) axis, then go up to the ATC curve.

10. a. AFC = ATC − AVC = 12 − 8.

11. d. Equal to ATC times quantity (13 × 10).

12. b. AFC times quantity. AFC is ATC minus AVC or 13 − 7 = 6, so 6 × 10 = 60.

13. a. Find 10 on the horizontal (quantity) axis, then go up to the MC curve.

14. c. This is where the ATC curve is at its minimum.

15. a. This is where the MC curve is at its minimum.

16. b. The $300 will have to be paid whether the house is rented or not. It is a sunk cost and should not be considered. Any rent over $100 will allow the family to pay the $100 utilities and at least have some left over to put toward the mortgage payment.

17. c. The decision at hand is whether to pay $2 to watch a movie you value at $5. The $3.50 paid originally is a sunk cost because the movie store will not refund it if you bring it back and say that you did not get a chance to watch it.

18. c. The others shift it upward.

19. a. Economic profits subtract more costs (the opportunity costs) and are thus generally lower.

20. d. When per-unit costs fall as plant size is expanded, the LRATC curve will slope downward.

21. b. This is a definition.

22. b. Rules are implemented to minimize employee shirking.

23. c. Limited liability makes investing in a corporation less risky than in other forms of business because the remainder of your assets are not held against the debts of the company.

24. c. Accounting profit is $100,000 − $60,000, while economic profit is $100,000 − $90,000. Her economic cost is the accounting cost of $60,000 plus the opportunity cost of her equity capital (the forgone interest of $2,000) plus her forgone wages of $28,000.

25. c. Zero economic profit means accounting profits equal opportunity costs.

26. c. In the long run, all factors of production can be changed.

27. c. Remember, MC always "pulls" ATC.

28. b. Most of the information is irrelevant. To find AFC at 20 units, we need to know TFC and then divide it by output. We know AFC is $14 when output is 10, so TFC is $140. Then $140 divided by 20 gives the answer.

29. b. This is just an application of the law of diminishing returns. Do not confuse it with the law of diminishing marginal utility which applies to consumers.

30. b. This is one of the reasons for economies of scale listed in the book.

CHAPTER TWENTY-TWO

TRUE OR FALSE

The following are true: 1, 2, 4, 5, 7, 8, 9, 11, 15.

The following are false:

3. For a price taker, marginal revenue is equal to price.

6. A firm's short-run supply curve is its marginal cost (MC) curve above average variable cost (AVC).

10. They always produce where MC = MR but only produce where ATC is at its minimum in the long run.

12. Zero economic profit means that the firm is earning an accounting profit that is typical of the profit it could earn elsewhere in other industries. There is no reason for the firm to leave or for firms from other industries to enter.

13. In a constant cost industry, long-run supply is horizontal and market price will return to its original level. It would rise for an increasing cost industry.

14. Fixed costs remain present when a firm shuts down in the short run.

PROBLEMS AND PROJECTS

1. a. Total Revenue: $0, 25, 50, 75, 100, 125, 150
    b. Marginal Revenue: $25, 25, 25, 25, 25, 25; equal to price
    c. Marginal Cost: $10, 5, 10, 20, 30, 40
    d. Profit: $–20, –5, +15, +30, +35, +30, +15
    e. Produce all units up to where marginal cost equals price ($MC = P$)
    f. Yes; it falls when the unit is produced.
    g. 4; 4; yes
    h. 6
    i. No change; profit equals $105 for both.

2. a. Total Cost: $0, 10, 30, 60, 100, 150
    b. Marginal Cost: $10, 20, 30, 40, 50
    c. 3
    d. $60; $20; $10
    e. 3 tons × $10 per unit profit equals $30; $90 total revenue minus $60 total cost equals $30; yes.

3. a. Output is 1,000 (total revenue divided by price); total cost is $8,000 (average total cost times quantity); marginal revenue is 8 (marginal revenue equals price); marginal cost is 8 (marginal cost equals marginal revenue when maximizing profits); total profit is $0 (total revenue minus total cost).
    b. Yes (zero economic profit).
    c. Stay the same.

4. a. 60 (the output level where $MC = MR$)
    b. $1,200 total revenue ($20 price × 60 units); $600 total cost ($10 average cost per unit × 60 units); $600 profit ($1,200 total revenue minus $600 total cost).
    c. It is the rectangle above $10 and below $20 from the price axis out to 60 units.
    d. $550; less.
    e. 200 firms (12,000 total units of output ÷ 60 units per firm)
    f. Firms would enter because there are economic profits; price would fall to minimum average total cost which is $9.

5. a. Economic profit; increase
    b. Zero economic profit; stay the same
    c. Economic loss; decrease; remain open in short run

6. a. New market price where D_2 intersects S.
    b. Profits increase; firm output increases.
    c. More firms will enter.

7. a. Price: $60, 40, 30, 50
        Rooms rented: 30, 20, 0, 25
        Profits: +, –, –, 0
    b. No; shut down during summer because price is below AVC, thus you will rent no rooms during the summer.
    c. You would see whether the profits during some seasons are enough to offset the losses during others so that you did not have losses for the entire year.

MULTIPLE CHOICE

1. c. In a price-taker market, there are a large number of small firms producing identical products. They must take the market price as given and will earn zero economic profits in the long run.

2. a. This is the definition. A price-searcher firm can set its own price, but the number of units sold will depend on the price chosen because the firm will face a downward-sloping demand curve.

3. a. For a price taker, marginal revenue equals price.

4. c. This is the rule for profit maximization. For a price-taker firm, because price equals marginal revenue, this could also be correctly stated as marginal cost equals price.

5. a. This unit adds more to revenue than it does to cost.

6. c. It is earning $4 profit on each unit, times 50 units.

7. d. These are the two important things to remember about marginal revenue for the price-taker firm.

8. c. Zero economic profit means that the firm is doing as well as it could in other alternative industries. There is no incentive for the firm to exit or for other firms to enter.

9. c. Marginal revenue is the change in total revenue, while marginal cost is the change in total cost.

10. a. This is an alternative term that you might run into in another economics class.

11. d. This is how a price-taker market reaches long-run equilibrium.

12. d. Higher demand increases price, firms expand output, and the profits attract new competition.

13. b. Short-run profits (price above average total cost) attract new firms into the industry until zero economic profit (price equal to average total cost) is restored.

14. d. All of these are true.

15. d. Lower demand reduces price, causing losses and firms to exit.

16. b. A firm's short-run supply curve is its marginal cost curve above average variable cost.

17. a. Both *b* and *c* are opposites of what is correct.

18. a. In an increasing cost industry, all firms' costs rise with the entry of new additional firms because resource prices in the industry are bid upward.

19. d. It will create losses in the short run, some firms will go out of business, and the market price will rise until the remaining firms can cover their costs (including the cost of the antipollution devices).

20. b. As long as a market is "open" and firms are free to enter and exit, the industry can earn neither abnormally high nor abnormally low profits in the long run.

21. b. Because the firm will shut down in the short run at prices lower than *AVC*, the short-run supply curve is only the portion of MC above AVC.

22. a. Total revenue ($400) is larger than total variable cost ($300), so you should remain open. If you shut down, your loss is equal to your rent and other fixed costs of $200. If you remain open, you lose only $100. Put in another way, even though you cannot cover your entire rent, you are at least making $100 from being open to put toward your rent.

23. c. It should continue to operate until the lease expires because it can cover its variable cost. This answer is similar in logic to the previous question.

24. a. In his own words he has said that he follows the marginal-cost/marginal-revenue rule and also that he is out to maximize profit. This producer is exactly what is being modeled in "fancy" economic theory.

25. d. This is how price changes in a market economy help to redirect resources when consumer tastes (or other conditions) change.

26. c. Profit is equal to $10 at an output level of three units. You can work this problem in two ways, either by computing marginal cost and producing every unit with marginal cost less than price or by computing total revenue and finding actual profit for each level of output, then selecting the level with the highest profit.

27. c. This is the level of output where *MC* equals *MR* (at point *F*).

28. b. It is a profit, not a loss, because *P* is greater than *ATC*. Profit is the area that represents per unit profit times quantity $[(P - ATC) \times q]$.

29. a. Positive economic profits will attract new firms into the industry.

30. d. Because price equals *ATC*, there is zero economic profit; the industry is in long-run equilibrium.

31. c. This is the level of output where *MC* equals *MR* (at point *H*). The firm would not shut down in the short run because price exceeds *AVC*.

32. c. It is a loss because *P* is lower than *ATC*. The loss is the area that represents per unit loss times quantity $[(P - ATC) \times q]$.

33. b. Some of the firms experiencing losses will shut down, and market price will rise until the remaining firms earn zero economic profit.

34. a. Price is less than *AVC*; the firm should shut down in the short run.

35. a. An upward-sloping long-run supply curve shows that it is an increasing cost industry.

CHAPTER TWENTY-THREE

TRUE OR FALSE

The following are true: 2, 5, 6, 7, 9, 10, 12, 14, 16, 17.

The following are false:

1. All firms, regardless of market conditions or industry, maximize profits by producing at $MR = MC$.

3. Price discrimination is the practice of charging different prices to different customers for the same product.

4. For a price searcher, marginal revenue is less than price, so the marginal revenue curve lies below the demand curve for the firm.

8. The entry of new firms will result in a reduction in demand for existing firms in the market.

11. A contestable market is one in which the barriers to entry are low, in other words, the cost of entry and exit is low.

13. Price will be greater than marginal cost. The firm will equate marginal cost and marginal revenue, but for a price-searcher firm, marginal revenue is less than price. Thus, marginal cost is also less than price.

15. Marginal revenue is the change in total revenue. Three units at a price of $5 yields total revenue of $15, while four units at a price of $4 yields total revenue of $16. Thus, the marginal revenue from the sale of the fourth unit is $1 (the difference, $16 − $15). Note that this is less than the price at which the fourth unit is sold.

PROBLEMS AND PROJECTS

1. a. Total Revenue: $0, 60, 110, 150, 180, 200, 210
        Marginal Revenue: $60, 50, 40, 30, 20, 10
        Marginal Cost: $50, 20, 25, 29, 40, 50
        Profit: $−40, −30, 0, 15, 16, −4, −44
    b. To maximize profit, charge a price of $45 and produce a total of 4 units. You can find this either by finding the row in the table with the highest total profit or by using the marginal-cost/marginal-revenue rule.
    c. Price of $45 is greater than marginal cost of $29.
    d. The demand curve for your firm would drop as other firms entered the business, drawing away some of your customers. This would continue to occur until all firms earned only zero economic profit.

2. a. The firm is a price searcher because it faces a downward-sloping demand curve.

b. The output is where $MR = MC$; the price is the price on the demand curve associated with the profit-maximizing output.
c. The firm is making a profit because its price is greater than its ATC.
d. The positive economic profits will attract competitors to the industry. As new firms enter the market, the demand curve for this firm will decrease (shift downward and to the left) until it is exactly tangent to the ATC curve.

3. a. The output is where $MR = MC$; the price is the price on the demand curve associated with the profit-maximizing output.
    b. The firm is making a loss because its price is less than its ATC. It will remain open in the short run because price is still above AVC.
    c. The economic losses will cause some firms to exit the industry until the demand curves for the remaining firms increase enough to restore zero economic profit. This will happen when this firm's demand curve shifts upward and to the right until it is exactly tangent to the ATC curve.

4. a. 1, students have more limited budgets and more substitute activities available to them.
    b. 2, they have more options available (different possible dates of travel, different possible transportation such as a car or bus, etc.)
    c. 1, these people have the option of continuing to drive their current car.
    d. 1, the poor will have more limited budgets and will be more sensitive to price.

MULTIPLE CHOICE

1. d. Differentiability of goods and services is an important reason why competitive price searchers experience downward-sloping demand curves, unlike the horizontal demand curve confronting price takers.

2. d. All of these conditions will be met.

3. d. To maximize profit, all decisions should be made with this rule.

4. a. The money lost on the earlier units (for which price was lowered) is why producing an additional unit adds less to revenue than the price at which it is sold.

5. c. A price searcher is different because they face a downward-sloping demand curve. The demand curve for a price taker is a horizontal line at the market price.

6. a.   These are the conditions that define a competitive price-searcher market. Note that answer *d* contains the conditions for an open price-taker market.

7. a.   This is the difference in total revenue. Four units at a price of $6 yields total revenue of $24, while five units at a price of $5 yields total revenue of $25. By producing and selling this additional unit, revenue increases by $1.

8. b.   This is how the market will return to zero economic profit in the long run.

9. d.   Answer *c* is incorrect because $P > MC$ for the price searcher.

10. d.   This is the definition of a contestable market. It has low barriers to entry.

11. c.   This is the main result both markets share in common.

12. d.   Answer *c* is incorrect because a price searcher does not maximize profits at this point, see the next question.

13. c.   This is a potential source of inefficiency in price-searcher markets.

14. b.   The standard model of competitive price searchers does not account for the benefits consumers derive from product differentiation. As a specific example, the model simply shows that if all brands of beer were exactly identical, beer could be produced at a lower per-unit cost and sold at a lower price to consumers.

15. c.   Since entry barriers are low, economic profits will attract new entrants. Existing firms will experience a drop in the demand for their product, and prices will fall until zero economic profits are restored.

16. b.   Firms charge those groups with the more elastic (or less inelastic) demand lower prices, and those groups with the more inelastic (or less elastic) demand higher prices. The result is generally a larger output and an improvement in allocative efficiency.

17. a.   This is a basic similarity between price-taker and competitive price-searcher industries. This condition is true for any contestable market (any market in which the cost of entry and exit is low).

18. a.   Quantity (*E*) is where $MR = MC$, and the demand curve gives the price that firms are able to charge for that quantity (*A*).

19. a.   Profit = $TR - TC = (P \times q) - (ATC \times q) = q \times (P - ATC)$, or in words, profit is equal to per-unit profit $(P - ATC)$ times the quantity sold (*q*). Per-unit profit is equal to the height *KG* and the quantity is equal to the width of *CK*. This is a profit, not a loss because price exceeds *ATC*.

20. b.   Profits attract new competitors into the industry who will draw away some of this firm's customers, reducing demand.

21. b.   Quantity *I* is where $MR = MC$, and the demand curve gives the price firms are able to charge for that quantity *C*.

22. d.   This is a loss because price is less than *ATC*. Per-unit loss is equal to the height *EF* and the quantity is equal to the width of *CF*. The entire area is the total loss.

23. b.   Some firms will exit due to the losses, and the demand for the remaining firms will increase.

24. b.   Total profit is $12 at this price and output, higher than at the other levels. You can find this answer either by finding the row in the table with the highest total profit or by using the marginal-cost/marginal-revenue rule.

25. b.   The new, rival businesses that drive out old competitors tend to be the ones that find new, more efficient and creative ways of satisfying consumers. The failure of the old businesses allows the assets and resources from that failed business to move into other areas where those resources are now more productive and highly valued.

26. a.   Entrepreneurial discovery and innovation are important keys to economic prosperity. The traditional, profit-maximizing graphical model of the firm does not fully incorporate the role of the entrepreneur.

CHAPTER TWENTY-FOUR

TRUE OR FALSE

The following are true: 1, 5, 7, 8, 9, 11, 12, 13, 14.

2. High barriers preventing the entry of new competitors make it possible for monopolies to earn economic profits in the long run.

3. To maximize profits, all firms produce the output level where $MR = MC$.

4. Inefficient production means higher costs that lead to lower profits, so the monopolist still has some incentive to produce efficiently.

6. A market dominated by a monopoly will have a higher price and a lower level of output than if it were competitive.

10. Market power refers to the ability of the firm to earn abnormally high profits. A firm facing heavy competition has the least market power.

PROBLEMS AND PROJECTS

1. a. Since the *LRATC* curve decreases over the range of quantities that are demanded, a single firm would be the lowest-cost producer. This is a situation of natural monopoly.
   b. The firm will produce the Q where $MR = MC$.
   c. The firm will charge the price from the demand curve associated with the quantity in part *b*.
   d. It is the area between the demand curve and *ATC* out to the profit-maximizing level of output.

2. a. *TR*: 6,400, 7,000, 7,800, 8,400, 8,800, 9,000, 9,000
      MR: 600, 800, 600, 400, 200, 0
      MC: 400, 400, 500, 700, 1,000, 1,200
   b. $1.20
   c. Yes; $1,100 per month
   d. Approximately $13,200 ($1,100 per month times 12 months) or the present value of the expected economic profit; the university would then reap the monopoly benefits.

3. a. P_4, Q_1, the area with height of P_2 to P_4 and width out to Q_1
   b. Q_2, P_3 (where *MC* intersects *D*)

4. a. P_1, Q_2
   b. P_2, Q_1

5. a. 50,000 units of output
   b. 30 cents.
   c. It will increase to 40 cents.

d. no; 3 (150 ÷ 50); 6 (300 ÷ 50)

6. a. Upper left: Tom's $6,000; Bob's $6,000
      Upper right: Tom's $2,000; Bob's $9,000
      Lower right: Tom's $8,000; Bob's $8,000
   b. $30 (yields $6,000, which is larger than the profit of $2,000 at a price of $40)
   c. $30 (yields $9,000, which is larger than the profit of $8,000 at a price of $40)
   d. No, set price at $30 is best strategy in both cases.
   e. $30; no
   f. Both earn $6,000; yes, both would earn $8,000.
   g. No, both have an incentive to cheat (lower price to $30) to increase profits.

7. a. P_3 and Q_1 (at point A); yes
   b. P_2 and Q_2 (at point B); zero
   c. P_1; an economic loss; the monopolist would shut down, so output in the long run would be zero

MULTIPLE CHOICE

1. b. This is the definition of a monopoly market.

2. b. The others violate at least one of the market conditions necessary to be a monopoly.

3. c. The elasticity of demand has nothing to do with how easy it is for new firms to enter the market. The only other barrier not listed is economies of scale.

4. a. Economies of scale are present if per-unit costs fall as a firm increases its size in the long run. If present, one large firm will have lower costs than several smaller firms.

5. d. They "restrict" output to increase price. Alternatively, you may remember that monopolies charge higher prices and thus sell fewer units of output.

6. d. It results in higher prices and positive economic profit opportunity while the barrier to entry is in place.

7. d. A monopolist can lose money if costs exceed the price consumers are willing to pay, it will charge the price that maximizes their profit, and will make higher profits the more it can reduce costs.

8. d. All of these conditions are true.

9. b. At a price of $5 and an output of 3 units, the monopolist earns a profit of $5 (total revenue of $15 minus total cost of $10), higher than for any other level of output in the exhibit.

10. d. This is the major difference between the markets that arises due to the barriers to entry under monopoly.

11. d. Produce the level of output where $MC = MR$, and set price up along the demand curve.

12. c. Produce the level of output where $MC = MR$, set price up along the demand curve, profit is equal to the difference between price and ATC (which is per-unit profit) times the number of units sold.

13. a. This is the definition of an oligopoly market.

14. b. OPEC is an example of a specific cartel. They attempt to act like a single monopoly and maximize joint profit.

15. a. A higher market price for oil, for example, will only come about if less oil is produced.

16. c. Cartels restrict output and raise price, in any industry.

17. a. The first major antitrust law was the Sherman Act.

18. c. The others would make successful collusion less likely.

19. d. This is why collusive agreements are so unstable. The prisoners' dilemma is one frequently used tool to demonstrate these incentives.

20. a. Cartels result in higher prices and lower output. Don't forget the law of demand; as funeral prices rise, some people will be cremated, while others might be buried in other nearby towns. There is no such thing as a perfectly inelastic demand curve.

21. d. More often than not, regulatory agencies end up using their power to help the established firms in the industry at the expense of consumers.

22. a. The only way you can earn positive economic profits in the long run is to prevent new firms from entering and offering your customers cheaper prices. This can only be done by legal restrictions on the ability of new firms to enter.

23. d. While regulation "ideally" could improve the situation, the real-world problems are generally very large in implementing the ideal outcomes.

24. c. Without a profit motive, government agencies have no incentive to conserve on resources to cut costs.

CHAPTER TWENTY-FIVE

TRUE OR FALSE

The following are true: 2, 3, 5, 7, 11, 12, 13, 14.

The following are false:

1. Machines can be substituted for workers and vice versa.

4. When the demand for a final product increases, the demand for resources used to produce the good will increase as well.

6. This is true for a price-taker firm, not a price-searcher firm. For a price-searcher firm, marginal revenue (MR) is less than price (P), so MRP is less than VMP.

8. They will stop hiring before that point because they will hire only until marginal revenue product falls to equal the market wage rate.

9. The correct formula is marginal product (MP) divided by price (P), not MRP divided by price.

10. With more time to adjust, the long-run supply will be more elastic, not more inelastic.

PROBLEMS AND PROJECTS

1. a. MP: 5, 4, 3, 2, 1
    TR: 500, 900, 1200, 1400, 1500
    MRP: 500, 400, 300, 200, 100
    b. three
    c. two
    d. New TR: 750, 1350, 1800, 2100, 2250
    New MRP: 750, 600, 450, 300, 150
    New employment level = 4, so she hires one more worker relative to part b.

2. a. MP: 5, 7, 6, 3.5, 2.5, 1
    TR: 500, 1200, 1800, 2150, 2400, 2500
    MRP: 500, 700, 600, 350, 250, 100
    b. five
    c. four

3. a. 0, –, +, –
    b. +, 0, +, +
    c. 0, +, –, +
    d. –, 0, –, –
    e. +, 0, +, +

4. a. No, MP of Vitacorn/P of Vitacorn = 200/800 < 400/1200 = MP of Cornpower/P of Corn-power.
    b. The farmer could produce the same output for $400 less.

c. Yes, the decrease in the *MP* of Cornpower as its usage increases will cause the ratio of the *MP* of Cornpower to its price to decrease, eventually fulfilling the condition for cost minimization: *MP* of Vitacorn/*P* of Vitacorn = *MP* of Cornpower/*P* of Cornpower.

5. a. For U.S. workers, *MP/P* = 60/10 = 6. For Mexican workers, *MP/P* = 30/6 = 5. This means the firm is getting six units of output per dollar spent on U.S. labor, while it would get only five units of output per dollar spent on Mexican labor.

b. Because *MP/P* is lower in Mexico, costs would be higher. As an easy example, to produce 60 units would require one U.S. worker at a cost of $10, while it would take two Mexican workers (with *MP* of 30 each) to produce 60 units at a cost of $12 total (two workers at $6).

c. *MP/P* would become equal at a Mexican wage rate of $5. So at any wage rate below $5, it would be profitable to move to Mexico to lower costs.

MULTIPLE CHOICE

1. c. There will be many workers with these skills (many close substitutes).

2. a. The demand for resources is derived from the demand for the product.

3. a. A small change in resource price raises product cost and reduces sales greatly. Again, the demand for resources is derived from the demand for the product.

4. b. Additional employment would add more to revenue than it would add to cost.

5. a. We say it is derived from the demand for the product.

6. b. In the long run, it is easier to change production methods to use more or less substitute resources.

7. c. Since *P* = *MR*, *MRP* = *VMP*.

8. d. This would equate *MP/P* for skilled and unskilled labor.

9. a. This is the condition for a firm to minimize its costs (or maximize its profits)

10. d. All of these are listed in the text as shifting the demand curve for a resource.

11. b. Currently *MP/P* for labor is 40 ÷ 20 = 2, while *MP/P* for capital is 10 ÷ 10 = 1, so the firm is not minimizing its costs. It should substitute into the one with the higher ratio (labor) and away from the one with the lower ratio (capital).

12. d. The aid would attract more students, increasing the supply of college graduates and lowering their wages.

13. b. In competitive labor markets, wages equal workers marginal revenue products. If college graduates did not have higher MP, their wages would not be higher.

14. b. Human capital is the skills and knowledge of a person. Investing in human capital is when a person spends money or other resources to increase their human capital.

15. b. Higher worker wages will mean a higher price for the final product. If the demand for the final product is very elastic, then sales of the final product will fall substantially, meaning fewer workers will be needed to produce the steel.

16. b. *MRP* equals *MP* times price. *MP* of the fifth worker is the change in total output that the fifth worker causes, which is 20 − 18 = 2. So *MP* times price is 2 × $2 = $4.

17. b. The firm should hire only those workers for which *MRP* is greater than the wage of $5.

18. a. The firm should hire only those workers for which *MRP* is greater than the wage of $7.

19. c. The fifth workers marginal product is 20 − 17 = 3. So *MP* times price is 3 × $200 = $600.

20. d. Hire only if the additional revenue (*MRP*) exceeds the additional cost.

21. d. It is the change in units of output multiplied by the price they can be sold for, so this is the same as the change in the firm's revenue.

22. b. This is why they are the same for a price-taker firm because *P* = *MR*.

23. d. Higher demand raises price and creates an incentive to supply more of the resource.

24. b. Or alternatively, you might say it is more inelastic in the short run.

25. b. Never employ a resource that costs more to hire than its value to the firm.

CHAPTER TWENTY-SIX

TRUE OR FALSE

The following are true: 2, 3, 6, 7, 9, 10, 11, 12, 13, 15.

The following are false:

1. This is not sufficient. Workers would have to have identical preferences, jobs would all have to be equally attractive, and labor would have to be perfectly mobile.

4. There is a strong positive relationship. More education leads to higher earnings.

5. The top performer gets a wage greater than MRP, the others get wages less than MRP.

8. It will have a higher wage to compensate the worker for taking on the higher level of risk.

14. Automation can increase employment in the industries that it affects. In addition, consumers will save money on goods and services that are cheaper due to automation, they will use that saved money to demand other goods and services.

PROBLEMS AND PROJECTS

1. a. –
    b. +
    c. +
    d. –
    e. +
    f. –

2. a. Jane earns more in the form of money earnings.
    b. Both have identical total compensation (they are in identical jobs). The compensation is just given differently at the two companies.
    c. Yes, Bob would gain more value from the benefits to make it worthwhile to give up $5,000 in money earnings to get these benefits.
    d. Jane would have to decide whether these benefits were worth $5,000 to her. For example, she might be able to buy a private health-insurance plan outside her employer for $2,000 and get her own child care locally for $2,000, in which case it would not make sense to pay the employer $5,000 to provide these for her.

3. a. Q = 3,000; P = $300
    b. Q = 4,000; P = $200
    c. Originally the industry employed 50 workers for every 1,000 calculators produced, or a total of 150 (50 × 3) workers when it produced 3,000 calcula-

tors. Now it employs 40 workers for every 1,000 produced, or a total of 160 (40 × 4). Employment has risen by 10 workers due to the increased output afforded by the automation lowering the price to consumers.
    d. See the "Myths of Economics" box in this chapter for a good refutation of this statement.

4. a. A1
    b. B1
    c. B2
    d. B3

MULTIPLE CHOICE

1. a. A college education increases your productivity on the job.

2. a. Security of income attracts more workers (increases supply) and lowers wages in secure professions relative to insecure ones.

3. d. All of these make the job more attractive, increasing the supply of labor into the occupation and lowering the wage rate.

4. a. Worker preferences, like other differences across people, create earnings differences.

5. a. Tournament pay is a theory to describe situations where the "winner" receives a very high reward, while those just underneath the winner receive substantially less.

6. d. All of these are possible sources of earnings differences.

7. b. The market punishes discriminatory firms by lowering their profits when the discrimination is rooted in the employer (not the customers). To be more selective, the firm's costs will have to rise.

8. a. Productivity growth has risen in recent years, most likely because of the improvements in computer speed and technology.

9. c. Growth of the physical capital stock through investment increases labor productivity and is a major driving force for real wage growth.

10. a. Services of more productive workers are worth more; undesirable jobs would pay more.

11. c. True, although automation can harm specific individuals or groups.

12. b. Higher supply of labor into the occupation would lower wages.

13. b.   Customers will be willing to pay higher prices or buy more from the discriminating firm.

14. d.   The benefit of a tournament pay system is that it increases effort among all workers.

15. d.   This is an example of a situation where a firm may discriminate in its hiring based upon customer preferences.

CHAPTER TWENTY-SEVEN

TRUE OR FALSE

The following are true: 1, 2, 3, 4, 6, 7, 10, 12, 13, 14.

The following are false:

5.   It will rise if the interest rate falls.

8.   The real rate of interest represents the true cost.

9.   More risk increases the interest rate.

11. Stock prices adjust rapidly to reflect any changes in how the market perceives the profitability of a given corporation.

PROBLEMS AND PROJECTS

1. a.   A (because A has the higher inflation premium)
    b.   C (because C has higher demand for borrowing loanable funds)
    c.   F (because F has the lower supply of loanable funds)
    d.   G (because G has the higher risk premium)

2. a.   At a price of $2 per board foot, the extra 10,000 board feet is equal to $20,000 in future revenue received 30 years from now. Discounted to present value, this is equal to $4,627.55 (found as $20,000 $\div [1 + 0.05]^{30}$) when the interest rate is 5 percent, so it is a worthwhile investment because it costs less than this amount. At 10 percent, the present value is $1,146.17 (found as $20,000 $\div [1 + 0.1]^{30}$), still enough to make the investment worthwhile, but at 15 percent the value falls to $302.06 (found as $20,000 $\div [1 + 0.15]^{30}$), below the cost of $500, so it is no longer worthwhile.
    b.   At a price of $1 per board foot, the extra 10,000 board feet is equal to $10,000 in future revenue received 30 years from now. Discounted to present value, this is equal to $151.03, less than the $500 cost of the investment. At a price of $2, the present value becomes $302.06 still below the cost, but at a price of $4, the present value is $604.12, so it becomes worthwhile.

3. a.   The present value of receiving $1,000 per year forever at an interest rate of 8 percent (found as $1,000 $\div$ 0.08) is $12,500. This is a fairly close approximation to the true value of $12,234.
    b. $4,761,900 (found as $333,333 $\div$ 0.07), which is a fairly close approximation to the true value of $4,136,329
    c. $15,000 (found as $150,000 $\times$ 0.10), which is a fairly close approximation to the true value of $15,912

(Note that an approximate monthly payment could be found by dividing these annual amounts by 12.)

4. a. $150,000
    b. $50 million
    c. $46.15
    d. $12,434.26
    e. $36,000

MULTIPLE CHOICE

1. d. More resources devoted toward investment requires less resources be devoted toward current consumption.

2. a. A positive rate of time preference means sooner is preferred to later. Different people may have different rates of time preference, some might prefer to have $75 now rather than $100 later, while others would prefer waiting and receiving the $100 rather than having $75 now. But everyone should prefer having $100 now rather than $100 later.

3. a. Present value is inversely related to the interest rate. (Note that the interest rate is in the denominator of the present value equation.)

4. a. The answer is found as $100 \div (1 + 0.06)^1 = \$100 \div 1.06$.

5. a. The answer is found as $100 \div (1 + 0.06)^2 = \$100 \div 1.1236$.

6. c. This is the sum of the answers to questions 4 and 5.

7. d. When the payments are to be received each year forever, use the asset formula given in the text ($100 \div 0.06$).

8. c. It would fall with the interest rate, it would fall if further into the future, and would only be worth $90.91 if the interest rate was 10 percent.

9. b. It also applies to investing in your education (human capital) in the same manner as for an investment in physical capital.

10. d. A government law holding the interest rate below equilibrium would reduce the quantity of savings and increase the quantity of loans demanded. There would be a shortage of money available for loan.

11. c. The value of an asset is the discounted present value of future profits. This present value falls immediately.

12. c. Growth requires high investment (and thus high savings), but it also requires that the money is invested in the most beneficial and productive activities (the function of a capital market).

13. a. These are listed in the book as the items leading to economic profit.

14. d. All of these would lower present value (lower interest rate, fewer years of repayment, and less increase in earnings).

15. a. We prefer shorter time until acquisition of an item.

16. b. Answer *c* refers to pure interest yield, a slightly different concept.

17. a. the difference between 10 percent and 7 percent

18. b. Pure interest is the nonrisk component.

19. b. The present value of these three payments added together is approximately $8,170 (found as [$3,000 \div (1 + 0.05)^1] + [\$3,000 \div (1 + 0.05)^2] + [\$3,000 \div (1 + 0.05)^3]$).

20. d. The resulting present value is greater than the project's current cost for any interest rate less than 5.4 percent. (Hint: There is no simple way of working this, you must try several different values to find the answer.)

21. c. At an interest rate of 10 percent, the value of an asset generating $15,000 per year is $15,000 \div 0.10 = \$150,000$.

CHAPTER TWENTY-EIGHT

TRUE OR FALSE

The following are true: 1, 2, 4, 5, 6, 7, 9, 12, 14, 15, 16.

The following are false:

3. Only one in five millionaires in the United States inherited their fortunes.

8. Means-tested income transfer programs are the only programs for which eligibility is dependent upon having a low income status. Less than one-fourth of government income transfers are means-tested.

10. While cash benefits are counted as income, in-kind benefits are not.

11. It is just the opposite. Transfer payments to the poor reduce the cost of choices that lead to poverty.

13. Despite a rather large growth in transfer payments, income inequality and poverty among the nonelderly have risen.

PROBLEMS AND PROJECTS

1. a. $7,568; $7,448; $9,229
    b. $5,509; will fall by $120 (from $7,568 to $7,448)
    c. Less. The $2,000 cost of transportation and child care exceeds the increase in disposable income of $1,661 ($9,229 – $7,568).
    d. $120 less in 1984 ($7,448 – $7,568); $2,109 more in 1994 ($9,657 – $7,548)
    e. $1,661 more in 1984 ($9,229 – $7,568); $3,389 more in 1994 ($10,937 – $7,548)
    f. increased her incentive to work

2. a. B
    b. C
    c. F
    d. H
    e. They would be the same. While most people would think country I should be considered to have more inequality, this is a drawback of traditional income distribution statistics based upon annual income data.

3. a. 4.5 percent; slightly more likely to remain (53 percent remained, so 47 percent fell)
    b. 53.5 percent; 5.0 percent; slightly more likely to remain (53.5 percent remained, so 46.5 percent rose)
    c. 28.0 percent; 36.5 percent (14.0 + 22.5); 36.0 percent (24.0 + 12.0)
    d. 10.5 percent (5.5 + 5.0); 11.0 percent (4.5 + 6.5)

    e. 30.5 percent (5.5 + 4.5 + 14.0 + 6.5); 30.5 percent (5.5 + 12.5 + 5.0 + 7.5)

4. Case 2: 50 percent; 30 percent; 20 percent
    Case 3: 45 percent; 30 percent; 25 percent
    Case 4: 55 percent; 30 percent; 15 percent
    a. Case 4 is the most unequal; Case 3 is the most equal.
    b. same; all have more money income
    c. more equal; all have less money income
    d. less equal; all have more money income
    e. All would prefer Case 4 as all have the highest money income in that case.
    f. No, distributions reflect percentages of income, and not the true level of income. It is possible for all incomes to rise, or for all incomes to fall, when the distribution becomes either more or less unequal. There is no clear relationship.

MULTIPLE CHOICE

1. a. There has been steadily rising income inequality since the 1970s.

2. b. Lifetime income is distributed much more equally than annual income.

3. b. A progressive tax system takes a larger share of income as earnings increase, reducing the after-tax income of the rich by a larger percentage than the poor. Additionally, transfers are proportionately larger to lower income individuals. Both work to lessen the inequality of the income distribution.

4. d. All of these have contributed to the rise in income inequality.

5. c. Income is determined by resources supplied. This income is created by the individuals who supply the resources.

6. a. These are the reasons why large transfer programs can actually lead to more poverty.

7. c. The others would be the same given the statement in the question. Even if we all earned the same identical amount at each age, it would not be the case that different people who are different ages would earn the same amount.

8. b. Only money income is counted.

9. a. This is the poverty threshold for this family. It is adjusted for family size and inflation.

10. c. This is a major shortcoming of income distribution statistics based upon annual incomes at any one point in time.

11. d. All of these are true.

12. b. When more persons in a family work, that family will have higher income.

13. b. It fell from the 1950s to the 1970s but has risen ever since.

14. a. In net, taxes and transfers raise the disposable income of the poor and lower the disposable income of the nonpoor.

15. b. Some data on this is given in the book.

16. b. Because of substantial income mobility, lifetime income is more equally distributed than annual income.

17. a. A means-tested income transfer is limited to persons or families with income below a certain cutoff point. Eligibility is thus dependent on low-income status.

18. b. It reduces the incentive to work and earn just like having high marginal income tax rates.

19. c. Because they have lost one-half of their income in the form of reduced benefits.

20. a. This is the definition of the Samaritan's dilemma.

21. d. There is a more unequal distribution of income, a higher poverty rate among the nonelderly, and more single-parent families.

22. d. Opponents stress that a fair process is more important than the outcome produced and that high tax and transfer rates reduce the total economic pie.

SPECIAL TOPIC ONE

TRUE OR FALSE

The following are true: 1, 2, 5, 7, 9, 10, 11, 13, 14, 15, 16.

The following are false:

3. These items account for less than 13 percent of the budget. Spending on income transfers, health care, national defense, and interest on the national debt together account for 87 percent of federal spending.

4. A sales tax is levied by 45 of the 50 states. (Alaska, Delaware, Montana, New Hampshire, and Oregon are the exceptions.) Personal income taxes are imposed by 41 states. (Alaska, Florida, Nevada, New Hampshire, South Dakota, Tennessee, Texas, Washington, and Wyoming are the exceptions.)

6. Federal spending remained roughly constant with not much growth throughout the 1800s, and only beginning in the 1900s did spending begin to grow rapidly.

8. It is just the opposite—transfers have grown rapidly and defense has fallen substantially.

12. The top 1 percent of earners accounted for 39.9 percent of federal personal income tax revenue in 2006, compared to 3.0 percent for the bottom half of earners.

PROBLEMS AND PROJECTS

1. a. 23.2 (127.7 ÷ 549.5), 52.2 (285.8 ÷ 547.7), 12.6 (68.9 ÷ 547.7)

   b. 33.8 (636.5 ÷ 1,883.0), 15.5 (274.1 ÷ 1,765.7), 14.6 (258.0 ÷ 1,765.7), 12.2 (215.2 ÷ 1,765.7)

   c. fallen from 52.2 percent of the budget to 15.5 percent of the budget

   d. risen from 12.6 percent of the budget to 23.1 percent of the budget

   e. risen from 7.5 percent of the budget to 12.2 percent of the budget

   f. risen from 0.9 percent of the budget to 20.9 percent of the budget

   g. risen from 8.0 percent of the budget to 14.6 percent of the budget

   h. national defense in 1960, Social Security in 2000

   i. fallen from 23.2 percent of revenue to 10.1 percent of revenue; no, because business cannot pay taxes, only people can—business taxes are borne by consumers, workers, and/or shareholders

   j. individual income taxes are the largest revenue source in both years

   k. because the data are in nominal terms and they are not corrected for inflation

2. a. 40.42 (450,926 ÷ 1,115,504), 71.22 (794,432 ÷ 1,115,504), 86.59 (965,875 ÷ 1,115,504), 97.11 (1,083,243 ÷ 1,115,504)

    b. risen

    c. fallen

    d. There is, of course, no right answer to this question, but most people examining this data are surprised to see that the rich pay such a large share of the tax burden.

MULTIPLE CHOICE

1. c. The personal income tax is the largest source of federal government revenue.

2. a. Both of these are true statements.

3. c. While the tax code is adjusted for inflation, it is not adjusted for changes in real income that occur through time. As Americans get richer through time, more and more of their income is taxed at a higher rate.

4. a. In fact, real per capita federal spending was actually slightly lower in 2000 than in 1990.

5. d. All of these statements are true regarding the federal budget.

6. c. Taxes impose compliance and administration costs as well as creating an excess burden through the elimination of productive exchanges.

7. c. This is the IRS data given in the textbook.

8. a. This is the IRS data given in the textbook.

9. b. This is the U.S. Treasury Department data given in the textbook.

10. a. This is the U.S. Treasury Department data given in the textbook.

11. c. The percent of income taken by federal taxes rises sharply with income.

12. a. The Earned Income Tax Credit is a provision in the tax code that provides a credit or rebate to persons with low earnings and is phased out as earned income rises.

13. b. Relative to other major industrial countries, the United States has a low level of government spending as a share of GDP.

14. a. No private business can legally use coercive force to require a person to pay for something like the government can.

15. b. When government gets too large, it begins to lower growth.

SPECIAL TOPIC TWO

TRUE OR FALSE

The following are true: 1, 2, 4, 5, 6, 9, 10.

The following are false:

3. Approximately three-fourths of the population, or 227 million people, in the United States use the Internet.

7. The Internet generally makes it easier for consumers to do this.

8. The Internet has also made it easier for businesses to purchase from each other.

PROBLEMS AND PROJECTS

1. The answers to this problem will depend on the list as you do this problem.

2. The answers to this problem will depend on your favorite CD. Generally I own most of the other CDs listed in the section of what others bought, and frequently I find a new one I didn't know about that I really like.

3. Without the college bookstore acting as a middleman, you should be able to get a higher used price for selling your textbooks on-line; however, the transaction cost of having to ship your book or find the seller may be high enough that this is not worth it to you. The bookstore provides value because it acts as a middleman helping to lower the transaction costs for buyers and sellers trading used books.

MULTIPLE CHOICE

1. c. This is the data given in the book.

2. d. These are the three major sources of economic gains from the Internet listed in the textbook.

3. b. This is a number given in the text.

4. a. Computer hardware and software has the highest percent of on-line sales.

5. d. Automobiles have the smallest on-line sales of those listed, but food is even lower.

6. d. All of these are reasons why on-line retail stores can potentially have lower costs.

7. a. This is one of the drawbacks to purchasing on-line. A potential solution is to have only a few items on display in hybrid stores that act as showrooms.

8. d. All of these are advantages of job-posting Web sites over traditional newspaper ads.

9. d. Job turnover may increase because many employed workers routinely search for new jobs on the Internet.

10. c. This is the data shown in the text.

11. b. Telecommuting is the use of the Internet to work from home or another location.

SPECIAL TOPIC THREE

TRUE OR FALSE

The following are true: 2, 3, 6, 7, 8, 9, 11, 12, 13.

The following are false:

1. The system takes the current tax revenue and pays it out to current retirees. Only recently has Social Security begun to save a fraction of current revenue in anticipation of the retirement of the baby boom generation.

4. Current workers will fare much worse than those before them.

5. A worker aged 40 or younger can expect a rate of return of about 2 percent, about one-fourth that of an average stock market return.

10. On average, blacks have a shorter life expectancy than whites, so Social Security adversely affects the economic welfare of blacks relative to whites.

PROBLEMS AND PROJECTS

1. a. Taxes of $1,000 per worker would support a benefit level of $15,000 per retiree in the 1950s.
    b. Taxes of $5,000 per worker would support a benefit level of $15,000 per retiree in 2000.
    c. Taxes of $7,500 per worker would support a benefit level of $15,000 per retiree in 2030.
    d. Benefits would have to be cut from $15,000 to $10,000 per retiree.

2. a. Yes, technically you have savings of $5,000, and your spouse has a debt of $5,000.
    b. Your spouse would have to run a "surplus" (spend less than he or she earns) to repay the money.
    c. It is the same. The Social Security trust fund holds U.S. Treasury bonds, which will have to be repaid by the federal government (either through higher taxes or spending cuts in other areas) when Social Security needs to use the money in the trust fund. In essence, it is no different than if the surplus had never been saved.

3. a. At 1.8 percent, the money would have doubled once by age 65, so you would have only $40,000 instead of $320,000. While this is an oversimplified problem, the amount is similar to the real difference, which amounts to about $200,000 for the average baby boomer.
    b. At 3.6 percent, the money would double every 20 years. So $20,000 invested at age 25 would grow to $40,000 at age 45 and to $80,000 at age 65. This is double the amount that would be present at a 1.8 percent return ($80,000 versus $40,000).
    c. The economy would be double its current size.
    d. $160,000; $240,000; $20,000; $40,000

MULTIPLE CHOICE

1. c. This is what is meant by a pay-as-you-go system.

2. d. The ratio was sixteen workers per retiree in the 1950s, three workers per retiree in 2008, and will fall to two workers per retiree by 2030.

3. c. By using the trust fund to purchase bonds, the money was available for the government to spend on other current programs. When these bonds come due, the federal government will have to repay this money it has borrowed from the Social Security trust fund.

4. b. This is when Social Security will begin to draw down the trust fund.

5. d. This is the definition of an unfunded liability from the text.

6. d. A young worker today is expected to earn a negative real rate of return on their contributions, meaning that the real value of the benefits received will be less than the real value of the taxes paid.

7. a. These are essentially IOUs from the federal government that will have to be repaid in the future.

8. b. To repay the bonds, the government will have to either raise taxes or cut spending.

9. d. These are the only options available besides substantial reform.

10. c. Above this level of income, total annual Social Security taxes remain constant.

11. a. Blacks have a lower life expectancy than whites or Hispanics, life expectancy rises with education, and females have a longer life expectancy then males.

12. c. A spouse can collect benefits based upon either their own average annual salary or 50 percent of their spouse's average annual salary. A married woman who does not work will receive the same benefits as if she had worked and earned an average annual salary equal to 50 percent of her husband's.

13. d. Both of the statements are true.

14. a. All of the other countries have taken steps toward privatization.

SPECIAL TOPIC FOUR

TRUE OR FALSE

The following are true: 2, 3, 4, 6, 7, 8, 9, 11, 12, 13.

The following are false:

1. Real returns have averaged far greater than the 7 percent long-term average.

5. This will generally lead to good performance of the stock market.

10. They are buying ownership rights to a fraction of future earnings generated by the firm.

14. The operating costs of indexed funds are lower because there is less trading (buying and selling of stock shares) involved in maintaining a portfolio of stocks that mirrors a broad index, and there are no research costs involved in evaluating the future prospects of companies for indexed funds.

15. Mutual funds with good performance over a 5- or 10-year period often tend to be among the worst performers in the future.

PROBLEMS AND PROJECTS

1. a. decrease
    b. increase
    c. increase

2. a. $173.55 = (\$100 \div (1.10)^1) + (\$100 \div (1.10)^2)$
    b. $185.94 = (\$100 \div (1.05)^1) + (\$100 \div (1.05)^2)$
    c. $177.69 = (\$150 \div (1.10)^1) + (\$50 \div (1.10)^2)$
    d. $214.88 = (\$100 \div (1.10)^1) + (\$150 \div (1.10)^2)$
    e. $260.33 = (\$150 \div (1.10)^1) + (\$150 \div (1.10)^2)$

MULTIPLE CHOICE

1. a. Answers *b* and *c* would increase risk.

2. c. Both will lower risk.

3. c. This is even true compared to investing in U.S. Treasury bonds.

4. c. Both are true.

5. b. This is the definition of a managed equity mutual fund.

6. a. The concept of a price/earnings (P/E) ratio provides an interesting look at how interest rates affect stock prices.

7. b. A lower interest rate is associated with a higher present value of future income streams. The higher present value leads to an increase in the market value of stocks.

8. d. The random walk theory is consistent with all of the statements.

9. d. All are ways for firms to obtain additional funding.

10. a. The value of the option to purchase the stock would increase.

SPECIAL TOPIC FIVE

TRUE OR FALSE

The following are true: 1, 5, 6, 9, 10

The following are false:

2. Sub-prime loans are loans made to individuals with poor and/or incomplete credit histories, and, therefore, involve a higher interest rate.

3. Adjustable rate mortgages are tied to short-term interest rates, and thus, the interest rate and the monthly payment will vary over the life of the loan.

4. Malinvestment is misguided investment caused when the Fed holds interest rates artificially low, which encourages too much borrowing.

7. The Fed has had a difficult time using discretionary monetary policy as a stabilization tool, usually because of the timing lags involved with the use of such policy. The financial crisis of 2008 is the most recent example of this inability.

8. Regulations are unlikely to be effective at preventing a future financial crisis as regulations carry with them secondary effects and a tendency for the regulators to be influenced by those they intend to regulate.

PROBLEMS AND PROJECTS

1. a. +
    b. +
    c. +
    d. +
    e. -

2. a. 8
    b. 2
    c. 3
    d. 1
    e. 6
    f. 5
    g. 4
    h. 7

MULTIPLE CHOICE

1. b. Fannie Mae and Freddie Mac are both government-sponsored enterprises, so it was widely believed that the government would back their bonds if they ever ran into financial trouble. As a result, they could borrow funds cheaper than private lenders could.

2. a.   The Community Reinvestment Act loosened mortgage lending standards, which required banks to reduce their lending standards and extend more loans to borrowers who did not meet the conventional credit criteria.

3. c.   The lower lending standards resulting from the government sponsored enterprises and the Community Reinvestment Act increased the percentage of subprime and Alt-A loans to 33 percent of all loans by 2006. Over the same time period, the number of conventional loans fell to about one-third of all loans.

4. c.   The Fed's artificially low short-term interest rates substantially increased the attractiveness of adjustable rate mortgages to both buyers and sellers. This made it possible for homebuyers afford to pay smaller down payments along with higher monthly payments on larger and more expensive homes.

5. a.   Between 2002 and 2004 (during the recovery from the 2001 recession), the Fed instituted expansionary policy in the form of extremely low short-term interest rates in an effort to stimulate the economy.

6. b.   The combination of the mortgage lending regulations and the Fed's artificially low interest rate policies encouraged decision makers to borrow more money and make additional investments then they would have done otherwise. As a result, the foreclosure rates on the adjustable rate mortgages for both prime and subprime lenders soared, while foreclosure rates on fixed interest loans remained relatively stable.

7. b.   The Securities and Exchange Commission (SEC) rule change made it possible for investment banks to increase the leverage of their investment capital by expanding their mortgage financing activities, which eventually lead to their collapse.

8. d.   When the default rates increased sharply in 2006 and 2007, it became apparent that these mortgage-backed securities were a lot more risky than had been previously thought. This caused their value to plummet which is why the investment banks collapsed so quickly.

9. b.   Those securities with a Triple-A rating were deemed less risky and, thus, more valuable. This gave rating agencies an incentive to give more Triple-A ratings as they were often paid attractive fees and given more business for doing so.

10. c. The debt to income ratio has increased dramatically in recent years. By 2008, it had soared to 135 percent, more than twice the level of the mid-1980s.

11. b. People expectedly respond to incentives by shifting their debt to where it is tax-deductible, such as home mortgages and home equity loans.

12. b. Timing lags make it difficult to use monetary policy as a stabilization tool.

13. c. Regulations have difficulty dealing with future issues and keeping pace with the adjustments of an ever-changing economy. Regulations are also subject to secondary effects and the threat of being undermined by a close relationship between the regulators and those whom they intend to regulate.

14. c. When monetary policy makers attempt to manipulate real output and employment, their actions will generate instability rather than stability. The primary focus of the Fed should be the achievement of price stability.

SPECIAL TOPIC SIX

TRUE OR FALSE

The following are true: 3, 5, 6, 7, 8

The following are false:

1. While many believe that the Great Depression was caused by the stock market crash that occurred on October 22, 1929, in reality, the stock market had nearly recovered back to its original level within months of the crash. It was not until the government began instituting the policies described in this chapter that the stock market started to decline steadily again.

2. The government actually raised tax rates. In fact, personal income tax rates were increased by 150 percent at all levels of income.

4. The government used contractionary monetary policy by increasing the discount rate and aggressively selling bonds during the Great Depression.

9. Unfortunately, the political incentive structure encourages politicians to do something during severe economic downturns to avoid looking unresponsive. This means that even bad policies are at least temporarily more popular than no policy changes at all.

10. While it is a popular notion that the New Deal policies ended the Great Depression, the data shows that the economy was still struggling seven years after the beginning of the New Deal. The Great Depression was eventually diminished by the increase in demand for military goods during World War II.

PROBLEMS AND PROJECTS

1. a. E, G, E, G, E, G, G, E, G, G, E
    b. No, the government policies incorporated during the great depression did not follow what economic theory suggests a government should do to combat a recession
    c. This would indicate that the government policies were responsible for the extended length and severity of the Great Depression.
    d. The failure of the government to use the appropriate economic policies are likely the result of a combination of ignorance about which policies to use (much of what we have learned about fiscal and monetary policy comes from the experience of the Great Depression) and pressure from the public and special interest groups to invoke policies that would be in the interest of a few, but to the detriment of many.

MULTIPLE CHOICE

1. b. The length and severity of the Great Depression was heightened by the government's poor use of monetary policy, high taxes, restriction of free trade, and constant structural changes that lead to an unstable economic climate.

2. c. The Dow Jones Industrial Average was above 300 before the initial crash on October 29, 1929 when it plunged to 230. However, by mid April of 1930, it had risen back up to 294, but then steadily declined in response to the Smoot-Hawley Tariff signed on June 17, 1930.

3. b. The Fed instituted contractionary monetary policy over these time periods by increasing the discount rate and aggressively selling bonds. This policy reduced the money supply, and consequently, prices, which further exacerbated the severity of the Great Depression.

4. b. High tariffs and other restraints on trade increase the costs of trade, which lowers the amount of exchange and reduces the gains from specialization and competition that are associated with it.

5. d. Even with higher tax rates, the size of the tariff reduced the volume of international trade so drastically that total tariff revenue fell as a result.

6. a. The highest marginal tax rate went from 25 percent to 63 percent and later to 79 percent, and personal income tax rates increased at all levels by 150 percent. This reduced both after-tax income as well as the incentive to earn and invest.

7. c. The government increased taxes drastically at this time in an effort to keep the budget balanced and pay for all of the additional government spending.

8. b. The National Industrial Recovery Act organized businesses into government-sponsored cartels that were designed to keep prices high.

9. d. All of these government actions contributed to the Great Depression.

10. c. The massive new programs and regulations associated with the New Deal created regime uncertainty, a situation where people are reluctant to undertake business ventures and investments because the government is frequently changing the rules.

11. d. Measured as a share of the economy, the increases in government spending and federal deficits during the 1930s were relatively small. Thus, there is little

reason to believe that fiscal policy exerted much impact on the economy.

12. b. The Great Depression is a clear example that discretionary monetary policy can result in economic instability if timed and used inappropriately.

13. c. To combat a recession, the government should use expansionary fiscal and monetary policy by decreasing taxes and increasing the money supply.

SPECIAL TOPIC SEVEN

TRUE OR FALSE

The following are true: 1, 3, 5, 7, 9

The following are false:

2. The United States has a more dynamic business environment with higher labor mobility, a characteristic that many believe will help the United States adjust more quickly when faced with economic downturns.

4. Just the opposite is true. Japan's fiscal policy was very expansionary during the recession of the 1990s. The government increased spending and financed it with borrowing, which brought about large budget deficits.

6. Even well-educated and highly skilled young workers lack experience. Productivity tends to reach its peak as workers gain more experience and move into their prime working years (age 35 to 59).

8. The opposite is true; Japan has a higher savings rate compare to the United States.

10. The United States practiced expansionary monetary policy during the 2008 economic downturn, which may lead to a stronger recovery than the one Japan experienced after their recession during the 1990s. However, it is also possible that this expansionary monetary policy may lead to future economic instability.

PROBLEMS AND PROJECTS

1. a. B
    b. B
    c. B
    d. U
    e. J
    f. B
    g. J
    h. U

MULTIPLE CHOICE

1. b. Both Japan in the 1990s and the United States in 2008–2009 experienced significant declines in the asset prices that was a major cause of the economic downturn in the respective countries.

2. d. This reduced the cost of buying and holding both real estate and business assets. Persistently strong growth, optimism, and easy credit caused asset prices in Japan to soar.

3. b. Japan had incredibly high growth of 6 percent for much of the period following World War II, but Japan's growth rate fell to 1 percent in the 1990s, a period Japan refers to as its lost decade.

4. a. Keynesians believe that it is appropriate for the government to run a budget deficit during times of recession in order to further stimulate the economy.

5. d. Expansionary fiscal policy involves running a budget deficit by lowering taxes and/or increasing government spending. This is what Japan did in the 1990s.

6. b. Nominal interest rates are influenced by the expected rate of inflation. When people expect a decline in the general level of prices (deflation), then annual interest rates will be low.

7. c. Both Japan in the 1990s and the United States during the Great Depression made the same error of using restrictive monetary policy during a recession.

8. c. If Japan wanted to use both fiscal and monetary policy to pull the economy out of a recession, then economic theory indicates that it would be most appropriate to use countercyclical policy, which involves an increase in government spending and expansionary monetary policy.

9. b. A larger elderly population means more expenditures for retirement benefits and health care, a lesson being learned in both Japan and the United States.

10. a. Demographic changes in Japan have adversely affected the growth of the Japanese economy since 1990. The United States, which is going through similar demographic changes, faces the same potential difficulties.

11. d. The fact that the U.S. economy is more dynamic and has a more flexible labor market could hasten the adjustment process resulting from the financial crisis.

12. c. Give the number of similarities between the economic downturns of Japan in the 1990s and the United States in 2008, it is reasonable to expect that U.S. housing and stock market prices will take a while to recover, as was the case in the Japanese experience.

SPECIAL TOPIC EIGHT

TRUE OR FALSE

The following are true: 1, 2, 5, 7, 8, 11, 12.

The following are false:

3. When current resources (labor, machines, buildings, etc.) are used to produce government goods, the forgone production in other areas must be forgone today. This opportunity cost cannot be pushed into the future.

4. A larger capital stock means higher labor productivity and thus *higher* wages.

6. Privately held debt is the portion owned by all private investors, domestic and foreign (in essence, all debt not owned by U.S. government agencies). External debt refers to the portion owned by foreign investors.

9. Under the traditional view, investment is crowded out and the future capital stock is lower. This is not true under the new classical view.

10. The United States is about average.

PROBLEMS AND PROJECTS

1. Year 1: Total expenditure is $150 (equal to revenue because no surplus or deficit).

   Year 2: Total revenue is $150 ($50 less than total expenditure with a $50 deficit).

   Year 3: +$20 surplus (amount by which revenue exceeded expenditures).

   Year 4: –$10 deficit (revenue minus expenditure) and $40 debt ($30 old debt plus $10 more from this year's deficit).

   Year 5: $70 debt ($40 old debt plus $30 more from this year's deficit).

   Year 6: $190 total expenditure and $70 surplus (necessary to pay debt down to zero).

2. a. Total receipts: $1,039.9; $1,150.0
      Total outlays: $1,235.9; $1,273.4
   b. –196.0; –123.4
   c. In 1997, the actual deficit was larger than reported, and in 1998, there was actually a deficit despite a reported surplus.

MULTIPLE CHOICE

1. b. The debt is the total amount owed at any one point in time. The deficit (or surplus) is the annual amount by which the debt changes.

2. a. External debt is debt owned by foreigners.

3. b. It is the portion not owned by government agencies but by private investors. It represents a true net interest burden from the government to persons.

4. c. Answers *a* and *b* are untrue myths about the burden of the debt addressed in this application chapter.

5. a. Higher government borrowing pushes up interest rates, reducing private borrowing and investment. The inflow of foreign capital looking to earn the higher interest rate offered in the U.S. will appreciate the dollar, reducing net exports.

6. b. Expenditures have risen very rapidly, much more so than revenue.

7. a. The national debt is the sum of all prior deficits and surpluses.

8. b. Prior to the acceptance of Keynesian theory, the general practice was to follow a balanced budget except in war time or other emergencies. Keynesian theory called for deficits to be run to actively manage the state of the economy.

9. c. In year 1, expenditures of $100 exceed revenue of $100 by $10, thus a deficit.

10. b. In year 2, revenue of $150 exceeds expenditure of $120 by $30, thus a surplus.

11. d. In year 3, there is a $50 deficit ($250 expenditure versus $200 revenue). The national debt is the sum of all the deficits and surpluses over all three years ($-10 + 30 - 50 = -30$).

12. c. The interest on these bonds will be paid from one agency of the government to another.

13. b. This is a statistic given in the text.

14. d. While taxes will be increased in the future to repay the debt, people holding bonds at that same time in the future will get the repayment of the debt with interest.

15. b. This is the primary concern about how the debt harms future generations.

16. b. Social Security is running a surplus in preparation for the retirement of the baby boom generation. This surplus is counted in the budget calculations, lowering the size of the reported deficit.

17. a. The deficit would be larger (or alternatively, the surplus would be smaller).

SPECIAL TOPIC NINE

TRUE OR FALSE

The following are true: 2, 3, 4, 6, 9, 10, 11.

The following are false:

1. Health-care expenditures have risen quite dramatically over this period.

5. There are two reasons why it would increase the price of medical services. First, lower out-of-pocket cost for consumers causes them to increase their demand for medical-care services, which pushes up prices. Secondly, it gives consumers less of an incentive to economize and shop for low-cost services and producers less of an incentive to provide the goods at a low price.

7. It is generally less effective.

8. The aging of the baby boomers is expected to cause even more rapid growth in health-care prices and expenditures unless major structural changes are made in health-care markets.

12. Only one new medical school has been established in the United States during the last two decades.

PROBLEMS AND PROJECTS

1. a. This would increase the demand for medical services, increasing price and increasing quantity.
    b. This would increase the demand for medical services, increasing price and increasing quantity.
    c. This would be illustrated as a horizontal line in the graph below the equilibrium price. The quantity demanded would rise (moving down along the original demand curve) and the quantity supplied would fall (moving down along the original supply curve). Neither curve would shift. There would be a shortage of medical-care services. The price would be lower and the quantity provided would be lower.
    d. This would increase the supply of medical services, decreasing price and increasing quantity.
    e. This would increase the supply of medical services, decreasing price and increasing quantity.

2. a. Erin faces a combined marginal tax rate of 49.3 percent. Thus for every dollar she uses to purchase the plan through her employer, her taxes will fall by 49.3 cents and her net take home pay will fall by 50.7 cents. For the $6,000 health-care policy, her net take home pay will fall by only $3,042.
    b. $3,042 rather than $6,000, a difference of $2,958.
    c. This price differential is probably large enough to cause Erin to purchase it through her employer.

d. Auto insurance is not treated as a pre-tax deduction if it is employer provided, thus there is no preferential tax treatment of auto insurance when it is purchased through an employer. Consumers would prefer to get it outside of their employer (just as they would with health insurance) so they don't lose it when they lose their job or change jobs.

MULTIPLE CHOICE

1. b. When price is not used to ration a good, some other mechanism must be used.

2. b. This is a statistic given in the text. It includes both private and government financed expenditures.

3. d. The names of the programs are switched in that (I) refers to Medicaid and (II) refers to Medicare. Other than the switched names, the statements are true.

4. d. All of these are true. A lower-middle-income family can purchase a $6,000 health-care insurance plan through an employer with only a $4,200 reduction in net wages.

5. d. This is the combined payments of the public sector and private health insurance.

6. d. All of these are reasons why the increase in third-party payments has caused the prices of medical-care services to rise.

7. b. The ratio of the medical care price index to the general consumer price index has doubled since 1965, meaning medical-care prices have risen on average twice as rapidly as consumer prices in general.

8. b. Competition and consumer choice are a more effective way to control costs than through the use of rules and regulations.

9. a. There will be a rapid increase in the demand for medical-care services as the baby boomers retire.

10. d. Perverse public policy is the primary factor underlying the soaring expenditures and rising prices in the health-care industry.

11. b. This is the term used to refer to these accounts. Giving these accounts similar tax treatment compared to employer-provided health insurance and reducing the regulatory restrictions on their use could help to improve the situation in the health-care industry.

12. d. These are three of the five reforms listed in the text that could improve the operation and efficiency of health-care markets.

13. a. The others are the opposite of what is true.

SPECIAL TOPIC TEN

TRUE OR FALSE

The following are true: 3, 4, 6, 7, 8, 9, 11.

The following are false:

1. Average achievement scores today are lower than they were 35 years ago. They fell quite a bit during the 1970s, remained roughly constant during the 1980s, and rose slightly during the 1990s.

2. Comparisons made using eighth-grade science achievement scores show that U.S. students lag well behind those of most other developed countries.

5. Spending in the United States has been rising rapidly and is among the highest in the world, so a lack of funding does not explain the poor (and worsening) performance.

10. Charter schools are not permitted to be religious schools.

12. Both of these are incorrect; voucher programs tend to increase scores and lower segregation.

PROBLEMS AND PROJECTS

1. a. +
    b. −
    c. +
    d. −
    e. +
    f. ?, some critics argue that this might be (−) but based on existing evidence from such programs it appears that the effect is a (+)
    g. +
    h. ?, but likely − based on existing evidence from such programs
    i. −

2. a. 16.5; 15.2; private schools have fewer students per teacher
    b. 520; 216; private schools have fewer students per school
    c. $6,898; $4,676; private schools have lower costs per student
    d. $3,116 ÷ $6,898 = 45.2% (less than half)
    e. The proficiency test scores are higher for private schools in both categories.
    f. Private schools appear to have better academic performance at a significantly lower cost per student.

MULTIPLE CHOICE

1. d. All of these statements are true regarding achievement scores.

2. a. In international rankings in both science and mathematics, U.S. students scored well below average.

3. a. Real spending per pupil has more than doubled during the last three decades.

4. d. Average spending per pupil was $10,585 in 2005.

5. c. U.S. spending is among the highest in the world. It is 46 percent more than the average across the 29 countries in the comparison.

6. d. In fact, U.S. spending is almost twice as high per pupil as in Australia and France and is about 26 percent higher than in Japan.

7. d. All of these are true.

8. b. The others are the opposite of what is true.

9. b. Public provision and financing through taxation both lower the efficiency of educational markets.

10. a. The higher education system is a good example of how different incentives can make a big difference in school performance.

11. d. All of these are true about a voucher system.

12. d. All of these are true about charter schools.

13. c. This is a figure given in the textbook.

14. b. This is a figure given in the textbook.

15. d. All of these statements are true.

SPECIAL TOPIC ELEVEN

TRUE OR FALSE

The following are true: 1, 2, 3, 4, 9, 10.

The following are false:

5. There is no gap for singles, the group least influenced by actual and potential differences in specialization within the traditional family.

6. In 1968, only 27 percent expected to be working at age 35. By 1979, this figure had risen to 72 percent.

7. It has increased in all of the fields listed.

8. There was relatively little change in the differential in the 1960s and 1970s.

PROBLEMS AND PROJECTS

1. a. 73.8, 97.1, 67.3, 73.5, 83.3, 73.0, 71.4 (each of these is calculated by dividing the value for females by the value for males)

   b. The F/M ratio is higher for single workers than for married workers.

   c. The ratio for singles who have never been married is much higher. In fact, the F/M ratio for never-married single workers is 100 percent, which means no earnings differential between males and females.

   d. The F/M ratio is higher for black workers than for white workers.

   e. The F/M ratio is slightly higher for workers with only a high school education than for college-educated workers.

   f. The gap is the largest when the ratio is the smallest, so the gap is the largest among married workers. The gap is the smallest among single workers.

2. a. 70.0% (35,000 ÷ 50,000)

   b. $21.85 for males, $17.71 for females

   c. $40,520 ($17.71 × 2,288); 81.0%

   d. $44,520 [$40,520 + ($1,000 × 4)]; 89.0%; accounting for these two factors has accounted for approximately two-thirds of the observed difference in annual earnings between males and females (89.0% F/M ratio compared to a 70.0% F/M ratio).

MULTIPLE CHOICE

1. c. This is a figure given in the textbook.

2. b. This is a figure given in the textbook.

3. c. This is a figure given in the textbook. It is less than the annual earnings differential because women

worked approximately 7 percent fewer hours on average than men.

4. a. The employer could cut their labor costs by 20 percent by replacing their male employees with female employees.

5. d. All of these were, historically, the result of males typically being more likely to be the person in the family pursuing paid employment.

6. b. It is nonexistent for singles, the group least influenced by actual and potential differences in specialization within the traditional family.

7. d. It has increased in all of the fields listed.

8. c. There was little change in the differential in the 1960s and 1970s.

9. a. This has resulted in a narrowing of the wage differential, and this trend is expected to continue into the future.

10. b. This will happen as more and more women who have prepared themselves for professional and business careers acquire experience and move into the prime earning years of life.

11. d. All of the items listed would tend to cause the earnings of women to be lower than for men.

12. c. If equally qualified women have a lower wage rate, there will be a rather large cost advantage for firms if they hire women.

SPECIAL TOPIC TWELVE

TRUE OR FALSE

The following are true: 2, 3, 4, 5, 8.

The following are false:

1. Union membership has continuously declined over this period.

6. A much higher proportion of male workers are union members.

7. It is one of the least unionized.

9. The southern states tend to have the lowest rates of union membership.

10. While unions increase the wages of their members, they probably end up decreasing the wages of nonunion workers because of the expanded supply of workers in the nonunion sector.

PROBLEMS AND PROJECTS

1. a. +
    b. −
    c. +
    d. −
    e. Higher wages increase tuition, and then enrollment declines, and thus the university needs fewer professors. In addition, the university will substitute away from labor to other factors of production (say building new buildings with larger classrooms), which will further reduce the number of professors needed by the university.

2. a. 3, +
    b. 1, −
    c. 3, +
    d. 2, −
    e. 3, +
    f. 1, −

MULTIPLE CHOICE

1. b. The others are all opposites of what is true.

2. d. There has been a decrease in the desire of workers to form unions.

3. c. The others are the three listed in the book. A union wage increase makes a firm less competitive because it must raise price to cover the added cost of labor.

4. b. Right-to-work laws forbid union shop contracts.

5. a. When only one firm raises prices, their sales fall substantially as consumers switch to substitute products. When all firms in an industry raise price, consumers cannot as easily avoid the higher prices caused by union wage increases.

6. b. When union labor becomes more expensive, firms will use less union labor and more of substitute inputs such as machines and nonunion labor.

7. b. But the percentage differs substantially between industries and occupations.

8. a. Since the 1950s, it has fallen by more than half.

9. b. Consumers do not like to pay high prices. Whenever competition is present, consumers will switch to nonunion products, limiting the ability of the union to increase wages.

10. c. The evidence shows no linkage between unionization and the share of national income going to labor.

11. a. When there are no good substitutes, it will be hard for the firm to switch to other inputs to avoid paying the higher wages.

12. c. This is known as the union wage premium.

SPECIAL TOPIC THIRTEEN

TRUE OR FALSE

The following are true: 2, 3, 4, 5, 7, 8, 9, 10.

The following are false:

1. The evidence suggests that resource scarcity has fallen over the past century, and as a result most real resource prices are much lower than in the past.

6. Timber is an example of a renewable resource.

11. Government subsidies do just the opposite by leading to improper allocation of water resources.

PROBLEMS AND PROJECTS

1. a. 30.9 years worth of supply "remained" (185.6 ÷ 6.0). So we "should" have run out of natural gas in about 1981!

    b. Proved reserves are only the amount that is known to exist and can be extracted at current (here 1950) prices and technology. New finds, better technology, and higher prices increased proved reserves.

    c. While total proved reserves are falling, they are not falling by nearly as much as they would have if no new proved reserves were found. Because consumption was about 200 trillion, while reserves fell by only 2 trillion, approximately 198 trillion of new reserves were found during this ten-year period. The rate of increase in proved reserves has been just slightly less than the rate of consumption.

    d. The price of natural gas more than tripled, and consumption fell as a result. Because demand is more elastic in the long run, consumption continued to decline past the change in the price.

    e. The price fell between 1990 and 2000. We would expect natural gas consumption to fall in response to this price increase.

    f. The correct answer is never, even though the data "tell" us that there is only a 7.4 year's supply remaining!

2. a. They correspond very well to the price data. There was a large price jump between 1970 and 1980, and this is when usage fell the most. The price almost was the same in 1960 and 1970, and usage of homes built in these periods was almost the same as well.

    b. The higher prices have provided an incentive for new homes to be built using more electric power instead of natural gas. In addition, they have provided an incentive to spend more on making the home more energy efficient (insulation, thicker windows, etc.), reducing overall energy consumption by homes.

c. This is almost entirely due to the incentives created by market prices. When homeowners began receiving very high fuel bills for using natural gas, they wanted to switch to electric to save their own money, not in an effort to "save" the remaining supply of natural gas!

d. Yes, the recent changes correspond fairly well.

3. a. A movement from point A to B caused price to rise from P_1 to P_2 and quantity to fall from Q_1 to Q_2 in the short run.

b. A movement from point A to C caused price to rise from P_1 to P_3 and quantity to fall from Q_1 to Q_3 in the long run. Relative to the short run, the price in the long run falls from P_2 to P_3, and quantity falls further from Q_2 to Q_3.

c. There is a greater reduction in quantity used in the long run. Demand is always more elastic in the long run because it takes time for people to fully adjust to a change.

4. a. −
    b. −
    c. +
    d. +

MULTIPLE CHOICE

1. c. They ignore the increased finding and extraction of reserves, as well as the reduction in consumption, that result from the higher prices that occur as a resource is depleted.

2. d. All of these affect how much resources a person consumes.

3. d. This is a definition and is the reason why doomsday predictions using this data are wrong.

4. d. For example, in 1926 the U.S. government informed people that the supply of oil would only last another seven years. These types of predictions happen very frequently but have always proved incorrect.

5. d. All of these would occur as the result of higher titanium prices.

6. a. The real prices of most resources continue to decline suggesting that supply is growing faster than demand. These resources are thus becoming relatively less scarce.

7. b. This is the definition of a nonrenewable resource.

8. c. Timber is a renewable resource because trees can be replanted and replenished relatively quickly.

9. c. We have about the same amount of forest land as in 1920 and are producing even more timber than before on that same amount of land.

10. a. Indur Goklany has estimated that if agricultural technology had been frozen at 1961 levels, the 1998 level of food production would have required more than double the amount of land used today for farming.

11. a. When natural resources are not traded, or where markets are not allowed to function as well as the markets described above, problems of waste and scarcity are common. Water suffers from the lack of well-functioning markets.

SPECIAL TOPIC FOURTEEN

TRUE OR FALSE

The following are true: 1, 2, 5, 7, 8, 9, 10.

The following are false:

3. Scientists and some firms act as special interest groups with incentives to advocate funding toward their own purposes, which is directly influenced by the Kyoto Protocol.

4. The debate over global warming is far from being settled. Many reputable scientists disagree with the assertion that global warming is a problem. Scientists are not even sure whether a warmer world would, on the whole, be better or worse.

6. Total reductions in pollution will not change, but the costs may be much lower.

PROBLEMS AND PROJECTS

1. a. Column 2 only.
   b. Column 1 only.
   c. Yes, the animals that are going extinct are the ones that the government has forbid private ownership of.
   d. Cows, pigs, and chicken are slaughtered at rates hundreds of times greater than any other animals, but are the ones that are the least subject to extinction. Indeed it is their value to humans for consumption that provides the incentive to breed them and keep massive numbers of them alive.
   e. The ranchers who own and kill cattle for beef are identical to those who would kill elephants for ivory. The only difference is in the ownership. If ivory poachers could own the elephants, they would breed them so that they do not go extinct. After all, if the elephants go extinct, the poachers are out of income, just like if a cattle rancher killed all of his cattle.

2. a. The Audubon Society does this to generate more revenue with which to buy additional lands to preserve. Yes, both parties are better off.
   b. They only allow drilling during certain times of the year and also only if it will create very little (or no) lasting damage to the environment.
   c. No. Because the cost of the road exceeded the value of the timber, it would not have been profitable to do so.
   d. Yes. Yes. It is $5 million cheaper for the environmental group, and $5 million more profitable for the oil company.

MULTIPLE CHOICE

1. d. All of the these examples involve either a large number of people being affected by emissions or a large number of polluters that will undermine the effectiveness of the market exchange approach because of high transaction costs.

2. d. The examples listed are all possible problems associated with a regulatory approach.

3. a. Over the past century, a 1.4 degree (F) of warming of the earth has occurred that may be attributed to higher levels of carbon dioxide.

4. d. All of this is under debate and is far from being settled conclusively.

5. c. Government regulation tends to promote special interest lobbying, leading to inefficiencies.

6. a. Wealthier people can respond to environmental threats by taking precautions that poorer people cannot afford, such as better health care, safer cars, and routine safety measures.

7. a. The process will be efficient if the emission charges equal the marginal cost to those being harmed.

8. b. Overfishing was used as an example in the text—without ownership of the fish, each fisher has little incentive to conserve.